Eversheds Sutherland
Practitioner's Guide to
Key Aspects of the Re

Eversheds Sutherland: The Employment Practitioner's Guide to Financial Institutions: Key Aspects of the Regulatory Framework

General editors
Paul Fontes, Partner
Elizabeth Graves, Partner
Susan Mayne, Consultant

Contributors
Gregory Brandman, Partner
Simon Collins, Managing Director – Regulatory/ES Consulting
Dawn Dickson, Partner
Jake McQuitty, Partner
David Saunders, Partner
Sophie White, Partner
Daniel Allan, Senior Associate
Alice Heatley, Senior Associate
Fiona McMutrie, Principal Associate
Holly Short, Principal Associate
Olivia Toulson, Principal Associate
Jessica Wicker, Senior Associate
David Williams, Senior Associate

Bloomsbury Professional

LONDON • DUBLIN • EDINBURGH • NEW YORK • NEW DELHI • SYDNEY

BLOOMSBURY PROFESSIONAL
Bloomsbury Publishing Plc
41–43 Boltro Road, Haywards Heath, RH16 1BJ, UK

**BLOOMSBURY and the Diana logo are trademarks of
Bloomsbury Publishing Plc**

First published in Great Britain 2019

British Library Cataloguing-in-Publication Data

A catalogue record for this book is available from the British Library.

ISBN:	PB:	978-1-52650-420-3
	ePDF:	978-1-52650-422-7
	ePub:	978-1-52650-421-0

Typeset by Evolution Design and Digital Ltd (Kent)
Printed and bound by CPI Group (UK) Ltd, Croydon, CR0 4YY

To find out more about our authors and books visit
www.bloomsburyprofessional.com. Here you will find extracts, author
information, details of forthcoming events and the option to sign up for
our newsletters

Preface

The last few years have been a time of great change for financial institutions. In the wake of the LIBOR scandal the Parliamentary Commission on Banking Standards was established in 2012 to conduct an inquiry into professional standards and culture in the banking sector. Radical changes were proposed in the Commission's report 'Changing Banking for Good' which revolutionised the way financial institutions and larger insurance and reinsurance firms are run.

Noting that a lack of personal responsibility had been commonplace across the industry the new regime which was implemented as a result of the report places more responsibility upon staff and firms to manage their own staff and on individual responsibility.

In March 2016 the new senior managers and certification regime (SMCR) was ushered in, initially for deposit takers (banks, building societies and credit unions) and certain PRA regulated investment banks. A separate regime, the senior insurance managers regime, was simultaneously introduced for larger insurance and reinsurance firms. It had always been the intention to extend the regime across the financial services sector and policy statements setting out details of the extension were duly published in July 2018.

Together with the SMCR new rules were also introduced in respect of regulatory references and whistleblowing and the rules on remuneration have been significantly tightened up to align risk and reward.

Employment lawyers working for financial institutions have had to quickly get themselves up to speed with regulatory issues which were hitherto unfamiliar to them. Human resources professionals have found themselves working hand in glove with compliance and legal departments to implement and manage these new challenges. Drafting employment documentation and settlement agreements now need to take into account the myriad issues raised by the new regime. Disciplining and appraising staff now has the added complexity of fit and proper assessments and potential notifications to the regulator. Employers will need to comply with the onerous rules on regulatory references when staff depart. From recruitment to departure and beyond, the landscape has changed for financial institutions and insurers.

The complexity of the rules and the difficulty for practitioners in finding resources to help them understand the new regime has led to confusion and uncertainty. This book will provide an invaluable guide to the new regime and to how to handle the many issues raised by it. The publication will be timely given the rollout of the regime across the regulated industry in December 2018 for insurers and December 2019 for other financial institutions.

We would like to thank all those involved with this book. All the contributors are experts in their fields and have shared their knowledge and experience. Thanks too to our trainee solicitors who have checked references and carried out essential research.

The law is stated as at 1 December 2018. Where possible, we have sought to highlight any forthcoming legal developments of note or interest.

Paul Fontes
paulfontes@eversheds-sutherland.com

Elizabeth Graves
elizabethgraves@eversheds-sutherland.com

Susan Mayne

List of Abbreviations

AIFMD	–	Alternative Investment Fund Managers Directive 2011/61/EU
AFM	–	authorised fund manager
APER	–	Approved Persons Regime (FCA)
AR	–	appointed representatives
BEIS	–	Department for Business, Energy and Industrial Strategy
BSB	–	Banking Standards Board
BIPRU	–	the Prudential sourcebook for banks, building societies and investment firms in the FCA Handbook
CASS	–	Client Assets sourcebook
CEBS	–	Committee of European Banking Supervisors
COCON	–	Code of Conduct sourcebook in FCA Handbook
CP	–	consultation paper
CRD IV	–	Capital Requirements Directive IV 2013/13/EU
CRR	–	Capital Requirements Regulation No. 575/2013
DBS	–	Disclosure and Barring Service
DEPP	–	Decisions and Enforcement manual in FCA Handbook
DP	–	discussion paper
DPA	–	Data Protection Act 2018
DTR	–	Disclosure and Transparency Rules (FCA)
EG	–	FCA enforcement guide
EBA	–	European Banking Authority
EHRC	–	Equalities and Human Rights Commission
EIOPA	–	European Insurance and Occupational Pensions Authority
ERA	–	Employment Rights Act 1996
ESMA	–	European Securities and Markets Authority
FCA	–	Financial Conduct Authority
FEMR	–	Fair and Effective Markets Review
FG	–	finalised guidance
FIT	–	the Fit and Proper test for approved persons in the FCA Handbook
FRC	–	Financial Reporting Council
FS	–	feedback statement
FSA	–	Financial Services Authority
FSB	–	Financial Stability Board
FSMA	–	Financial Services and Markets Act 2000
FUND	–	Fundamental Principles in FCA Handbook
GC	–	guidance consultation
GDPR	–	General Data Protection Regulation 2016/679/EU
GEO	–	Government Equalities Office

GPG Regulations	–	Gender Pay Gap Regulations 2017, SI 2017/172
IA	–	Investment Association
ICO	–	Information Commissioner's Office
IFPRU	–	the Prudential sourcebook for investment firms in FCA Handbook
KFH	–	key function holder
LIBOR	–	London Interbank Offered Rate
LTIP	–	long term incentive plan
MiFiD	–	Markets in Financial Instruments Directive 2014/65/EU
MRM	–	management responsibility map
MRT	–	material risk taker (as defined with reference to criteria in Commission Delegated Regulation (EU) No 604/2014
NDF	–	non-Solvency II Directive firm
PCBS	–	Parliamentary Commission on Banking Standards
PIDA	–	Public Interest Disclosure Act 1998
PPI	–	Payment Protection Insurance
PR	–	prescribed responsibility
PRA	–	Prudential Regulation Authority
PRIN	–	Principles in FCA Handbook
PS	–	policy statement
RAPs	–	relevant authorised persons, namely deposit takers, certain PRA-regulated investment banks and certain branches of foreign banks
RBA	–	role based allowance
S II	–	Solvency II Directive 2009/138/EC as amended by Directive 2014/51/EU
SIB	–	Securities and Investment Board
SIMR	–	Senior Insurance Managers Regime
SIMF	–	senior insurance manager function
SM	–	senior manager
SMF	–	senior manager function
SMCR	–	Senior Managers and Certification Regime
SMR	–	senior managers regime
SoP	–	statement of policy
SoR	–	statement of responsibilities
SS	–	supervisory statement
SUP	–	Supervision part of FCA Handbook
SYSC	–	Systems and Controls Sourcebook in the FCA Handbook
UCITS	–	Undertakings for Collective Investment in Transferable Securities Directive 2009/65/EC

Contents

Table of Statutes

Table of Statutory Instruments

Table of Cases

Table of EU Material

CHAPTER 1

Background to the accountability regime

Paul Fontes, Partner, Elizabeth Graves, Partner and Susan Mayne, Consultant

I THE FINANCIAL CRISIS

1.01 The global financial crisis combined with multiple conduct failures (such as payment protection insurance mis-selling and benchmark manipulation) prompted widespread concerns about the lack of personal accountability in the financial sector, undermined trust in the banking and financial markets and raised questions about the alignment of risk and reward in financial institutions.

1.02 In early 2008 following the collapse of major banks such as Bear Stearns and Lehman Brothers the US federal reserve took on most of the losses of about US$306bn of Citigroup Inc's risky assets and injected new capital to ensure its survival. Estimates produced by the Boston Consulting Group in 2017 show that for the period 2009–2016 major banks incurred conduct fines and costs in excess of US$320bn worldwide.

Royal Bank of Scotland

1.03   In the UK, the Royal Bank of Scotland (RBS) asked its shareholders in 2008 to inject around £12bn of capital after disclosing £5.9bn of write-downs. RBS chief executive (Sir) Fred Goodwin finally resigned (after resisting government pressure for him to step down) a month before the RBS revealed losses of £24.1bn – the largest loss in UK corporate history – and the government took on a 58% stake in RBS for £15bn. It was widely believed that the reason for the near collapse of RBS was partly due to Goodwin's strategy of aggressive expansion, underwriting of collateral debt obligations and liquidity.

HBOS

1.04   At Halifax Bank of Scotland (HBOS) Paul Moore, Head of Group Regulatory Risk, was dismissed in 2004 after warning the board about HBOS's risky sales strategies. The then Financial Services Authority (FSA) accepted the conclusions of KPMG's investigation that HBOS had appropriate risk controls in place. In March 2008 HBOS shares fell 17% amid unfounded rumours that the Bank of England had been asked for emergency funding. The FSA conducted an investigation into whether short selling was a problem but concluded that there was no deliberate attempt to drive the share price down.

1.05   Following the takeover of HBOS in 2009 Lloyds TSB announced that HBOS had made a pre-tax loss of £10.8bn in 2008. The regulators that succeeded the FSA, the Financial Conduct Authority (FCA) and the Prudential Regulation Authority (PRA), subsequently identified the causes of failure in their November 2015 report, which found:

- The HBOS board had failed to instil a culture that balanced risk and return appropriately and lacked sufficient experience and knowledge of banking.

- There was a flawed and unbalanced strategy and a business model with inherent vulnerabilities arising from an excessive focus on market share, asset growth and short-term profitability.

- The firm's executive management had pursued rapid and uncontrolled growth of the Group's balance sheet. This led to an over-exposure to highly cyclical commercial real estate at the peak of the economic cycle.

- The board and control functions had failed to effectively challenge executive management.

- The underlying weaknesses of HBOS's balance sheet made the Group extremely vulnerable to market shocks and ultimately failure.

2 PARLIAMENTARY COMMISSION ON BANKING STANDARDS: 'CHANGING BANKING FOR GOOD'

1.06   The Parliamentary Commission on Banking Standards (PCBS), led by the chair of the Treasury Select Committee, was established in July 2012 in the wake of the LIBOR scandal (a series of fraudulent actions connected to the London Interbank Offered Rate) and other failings in the financial services industry. The aim of the PCBS was to conduct an inquiry into professional standards and culture in the banking sector. At that time the FSA was the sole regulator for the financial services industry.

1.07   The PCBS was appointed by both Houses of Parliament to consider and report on:

- professional standards and culture of the UK banking sector, taking account of regulatory and competition investigations into the LIBOR rate-setting process;

- lessons to be learned about corporate governance, transparency and conflicts of interest, and their implications for regulation and for government policy;

and to make recommendations for legislative and other action.

APER

1.08   Prior to the introduction of the Senior Managers and Certification Regime (SMCR) the main way in which individuals who worked in the financial services industry had been regulated was through the Approved Persons Regime (APER) contained in Part V of the Financial Services and Markets Act 2000 (FSMA). Under APER, financial services firms may not employ a person to perform a *'controlled function'* unless that person has been approved by the regulator following an application by the firm. Approved persons must comply with statements of principle, which are a series of binding standards of professional conduct. As detailed elsewhere in this book, under the extension of the SMCR, for most regulated financial services firms APER will be replaced by the SMCR and statements of principle will be replaced by the conduct rules (individual conduct rules for most staff and senior manager conduct rules for senior managers who continue to be approved by the regulator).

1.09   The PCBS criticised APER, noting that it acted as an initial gateway rather than as a system for effective ongoing supervision of the most important individuals in a firm. It found that there was a lack of clarity of responsibilities of individuals at senior level and that firms did not take enough responsibility for the fitness and propriety of their own staff at more junior levels. It also found gaps in the regulator's enforcement powers. This book does not attempt to address the detail in APER as this regime will be replaced by the SMCR following the extension of the regime to all FSMA-authorised firms in 2019 (December 2018 for insurers).

Changing banking for good

1.10   In June 2013, the PCBS published a final report entitled 'Changing banking for good' which outlined the radical reform it considered was required to improve standards across the banking industry. The PCBS noted that a lack of personal responsibility had been commonplace throughout the industry, risks and rewards in banking had been out of kilter and rewards for success needed to be better focused on generating long-term benefits for banks and customers. There needed to be clear lines of accountability and enforceable sanctions.

1.11   It also considered that it was not just bankers that needed to change – the actions of regulators and governments had contributed to the decline in standards. The PCBS's key recommendations were for the introduction of:

● A new senior persons regime, replacing APER, to ensure that the most important responsibilities within banks are assigned to specific, senior individuals so they can be held fully accountable for their decisions.

● A new licensing regime underpinned by Banking Standards rules to ensure that those who can do serious harm are subject to the full range of enforcement powers.

● A new criminal offence for senior persons of reckless misconduct in the management of a bank, carrying a custodial sentence.

● A new remuneration code to align risks taken and rewards received in remuneration, with much more remuneration to be deferred and for much longer periods.

● A new power for the regulator to cancel all outstanding deferred remuneration along with unvested pension rights and loss of office or change of control payments for senior bank employees in the event of their banks needing taxpayer support.

1.12   Introducing the report, Andrew Tyrie, the Chairman of the PCBS, commented:

> 'A lack of personal responsibility has been commonplace throughout the industry. Senior figures have continued to shelter behind an accountability firewall. Risks and rewards in banking have been out of kilter. Given the misalignment of incentives, it should be no surprise that deep lapses in banking standards have been commonplace. The health and reputation of the banking industry itself is at stake. Many junior staff who may have done nothing wrong have been impugned by the actions of their seniors. This has to end. Rewards for success should be better focussed on generating long-term benefits for banks and their customers. Where the standards of individuals, especially those in senior roles, have fallen short, clear lines of accountability and enforceable sanctions are needed. They have both been lacking. It is not just bankers that need to change. The actions of regulators and Governments have contributed to the decline in standards.'

1.13   The PCBS recognised that there were many players in the development of the banking crisis that had unfolded since 2007. The behaviour of bankers was recognised to be 'appalling' but regulators, credit ratings agencies, auditors, governments, many market observers and many individual bank customers in their approach to borrowing created pressures in the same, wrong direction.

1.14   Damningly, the report concluded:

'One of the most dismal features of the banking industry to emerge from our evidence was the striking limitation on the sense of personal responsibility and accountability of the leaders within the industry for the widespread failings and abuses over which they presided. Ignorance was offered as the main excuse. It was not always accidental.'

1.15   Further:

'Banking history is littered with examples of manipulative conduct driven by misaligned incentives, of bank failures born of reckless, hubristic expansion and of unsustainable asset price bubbles cheered on by a consensus of self-interest or self-delusion. An important lesson of history is that bankers, regulators and politicians alike repeatedly fail to learn the lessons of history: this time, they say, it is different. Had the warnings of past failures been heeded, this Commission may not have been necessary.'

Changes following the PCBS report

1.16   The recommendations in the PCBS report led to the Financial Services Act 2012 and the Financial Services (Banking Reform) Act 2013 which amended FSMA to make sweeping changes to the way in which individuals who work in banking are regulated. In 2014 the FCA and the PRA consulted over a new accountability framework for individuals together with other measures including remuneration and whistleblowing.[1]

1.17   In the FCA's consultation paper CP14/13 the regulators proposed changes to the way in which individuals working for UK banks, building societies, credit unions and PRA-designated investment firms were assessed and held accountable for the roles they performed.

1.18   In particular, as part of implementing the recommendations in the PCBS report, the SMCR and senior insurance managers regime (aimed at larger insurers and largely replicating features of the accountability regime) came into force on 7 March 2016, aimed at larger and more significant financial institutions and insurers regulated by the FCA and/or the PRA. The stated aim of the SMCR was to reduce harm to consumers and strengthen market integrity by making individuals more accountable for their conduct and competence.

1   FCA CP14/14.

3   INTRODUCTION OF THE SENIOR MANAGERS AND CERTIFICATION REGIME

1.19   The SMCR aims to encourage a culture of staff at all levels taking personal responsibility for their actions and to make sure firms and staff clearly understand and can demonstrate where responsibility lies.

1.20   FSMA was further amended in 2016[2] to enable the extension of the SMCR which resulted from the PCBS report to *all* firms authorised to provide financial services. On 9 December 2019 the SMCR will replace APER for nearly every firm regulated by the FCA and/or PRA (implementation of the SMCR for insurers was 9 December 2018).

1.21   Alongside the implementation of the SMCR, new rules were also introduced on whistleblowing and regulatory references as well as extensive changes to rules on remuneration. This means that financial institutions must have regard not only to general employment legislation and common law duties but also to regulatory rules and guidance which affect most aspects of the employment life cycle. These range, for example, from carrying out fit and proper assessments and proper checks at recruitment and throughout employment, the drafting of employment contracts and other documentation, through managing conduct and disciplinary issues to negotiating settlement agreements and providing/requiring/updating a regulatory reference.

Outline of SMCR

1.22   In outline, the SMCR comprises the following:

- *The senior managers regime (SMR)*: the SMR focuses on individuals holding key roles and responsibilities ie relevant authorised persons (RAPs). The regime entails allocating and mapping out responsibilities and preparing statements of responsibilities for individuals who carry out key functions (known as senior management functions (SMFs)). Individuals who fall under this regime must still be pre-approved by regulators, but firms are also legally required to ensure that they have procedures in place to assess their fitness and propriety before applying for approval and at least annually afterwards.

- *The certification regime*: this regime applies to other staff who could pose a risk of significant harm to the firm or any of its customers (for example, staff who give investment advice). These staff are *not* pre-approved by regulators. Firms must put in place procedures to assess for themselves the fitness and propriety of staff, for which they will be accountable to the regulators. These preparations will be important not only when recruiting for roles that come under the certification regime but when reassessing the fitness and propriety of staff who are subject to the regime.

---

2   Bank of England and Financial Services Act 2016, s 21.

● *The conduct rules*: the conduct rules are high level and set out a basic standard for behaviour that all those covered by the regimes will be expected to meet. Firms subject to the SMCR must ensure that staff who are subject to the conduct rules are aware of them and how they apply to them. Individuals subject to either the SMR or the certification regime have been subject to the conduct rules from the commencement of the new regime on 7 March 2016, while the wider application of the conduct rules to other staff working for SMCR firms under the first rollout of the regime came into force on 7 March 2017.

1.23   Further details on these aspects of the regime are set out in the relevant chapters in this book.

1.24   The regime ensures that all significant areas of a firm's operations have a senior manager who is responsible for them. Clarity as to a senior manager's specific responsibilities is provided by the statement of responsibilities, management responsibilities map, conduct rules and assessment of fitness and propriety to perform their role. The regulators emphasise[3] that senior managers should understand the business or oversight functions for which they are responsible. They are not expected to be experts but should understand and inform themselves about the business sufficiently to understand the risks of trading, credit and other relevant business activities.

1.25   Enforcement action against individuals has also been strengthened (see Chapter 13). Senior managers who breach the conduct rules could face sanctions which include censure, fines and industry bans. Such actions against senior managers include circumstances where the senior manager has failed to take reasonable steps to prevent a regulatory breach by staff for whom they are responsible.

1.26   Separately the certification regime puts upon firms the obligation to assess for themselves on recruitment and at least annually the fitness and propriety of staff who are potentially capable of causing significant harm to the firm or its customers.

1.27   New enhanced remuneration rules further ensure the proper conduct of staff who are classified as material risk takers (see Chapter 7). As the Bank of England points out, pre-crisis there were no restrictions on how variable remuneration was awarded, the form it took and the period over which it was paid. Following the changes made to the regulatory regime large banks must now pay at least 50% of any variable remuneration in non-cash elements. 40% of total variable remuneration awarded should be deferred (60% in the case of senior executives or for those with total variable remuneration of £500,000 or more). Deferral must take place between three and seven years (seven years for senior managers) and must be capable of being adjusted downwards by way of malus

---

3   See for example Bank of England Quarterly Bulletin 2018 Q3 'strengthening the link between seniority and accountability'.

and clawback in the case of misconduct, risk management failings or downturns in financial performance.

4   THE FINANCIAL CONDUCT AUTHORITY AND THE PRUDENTIAL REGULATION AUTHORITY

1.28   A practitioner must first determine whether the firm it is dealing with is a regulated firm. FSMA, s 19 states that a person (which includes a legal entity) must not carry on a regulated activity in the UK unless they are an authorised or exempt person. To determine whether an activity is regulated the practitioner must first ask whether the activity is carried out by way of business (ie there is a commercial aspect) in the UK and is in relation to a specified investment. Specified activities are set out in Part II of the Financial Services and Markets Act 2000 (Regulated Activities) Order 2001 (RAO)[4] and include accepting deposits; consumer credit activities; insurance-related activities; mortgage-related activities; and investment activities. Part III RAO sets out specified investments and their exclusions.

1.29   The Financial Services Register[5] is a public record of firms, individuals and other bodies that are, or have been, regulated by the FCA or the PRA and can be searched to determine whether a firm is regulated. It also lists senior managers and their status (ie whether they have been approved). The FCA is consulting over a wider directory to include details of certified and other key staff.

Predecessors to the FCA and PRA

1.30   The Securities and Investment Board (SIB) was created in 1985 in order to reverse the self-regulation of the financial services sector and to consolidate regulatory responsibilities. The SIB's name was changed in 1997 to the Financial Services Authority (FSA), which exercised powers given to it under FSMA.

1.31   Following the financial crisis the government decided to abolish the FSA from 1 April 2013. In its stead, two new regulators took the place of the FSA, splitting the regulatory responsibility for regulated financial firms between the Prudential Regulation Authority (PRA) and the Financial Conduct Authority (FCA). The two regulators cooperate closely in light of their different statutory objectives (see 1.32–1.39).

The PRA

1.32   The PRA was initially a subsidiary of the Bank of England (from March 2017, it has been brought within the single legal entity of the Bank). It is

4   SI 2001/544.
5   https://www.fca.org.uk/firms/financial-services-register.

responsible for the *micro-prudential regulation* of systemically important firms, including banks and insurers and it looks at the safety and soundness of firms.[6] The PRA has three statutory objectives which are set out in FSMA:

- to promote the safety and soundness of financial firms;
- (specifically for insurers) to contribute to the securing of an appropriate degree of protection for policyholders; and
- a secondary objective to facilitate effective competition.

1.33   The PRA regulates only insurers, deposit takers (banks, building societies and credit unions) and the largest investment firms.

1.34   Rules for firms regulated by the PRA are found in the PRA Rulebook.[7]

The FCA

1.35   The FCA is the UK financial services regulator responsible for the *conduct* of all firms authorised under FSMA. Around 56,000 financial services firms and markets in the UK are regulated by the FCA. It is also the prudential regulator for more than 18,000 of those businesses, including asset managers, financial advisers, and mortgage and insurance brokers. As with its conduct supervision, the FCA's prudential supervision goes beyond a quantitative analysis of firms' financial resources. It considers systems and controls, governance arrangements, and risk management capabilities including the risk of misconduct.

1.36   The FCA is also responsible for the regulation of conduct in retail and wholesale financial markets and its aim is to ensure that markets work well so that consumers get a fair deal.

1.37   The FCA has three statutory objectives:

- to protect consumers;
- to enhance the integrity of the UK financial system; and
- to help maintain competitive markets and promote effective competition in the interests of consumers.

1.38   The rules for firms regulated by the FCA are found in the FCA Handbook.[8] The Handbook contains the complete record of FCA legal instruments. All FCA-regulated firms must comply with the rules in the Handbook.

---

6   The PRA's approach to banking supervision is set out in: http://www.bankofengland.co.uk/publications/Documents/praapproach/bankingappr1304.pdf.

7   prarulebook.co.uk.

8   https://handbook.fca.org.uk.

The rules pursuant to the FCA's statutory supervisory duty[9] are set out in the FCA's Supervision Manual (SUP).[10] With regard to conduct supervision, the FCA states that its three main approaches are:

- proactive supervision for the biggest firms;

- event driven, reactive supervision of actual or emerging risks; and

- thematic work that focuses on risks and issues affecting multiple firms or a sector as a whole.

1.39 The FCA states that it will intervene early where it sees poor behaviour, taking action to prevent harm to consumers and markets.

Solo regulated and dual regulated firms

1.40 Most smaller firms within the regime are regulated by the FCA only – these are known as solo regulated firms. A solo regulated firm will be regulated by the FCA in relation to its prudential aspects as well as for conduct.[11]

1.41 Firms regulated by *both* the PRA and FCA are called dual regulated firms, which means that such firms must comply with both the FCA's and the PRA's rules.

1.42 The PRA and FCA have the same set of disciplinary powers and most versions of SMCR proposals have an FCA and a PRA version, but some aspects are only imposed by one regulator. Dual regulated firms will need to consider both the FCA and PRA rules in the FCA Handbook and the PRA Rulebook.

1.43 The PRA sets out its rules in the PRA Rulebook which imposes direct requirements on firms and the FCA's requirements are contained in the FCA Handbook. Non-rule material is set out in supervisory statements. In the FCA Handbook, guidance is marked by 'G' in the margin (rules are marked with the letter 'R').

1.44 Firms are expected to engage directly with policy materials.

Financial Policy Committee

1.45 Separately, the Financial Policy Committee of the Bank of England is responsible for the *macro-prudential* regulation of financial institutions and the Payment Systems Regulator is the economic regulator for the payment systems industry.

---

9 FSMA, s 1L.
10 https://www.handbook.fca.org.uk/handbook/sup/.
11 See the FCA factsheet for background: https://www.fca.org.uk/publication/other/factsheet.pdf.

5   EUROPEAN LEGISLATION AND REGULATION

1.46   Policy standards which are agreed internationally are implemented by way of Directives or directly-applicable regulations. The legislative programme must be implemented in the UK subject to what proposals are agreed for financial services under Brexit. The FCA has confirmed that it has no proposals to change existing regulation, although once the UK is no longer subject to EU law it is open to it in principle to change legislation and, more pertinently, not to adopt any new laws that are unpalatable. However, the chief executive of the FCA has stated that the FCA intends not only to enforce existing rules but to work to implement laws that have been agreed but are not yet in place. In the meantime the regulators have prepared for the possibility of a no-deal Brexit by publishing proposals to transpose EU regulation and technical standards into its rulebook to ensure a functioning regulatory framework.

1.47   The regulation of financial services across Europe is comprised of three European supervisory authorities (ESAs):

● the European Banking Authority (EBA);

● the European Securities and Markets Authority (ESMA);

● the European Insurance and Occupational Pensions Authority (EIOPA).

1.48   Part of the role of the ESAs is to improve coordination between national supervisory authorities in the EU. They have significant powers to propose draft rules and to take decisions binding on national supervisors and, to a lesser extent, firms.

6   REGULATORS' RULES, POLICY STATEMENTS ETC

1.49   The policy framework for the regulators' supervision is largely agreed internationally, both at global level and within the EU. Binding EU regulations form part of the UK regulators' requirements of firms and EU Directives must be transposed into national law.
Firms are also subject to guidance by the EBA, ESMA and EIOPA.

FCA publications

1.50   The different types of FCA publications as defined on the FCA website are:

● *Policy Statements (PS)*: A policy statement follows a consultation paper (CP) once the consultation period is over and the FCA has considered the responses. In a PS the FCA publishes its response to the answers it received to the original CP questions and sets out its rules. The PS contains the final legal instrument (Handbook rules).

- *Finalised Guidance (FG):* Finalised Guidance sets out the feedback to the guidance consultation and the final guidance.

- *Consultation Papers (CP):* In consultation papers the FCA consults on proposed changes to the FCA Handbook rules. It outlines its proposals, asks questions and invites responses from its varied audiences, including the financial services industry and consumer organisations. CPs contain draft Handbook rules.

- *Guidance Consultations*: In Guidance Consultations the FCA consults with firms on proposed non-Handbook guidance.

- *Feedback Statements (FS):* A Feedback Statement provides an overview of the key messages from a Discussion Paper (DP) or a call for inputs.

- *Discussion Papers (DP)*: Discussion Papers focus on a particular topic or area of interest. The main aim of a DP is to create a conversation or debate on the issue.

- *Calls for Input*: A call for input gives interested parties an opportunity to identify areas within a sector which could be improved in the interests of consumers, or highlight areas where competition is working well.

PRA publications

1.51   The different types of PRA policy publications as defined on the PRA website are:

- *Discussion Papers (DP)*: DPs are used to stimulate debate on issues about which the PRA is considering making rules or setting out expectations. The PRA uses the responses it receives on DPs to help formulate its policy. Once the PRA establishes a preferred position, draft rules and supervisory statements will be prepared and then the formal consultation process, by way of a consultation paper, will commence.

- *Consultation Papers (CP)*: CPs are the formal document by which the PRA sets out draft proposals and invites comments from the public on those proposals. CPs either deal with one discrete issue of significance or a number of small and/or uncontroversial topics in Occasional CPs.

- *Policy Statements (PS)*: PSs set out the PRA's feedback on consultation responses, together with the PRA's policy line. Feedback is only issued where there have been extensive comments by the public and industry.

- *Supervisory Statements (SS)*: SSs set flexible frameworks for firms, incorporating new and existing expectations. They focus on the PRA's expectations and are aimed at facilitating firm and supervisory judgement in determining whether they meet those expectations. They do not set absolute requirements which are contained in rules.

- *Statements of Policy (SoP)*: Statements of policy are the formal document by which the PRA details its policy on a particular matter. Statements of policy usually set out the PRA's approach to the exercise of powers conferred by the FSMA. They do not contain the PRA's expectations which are set out in a supervisory statement.

7　WHERE TO FIND THE REGULATORS' RULES

Sources

1.52　The regulators' rules applicable to the SMCR and remuneration are set out in various parts of the FCA Handbook[12] and PRA Rulebook.[13]
In particular, for the purposes of the following aspects of the regime, the rules can be found in the parts indicated in the table below.

Definitions

1.53

COCON	–	FCA code of conduct sourcebook (in 'high level standards' in FCA Handbook)
DEPP	–	FCA decision procedure and penalties manual (in 'regulatory processes' in FCA Handbook)
FIT	–	the fit and proper test for approved persons (in 'high level standards' in FCA Handbook)
FUND	–	Fundamental rules in the PRA Rulebook
PRIN	–	Principles of Business in FCA Handbook (in 'high level standards' in FCA Handbook)
S II	–	Solvency II part of the PRA Rulebook
CRR	–	for Capital Requirements Regulation firms (in the PRA Rulebook)
SUP	–	Supervision (in 'regulatory processes' in FCA Handbook)
SYSC	–	Senior management arrangements, systems and controls (in 'high level standards' in FCA Handbook)

See also the reader's online guide to the FCA Handbook.[14]

1.54　The table also refers to relevant policy and supervisory statements and other relevant guidance material.

12　handbook.fca.org.uk.
13　prarulebook.co.uk.
14　https://www.fca.org.uk/publication/handbook/readers-guide.pdf.

Aspect of the regime	FCA rules in FCA Handbook	PRA rules in PRA Rulebook	Extension of regime – FCA/PRA rule
Definitions of SMCR firm			
Core SMCR firm	Glossary of definitions		SYSC 23 Annex 1 (See FCA PS18/14)
Enhanced scope SMCR firm			SYSC 23 Annex 1 (See FCA PS18/14)
Limited scope SMCR firm			SYSC 23 Annex 1 (See FCA PS18/14)
Definitions and types of firms covered by SMCR (dual and solo regulated)[15]			SYSC 23.2
Overview of the SMCR (tracking components of regime to types of firm and handbook provisions)	SYSC 23.3		SYSC 23.3.3G (application to solo regulated firms)
Senior Managers Regime			
Policy statements introducing rules on SMCR See also FSMA, Pt V	CP15/22 PS18/14 (extension of SMCR) PS18/15 (extension to insurers)	PS16/15 PS15/18 (extension to insurers)	FCA PS18/14 FCA PS18/15 PRA PS15/18
Proposed extension of SMCR to all FSMA authorised firms See also Bank of England and Financial Services Act 2016	CP 17/25 PS18/14 (extension to all regulated firms) PS18/15 (extension to insurers)	CP14/17 PS16/15 PS15/18 (extension)	See SYSC 23 FCA PS18/14 FCA PS18/15 PRA PS15/18
UK branches of overseas banks	SYSC 4.8.11 PS15/30	PS29/15 SS28/15 (updated May 2017)	SYSC 26.6.4G
Senior management functions See FSMA, ss 59ZA, 59ZB	SUP 10C.4.3, SYSC 2 and 4 FS16/6	CRR firms – Senior Management Functions and Allocation of Responsibilities and guidance in SS28/15 (updated May 2017)	*Insurers* – CP14/17 Appendix 2, amended SS35/15 FCA CP17/26 (all insurers)

---

15 There is a helpful flow diagram in SYSC 23.3 to assist firms in determining what type of SMCR firm they are.

Aspect of the regime	FCA rules in FCA Handbook	PRA rules in PRA Rulebook	Extension of regime – FCA/PRA rule
List of senior management functions	SUP 10C.4.3R	CRR firms – Allocation of responsibilities CRR firms – Senior management functions 2–7 SS28/15 (updated May 2017)	SYSC 24.2.6 *Insurers* – CP14/17 Appendix 2, amended SS35/15
Apportionment of responsibilities	SYSC 4.7, 4.7.30G, 4.7.35G SYSC 2.1, 4.4.3R–4.4.6R (NED) SYSC 4.1.14		SYSC 24 Annex 1 *Insurers* – CP14/17 Appendix 2, amended SS35/15
Statement of responsibilities See FSMA, s 62A	SUP 10C.11 SUP 10C Annex 5D – statement of responsibilities form CP15/22 para. 2.58 FS16/6	CRR firms – Allocation of responsibilities 2.1 SS28/15 (updated May 2017) Also, CP34/16	*Insurers* – CP14/17 Appendix 2, amended SS35/15 FCA CP17/26 (all insurers)
Prescribed responsibilities	SYSC 4.7.7 R	CRR firms – Allocation of responsibilities 4.1	SYSC 24.2.6R *Insurers* – CP14/17 Appendix 2, amended SS35/15 FCA CP17/26 (all insurers except EEA branches) SYSC 24.3.1-2
Which PRs apply to which kind of firm			SYSC 24 Annex 1
Overall responsibility	SYSC 4.7, SYSC 4.7.11 SUP 10C.7		SYSC 26.6, SYSC 26.7.2G SUP 10.7 FCA CP17/26 (Solvency II firms and large NDFs only)
Guidance on overall responsibility	SYSC 4.7.9G		SYSC 26.2 (replacing SYSC 4.7.9G)
Management responsibilities maps	SYSC 4.5–4.5.15G FS16/6	CRR firms – Allocation of responsibilities 7.2–7.4 SS28/15 (updated May 2017) Also, CP34/16	FCA SYSC 25 (25.2–25.8) *Insurers* – CP14/17 Appendix 2, amended SS35/15 FCA CP17/26 (Solvency II firms and large NDFs only)
MRMs for non-UK RAPs	SYSC 4.6.1R		SYSC 25.1.4R

Aspect of the regime	FCA rules in FCA Handbook	PRA rules in PRA Rulebook	Extension of regime – FCA/PRA rule
MRMs for EEA authorised persons	SYSC 4.6.17G(1)-(4)		SYSC 25.6.2G(1)-(4)
MRMs – record keeping			SYSC 25.8
Guidance on what should be in MRM			SYSC 25.4
Guidance on what should be in MRM for EEA firm	SYSC 4.6.26G-28G		SYSC 25.6.10G
MRMs – exclusion of non-financial services activities for some firms			SYSC 25.3
SMR handovers	SYSC 4.9 See also COCON 4.2.8 G	CRR firms – senior management functions 2.7	SYSC 25.9 *Insurers* – FCA CP17/26 (Solvency II firms and large NDFs only)
Contents of handover document	SYSC 4.9.7G		SYSC 25.9.6G
Handover arrangements and certificates	SYSC 4.9.8		SYSC 25.9.8G
SM absence of less than 12 weeks ('the 12-week rule')	SUP 10C.3.13R-17R COCON 1.1.2R	SS28/15 (updated May 2017)	SYSC 26.4.6-11 SUP 10C.3.13R SUP 12.18
12-week rule – time spent before commencement of extension			SUP 12.18
Sharing a SMF	SYSC 4.7.25G – 4.7.29G SUP 10C.11.31 FS16/6	SS28/15 (updated May 2017) 2.10 – 2.11	SYSC 26.9.6 *Insurers* – CP14/17 Appendix 2, amended SS35/15
Ceasing to perform a FCA designated SMF	SUP 10C.14.5R		
Duty of responsibility See FSMA, s 66A(5)	DEPP 6.2 (6.2.9-A G–6.2.9-F) PS17/9 (and CP16/26) Guidance in FCA PS17/9	Guidance in PRA SS28/15 (updated May 2017)	*Insurers* – CP14/17 Appendix 2, amended SS35/15 Guidance on duty of responsibility for insurers and solo regulated firms FCA PS18/16

Aspect of the regime	FCA rules in FCA Handbook	PRA rules in PRA Rulebook	Extension of regime – FCA/PRA rule
Feedback on implementation of SMR	FS16/6 (UK firms subject to SMR) FS16/7 (non-EEA branches) FS16/8 (EEA branches) FS16/9 (credit unions)		
Firm's obligation to disclose to regulator anything of which the regulator would reasonably expect notice	PRIN 2.1.11		
Record keeping			
Requirement to make and retain adequate records	SYSC 3.2.20R SYSC Schedule 1 Handbook SYSC 9.1		
Record of management responsibilities maps	SYSC 4.5.21G – 4.5.22G		SYSC 25.8.1G
Senior Insurance Managers Regime			
Senior insurance managers regime	SUP Chapter 10A COCON FIT	S II firms/(non-S II firms) and guidance in SS35/15 (updated May 2017) PS 5/16, PS 27/16	See: SYSC 23 Extension to SMCR – see new parts set out in Annexes A-Y in Appendix 1 to PRA CP14/17 Appendix 2 sets out amended SS 35/15 FCA CP17/26
SIMR prescribed responsibilities		SII firms 3/SII Insurance/allocation of responsibilities 3	
Governance map		SII firms 5.1/SII Insurance/allocation of responsibilities 5	
Conduct Standards		S II firms – Insurance – conduct standards	
Individual and SM conduct standards		S II firms – Insurance – conduct standards 3	
SIMR key functions		SII firms 4/ SII Insurance/allocation of responsibilities 4	

Aspect of the regime	FCA rules in FCA Handbook	PRA rules in PRA Rulebook	Extension of regime – FCA/PRA rule
Application of SIMR to NEDs		S II firms – Insurance – conduct standards 1.1(6)	
Proposed extension of SMCR to insurers	CP 17/26	CP 14/17	
Certification regime			
Certification regime See FSMA, ss 63E, 63F	SYSC 5.2	CRR firms – Certification SS28/15 (updated May 2017)	*Insurers* – Insurance-Certification Amended SS35/15 (all insurers)
Significant harm functions	SYSC 5.2.3G SYSC 5.2.30R		SYSC 271.4G SYSC 27.6.3R
Significant risk taker		CRR firms – Certification 1.2	
Definition of material risk taker			SYSC 27.8.15
Temporary absence of less than four weeks	SYSC 5.2.27R	CRR firms – Certification 2.4	SYSC 27.5
Fit and proper assessment See FSMA, s 63F	SYSC 5.2.6 G–5.2.17G FIT 1.3	CRR firms – Fitness and propriety 2	SYSC 27.2.3G – 27.2.16G
Temporary UK role – '30' day rule. Significant harm functions do not apply where individual is based outside the UK and performs significant function for no more than 30 days in 12 months	SYSC 5.2.28A R, SYSC 5 Annex 1G		SYSC 27.5.3 R
Record keeping of certificates	SYSC 5.2.15G, SYSC 9.1		SYSC 27.2.13G
Regulatory references			
Regulatory references	SYSC 22 PS 16/22 SUP 10A.15.1G PS16/22	CRR firms – Fitness and propriety 5 SS28/15 (updated May 2017) PS 27/16	SYSC 22 (applicable to *all* SMCR firms including insurers) *Insurers* – CP14/17 Appendix 2, amended SS35/15 (all insurers)

Aspect of the regime	FCA rules in FCA Handbook	PRA rules in PRA Rulebook	Extension of regime – FCA/PRA rule
Factors to take into account when asking for and giving references	SYSC 22 Annex 2	SS28/15 (updated May 2017)	SYSC 22 Annex 2 *Insurers* – CP14/17 Appendix 2, amended SS35/15
Distinction between SMCR and other firms (appointed representatives)			SYSC 22.1.1AG
Territorial scope	SYSC 22.1.3R–22.1.7R		SYSC 22.1.3R–22.1.7R
Getting, giving and updating references (including for board directors)			SYSC 22.2
Regulatory references and sole traders			SYSC 22.2.8R–22.2.10G
When to ask for a reference	SYSC 22.2R/SYSC 22.2.3R	CRR firms – fitness and propriety 2.7.1 SS28/15 (updated May 2017) 6.18–6.24	SYSC 22.2R–22.2.3R
Right of reply	SYSC 22.5.4 PS 27/16	SS28/15 (updated May 2017) 6.45–6.48	SYSC 22.5.5 G
Obligation to update reference	SYSC 22.2.4R		SYSC 22.2.4R *Insurers* – CP14/17 Appendix 2, amended SS35/15
Regulatory reference template	SYSC Annex 1	CRR firms – Fitness and propriety 7.1	SYSC 22 Annex 1R
Need for complete and accurate information – settlement agreements	SUP 10A.15.4G	CRR firms – fitness and propriety 5.3 SS28/15 (updated May 2017) 6.28, 6.31	
Whistleblowing			
Whistleblowing	SYSC 18 PS 15/24	CRR firms – General organisational requirements 2A SS 39/15 PS 24/15	
Duty to notify regulator of successful complaint	SYSC 18.3.f(ii)	SS 39/15 section 2	

Aspect of the regime	FCA rules in FCA Handbook	PRA rules in PRA Rulebook	Extension of regime – FCA/PRA rule
Training obligations	SYSC 18.3.4, 18.3.4(2), (3)	CRR firms – general organisational requirements 2A SS 39/15 section 3	
Whistleblowers champion	SYSC 4.7.7R part 1 of table	PRA prescribed responsibility – CRR firms – allocation of responsibilities 4.1.19 SS 39/15 PS24/15, section 5	
Whistleblower's champion's responsibilities	SYSC 18.4.4R	CRR firms – allocation of responsibilities 4.1.19 SS 39/15	
Whistleblowing and settlement agreements	SYSC 18.5.1	CRR firms – general organisational requirements para. 2A.6 PS 24/15, section 4	
UK branches of overseas firms	SYSC 18.3.g PS 17/7	CRR firms – general organisational requirements para. 2A.7 PS 8/17	
Fitness and propriety			
Assessing fitness and propriety See FSMA, s 60A	SYSC 5.2.6 G FIT 1.2, FIT 1.3 FIT 2.1, 2.2, 2.3	CRR firms – fitness and propriety SS28/15 (updated May 2017)	SYSC 27.2.4G–27.2.7G *Insurers* – CP14/17 Appendix 2, amended SS35/15 (all insurers)
Performance management in retail finance firms			
Guidance on performance management practices	FG15/10		
Conduct Rules			
Conduct rules – application See FSMA, ss 64A–64C	COCON 1 CP 15/22	CRR firms – fitness and propriety SS28/15 (updated May 2017) PS 16/15	*Insurers* – CP14/17 Appendix 2 (all insurers), amended SS35/15
Individual conduct rules	COCON 2	CRR firms – fitness and propriety 3.1 SS28/15 (updated May 2017)	

Aspect of the regime	FCA rules in FCA Handbook	PRA rules in PRA Rulebook	Extension of regime – FCA/PRA rule
Senior manager conduct rules	COCON 2.2	CRR firms – fitness and propriety 3.2 SS28/15 (updated May 2017)	
Conduct rules – training	COCON 2.3		
Application of conduct rules to NEDs – guidance	COCON 1 Annex 1 (guidance) PS 17/8	CRR firms – fitness and propriety – conduct standards (also notified NEDs – notifications) SS28/15 (updated May 2017)	
Specific guidance on SM conduct rules	COCON 4.2	SS28/15 (updated May 2017)	
Factors to assess compliance with conduct rules	COCON 3.1	SS28/15 (updated May 2017)	
Specific guidance on individual conduct rules	COCON 4.1	SS28/15 (updated May 2017)	
Notification of breaches to regulator See FSMA, s 64C	SUP 15.11 (material breaches SUP 15.36)	CRR firms – notifications 2.4	
When to notify the regulator	PS 16/6	PS 9/16	
Criminal record checks			
Criminal record checks	FIT 2.1.1AG FIT 2.1.3G SUP 10C.10.16R CP15/22 para 3.10	CRR firms – fitness and propriety 2.8 SS28/15 (updated May 2017)	*Insurers –* CP14/17 Appendix 2, amended SS35/15 FCA CP17/26 (all insurers)
Checking for criminal convictions under FIT (Certification and other staff being assessed under FIT)	FIT 2.1.1A		
Criminal records checks for non-SMF directors (enhanced and core firms)	PS18/14 Guidance in SUP 10C.10.17G, 10C.10.18G, 10C.10.21G		SYSC 23.4

Aspect of the regime	FCA rules in FCA Handbook	PRA rules in PRA Rulebook	Extension of regime – FCA/PRA rule
Criminal records checks and regulatory references – pre implementation applications			SUP 12.14
Remuneration			
New remuneration rules (PSs)	PS 15/16 PS 17/10	PS 12/15 PS 7/17, SS 2/17	
CRD IV requirements	SYSC 19A, 19D		
Remuneration code for CRR firms	SYSC 19 D	CRR firms – Remuneration	
Remuneration code for IFPRU investment firms	SYSC 19A		
Remuneration code for dual regulated firms/CRR firms	SYSC 19D	CRR firms – Remuneration	
Remuneration code for alternative investment firm managers	SYSC 19B		
Remuneration code for BIPRU investment firms	SYSC 19C		
Remuneration code for UK UCITS management companies	SYSC 19E		
Proportionality	SYSC 19A.3.3 SYSC 9D.3.3 FG17/6 (for SYSC 19A) FG 17/8 (for SYSC 19D)	CRR firms – Remuneration 5.1 SS 2/17	
Material risk taker	FG 17/5 and 'code staff' in SYSC 19A, 19D SYSC 19A.3.4R SYSC 19D.3.4R	CRR firms – Remuneration 3 SS2/17 PS7/17	Definition of MRT – SYSC 27.7.15 R
Deferral	SYSC 19A.3.49R, SYSC 19D.3.59R PS 15/16	CRR firms – Remuneration 15.17–19 PS 12/15 SS2/17	

Aspect of the regime	FCA rules in FCA Handbook	PRA rules in PRA Rulebook	Extension of regime – FCA/PRA rule
Ratio between fixed and variable elements of remuneration (bonus cap)	SYSC 19A.3.34G/ SYSC 19A.3.35AR–35BR/SYSC 19A.3.44R–3.44E SYSC 19D.3.48R–53R PS17/10	CRR firms – Remuneration 15.2, 15.9–15.13 SS2/17 PS7/17	
Payments on early termination	SYSC 19A.3.45R SYSC 19D.3.54R	CRR firms – Remuneration 15.14	
Retained shares or other instruments	SYSC 19A.3.47R SYSC 19D.3.56R	CRR firms – Remuneration 15.15	
Notification to FCA/ PRA	SYSC 19A Annex 1 8G	SS2/17	
No variable remuneration to a NED	SYSC 19D.3.38R	CRR firms – Remuneration 15.3	
Hedging strategies	SYSC 19A.3.30R SYSC 19D.3.32R	CRR firms – Remuneration 13.1	
Guaranteed variable remuneration	SYSC 19A.3.40R SYSC 19D.3.44–47	CRR firms – Remuneration 15.7 SS2/17	
Ex post risk adjustment (malus and clawback) – guidance	General guidance on the application of ex-post risk adjustment to variable remuneration, 1 July 2015	SS2/17 PS12/15	
Ex post risk adjustment rules	SYSC 19A.3.51R–53G SYSC 19D.3.61R–65R	CRR firms – Remuneration 15.20–15.23 SS2/17	
Buy-outs *NB PRA regulated firms must comply with rules on remuneration statement/ buy out notice	SYSC 19A.2.4R, 19A.3.40R SYSC 19D.2.3R, 19D.3.45R	CRR firms – Remuneration 15A PS26/16	
Record keeping (inc performance appraisal processes)	SYSC 19A.2.4, SYSC 19A.3.53G SYSC 19D.2.3, SYSC 19D.3.6R	CRR firms – Remuneration 3.4, 6.5	
De minimis provisions	SYSC 19A3.34G, 19A.3.54R SYSC 19D.3.67R	CRR firms – Remuneration 16.7	
Retention awards	PS17/10	SS2/17	

Aspect of the regime	FCA rules in FCA Handbook	PRA rules in PRA Rulebook	Extension of regime – FCA/PRA rule
Freezing of variable remuneration pending conclusion of investigation	Para 4.5 general guidance on ex post adjustment – variable remuneration	Para 4.15 SS2/17	
Notifications to the regulator			
Overarching obligation to disclose anything of which the regulator would reasonably expect notice	Principle 11 of PRIN 2.1.1R	CRR firms – FUND – Rule 7 in 2.7 CRR firms – Notifications 2.1 and 2.2	
Consequences of breaching Principles	PRIN 1.1.7		
How to make notifications	SUP 15.7	CRR firms – Notifications 7 SS28/15 (updated May 2017)	
Notifications of code of conduct breaches and disciplinary action	SUP 15.11	CRR firms – Notifications 11.2	*Insurers –* CP14/17 Appendix 2, amended SS35/15
Notifications re changes to a FCA-approved person's details	SUP 10C.14		
Reporting under SUP 15.11 from commencement of SMCR extension			SUP 12.21
Termination payments			
Requirement that severance payment must be treated as variable pay subject to bonus cap (EBA guidelines)		PRA has acknowledged this rule must be implemented by CRR firms but has not yet made changes to Remuneration handbook	

CHAPTER 2

The Senior Managers Regime

Elizabeth Graves, Partner, Simon Collins, Managing Director –
Regulatory/ES Consulting and Susan Mayne, Consultant

I   BACKGROUND

SMCR replaces APER for 'relevant authorised persons'

2.01   Until the Senior Managers and Certification Regime (SMCR) came into effect on 7 March 2016 individuals who worked in the financial services sector were chiefly regulated through the Approved Persons Regime (APER) as set out in Part V of the Financial Services and Markets Acts 2000 (FSMA).

2.02   APER remained in place for the time being for firms not yet covered by the SMCR (but see 2.17). Under APER, FSMA-authorised firms could not engage or employ an individual to perform a 'controlled function'[1] unless the appropriate regulator (either the Financial Conduct Authority (FCA) or the Prudential Regulation Authority (PRA) depending on the nature of the controlled functions) had already approved that person to carry out the relevant functions on behalf of the firm.

2.03   Once approved by an appropriate regulator, an individual's details would be listed on the public Financial Services Register maintained by the FCA in accordance with its statutory duty.[2] Such approved persons must comply with statements of principle issued by the regulators, who may take enforcement action against an individual for breach of the statements of principle or for being knowingly concerned in a breach of regulatory requirements by the firm.

2.04   As outlined elsewhere in this book (see Chapter 1) the government made amendments to FSMA[3] to provide a legislative framework to implement the recommendations from the Parliamentary Commission on Banking Standards (PCBS) report, 'Changing banking for good'. The PCBS believed that the deficiencies it had highlighted in APER extended beyond banking firms but did not want to delay the implementation timetable. A new accountability regime was therefore first targeted at the banking sector ('relevant authorised persons' – see 2.15) with the intention of further extending it at a later date.

2.05   The Bank of England and Financial Services Act 2016 ('the 2016 Act') provided for the extension of the SMCR to all FSMA Part 4A authorised firms. HM Treasury published a policy paper on this extension in October 2015.[4] The aims behind the expansion of the regime included enhancing personal responsibility for senior managers (SMs) as well as providing an effective and proportionate means to raise standards of conduct of staff. Consultation proposals by the regulators were published in July 2017 setting out plans to extend the SMCR across the financial services industry in December 2019 (10 December 2018 for the insurance sector) (see 2.24).

---

1   FSMA, s 59(3) and as specified in FCA/PRA rules.
2   FSMA, s 347.
3   By way of the Financial Services (Banking Reform) Act 2013 ('the 2013 Act').
4   HM Treasury, 'Senior Managers and Certification Regime: extension to all FSMA authorised persons' October 2015.

2.06   In July 2018 the regulators published policy statements[5] with near-final rules extending the SMCR to all FCA regulated firms and insurers and reinsurers. Implementation for insurance firms is 10 December 2018 and 9 December 2019 for other financial services firms. On 20 November 2018, the PRA published a policy statement[6] confirming that there would be no changes to the final rules as consulted on for insurers. Details of the extended regime are set out in this chapter (and in Chapter 12 for insurers).

Introducing the new accountability regime: background to the senior managers regime final rules

2.07   As detailed more fully in Chapter 1, the regulators first consulted in 2014[7] on a new way to hold individuals to account following the PCBS recommendations. The proposals in the consultation paper were aimed at implementing the changes required by the amendments to FSMA following these recommendations.

2.08   Further proposals included changes to existing rules on remuneration[8] and, later in 2015, proposed new whistleblowing rules.[9]

2.09   In the regulators' joint consultation paper, 'Strengthening accountability in banks: a new regulatory framework for individuals', the PRA and FCA proposed the introduction of:

- a new senior managers regime (SMR) which would clarify the lines of responsibility at the top of banks, enhance the regulators' ability to hold senior individuals in banks, building societies, insurers and credit unions to account and require these institutions to regularly vet their senior managers (SMs) for fitness and propriety;

- a certification regime requiring firms to assess fitness and propriety of staff in positions where the decisions they make could pose significant harm to the bank or any of its customers; and

- a new set of conduct rules, which would take the form of brief statements of high-level principle, setting out the standards of behaviour required of bank employees.

2.10   Feedback on the consultation was addressed in a further feedback and consultation paper[10] which contained a set of near-final rules for the SMR and

---

5   FCA PS18/14; FCA PS18/15; PRA PS15/18.
6   PRA PS27/18, 'Strengthening accountability: implementing the extension of the SM&CR to insurers (Part 2)'.
7   FCA CP14/13; PRA CP14/14.
8   FCA CP14/14 and PRA 15/14, 'Strengthening the alignment of risk and reward: new remuneration rules'.
9   FCA CP15/4 and PRA CP6/15, 'Whistleblowing in deposit-takers, PRA designated investment firms and insurers'.
10   FCA CP15/9; PRA PS16/15.

consultation proposals on guidance on the presumption of responsibility that applied to SMs under the 2013 Act. This 'presumption' of responsibility was later superseded by a statutory 'duty of responsibility' on SMs to take reasonable steps to prevent regulatory breaches in their areas of responsibility. In the event of such misconduct, SMs can be guilty if they fail to take reasonable steps. The burden of proving misconduct will fall on the regulator, as with other regulatory enforcement actions. This duty is considered in more detail at 2.173 ff.

SMR – the final rules

2.11 In July 2015, the PRA and FCA set out final rules for the new accountability regime, the SMCR.[11] Separately, the PRA also introduced a senior insurance managers regime for insurance firms subject to EU Solvency II Directive 2009/138/EC (the Senior Insurance Managers Regime (SIMR)). At the same time as implementation of the SMCR, the SIMR came into force. Under the extension of the SMCR, the SIMR was replaced by the SMCR which now applies to all regulated insurers and reinsurers in a proportionate manner (see Chapter 12). Full details of the extended regime are set out in this chapter and elsewhere in this book.

2.12 The regulators also published rules on whistleblowing, regulatory references and remuneration (which are dealt with fully elsewhere in this book, see Chapters 10, 5 and 8 respectively).

2.13 The SMR focuses on individuals who hold key roles or have overall responsibility for whole areas of relevant firms. While individuals who fall under this regime must be pre-approved by regulators, firms are also legally required to ensure that they have procedures in place to assess the fitness and propriety of candidates before the firm applies to the appropriate regulator for approval, and at least annually thereafter.

2.14 Alongside its policy statement, the PRA also published a supervisory statement[12] setting out its expectations of firms in relation to the new regimes. This supervisory statement contains helpful guidance on aspects of the SMCR.

2.15 The regulators' final rules on the SMCR are contained in the FCA Handbook and PRA Rulebook. The SMCR initially only applied to *relevant authorised persons* (RAPs)[13] namely:

> 'a. deposit takers (banks, building societies and credit unions);

---

11 FCA CP15/22, 'Strengthening accountability in banking: Final rules (including feedback on CP14/31 and CP15/5) and consultation on extending the Certification Regime to wholesale market activities'; PRA PS16/15 'Strengthening individual accountability in banking: responses to CP14/14, CP28/14 and CP7/15'; and PS3/15 'Strengthening individual accountability in banking and insurance — responses to CP14/14 and CP26/14'.

12 SS28/15.

13 Defined in FSMA, s 71A.

b.   certain PRA regulated investment banks;

c.   branches of foreign banks operating in the UK (known as "incoming branches"). Incoming branches were brought within the ambit of "RAPs" by the FSMA 2000 (Relevant Authorised Persons) Order 2015, SI 2015/1865.'

2.16   From 7 March 2016, APER was replaced by a three-tier system for RAPs:

'a.   tier 1 – "senior managers" (SMs);

b.   tier 2– "certified persons";

c.   tier 3 – "relevant persons" to whom high level conduct rules apply (these rules also apply to certified staff and SMs and another tier of conduct rules apply specifically to SMs).'

2.17   Until the extension of the SMCR regime across the financial services industry comes into force in 2019, APER remains in place for the time being for financial institutions that were not otherwise caught by the SMCR. However, as noted, the regulators will extend the regime to *all* firms authorised under FSMA from 2019 (see 2.24) at which point APER will no longer apply. The only exception to this is appointed representatives[14] as the legislation did not empower the regulators to extend the SMCR to them.

UK branches of overseas banks

2.18   The definition of a 'relevant authorised person' (see 2.15) was extended to include overseas branches of UK firms.[15] The regulators have set out specific rules[16] for applying the SMCR to overseas branches of UK firms, modifying some of the requirements. The regulators refer to 'EEA' (European Economic Area) branches and 'non-EEA' branches, which have different rules and requirements.

2   EXTENSION OF SMCR TO ALL FINANCIAL SERVICES FIRMS

2.19   The PCBS was aware that the problems with APER would not just be confined to banking. However, it was concerned that attempting to extend the reforms it proposed to all sectors would delay the timetable for implementation for banks and so it recommended that the reforms should initially be introduced only for banking. In October 2015, the government announced that it would extend the SMCR to 'all sectors of the financial services industry'.[17]

---

14   See FCA PS18/14, para 2.15.
15   Financial Services and Markets Act 2000 (Relevant Authorised persons) Order 2015 (SI 2015/1865).
16   FCA PS15/30 (see also FCA CP15/10).
17   See: www.gov.uk/government/uploads/system/uploads/attachment_data/file/468328/SMCR_policy_paper_final_15102015.pdf.

2.20   The government's intention was to ensure the same high standards in both the banking and so-called 'shadow banking' sectors and therefore it was decided to extend the SMCR to all sectors of the financial services industry, including insurers, investment firms, asset managers, insurance and mortgage brokers and consumer credit firms. Provision for this extension is made in s 21 of and Sch 4 to the 2016 Act. Under the proposed extension the SMCR will replace APER.

2.21   The FCA published a consultation paper[18] in July 2017 on extending the SMCR across the financial services industry and for insurers[19] and on the same day the PRA published its consultation[20] on extending the regime to insurers.

2.22   For Solvency II insurers already subject to SIMR, the extension of the SMR involves less change than for other FCA authorised firms coming within the reach of the SMCR for the first time. The most significant change for Solvency II insurers is the replacement of APER with the certification regime for the 'second tier' within those firms still regulated by APER alongside SIMR who will become subject to the certification regime for the first time in 2018.

2.23   The outcome will be that the burden of assessing certification staff as fit and proper will fall upon all firms that come into scope. The main effects for new firms being brought into the regime are expected to be:

- a substantial reduction in the number of appointments that are subject to prior regulatory approval;

- most current approved persons below SM level are expected to become certified persons.

2.24   The government intends that implementation of the newly extended regime should come into operation on 9 December 2019 (10 December 2018 for insurers and reinsurers; see 2.26) and policy papers were published in July 2018[21] setting out the detail of the extended regime.

2.25   The proposals introduce some new concepts, most notably a three-tiered approach to compliance depending on the size, scale and complexity of a firm.

2.26   The FCA will consult further on how it proposes to implement the regime, including proposals to transition approved persons into the regime. For insurers, the SIMR was replaced by the SMCR when the new regime came into effect on 10 December 2018 (see Chapter 13).

---

18 FCA CP17/25, 'Individual accountability – extending the Senior Managers and Certification Regime to all FCA firms'.
19 FCA CP17/26, 'Individual accountability – extending the Senior Managers and Certification Regime to insurers'.
20 PRA CP14/17, 'Strengthening individual accountability in insurance – extension of the Senior Managers & Certification Regime to insurers'.
21 FCA PS18/14 (FCA PS18/15 and PRA PS15/18 for insurers).

2.27   The FCA and PRA also published consultation papers[22] in December 2017 on transitioning firms, insurers and individuals to the SMCR, the duty of responsibility for insurers and FCA solo regulated firms and implementing the extension of the SMCR to insurers.

2.28   Further guidance is provided in the FCA's 'Senior Managers and Certification Regime: Guide for solo regulated firms' published in July 2018 with the policy statements. An equivalent guide was also published for insurers.

2.29   Further details on the extended regime are set out in this chapter.

3   THE PROPOSED SMCR AFTER EXTENSION: WHO IS AFFECTED AND TO WHAT EXTENT?

Core firms

2.30   The FCA will apply a 'baseline' of requirements to every firm under the extension of the SMCR, which will be known as the 'core regime' and which will apply to approximately 14,000 firms. The three main elements of the SMCR (SMR, certification regime and conduct rules) will therefore apply to *all* firms.

2.31   The FCA also proposes some new responsibilities that firms will need to give their SMs ('prescribed responsibilities'). This will not apply to some firms (such as sole traders or firms with limited permissions, and EEA branches) known as limited scope firms and more responsibilities will apply to bigger firms. In its proposals, the FCA had intended to apply a prescribed responsibility for core firms to inform the governing body of their legal and regulatory obligations but, following consultation, this prescribed responsibility was removed.

2.32   The FCA will apply the following six senior management functions (SMFs)[23] (see 2.74 ff) for all core and enhanced firms (see 2.37 ff) where they have individuals performing the relevant roles:

Governing functions

- SMF9 – Chair (the chair can be executive or non-executive);

- SMF1 – chief executive;

- SMF3 – executive director;

- SMF27 – partner.

---

22 FCA CP17/40, 'Individual accountability: Transitioning FCA firms and individuals to the Senior Managers & Certification Regime'; CP17/41, 'Individual accountability: Transitioning insurers and individuals to the Senior Managers & Certification Regime'; CP17/42, 'The Duty of Responsibility for insurers and FCA solo-regulated firms'; PRA CP28/17, 'Strengthening accountability: implementing the extension of the SM&CR to insurers and other amendments'.
23 Each senior management function has a specific definition set out in FCA SUP 10C.

Required functions

- SMF16 – compliance oversight;

- SMF17 – money laundering reporting officer.

2.33   Some respondents to the consultation on extending the SMCR asked whether they could apply the enhanced SMFs (see 2.37) even if they were in the core tier. The FCA will not allow firms to adopt only parts of the enhanced tier as this could obscure accountability and make it more complicated for the FCA to supervise firms. However, it will be made easier for firms to opt into the enhanced tier as a whole.

2.34   The FCA adopts the term 'required functions' from APER which is aimed at categorising functions that the FCA requires some types of firms to have under certain sections of its Handbook.

2.35   The FCA will also apply the following prescribed responsibilities (PRs) to SMs in core and enhanced firms (core firms must apply only the first five of these PRs: (a) to (e)):

All firms

(a) Performance by the firm of its obligations under the SMR, including implementation and oversight.

(b) Performance by the firm of its obligations under the certification regime.

(c) Performance by the firm of its obligations in respect of notifications and training of the conduct rules.

(d) Responsibility for the firm's policies and procedures for countering the risk that the firm might be used to further financial crime.

(e) Responsibility for the firm's compliance with the Client Assets sourcebook (CASS) (if applicable).

Authorised fund managers (AFMs)

(f) Responsibility for an AFM's value for money assessments, independent director representations and for acting in investors' best interests. This PR only applies to AFMs.

Enhanced firms (additional PRs)

(g) Compliance with the rules relating to the firm's management responsibilities map.

(h) Safeguarding and overseeing the independence and performance of the internal audit function.[24]

---

24 SYSC 6.2.

(i) Safeguarding and overseeing the independence and performance of the compliance function.[25]

(j) Safeguarding and overseeing the independence and performance of the risk function.[26]

(k) If the firm outsources its internal audit function, taking reasonable steps to make sure that every person involved in the performance of the service is independent from the persons who perform external audit.

(l) Developing and maintaining the firm's business model.

(m) Managing the firm's internal stress-tests and ensuring the accuracy and timeliness of information provided to the FCA for stress-testing.

Practical guidance

The FCA has tried to be proportionate in its approach by introducing the tiered approach. It is clear from our experience that a number of firms are considering adopting the principles behind the enhanced regime even where they may be a core or limited scope firm by developing a management responsibilities map (see 2.138) and adopting handover procedures. Although the FCA has been clear that enhanced firms should meet certain criteria, they do recognise that firms, particularly within groups, where there may be an enhanced and a core firm, are looking to adopt one overall approach.

2.36   PRs will not apply to limited scope firms (see 2.44) and additional PRs apply to enhanced firms. Each PR should be given to the SM who is the most senior person responsible for that issue. They will need to have sufficient authority and an appropriate level of knowledge and competence to carry out the responsibility properly.

The enhanced regime

2.37   A number of significant, larger firms (accounting for fewer than 1% of regulated firms) will come within the enhanced regime and have additional responsibilities very similar to those under the existing regime for banks and building societies. These firms will need to have management responsibilities maps, handover procedures and will need to make sure that there is a SM responsible for every area of their firm ('overall responsibility') including operations, HR and IT. Details of these requirements are set out in this chapter. The enhanced tier is intended to capture systemically risky firms from a prudential perspective but also firms that are larger in size or have more complex structures.

---

25 SYSC 6.1.
26 SYSC 7.1.21R; SYSC 7.1.22R.

2.38   The FCA will use six objective criteria to identify firms to which the enhanced regime will apply. Once a firm meets the relevant criteria, the enhanced regime will automatically apply to them. This means that firms will need to monitor whether and how the criteria apply to them, particularly where they are close to meeting one of the relevant criteria. The types of firm caught will include:

- Firms that are significant IFPRU firms.

- Large CASS firms.

- Firms with assets under management of £50bn.

- Firms with a total intermediary regulated business revenue of £35m or more per annum.

- Firms with annual regulated revenue generated by consumer credit lending of £100m or more per annum.

- Mortgage lenders or administrators (that are not banks) with 10,000 or more regulated mortgages outstanding.

2.39   Enhanced firms will have additional SMFs (see 2.32) and additional PRs (see 2.35). The additional SMFs in enhanced firms (in all, 17 SMFs apply to enhanced firms) are:

- SMF2 – chief finance function;

- SMF4 – chief risk function;

- SMF5 – head of internal audit;

- SMF14 – senior independent director;

- SMF12 – chair of the remuneration committee;

- SMF10 – chair of the risk committee;

- SMF11 – chair of the audit committee;

- SMF13 – chair of the nominations committee;

- SMF7 – group entity senior manager;

- SMF24 – chief operations function;

- SMF18 – other overall responsibility.[27]

2.40   The FCA extended the transition period for firms moving into the enhanced tier to 12 months, which means that such firms will have 12 months to prepare and make the relevant changes.[28]

---

27 Many firms will not need this function as the people ultimately responsible for everything the business does will already be captured by other SMFs.
28 FCA PS18/14.

2.41   The FCA decided that it would not be proportionate to make all firms in a group with an enhanced firm automatically apply the enhanced tier.[29] However, it has made it easier for firms to opt into this tier if they want to by using a notification process and a new Form O. Nevertheless it should be noted that once a firm has opted into the enhanced tier it must comply with all of the rules; the firm cannot pick and choose.

2.42   The three financial criteria will now be worked out on a three-year rolling average basis.[30] The FCA made no changes to the absolute level of the thresholds which it felt were tailored appropriately to individual sectors. The FCA deliberately did not use employee numbers as a criterion by which to establish what tier a firm falls into in case this acted as a disincentive to hire staff.

2.43   The FCA is implementing 12 prescribed responsibilities that must be given to SMs at enhanced firms (see 2.35). There are also additional requirements under the SMR that only enhanced firms must apply; these are the overall responsibility requirement; management responsibilities maps; and handover procedures. Firms should ensure that appropriate handover procedures are in place before implementation.

Limited scope firms

2.44   There are a reduced set of requirements for limited scope firms where financial services activity is secondary to the main activity, such as retail firms, motor dealers etc, amounting to around 33,000 firms. For example, prescribed responsibilities will not apply to limited scope firms. These firms will need just one SM although there are three SMFs in the limited scope tier. The criteria for limited scope firms mirror how APER works, which reflects the different risks and business models of firms in this category.

Practical guidance

The regulators have never intended to require firms to change their governance structures to meet the requirements of the SMCR. While many firms in their planning have opted to undertake a governance gap analysis, this has tended to be useful in highlighting improvements around committee structure, board packs, reporting lines etc. It is certainly not the case that, unless you have a regulatory/legal requirement to appoint an individual to a role such as Chair of the Audit committee, you do not have to make an appointment or create specific committees if you consider your governance structure is appropriate for your firm. The regulator can of course challenge the structure at a later date, hence why a responsibilities map is an important document for the firm.

---

29   FCA PS18/14, para 6.14.
30   FCA PS18/14, para.6.9.

Appointed representatives

2.45 The extension of the SMCR does not affect individuals working as appointed representatives (ARs). This is because the relevant legislation did not give the FCA the power to extend the SMCR to ARs. As a result, the provisions of APER still apply to ARs. Principal firms remain fully responsible for their ARs and networks meeting the FCA rules. One exception is for limited permission consumer credit firms that also act as ARs for other business. These firms fall within scope of the extended SMCR as they are authorised firms.

4 SUMMARY OF REQUIREMENTS UNDER PROPOSED SMCR EXTENSION

2.46 The FCA published in its consultation paper[31] a summary of the proposed requirements under the extended regime and what aspects of the SMCR will apply to a particular type of firm. References are to sections of the consultation paper.

Summary of proposed requirements under extended regime – amended extract from consultation paper CP17/25 (see also FCA PS18/14)
Firms should note that the definition of 'employee' (P) is defined in FSMA, s 64A(6) to include a person who:

'(a) personally provides, or is under an obligation personally to provide, services to P under an arrangement made between P and the person providing the services or another person, and

(b) is subject to (or to the right of) supervision, direction or control by P as to the manner in which those services are provided, and 'employer' is to be read accordingly.'

TOOL	DESCRIPTION	WHO DOES IT APPLY TO?	WHERE CAN I READ MORE? (CP17/25)
Ancillary staff (in practice most firms to date have adopted the conduct rules for all staff through internal codes of conduct)	Employees (as defined widely by the FCA to include someone who is subject to the control or supervision of the firm) who are not covered by the Conduct Rules such as cleaners, receptionists etc	All firms	Section 7.14

31 FCA CP17/25.

TOOL	DESCRIPTION	WHO DOES IT APPLY TO?	WHERE CAN I READ MORE? (CP17/25)
Certification Function	A function performed by employees who are not senior managers (SMs) but who could pose a risk of 'significant harm' to the firm or its customers	All firms	Section 5.6
Certification Regime	The part of the regime that covers certification functions	All firms	Chapter 5
Criminal Records Checks	The requirement on firms to conduct criminal records checks for SMs and non-executive directors (where a fitness requirement applies) as part of checking that they are fit and proper	All firms	Section 6.8
Duty of Responsibility	Every SM will have a duty of responsibility as a result of FSMA. This means that when a firm breaks a regulatory requirement the SM responsible for that area could be held accountable if they did not take 'reasonable steps' to prevent or stop the breach	All firms	Section 4.20
Fit and Proper requirements	Firms must make sure all SMs and people performing Certification Functions are fit and proper to perform their role. This must be done on appointment and at least once a year	All firms	Chapter 6

TOOL	DESCRIPTION	WHO DOES IT APPLY TO?	WHERE CAN I READ MORE? (CP17/25)
Handover Procedures	A firm must take all reasonable steps to make sure that a new SM has all the information and materials they need to do the job	Enhanced firms only (although other firms may adopt these procedures as good business practice)	Section 8.36
Individual Conduct Rules	These are basic standards of behaviour that people performing financial services activities in firms are expected to meet. Firms need to train their staff in the conduct rules and how they apply to them. Firms will need to report breaches of Conduct Rules resulting in disciplinary action to the regulator every year	All firms	Chapter 7
Other overall responsibility function	A senior management function (SMF) that applies where a senior executive is the most senior person responsible for an area of the firm's business but they do not perform any other SMF	Enhanced firms only	Section 8.16
Overall responsibility	A requirement for every area, activity and management function of the firm to have a SM with overall responsibility for it	Enhanced firms only	Section 8.23
Prescribed responsibilities	FCA defined responsibilities that must be allocated to an appropriate SM	All firms except Limited Scope firms	Section 4.37 for Core Firms Section 8.19 for Enhanced Firms Section 9.11 for non-EEA branches

TOOL	DESCRIPTION	WHO DOES IT APPLY TO?	WHERE CAN I READ MORE? (CP17/25)
Regulatory references	Information that firms need to share with each other when an employee or director moves from one firm to another (for candidates of SMFs, Non-Executive Directors and Certification functions)	All firms	Section 6.12
Responsibilities Maps	A document setting out a firm's governance and management arrangements, and how responsibilities are allocated to individuals within a firm	Enhanced Firms only (although other firms may adopt as good business practice)	Section 8.33
Senior Management Functions	Roles where the people doing them need to be approved by the FCA. These are defined in the FCA Handbook	All firms	Section 4.12 for Core Firms Section 4.15 for Limited Scope firms Section 8.16 for Enhanced Firms Section 9.9 for non-EEA branches
Senior Manager Conduct Rules	These are additional Conduct Rules that apply to all SMs. Firms need to train SMs so that they understand what the Conduct Rules are and how they apply to them. Firms will need to report breaches of all individual and SM Conduct Rules by SMs resulting in disciplinary action to the FCA within 7 days	All firms	Chapter 7

TOOL	DESCRIPTION	WHO DOES IT APPLY TO?	WHERE CAN I READ MORE? (CP17/25)
Senior Managers	People who perform a SMF. These people need regulatory approval to do their jobs	All firms	Section 4.12 for Core Firms Section 4.15 for Limited Scope Firms Section 8.16 for Enhanced Firms Section 9.2 for EEA branches Section 9.9 for non-EEA branches
Senior Managers Regime	The part of the regime for SMs. This includes SMFs, Statement of Responsibilities, Duty of Responsibility, Fit & Proper, Conduct Rules, Prescribed Responsibilities, Regulatory References and criminal records checks For Enhanced Firms, it also includes Responsibilities Maps, Handover Procedures and Overall Responsibility	All firms	Chapter 4 for all firms Chapter 8 for Enhanced Firms Chapter 9 for EEA and non-EEA branches
Statement of Responsibilities	A document that every SM needs to have that sets out what they are responsible and accountable for. This needs to be submitted to the regulator when a SM is being approved and be kept up to date	All firms	Section 4.16

Transfer of individuals between insurance and banking firms

2.47   Following the extension of the SMCR to all insurance firms, the PRA proposes to enable individuals who have been approved for a senior insurance management function (SIMF) within insurance firms to be treated equivalently to individuals who have been approved for a SMF within banking firms.

5 GUIDES FOR INSURERS AND SOLO REGULATED FIRMS ON THE EXTENDED SMCR

2.48   The FCA has published guides[32] for insurers and solo regulated firms on the SMCR. These guides summarise the rules and guidance on the SMCR, what firms need to do under the new regime and how the FCA will move firms and individuals from APER to the SMCR. The Handbook will take precedence where there is conflict between the guidance and the rules but the guides provide useful information for transitioning firms and insurers. The guides are based on the near-final rules published in the FCA's policy statement PS18/14.

6 TRANSITIONING FIRMS TO THE SMCR

2.49   The FCA has assumed for the purposes of the near-final rules published in July 2018 that firms will have 12 months from the start of the regime to complete their fitness and propriety assessments and to get certification paperwork in place. For solo regulated firms, commencement is 9 December 2019. Firms must check that their approvals are correct on the Financial Services Register as soon as the new regime starts. If their approvals are incorrect then the relevant regulatory forms must be submitted as soon as possible. For all firms the conduct rules in COCON apply from commencement of the regime to staff holding a senior manager or certification function. Firms will have 12 months from commencement to apply the conduct rules to 'other conduct rules staff'.

Transitioning insurers to the SMCR[33]

2.50   The FCA's proposed approach to converting approved individuals from the APER to the SMCR differs according to the type of firm and the extent to which the SMCR applies to that firm. If the FCA currently approves a person for their role and the equivalent role exists under the SMCR, it will not be necessary to apply for re-approval.

2.51   The regulators propose that the requirement on insurers to certify employees performing certification functions as fit and proper would come into effect 12 months after the commencement of the SMCR for insurers. This means that firms would not need to obtain regulatory references for certified staff until the time they decide whether to issue a certificate to those employees.

2.52   The FCA proposed giving firms 12 months from commencement to prepare to apply the conduct rules to 'other conduct rules staff'.

---

32 https://www.fca.org.uk/publication/policy/guide-for-fca-solo-regulated-firms.pdf;   https:// www.fca.org.uk/publication/policy/guide-for-insurers.pdf.

33 CPs 17/41, 28/17; FCA PS18/15; PRA PS15/18.

7 SENIOR MANAGERS

2.53   A SM is a senior executive who carries out SMFs (see 2.74). The aim of the SMR was to ensure that SMs would be held accountable for their conduct. Under the accountability regime SMs are subject to far more scrutiny than under APER. There are some similarities with the approved persons regime under APER since a SM must be *pre-approved* by the appropriate regulator to carry out their role, has additional obligations under separate senior manager conduct rules (which replace the APER statements of principle) as well as a statutory duty of responsibility.

2.54   While the regulator must approve SMs, it is for the firm to ensure that proper due diligence is carried out on SMs to assess them as fit and proper to carry out the SMF(s) which the SM is to fulfil.

2.55   The SMR has no territorial limitation. This means that if a SM is based outside the UK but works for a RAP, they must comply with the rules applicable to SMs in the same way as UK-based SMs.

Practical guidance

The FCA and PRA did not expect to see an increased number of SMs as a result of the regime coming into force. They have made it clear that the SM appointment is for the most senior individuals within the firm and would largely have mirrored the firm's previous approved person population for governing and required functions. In addition they do not expect a SM to report to another SM (apart from the CEO/board). The extended regime adopts similar requirements.

What pre-employment checks should be carried out?

2.56   Full details about the fitness and propriety assessment for SMs are set out in Chapters 3 and 4. See also Chapter 5.

Before applying to the regulator for approval of a candidate for a SM role, a firm should ensure that the following checks are carried out:

- credit checks;

- criminal records checks (see Chapter 3);

- regulatory references (see Chapter 5);

- any checks necessary as part of the fitness and propriety assessment (see Chapters 3 and 4).

Drafting an offer letter for a senior manager

An offer letter to a candidate for a SM role should be drafted carefully given that there is no guarantee of regulatory approval. While the regulatory rules do not, of themselves, specify the content of offer letters, the requirements highlighted above mean that a firm will wish to include the following provisions in any offer letter.

The offer of employment should be made subject to regulatory approval being obtained and to the candidate's cooperation with that process, including consent to pre-employment checks. The employment contract should separately provide that employment is conditional upon regulatory approval being maintained.

The offer should also be made subject to the receipt of satisfactory regulatory references and the relevant checks (credit and criminal records checks) and the firm's own fitness and propriety assessment in addition to regulatory approval. Circumstances may arise in which the firm's own due diligence processes flag a fitness and propriety issue which the firm believes will result in the regulator declining to approve the individual, for example a regulatory reference discloses an issue which has arisen after the candidate's departure from a previous firm. Clearly, the firm will want to have the option to withdraw its offer of employment without any obligation to submit an application to the regulator for SM approval.

The employee should be asked to give consent to the checks to be carried out as part of the vetting process (subject always to complying with data protection legislation).

The firm may also wish to consider including a warranty that the individual has given full disclosure during the recruitment process either in the offer letter or any fitness and propriety questionnaire that the candidate is required to complete.

The commencement date may need to be kept flexible given that regulatory approval may take some time. A date could be specified subject to regulatory approval being obtained ('DATE or as soon as practicable thereafter once regulatory approval has been obtained').

Where details of any variable remuneration are given in the offer letter, the rules on variable pay (see Chapter 7) must be borne in mind and the rules on deferral, malus and clawback should be set out or cross referenced (the individual should in the latter case be given a copy of any document with the relevant provisions during the recruitment process).

The candidate should be reminded of their regulatory obligations, in particular their obligation to comply with individual and SM conduct rules.

Applying to the regulator for approval

2.57   While the APER regime required a firm to carry out its own due diligence prior to submitting an application for approval for a candidate to carry out controlled functions, as noted at 2.56, when making an application to the regulator for a SM to be approved, firms need to carry out far more due diligence than under APER, since a far wider range of behavioural issues may affect a fit and proper assessment.[34]

2.58   This assessment could potentially result in delays in the recruitment process so firms may need to consider interim appointments (see 2.159) pending regulatory approval for a candidate. In any event the approval process itself is lengthy (there is a statutory time limit[35] of three months for regulatory approval starting from the date of receipt of the application) and there will be further delays when the new SM reviews handover material. However, the regulators will seek to approve applications earlier if they can and firms are advised to ensure that an application is as complete as possible. Where there is a particular urgency to the application, firms will wish to explore with the appropriate regulator whether it may be possible to submit an application prior to receipt of criminal records checks and/or regulatory references (since it is the requirement to obtain these that is the most common cause of delay in the process).

2.59   Any anticipated delays should be built into the recruitment process. On occasion, the regulator may ask to interview a candidate for a SMF although this is more likely at larger more systemically important firms. Once the regulator is satisfied that the individual is fit and proper it will grant approval, possibly subject to conditions or limitations.

2.60   Given that regulatory approval is not guaranteed, firms should ensure that offers of employment or promotion are conditional on a SM achieving and maintaining regulatory approval as a SM.

Practical guidance

From our experience with banks, building societies, credit unions and insurers etc the appointment of new SMs has created far more regulatory attention than under APER. Interviews of prospective executives, non-executive directors (NEDs) and compliance officers are more routine. In addition we have also seen the use of exit interviews by the regulators. While the request for an interview will be dependent on the firm's size, sector and complexity, closer regulatory scrutiny of SMs is inevitable.

2.61   The rules governing applications for approval under the SMR are set out in the FCA Handbook[36] and in the PRA Rulebook.[37] Where the senior function is a PRA function, the PRA can only grant approval with the FCA's consent

---

34 FCA SUP 10C.10; PRA 'Fitness and Propriety Assessments by Firms'.
35 FSMA, s 61(3A)(b).
36 SUP 10C.
37 Applications and notifications.

whereas where an application is made for approval of a FCA function, the FCA determines approval alone.[38]

2.62   Before a firm may apply for pre-approval of a SM,[39] the firm must be satisfied that the person in respect of whom the application is made is a *fit and proper* person to perform the function.[40] An application for approval must be accompanied by a statement of responsibilities (see 2.115) and any handover certificate or documentation that has been produced.[41]

2.63   The FCA rules governing the assessment by a firm of the fitness and propriety of an individual who is to be put forward for approval as a SM or a person whom it proposes to certify to perform a significant harm function are set out in the FIT section of the FCA Handbook. The equivalent rules for the PRA are set out in the Fitness and Propriety section in the PRA Rulebook.

2.64   In deciding whether a SM is fit and proper to be approved the RAP must have regard to a number of factors, such as whether the candidate:

- has obtained a qualification;

- has undergone or is undergoing training;

- possesses the requisite level of competence; or

- has the personal characteristics required[42] (under general rules made by the FCA[43]).

2.65   When carrying out the fit and proper assessment firms must take care to ensure that the proper questions are being asked and that the potential impact of any behavioural traits (such as an overbearing manner which may suggest bullying or a possible tendency to suppress a whistleblower) are taken into account. To this end, it is important that those carrying out the assessment are properly trained and understand the implications of the assessment process. Guidance for making the application is set out in SUP 10C.10.8G and PRA Fitness and Propriety Assessments by Firms and the PRA's supervisory statement SS28/15.

2.66   FSMA, s 59 provides that a firm must take *reasonable care* to ensure that no individual performs a SMF without having been approved to do so. If a SM performs a SMF without approval, the firm *and* the individual may be accountable.[44] A firm and the individual both owe duties to the regulator not to

---

38 FSMA, s 59(4)(a).
39 FSMA, s 59.
40 FSMA, s 60A(1); SUP 10C.10.14G. See also the main assessment criteria in the FCA's Fit and Proper Test for Approved Persons (FIT): www.handbook.fca.org.uk/handbook/FIT.pdf.
41 SUP 10C.10.11G and SUP 10C.10.13G.
42 FSMA, s 60A(2); PRA Fitness and Propriety Assessments by Firms.
43 SUP 10C.11 (PRA rules are in PRA Rulebook Allocation of Responsibilities 2).
44 FSMA, s 63A; SUP 10C.10.4G.

mislead,[45] to disclose anything of which the regulator would expect notice and must provide full information when applying for approval.

2.67   Before a firm applies for approval it must satisfy itself that the candidate is fit and proper (see Chapter 4). Firms should note that failing to disclose relevant information to the FCA may be a criminal offence.[46]

2.68   A firm should additionally check the Financial Services Register as part of its fitness and propriety assessment to verify information contained in the application for approval.[47] A criminal records check (see Chapter 3) and a search of any equivalent of the Financial Services Register outside the UK should be carried out.[48] The relevant provision of the FCA Handbook limits this obligation to 'where appropriate'. There is no guidance as to when such checks will be appropriate, but might include, for example, where a candidate has worked in another country or has disclosed involvement in criminal proceedings in another country.

2.69   Firms should also obtain appropriate regulatory references as part of the approval process (see Chapter 5).

2.70   The FCA emphasised in its final rules[49] that firms must allocate responsibilities to SMs under the SMR clearly and without gaps. In order to allocate responsibilities appropriately, firms need to make sure that they understand the following key concepts: 'senior management functions' (SMFs), 'prescribed responsibilities' (PRs) and 'overall responsibility'.

2.71   An application for approval is usually made using the relevant template Form A published by the FCA from time to time.[50] Notably, it is the firm which must submit the application (not the individual candidate for SM approval)[51] although the individual candidate must sign a declaration at the end of Form A by which he/she confirms, among other things, that:

- the information included in Form A is accurate and complete to the best of his/her knowledge and that he or she has read the notes to the Form published by the FCA (and PRA if applicable);

- he/she will notify the FCA and/or PRA if there is any material change in the information provided;

---

45   FSMA, s 398(1) and Principle 11 PRIN 2.1.1R; FSMA, s 400.
46   FSMA, s 398; SUP 10C.16.6G.
47   SUP 10C.10.20G.
48   SUP 10C.10.21G.
49   FCA CP15/22.
50   FCA SUP 10C.10.8 (which also prescribes the circumstances in which the application must be made using Form E). A short-form Form A application may be submitted where the candidate is already authorised as an approved person and there are no concerns about fitness and propriety.
51   If a firm has outsourced SMFs, SUP10C.10.6 and SUP10C.10.7 provide further guidance about who must submit the application.

- the statement of responsibilities attached to the Form accurately reflects the aspects of the affairs of the firm which it is intended that the candidate will be responsible for managing, and that the candidate has accepted all the responsibilities set out in the statement of responsibilities;

- the FCA/PRA are authorised to undertake further enquiries and seek such further information as they think appropriate to identify and verify information that either considers relevant to the assessment of the application in the course of their statutory duties;

- he or she understands the regulatory responsibilities of the proposed role as set out in the rules of conduct in the FCA's code of conduct (COCON) and/ or the PRA Rulebook: Conduct Rules.

2.72 Form A also requires the firm to submit any further relevant information in Section 6. This is likely to be the part of the Form in which the applicant firm will include any information disclosed to it by a former employer as being relevant to the firm's assessment of the candidate's fitness and propriety in the catch-up Box G of the Regulatory Reference template (see Chapter 5) together with details of the additional due diligence that the applicant firm has conducted upon receipt of that information to satisfy itself of the candidate's fitness and propriety. An example is a disclosure from a candidate or previous employer that the candidate is implicated in an investigation at the previous firm that is ongoing but where no findings of any fitness and propriety have been made.

2.73 Firms must consider at least annually[52] whether there are grounds on which regulatory approval might be withdrawn which means that a firm must in effect reassess a SM annually as fit and proper, usually as part of their annual performance appraisal. The same checks as are required for approval on appointment are not necessary, unless there is particular cause for concern about a specific issue. If the firm becomes aware of an issue of concern it must notify the regulator.

8 SENIOR MANAGEMENT FUNCTIONS

2.74 Section 59 of FSMA 2000 provides that controlled functions are those that are specified as SMFs by either the FCA or the PRA. Under APER approved persons that perform controlled functions[53] for authorised firms can exert significant influence over the firm's regulatory conduct. Each SMF has a specific definition that is set out in SUP 10C of the FCA Handbook. The FCA encourages firms to consider the definitions of each SMF when thinking about if and how they apply. The FCA gives this example:[54] if someone holds the title of director this does not necessarily mean they will hold the executive director SMF and members of an executive committee are not automatically SMs.

---

52 FSMA, s 63(2A).
53 FSMA, s 59(3).
54 FCA PS18/14, para.2.11.

2.75   In broad terms SMFs[55] replace the 'significant influence functions' under APER. A SMF is described[56] as any function (in relation to a RAP) if:

- the function will require the person performing it to be responsible for managing one or more aspects of the firm's affairs, so far as relating to the firm's regulated activity; and

- those aspects involve, or might involve, a risk of serious consequences for the firm or for business or other interests in the UK.

2.76   SMFs may be specified by either regulator on behalf of a RAP in the UK or overseas. Between the FCA and the PRA there are a number of specified SMFs plus SMF18 which is a catch-all 'overall responsibility' function. The list of FCA SMFs is set out in the supervision manual part of the FCA Handbook[57] and the PRA SMFs are set out in the 'senior management functions' part of the PRA Rulebook.[58]

2.77   PRA regulated firms should note specific requirements on SMFs set out in the PRA's supervisory statement.[59]

2.78   Before the FCA or PRA approve an individual as a SM, a firm must first ensure that procedures are in place to assess the SM's fitness and propriety. As noted above, a wider range of behavioural issues may now affect a fit and proper assessment and firms should ensure that their standard forms cover the right range and type of questions. This assessment should be carried out *before* applying for approval and at least annually afterwards.

2.79   A firm will also need to prepare a statement of responsibilities (SoR) (see 2.115) for individuals carrying out SMFs.

2.80   Individuals performing a SMF specified by the PRA will require pre-approval by the PRA with the FCA's consent. As noted above, the application for approval is submitted by the RAP using Form A where the individual will form both PRA and FCA senior management functions (Form A must be submitted to both regulators using the Connect System). Individuals performing a SMF specified by the FCA will require pre-approval by the FCA only and accordingly Form A needs to be submitted to the FCA only.

2.81   If a person performs more than one SMF, the firm will need to apply for approval for each function. This can be done at the same time and using the same Form A for all functions.

2.82   Some of the functions will exist in many larger and smaller firms, such as the function of chief executive (SMF1) while others will only be relevant for

---

55   Key responsibilities, defined in FSMA, s 59ZA.
56   FSMA, s 59ZA.
57   SUP 10C.4 (https://www.handbook.fca.org.uk/handbook/SUP/10C/4.html?date=2016-06-30).
58   http://www.prarulebook.co.uk/rulebook/Content/Part/212475/10-09-2017.
59   SS 28/15, 'Strengthening individual accountability in banking'.

some firms; for example the chairman of the nomination committee function (SMF13) will only be used where the firm has a committee that performs this function.

2.83 The FCA addresses the issue of partners.[60] It is for firms to decide whether a partner performs a SMF, based on the FCA's rules and guidance in SUP 10C.5. If a firm's principal purpose is not to carry on regulated activities (eg a professional services firm) then the partner function only applies to the extent that the partner has responsibility for a regulated activity.

9 APPROVALS

2.84 The regulators may grant an application for approval subject to any conditions that may be considered appropriate and/or grant approval only for a limited period.[61] For example, a time limitation may be imposed in relation to an interim appointment due to an ongoing or prospective enforcement investigation which has resulted in an existing SM being suspended from his/her SMFs.

2.85 An example of a condition is a competency-related condition, although the FCA firmly makes the point that firms should not see this as an opportunity to put forward a sub-standard candidate in the knowledge that they may scrape through with a qualified approval.[62]

2.86 Time-limited approval may also be granted where a firm needs to appoint a candidate on an interim basis while it seeks to appoint a permanent candidate. Such approval would not normally be given for a period of less than 12 weeks since a firm would be expected to use the '12-week rule' (see 2.159) in such a case.[63] The FCA would not expect to impose a time limitation of this type for longer than 12–18 months. The FCA gives the following example:[64]

> The head of compliance resigns unexpectedly from a firm. The firm wishes to appoint one of its deputies. The FCA and the firm believe the deputy to be capable of running the firm's compliance function on a day-to-day 'business as usual' basis but the deputy has no experience developing a long-term firm-wide strategy. The firm estimates that it could take up to a year to recruit a permanent head of compliance. It also believes that the deputy could be the ideal candidate if the deputy could outline a viable compliance strategy for the firm.

---

60 FCA PS18/14, para.2.11.
61 SUP 10C.12.3G.
62 SUP 10C.12.20G.
63 SUP 10C.12.8G; SUP 10C.3.13R.
64 SUP 10C.12.12G.

In this situation, it may be appropriate to approve the deputy as head of compliance subject to a 12-month time limit.

2.87 Before the end of that period, the deputy would have to prepare a new compliance strategy and the deputy's ability to do so would be taken into account when deciding whether to approve the deputy on a permanent basis.

10 PRESCRIBED RESPONSIBILITIES

2.88 There are around 30 prescribed responsibilities (PRs) between the FCA's and PRA's rules that must be assigned to individuals holding SMFs. Some of these PRs have been specified by both regulators and others by either FCA or PRA only. Not all of the PRs will be relevant to all firms as the SMR is applied proportionately to smaller firms. A firm does not decide its own PRs.

2.89 A list of senior management responsibilities are set out in the FCA Handbook and in the PRA Rulebook.[65]

2.90 When allocating PRs, firms should make sure that they understand who will have responsibility for all of the different functions and activities that the firm conducts. In practice, this will involve not only identifying the individuals who will hold SMFs and be assigned PRs, but also considering what other activities or areas of the firm exist, which may be the responsibility of individuals who report directly to the board but are not members of the board or the firm's wider governing body. In CP17/25 the FCA gives the example of a person performing the money laundering reporting officer SMF who is not responsible for all aspects of financial crime and/or reports to a more senior individual with responsibility for financial crime matters – in such a case the PR for financial crime should be allocated to the more senior individual and not the money laundering reporting officer.

11 SHARED PRESCRIBED RESPONSIBILITIES

2.91 While a PR should normally be held by only one person, the regulators state that PRs can be shared in some circumstances. Where a firm allocates a PR to more than one SM each of those individuals will, in principle, be deemed wholly responsible for it. PRs can therefore be shared but not split among two or more SMs.[66] Where responsibilities have been allocated to more than one individual, the firm must keep records to show clearly how those responsibilities are shared or divided between the individuals.[67]

---

65 SYSC 4.7 FCA Handbook, Senior Management Functions PRA Rulebook.
66 SUP 10C.11.33G.
67 SYSC 2.2.3G.

2.92   The FCA does not expect a firm normally to split an FCA prescribed senior management responsibility between several SMF managers, with each only having responsibility for part.[68] Nor does the FCA expect a firm normally to allocate responsibility for an FCA prescribed senior management responsibility or an overall responsibility for a firm's activities, business areas and management functions to two or more SMF managers jointly. However, the FCA states that although the norm should be for a firm to have a single individual performing each FCA prescribed senior management responsibility or function allocated, there may be circumstances in which responsibilities can be divided or shared.[69] It also says that a firm should only divide or share a responsibility where this is appropriate and can be justified. Firms should ensure no gap is left. The FCA gives examples[70] of when it may be justified to share a PR as where it is part of a job share, where departing and incoming SMs work together temporarily as part of a handover, or where a particular area of a firm is run by two SMs.

2.93   Key sections in the FCA's Supervision manual should also be considered for guidance on sharing and dividing responsibilities for drafting a statement of responsibilities (SoR) (see 2.115).[71] SoRs should show which responsibility or function is shared or divided between which SMF managers or other persons. It should be clear which responsibility or function and which SMF managers or other persons are involved. Where the responsibility is split between several SMF managers, the SoR for each SMF manager should explain why this has been done and give full details of the arrangements. In general, where responsibilities are shared, each SM will be jointly accountable for those responsibilities. When a firm moves a PR from one SM to another SM, the relevant SoRs will need to be updated to reflect these changes.

2.94   The PRA sets out guidance on shared responsibilities in its supervisory statement.[72] Where a function is genuinely shared, care should be taken that both SoRs (see 2.115) are identical. Firms should ensure that contracts of employment are consistent with the SoRs. In circumstances where a responsibility or function is shared or divided, the SoR for each function should make this clear and in the case of division, it should clarify for what part of which responsibility or function the SM has responsibility.[73]

Practical guidance

In planning for the regime for the banks and building societies a number of firms were initially inclined to share PRs amongst their senior managers. However, as time elapsed and managers looked more closely at their ultimate responsibilities, the sharing of a responsibility became the exception rather

---

68 SYSC 4.7.25G.
69 SYSC 4.7.26G.
70 FCA CP17/25.
71 SUP 10C.11.31G–SUP 10C.11.33G.
72 SS28/15.
73 SUP 10C.11.31G.

than the rule. While it is very much the firm and its senior management that decide on allocation, the regulator will certainly comment if it believes a responsibility has been allocated to someone who does not have the appropriate competency or the span of control is too wide. Firms should not underestimate the time required both individually and collectively to resolve the allocation of responsibilities.

12   OVERALL RESPONSIBILITY

2.95   Firms should think through what overall responsibilities their SMs have for the activities, functions and area of their business.

2.96   The FCA Systems and Controls Sourcebook (SYSC)[74] explains that a person having overall responsibility for a function (SMF18) means a person who has: (1) ultimate responsibility for managing or supervising that function; and (2) primary and direct responsibility for (a) briefing and reporting to the governing body about that function; and (b) putting matters for decision about that function to the governing body. Having overall responsibility does not mean that the person needs to have day-to-day management control of that function. They need to be the most senior person responsible for managing the area overall and be sufficiently senior and credible, and with sufficient resources and authority, to be able to exercise their management and oversight responsibilities effectively.

2.97   The FCA has published new Handbook guidance[75] to explain the purpose of the overall responsibility requirement. This guidance replaces the previous guidance[76] in the Handbook. Unregulated activities will come into the scope of overall responsibility where they meet the definition of 'SMCR financial activities' under the FCA Handbook.

2.98   Individuals who have overall responsibility for activities, functions or areas of the business need to be pre-approved for SMFs.

2.99   In some cases, the SM who has overall responsibility for an activity, function or area will already have been identified as performing a specific SMF but it is very important that firms also identify any other individuals who have overall responsibility for an activity, function or area. The FCA gives an example that if an individual is assigned the head of key business area function (SMF6), he or she is likely to have overall responsibility for the business area in question (and will not require approval for the 'other overall responsibility' function in addition to this). In other cases, it may depend upon the particular way that the firm is organised.

---

74   SYSC 4.7.11G meaning of overall responsibility.
75   SYSC 26.2.
76   SYSC 4.7.9G.

2.100   A firm does not have to assign overall responsibility for those areas where prescribed responsibilities exist and are assigned to SMs. Overall responsibility provisions do *not* apply to NEDs because, of course, the purpose of having NEDs is that they should not be involved in the day-to-day running of the business.

2.101   It is not possible to divide an overall responsibility because they are specific to how a firm is structured; but allocating overall responsibility for the same area or activity to two or more SMs is permitted ('sharing') where this is appropriate.

2.102   When considering which individual has overall responsibility for a particular area or function, such as for instance HR or Change, firms will need to ensure that they identify the individual who is genuinely accountable in regard to the entity in question, regardless of whether or not they are an employee or a director of the entity.

2.103   As stated at 2.55, the SMR has no territorial limitation so under the overall responsibility rules firms must allocate responsibility to a SM for all activities, business areas and management functions, including those carried out from a branch overseas.

2.104   If an individual who has overall responsibility for an activity, function or area is not otherwise included in the list of SMFs that person would need to be pre-approved for SMF18.

2.105   The FCA notes that banking firms sometimes find the overall responsibility function difficult to understand. In its consultation CP17/25 on extending the SMCR the FCA provided the following guidance:

- Firms should consider what activities, business areas and management functions they have. Firms may find it useful to refer to Annex 1 of SYSC 25 as a starting prompt to think about how their own business is organised, but this is not mandatory or exhaustive.

- Once a firm has set out each of its activities, business areas and management functions, the next step will be to think about who has overall responsibility at the most senior level for each of these.

- The most senior person with Overall Responsibility might be an existing Senior Manager, such as the Chief Executive, an Executive Director or Compliance Oversight. We expect that this will be the case most of the time.

- However, depending on how a firm is organised, the most senior person with Overall Responsibility for an area might not already be a Senior Manager. In this case, this person will need to be approved by the FCA as a Senior Manager under SMF18 – Other Overall Responsibility (explained in section 8.16). We expect that this will be the exception, rather than the rule, but welcome comments on whether this will be the case in practice.

- Where a Senior Manager has Overall Responsibility for an activity, business area or management function, this will need to be clearly set out in their statement of responsibilities and reflected in the Responsibilities Map.'

13   THE ROLE OF LEGAL COUNSEL

2.106   One of the principles of the SMCR is, as outlined at 2.95 ff, that a SM must have 'overall responsibility' for each area of the firm's business, ensuring complete coverage (ie no gaps). In feedback, many firms questioned how SMF18 – other overall responsibilities – applied to the legal function. A SM must have overall responsibility for all areas of the firm (including the management of the legal function) and this may mean appointing the head of the function as an SMF18 if they are not already captured as another SM (for example, as the head of compliance).

2.107   Many firms felt that it had not been clear that a SM must be appointed for overall responsibility of the legal function, while others considered it inappropriate for the SMR to apply to the legal function at all. Some firms were concerned that the regime required the general counsel or legal director to be captured as a SM in their role in providing legal advice to the firm.

2.108   The FCA published a press release on 27 January 2016 which disclosed its own uncertainty and announced its plans to publish a consultation paper on the issue. In September 2016, the FCA then published a discussion paper[77] (DP) in response to feedback from firms on the position of general counsel.

2.109   Responses to the DP were requested by January 2017. It is understood that the FCA will publish a consultation paper in early 2019 to take forward proposals.

2.110   The DP notes that the relevant legislative and regulatory framework does not contain any requirement that the role of general counsel be designated a SM within the SMR. The DP sets out reasons to exclude the head of the legal function from the SMR, including:

- it is an advisory function not an activity, business area or management function;
- the head of legal's ability to provide impartial and independent advice would be impaired;
- legal professional privilege may be prejudiced since the SM may need to disclose material to the regulators which might otherwise be privileged;
- the independence of the legal function may be affected;

---

77   FCA DP16/4, 'Overall responsibility and the legal function'.

- lawyers are already subject to regulation (Solicitors Regulation Authority and Bar Standards Board).

By contrast, reasons were also provided to keep the head of the legal function in the SMR:

- in the FCA's view the activities of the legal function fall within the ambit of an 'activity, business area or management function' per SYSC 4.7.8R;
- failings in the legal function could create systemic risks and impact on the wider business;
- the focus of the SMR is not on provision of legal advice but on effective management of the function.

14   DRAFTING A SERVICE AGREEMENT FOR A SENIOR MANAGER

2.111   With only two exceptions, the regulatory rules do not expressly require any specific terms to be included in a service agreement or employment contract for a SM.

2.112   The first exception is contained in the PRA's Rulebook, Fitness & Propriety. PRA authorised CRR firms must contractually require each of their PRA approved SMs to comply with both the PRA Individual Conduct Rules and the PRA's Senior Manager Conduct Rules. Accordingly, a PRA approved SM's service agreement must contain an express term that the employee will comply with the relevant Conduct Rules. Many firms have chosen to simply cross-refer to the PRA's Conduct Rules rather than incorporate the text of each into the individual's contract. The FCA Handbook does not contain a corresponding requirement in relation to the FCA Individual Conduct Rules and FCA Senior Manager Conduct Rules but requires that firms ensure employees understand and are trained on the applicable conduct rules. Despite this, most banks and building societies have updated the service agreements of their SMs to include express terms requiring them to also comply with the FCA's Conduct Rules.

2.113   The second exception can be found in the PRA's Supervisory Statement on Remuneration[78] which applies to banks and building societies and requires both remuneration policies and employment contracts to clarify that:

- variable remuneration awards are conditional, discretionary and contingent upon a sustainable and risk-adjusted performance, in excess of that required to fulfil the employee's job description as part of the terms of employment. Such awards may therefore be subject to forfeiture or reduction at the employer's discretion;
- variable remuneration including a deferred portion is paid or vests only if it is sustainable according to the financial situation of the firm as a whole and

---

78   Paragraph 4.5 of PRA SS2/17, 'Remuneration'.

justified on the basis of the performance of the firm, the business unit and the individual concerned; and

● variable remuneration awards should be reduced or clawed back according to specific criteria set by the firm under Remuneration 15.21(1) which should, as a minimum, cover each of the relevant scenarios outlined in Remuneration 15.22–15.23.

2.114 In addition to the above, all firms should consider including the following provisions in offer letters and service agreements for SMs:

● The offer of employment should be made conditional upon the firm being satisfied that the individual is fit and proper, and obtaining and maintaining regulatory approval for the individual to carry out SMFs.

● The SM should warrant that they have disclosed all and any matters which may have an impact on their approved status. Some firms may choose to include an express warranty in an employment contract, others may choose to rely on a self-declaration by the candidate in a fitness and propriety questionnaire completed during the recruitment process.

● The description of the SM's role must be consistent with their SoR (and when one is updated, the other should reflect the changes). Many firms choose to attach the SoR to the service agreement (see 2.134) and to include an express term that the SM shall perform the responsibilities set out in the SoR as amended from time to time.

● The employment should be made conditional upon the SM conducting themselves in a fit and proper manner in accordance with their regulatory obligations.

● The employment must be made conditional upon the receipt of satisfactory regulatory references; there should be provision that in the event that a reference is updated during the course of employment and discloses something which impacts upon the individual's fitness and propriety, the firm reserves the right to terminate employment, with or without notice. The firm should reserve the right to disclose the matter, where it considers it appropriate, to the regulator(s) (in accordance with its regulatory obligations) (see Chapter 6).

● The SM should agree to do all necessary things to ensure compliance by them, those individuals for whom they have responsibility and the firm with all regulatory requirements and guidance from time to time in force.

● A provision should be included that the SM's duties may be reallocated during any period of absence for whatever reason and that such reallocation shall not constitute a breach of contract.

● The SM should agree to provide all reasonable assistance at any time with any internal or regulatory investigation in connection with any matter with which they may be or may have been involved.

- The firm may wish to include a provision that the individual will cooperate with any post-termination investigation carried out by the regulator(s) for a specified period of time after termination. In such a case the individual may seek a term providing for reasonable access to documents (subject to confidentiality requirements).

- The SM should be required to comply with any firm and regulatory handover obligations (see 2.161 ff) including, where required, maintaining a living handover document.

- A deductions from wages clause should include deductions by way of malus and clawback in accordance with firm policy and regulatory requirements (see 7.85 ff in relation to those firms subject to the Remuneration Part of the PRA Rulebook). There should be no guaranteed bonus other than for new hires in the first year of service and subject to exceptional circumstances (see Chapter 7).

- The provisions on deferral, malus and clawback should be set out and cross referenced to the relevant plan/scheme.

- The regulator's whistleblowing rules should be referred to and cross referenced to the firm's compliant whistleblowing policy (see Chapter 10).

- Any confidentiality provision should not limit the SM's rights under the regulatory whistleblowing rules.

- The firm should reserve the right to suspend the individual on full pay pending any investigation, disciplinary process or in the event that the firm has grounds to believe the individual is not fit and proper.

- In the event of any investigation into the individual's alleged misconduct (or the misconduct of others in relation to any area of the business for which the SM is accountable or responsible), the firm should reserve the right to suspend the payment of any variable remuneration and vesting of any deferred compensation pending the outcome of the investigation, subject always to the firm's malus policy.

- During any period of suspension, the firm should reserve the right to reallocate the SM's SMFs without this constituting a breach of contract.

- The firm may wish to include the right to terminate employment summarily without compensation if it reasonably concludes that the individual is not fit and proper to carry out a controlled function or if the FCA/PRA withdraw approval for the employee as a SM or if the individual breaches any of the regulator(s)'s Individual or Senior Manager Conduct Rules or any other regulatory requirement.

15 STATEMENT OF RESPONSIBILITIES

2.115   Section 60(2A) of FSMA states that if an application is for the approval to perform a designated SMF and the employer is a RAP then the appropriate regulator must require the application to contain or be accompanied by a SoR.[79] This statement sets out the aspects of the firm's affairs which the SM will be responsible for managing in the performance of their function(s).

2.116 The regulatory rules dealing with SoRs are set out in the FCA Handbook[80] and the PRA Rulebook.[81] A SoR must be set out in the form of the regulatory template[82] and must set out both FCA and PRA SM responsibilities for a SM authorised to carry out PRA SMF.

2.117 As highlighted at 2.115, the SoR must accompany and be in support of a SM's application for approval from the regulator and responsibilities must be allocated clearly and without gaps. Each SM must therefore have a SoR which relates to their responsibilities.

2.118 The PRA states[83] that a SoR (and management responsibilities maps (MRMs) – see 2.138 ff) should promote clarity and transparency on the individual responsibilities of each SM and a firm's management and governance arrangements. The FCA believes that it should be possible for a person who understands the firm's business, but not the way that it is organised, to read a senior manager's SoR and identify what that person is individually accountable for.

2.119 Firms should note that in the event of any misconduct, the SoR will set out the extent of a SM's responsibility and so it will be a crucial document for assessing liability. There should be a separate SoR for each SM and SoRs should not be combined for several SMs.[84]

2.120 The PRA provides that a SoR and MRM provide for a more targeted assessment of the fitness and propriety of prospective and incumbent SMs by allowing their competence, knowledge, experience, qualifications, training and, where relevant, proposed time commitment to be measured against the responsibilities they have been allocated.

2.121 SoRs should be kept updated and past versions should be kept as part of a firm's record keeping obligations[85] under SYSC 9.1 (general rules on record keeping). When a SoR is updated it will replace the earlier version.

---

79 FSMA, s 60(2B).
80 FCA, SUP 10C.11.
81 PRA Rulebook, Allocation of Responsibilities 2. See also PRA guidance on SoRs in PRA SS28/15 (updated May 2017).
82 FCA SUP10C, Annex 5D.
83 PRA SS28/15 (updated May 2017).
84 SUP 10C.11.16G.
85 FCA SUP 10C.11.22G.

Completing the SoR template

2.122   The FCA and the PRA have provided useful guidance[86] for drafting the SoR and examples of SoRs for various SMFs. The SoR should be a self-contained document which records the allocation of responsibilities and does not cross-refer or link to other documents. There is an indicative (not absolute) 300-word limit to describe each responsibility.

2.123   The SoR is a potentially contentious area between employer and employee: the employer needs to ensure all SMFs are accounted for; the employee may wish to reduce the number of functions they are accountable for or to ensure they are adequately compensated for allocated functions.

2.124   Firms may provide supplementary relevant information as part of the SoR where this is necessary to record a person's responsibilities accurately. However, the SoR should not refer to other documents. Firms should also ensure SoRs match any job descriptions but the SoR is not a job profile. A SoR must be resubmitted when there is a significant change in the SM's responsibility.[87]

2.125   The allocation of responsibilities under a SoR should not reduce or alter the scope of any applicable prescribed responsibilities.[88] Where the description in the SoR goes beyond the prescribed responsibilities or the firm includes additional responsibilities and information the FCA rules state that the firm should not reduce or alter the scope of the prescribed requirements or dilute or undermine the prescribed requirements.[89]

2.126   The PRA notes that SoRs should also indicate where a SM has additional responsibilities not covered under prescribed or overall responsibilities. Typically, such additional responsibilities will include managing or overseeing material actions or projects specific to a firm or a SM. These should be set out at section 3.00 of the template.

2.127   The FCA expects a SoR for a non-executive director who is also a SM to be less extensive than that for an executive SM.[90]

Records of statements of repsonsibility

2.128   Firms should retain past copies of SoRs as part of their record keeping obligations.[91]

---

86   SUP 10C.11.24 G; FCA CP15/22, para 2.58; PRA SS28/15 and FCA GC18/4, 'Senior Managers and Certification Regime – Proposed guidance on statements of responsibilities for FCA firms'.
87   FSMA, s 62A(2).
88   SUP 10C.11.26G(3).
89   SUP 10C.11.26G(3)–(4).
90   SUP 10C.11.34–35G.
91   SUP 10C.11.22G.

2.129   Firms must at all times have a complete set of current SoRs for all their SMs.[92]

Revised statements of responsibility

2.130   If there has been any significant change to a SM's responsibilities a firm must provide the regulator with a revised SoR.[93] The FCA sets out guidance on what it considers to constitute 'significant change'.[94] The examples include the sharing or dividing up of a function.

2.131   If a SM ceases to carry out a SMF (but continues to perform another SMF) for a firm, the firm must submit a revised SoR.[95]

Feedback on statements of responsibility

2.132   The FCA, in a feedback statement,[96] noted that some firms submitted SoRs with additional information that was either not relevant to the individual's responsibilities or which focused on how the individual discharged their responsibilities, rather than what they were actually responsible for. In some cases this appeared to limit or caveat the responsibility to particular activities, which could result in a lack of clarity or gaps in responsibilities.

2.133   In other cases, not enough information was given to be able to understand what the SM was responsible for. The FCA provides as an example cases where job titles were given as overall responsibilities without sufficient information for the FCA to understand which business functions and activities fall into the SM's overall responsibilities. Some firms also provided SoRs that were not consistent with the MRM.

Interaction between the statement of responsibilities and the employment contract

2.134   The SoR is a regulatory document rather than a contractual one. However, since it will be a crucial document for the ongoing employment relationship and the SM's regulatory approval, both the SM and the firm would be advised to agree the content of the SoR before an offer of employment is accepted. To do this properly, the SM will also require sight of the handover notes from any previous SM he/she will succeed upon commencing employment. A prudent firm would not release such information to a candidate without having entered into

---

92   SUP 10C.11.20R.
93   FSMA, s 62A.
94   SUP 10C.11.6G.
95   SUP 10C.11.12R.
96   FCA FS16/6.

an appropriate non-disclosure agreement since handover notes will often contain confidential, commercially sensitive and legally privileged material.

Practical guidance

An important point to note with a SoR is ensuring that they are reviewed. This is very relevant when an individual will be taking on responsibility for a major project such as General Data Protection Regulation implementation. By way of example, at the time of publication of this book, it is also anticipated that SoRs will be reflecting who within the firm is responsible for the Brexit strategy. Firms and individuals need to think more widely than the required PRs to reflect business activities and other non-prescribed responsibilities in the SoR.

Guidance on the statement of responsibilities and management responsibilities maps

2.135   The FCA consulted[97] on detailed guidance in December 2018 on SoRs and MRMs (see 2.138 ff). The FCA makes clear that the guidance is not binding and it will not presume that a firm has breached the rules if it departs from the guidance. However, the guidance is particularly helpful in understanding how to assign prescribed responsibilities and how to complete the SoR and MRM, highlighting problem areas.

2.136   The guidance should be applied proportionately and sets out examples of good and poor practice as well as providing questions that firms should ask themselves. The examples are grouped according to whether a firm is limited, core (see 2.30) or enhanced (see 2.37).

2.137   With specific reference to the SoR, the FCA states that it should be clear and easy for regulators, the SM and others in the firm to understand it. It should not contain unnecessary detail. It is not the same as a job profile, so it should not describe the competencies and skills required for a job or how those responsibilities should be discharged.

16   MANAGEMENT RESPONSIBILITY MAPS

2.138   Firms must also produce MRMs to show how all responsibilities are allocated across the firm.[98] The rules for completing MRMs are set out in the regulators' rules.[99] One purpose of the MRM is to help the firm and the FCA

---

97 FCA GC18/4.
98 SYSC 4.5.7R.
99 SYSC 4.5 (https://www.handbook.fca.org.uk/handbook/SYSC/4/5.html); PRA Allocation of responsibilities 7 (http://www.prarulebook.co.uk/rulebook/Content/Part/212514/10-09-2017); and PRA guidance in PRA SS28/15 (updated May 2017).

satisfy themselves that the firm has a clear organisational structure. It also helps the FCA to identify who it needs to speak to about particular issues and who is accountable if something goes wrong.

2.139   The MRM must be consistent with the SoR.[100]

2.140   A key purpose of these maps is to ensure that, when looked at collectively, all areas and responsibilities are allocated to a SM with no gaps. The map is a single *up-to-date* document that describes a RAP's management and governance arrangements. It also sets out how responsibilities have been allocated, including whether they have been allocated to more than one person. The MRM must be an accessible, clear and comprehensive source of reference. MRMs must be kept as part of a firm's record-keeping obligations.[101]

2.141   The FCA has set out a list[102] of the main business activities and functions of a RAP in order to help a firm prepare its MRM.

2.142   In particular, a MRM must include:

- aggregate information on the allocation of responsibilities to SMs as set out in their individual, respective SoRs. Note, however, that it is not necessary for the MRM to duplicate or restate all the information in each SoR;

- the rationale for any shared or divided responsibilities and details of how each of the individuals responsible is expected to discharge the shared responsibility in practice;

- matters reserved for the board and the terms of reference of the key board committees, including their structures, membership, remit, interaction with other committees in the firm and, if applicable, the group;

- reporting lines of SMs to individuals and committees in the firm and, if applicable, the group, including those located overseas; and

- where firms are part of a larger group, the interaction of a firm's governance arrangements with group governance arrangements (for example, in areas such as internal codes of conduct and remuneration policies), including the extent to which the firm's management and governance arrangements are provided by, or shared with, other group entities.

2.143   There is no template for the map and it is up to firms to produce their own.[103] The PRA sets out further guidance for completing the MRM in a supervisory statement.[104]

---

100 SYSC 4.6.12G.
101 SYSC 9.1.
102 SYSC 4.7 Annex 1G.
103 By way of example, the FCA management responsibilities map is set out at: https://www.fca.org.uk/publication/corporate/applying-smr-to-fca.pdf.
104 PRA SS28/15.

2.144   The FCA sets out rules applying to small firms at SYSC 4.5.13. For such firms a MRM is likely to be simple and short. Small firms are defined as a 'small CRR firm' in the Allocation of Responsibilities part of the PRA Rulebook or a credit union that meets the small CRR firm requirements.

Feedback on MRMs

2.145   In a feedback statement[105] the FCA noted that many firms had not included all of the information required by the FCA rules.

2.146   Specific information that was missing included senior management responsibilities (as described in SoRs), details of and rationale for shared and divided responsibilities and the matters reserved to the board. This makes it difficult to understand how the complete picture of senior management responsibilities fits together across the firm, especially where they are shared or divided across multiple SMs.

2.147   Some firms provided only limited details on their governance arrangements so that the MRM did not provide relevant or sufficient information to understand how the management or governance of the firm worked. For example, some firms did not provide enough detail about reporting lines. There were sometimes few details of individuals in the wider group who were shown on the map and their relationship to the firm and its SMs.

2.148   The FCA also noted a number of MRMs for firms that were part of a larger group that did not fully or at all describe how the firm's arrangements interacted with group governance arrangements.

17   SHARING FUNCTIONS: CHIEF EXECUTIVE AND CHIEF OPERATIONS

2.149   The FCA states that if functions are allocated to joint chief executives under SYSC 2.1.4R column 2, they are expected to act jointly. This rule applies to a firm that is not a Solvency II or a small non-directive insurer and relates to the functions of dealing with the apportionment of responsibilities and overseeing the establishment and maintenance of systems and controls.[106]

2.150   A Solvency II firm must appropriately allocate to one or more senior managers the function of dealing with the apportionment of responsibilities and to one or more individuals the function of overseeing the establishment and maintenance of systems and controls.

105 FCA FS16/6.
106 SYSC 2.1.3A.

2.151   If the functions are allocated to an individual under SYSC 2.1.4R, column 3 the former may normally be expected to perform a leading role in the functions that reflects their position.[107] In other cases where the allocation is to more than one individual, they can perform the functions, or aspects of the functions, separately.

2.152   SMF24 (chief operations function[108]) is the exception to the rule that SMFs can be shared but not split.

2.153   The PRA's Supervisory Statement 28/15 envisages that SMF24 may be shared or split between two (but no more than three) individuals 'provided that the split accurately reflects the relevant firm's organisational structure and that comprehensive responsibility for operations and technology is not undermined'. For example, where a relevant firm has two distinct but equally senior individuals with overall responsibility for its internal operations and technology respectively, it may be appropriate for the SMF24 to be split between them. Where the SMF24 is split, the PRA does not expect it to be split between more than three individuals.

2.154   If a firm has two or more individuals who, between them, are responsible for internal operations and technology but there is a hierarchical relationship between them, only the most senior individual should be approved as SMF24.

2.155   Where a firm splits SMF24 between two or more individuals, the responsibilities of each relevant individual should be unambiguously clear and set out in their SoRs.

2.156   If a firm breaches a relevant requirement in an area relating to a PR which is shared by two or more SMs, each SM will have an opportunity to explain how the shared PR was discharged in practice when trying to demonstrate that they took reasonable steps to avoid the breach.

2.157   The FCA stresses that firms should think carefully about the responsibilities of any individual in any such situation and ensure that these are appropriately reflected in SoRs and MRMs. In particular:

- **Where responsibilities are jointly shared**, it follows that we would generally expect to see identical sections of the Statements of Responsibilities for each senior manager sharing the responsibility. If a firm was to contravene a relevant requirement in an area where a responsibility is shared in this way we, like the PRA, would consider all SMF managers sharing the responsibility to be jointly responsible.

- **If two individuals hold the same responsibility in relation to different aspects of a firm's business** (for example, the firm's European business and North American business) this would need

---

107 SYSC 2.1.6G.

108 SMF 3.00 defines the chief operations function as 'the function of having responsibility for the operations and technology of a firm'.

to be clearly set out in their Statements of Responsibilities and the firm's responsibilities map. The firm's map would also need to show that there were no gaps as a result of the arrangement. We would hold each individual responsible for the aspects of the responsibility assigned to them, but if it was unclear who was responsible all SMF managers with the relevant responsibility would be considered jointly responsible.'

Feedback on sharing functions

2.158   In a feedback statement[109] the FCA noted that some firms had not provided enough clarity or detail where responsibilities had been shared or divided, so that it was not clear which SMF manager was responsible for which areas. In some cases the descriptions of the split of responsibilities did not provide a consistent and complete picture of who was responsible for what across the relevant SMF managers. Also, in a number of cases, responsibilities were described as shared; however, it appeared from the description provided that the SMF managers were in fact responsible for different areas. In both the MRMs and the SoRs, firms had not always appropriately described the shared or divided responsibility in a way that provided comfort that all responsibilities had been allocated as required by the FCA rules. Neither did firms always state the reasons why they had divided or shared FCA prescribed responsibilities.

18 TEMPORARY COVER FOR SENIOR MANAGERS – THE '12-WEEK RULE'

2.159   Where the '12-week rule' applies, regulatory approval will not be required for an individual covering for the absence of a SM. Further, the FCA provides[110] that the SM conduct rules (see 2.167) do not apply to an employee of a RAP who would be a SMF manager but for the 12-week rule and regulatory approval will not be required for that interim appointment. This rule provides:

'If:

(1) a firm appoints an individual to perform a function which, but for this rule, would be a FCA-designated SMF;

(2) the appointment is to provide cover for a SMF manager whose absence is:

(a) temporary; or

(b) reasonably unforeseen; and

---

109 FCA FS16/6.
110 SUP 10C.3.13R.

(3) the appointment is for less than 12 weeks in a consecutive 12-month period;

the description of the relevant FCA-designated SMF does not relate to those activities of that individual.'

2.160   This rule enables cover to be given for (for example) holidays and emergencies and avoids the need for the precautionary approval of, for example, a deputy. However, as soon as it becomes apparent that a person will be performing a FCA designated SMF for more than 12 weeks, the firm should apply for approval.

19   HANDOVERS

2.161   The regulators each have specific rules for handovers where a SM is departing and 'handing over' his role and responsibilities to another SM.

PRA requirements

2.162   The PRA requires firms to take all reasonable steps to ensure that before a person begins to perform any new PRA SMF, that person is provided with all relevant information that they might reasonably expect. This requirement does not require a handover certificate to be produced by the departing SM.

FCA requirements

2.163   The FCA[111] sets out more detailed requirements. Note that the FCA's handover rules will only apply to enhanced firms (see 2.37–2.43). A firm must take all reasonable steps to ensure that:

(1) a person who is becoming a SM;

(2) a SM:
   (a) taking on a new job or new responsibilities; or
   (b) whose responsibilities or job are being changed; and

(3) anyone who has management or supervisory responsibilities for the SM in (1) or (2);
has, when the SM starts to perform his new or revised responsibilities or job, all information and material that a person in (1) to (3) could reasonably expect to have to perform those responsibilities or that job effectively.

2.164   A firm must have a policy about how it complies with SYSC 4.9R, including the systems and controls it uses and must make and maintain adequate records.

111 SYSC 4.9.

2.165   The information and material that should be made available includes details about:

- unresolved or possible breaches of the requirements of the regulatory system; and

- any unresolved concerns expressed by the FCA, the PRA or another regulatory body.

2.166   The handover document should be a practical and helpful document and not just a record. The material should include an assessment of what issues should be prioritised and should include judgment and opinion, not just facts and figures.

2.167   The FCA requires a firm to have arrangements for an orderly transition on the departure of a SM. As part of these arrangements, the firm should take reasonable steps to ensure that the predecessor contributes to the information and material all that would be reasonable to expect the predecessor to know and consider relevant, including the predecessor's opinions. One way of doing this could be for the predecessor to prepare a handover certificate. However, the FCA accepts that there may be cases in which it will be impractical to ask the predecessor to prepare a handover certificate and it is not mandatory to do so.[112] However, firms should ensure there is an orderly transition between SMs. Core and limited scope firms (see 2.44) do not have to comply with handover obligations. However, SMs in core and limited scope firms will still be subject to senior manager conduct rule 1 in the conduct rules (see Chapter 6) which requires SMs to ensure that the business of the firm for which they are responsible is controlled effectively. Handover procedures may be useful to support this.

2.168   A common problem that arises is how to ensure that a departing SM will abide by their handover obligations. Many firms choose to include a contractual obligation in service agreements for SMs and in any settlement agreement regarding exit arrangements. A more practical approach may be to ensure that all SMs regularly complete a 'living' handover document which is regularly maintained and kept up to date.

2.169   On some occasions, SMs have asked for firms not to apply clawback to any variable pay and in exchange they agree to comply with their handover obligations.

2.170   If a SM refuses to comply with any reasonable handover request this may constitute misconduct on their part.[113]

---

112 FCA PS18/14.
113 Conduct Rule SC1: 'you must take reasonable steps to ensure that the business of the firm for which you are responsible is controlled effectively'.

2.171   Handover obligations did not previously apply to insurers although both the FCA and the PRA apply new handover requirements for larger insurers under the extension of the SMCR regime (see Chapter 12).

2.172   The FCA expects a SM under senior manager conduct rule one to ensure an orderly handover between SMs under their oversight or responsibility.[114] The SM in charge of this function will therefore potentially be on the hook if they have failed to ensure that handover arrangements have been put in place.

Practical guidance

What we have seen over the past two years is that the handover process has been a valuable tool in succession planning for SMs, where a role is transitioning internally or an external candidate is being appointed. We have also seen the concept extended to certification roles and in some firms the overarching principle of a handover has been integrated into good business practice across the firm. While it is only enhanced firms who are obliged to have a handover policy in place, we have seen many core and limited scope firms looking to adopt the concept for their business.

---

20   STATUTORY DUTY OF RESPONSIBILITY AND CRIMINAL OFFENCE OF CAUSING A FINANCIAL INSTITUTION TO FAIL

Duty of responsibility

2.173   Under s 66 of FSMA the regulators may take disciplinary action against those they regulate. Section 66 previously provided that if there had been a contravention in respect of a function for which a SM had responsibility then there would be misconduct unless the SM could show he had taken reasonable steps to avoid the breach occurring. In other words, the burden of proof would fall upon the SM to show he had taken reasonable steps. The government replaced this reverse burden of proof with a *statutory duty of responsibility*. The burden is now on the regulators to prove that a SM has failed to take *reasonable steps* to prevent a regulatory breach from occurring.

2.174   Each SM now has a *duty of responsibility* (rather than a presumption of responsibility) for the management of his function. Under the duty of responsibility both the FCA and the PRA can take action against SMs if they are responsible for the management of any activities in their firm in relation to which their firm contravenes a regulatory requirement, and they do not take such steps as a person in their position could reasonably be expected to take to avoid the contravention occurring (or continuing).

---

114 COCON 4.2.8G.

2.175   On 3 October 2016, the FCA issued a consultation paper[115] on guidance on the duty of responsibility on SMs. The consultation identifies the factors that the FCA will take into consideration in determining whether to take disciplinary action against a SM where a firm has breached a regulatory requirement for which the SM had a management responsibility. The guidance addresses the formal considerations for regulatory action and considers the steps which a firm and a SM will need to take to satisfy themselves that the SM has discharged and continues to discharge his duty. It also highlights the importance of the SoR in this regard.

2.176   The FCA has issued final policy guidance in a policy statement[116] which made no changes to the guidance contained in the consultation and which applies from 3 May 2017. The rules are set out in the FCA Handbook.[117]

2.177   When determining whether a SM was responsible for the management of any of the firm's activities the FCA will consider the SoR, including whether the SM was performing an executive or non-executive role, the MRM, how the firm operated and how responsibilities were allocated, the SM's actual role and responsibilities and the relationship between the SM's responsibilities and those of other SMs in the firm.

2.178   When determining whether the SM took such steps as a person in their position could reasonably be expected to take, the FCA will take into account the following:

(1) the role and responsibilities of the SM;

(2) whether the SM exercised reasonable care when considering the information available to them;

(3) whether the SM reached a reasonable conclusion on which to act;

(4) the nature, scale and complexity of the firm's business;

(5) the knowledge the SM had, or should have had, of regulatory concerns, if any, relating to their role and responsibilities;

(6) whether the SM (where they were aware of, or should have been aware of, actual or suspected issues that involved possible breaches by their firm of relevant requirements relating to their role and responsibilities) took reasonable steps to ensure that the issues were dealt with in a timely and appropriate manner;

(7) whether the SM acted in accordance with their statutory, common law and other legal obligations, including, but not limited to, those set out in the Companies Act 2006, the FCA Handbook and, if the firm was listed on the London Stock Exchange, the UK Corporate Governance Code and related guidance;

115 CP16/26.
116 PS17/9.
117 FCA Decision Procedure and Penalties manual (DEPP) 6.2.9; FCA Handbook.

(8) whether the SM took reasonable steps to ensure that any delegation of their responsibilities, where this was itself reasonable, was to an appropriate person with the necessary capacity, competence, knowledge, seniority and skill, and whether the SM took reasonable steps to oversee the discharge of the delegated responsibility effectively;

(9) whether the SM took reasonable steps to ensure that the reporting lines, in relation to the firm's activities for which they were responsible, were clear to staff and operated effectively;

(10) whether the SM took reasonable steps to satisfy themselves, on reasonable grounds, that, for the activities for which they were responsible, the firm had appropriate policies and procedures for reviewing the competence, knowledge, skills and performance of each individual member of staff to assess their suitability to fulfil their duties;

(11) whether the SM took reasonable steps to assess, on taking up each of their responsibilities, and monitor, where reasonable, the governance, operational and risk management arrangements in place for the firm's activities for which they were responsible (including, where appropriate, corroborating, challenging and considering the wider implications of the information available to them), and whether they took reasonable steps to deal with any actual or suspected issues identified as a result in a timely and appropriate manner;

(12) whether the SM took reasonable steps to ensure an orderly transition when another SM under their oversight or responsibility was replaced in the performance of that function by someone else;

(13) whether the SM took reasonable steps to ensure an orderly transition when they were replaced in the performance of their function by someone else;

(14) whether the SM failed to take reasonable steps to understand and inform themselves about the firm's activities for which they were responsible, including, but not limited to, whether they:

    (a) failed to ensure adequate reporting or seek an adequate explanation of issues within a business area, whether from people within that business area, or elsewhere within or outside the firm, if they were not an expert in that area; or

    (b) failed to maintain an appropriate level of understanding about an issue or a responsibility that they delegated to an individual or individuals; or

    (c) failed to obtain independent, expert opinion where appropriate from within or outside the firm as appropriate; or

    (d) permitted the expansion or restructuring of the business without reasonably assessing the potential risks; or

    (e) inadequately monitored highly profitable transactions, business practices, unusual transactions, or individuals who contributed significantly to the profitability of a business area or who had significant influence over the operation of a business area;

(15) whether the SM took reasonable steps to ensure that, where they were involved in a collective decision affecting the firm's activities for which they were responsible, and it was reasonable for the decision to be taken collectively, they informed themselves of the relevant matters before taking part in the decision, and exercised reasonable care, skill and diligence in contributing to it;

(16) whether the SM took reasonable steps to follow the firm's procedures, where this was itself appropriate;

(17) how long the SM had been in role with their responsibilities and whether there was an orderly transition and handover when they took up the role and responsibilities;

(18) whether the SM took reasonable steps to implement (either personally or through a compliance department or other departments) adequate and appropriate systems and controls to comply with the relevant requirements and standards of the regulatory system for the activities of the firm.

Statutory duty of responsibility and insurers and solo regulated firms under the extension of the SMCR

2.179   The FCA has published new guidance on the statutory duty of responsibility setting out how it will apply this duty to insurers and FCA solo regulated firms[118] once the SMCR is extended to these firms (see 2.218 ff for more detail on this guidance).

Causing a financial institution to fail

2.180   Section 36(1) of the Financial Services (Banking Reform) Act 2013 created a new criminal offence which applies to SMs, which arises when:

- at a time when a person (S) is a SM in relation to a financial institution (F);

- S takes or agrees to the taking of a decision by or on behalf of F as to the way in which the business of a group institution is to be carried on;

- S fails to take steps that could be taken to prevent such a decision being taken; and

- at the time of the decision S is aware of the risk that the decision may cause F to fail.

2.181   S's conduct must fall far below what could reasonably be expected of a person in S's position and the implementation of the decision must actually cause F to fail.

---

118 FCA PS18/16.

2.182 The offence applies in relation to conduct that takes place on or after 7 March 2016. A SM is defined as someone performing a SMF, so that even if this is not a designated SM that person may be at risk of committing the offence. The individual must be 'aware of the risk' so there is an element of knowledge of the risk involved in determining culpability.

2.183 A person guilty of this offence is liable on summary conviction to imprisonment of up to 12 months and/or a fine; on indictment, to imprisonment for up to seven years and/or a fine. The criminal offence came into force on 7 March 2016 and it is expected that it will rarely occur.

21 REGULATORY FEEDBACK

2.184 In September 2016, the FCA published feedback on a number of topics including drafting SoRs and MRMs from:

- all UK banks, investment firms and building societies;[119]

- branches of banks outside the EEA;[120]

- branches of banks within the EEA;[121]

- unions.[122]

2.185 Nothing in the statements creates new guidance but provides a useful review, identifying issues and pitfalls.

2.186 A few points arising from the feedback are as follows.

2.187 In some cases it was not clear whether firms had identified sufficiently senior individuals to hold SMFs or particular responsibilities. Examples included where one SMF manager reports to another or where SMF managers do not appear to have sufficient seniority, resources or authority to discharge their responsibilities effectively.

2.188 In some firms' submissions it was not clear that all the business functions and activities of the firm had been allocated as overall responsibilities. Where responsibilities had been shared or divided, SoRs and MRMs were not always clear enough to enable the FCA to understand how the sharing or division of responsibilities worked.

2.189 Further, responsibilities as set out in the SoRs and MRMs were not always clear. Some firms did not provide enough detail in these documents to delineate the scope of an individual's responsibilities. In other cases, they were

---

119 FS16/6.
120 FS16/7.
121 FS16/8.
122 FS16/9.

not sufficiently focused on what an individual was actually responsible for. In a few cases, SoRs were not consistent with MRMs.

2.190 Some MRMs did not clearly set out SMs' responsibilities and many maps omitted other required information.

2.191 In a number of cases, MRMs did not give enough information around governance arrangements. This was particularly noticeable where firms are part of a larger group. These firms often provided quite limited information about how the firm's management and governance connects to the group. These omissions could make it difficult for supervisors to understand how a firm is managed and governed in practice.

2.192 The FCA reminded firms that a SM is responsible for the firm's performance of its obligations under the SMR.[123]

22 NON-EXECUTIVE DIRECTORS

2.193 Under the Capital Requirements Directive IV[124] (CRD IV), the Markets in Financial Instruments Directive[125] (MiFID) and the European Banking Authority's (EBA) suitability guidelines, all members of the management body must be fit and proper (this does not apply to credit unions).

2.194 CRD IV requires member states to ensure that board members of Capital Requirements Regulation (CRR) 575/2013 firms 'at all times be of sufficiently good repute and possess sufficient knowledge, skills and experience to perform their duties'.

2.195 The EBA suitability guidelines provide that this includes ensuring that the appointment of all board members is subject to a regulatory approval or notification process. In order to comply with EU obligations, the PRA provides that notified non-executive directors (notified NEDs) are subject to assessment and notification requirements in lieu of pre-approval.[126] Under these requirements, firms must assess the fitness and propriety of all NEDs not subject to regulatory approval on appointment and periodically thereafter. Firms should notify the PRA that such NEDs have been deemed fit and proper and also of any other information that would be reasonably material to the assessment of a NED's fitness and propriety.

2.196 The PRA and FCA initially published feedback[127] confirming that the only NEDs that would require regulatory pre-approval as SMs by either regulator

---

123 SYSC 4.7.7R(1).
124 2013/36/EU.
125 2014/65/EU.
126 PRA Fitness and Propriety 2.3.
127 FCA CP15/5.

would be the chairman, senior independent director and the chairs of the risk, audit, remuneration and nomination committees. All other NEDs ('notified' or standard NEDs) were not initially included in the regime although they had to comply with the PRA regulatory references rules (see 2.198).

2.197   However, in May 2017 the FCA introduced final rules in its policy statement[128] extending its conduct rules to standard NEDs[129] in banks, building societies, credit unions and dual regulated investment firms and insurance firms. This is dealt with in further detail in Chapter 6. Firms should ensure that NEDs are appropriately trained in the conduct rules and where any breach of COCON results in disciplinary action should be notified to the relevant regulator. The PRA requires firms to contractually ensure notified NEDs and credit union NEDs comply with their individual conduct rules.

2.198   The PRA regulatory reference regime applies to NEDs in CRR firms.[130]

2.199   The PRA rules provide that, when deciding whether a person is fit and proper on appointment as a notified NED or a credit union NED, a firm must obtain the individual's consent for the firm to request the fullest information in relation to that person that it is lawfully able to request under the Police Act 1997 (criminal records checks).[131]

2.200   The PRA requires firms to notify the PRA when a person becomes a notified NED and must provide the PRA with all of the information needed to assess whether that person is fit and proper.[132] If a firm becomes aware of information which might reasonably be material to the fitness and propriety assessment of a notified NED it must inform the PRA as soon as practicable. Where a firm replaces a notified NED because the person no longer fulfils the fitness and propriety requirements the firm must notify the PRA.

2.201   Where a notified NED assumes a new role with the firm or ceases to be a director of the firm, the firm must notify the PRA.

Practical guidance

When considering roles, the group entity function (SMF7) needs to be evaluated by enhanced firms where there is an overseas parent. We have seen a number of instances where an individual exercises significant influence over the firm's day-to-day business but holds a NED role and is based overseas. In such circumstances it may be more appropriate to

---

128 FCA PS17/8.
129 Standard or notified NEDs are non-executive directors who do not perform a senior management function. See https://www.handbook.fca.org.uk/handbook/glossary/G4573s.html; http://www.prarulebook.co.uk/rulebook/Glossary/FullDefinition/77799/08-05-2018/77800.
130 PRA Fitness and Propriety 5.1.
131 PRA Fitness and Propriety 2.9.
132 PRA Fitness and Propriety 4.2–4.6.

allocate the SMF7 function to such an individual which is executive in nature. The regime is very 'entity' centric and hence regulators are keen to ensure that they have visibility over individuals influencing the UK entity, to ensure mind and management is in the UK.

23 TRANSITIONING FCA FIRMS TO THE SMCR: CP17/40, PS18/14

2.202   As noted at 2.05 the regulators consulted on transitioning firms to the SMCR and set out their proposals in PS18/14.

2.203   The requirements for transitioning depend on whether a firm is classified as limited scope, core or enhanced.

2.204   The FCA sets out how it proposes to transition firms and individuals from APER to the SMCR. Given the disparity in size and nature of affected firms, the FCA suggests a proportionate approach to conversion. Most approved persons at core and limited scope firms will automatically convert into the corresponding new SMFs.

2.205   The FCA has also reviewed feedback with regard to their proposal to only list individuals holding SMFs on the Financial Services Register. Concerns were raised about the potential impact of excluding certified staff and the FCA is considering its next steps in this regard. Any changes will also apply to insurance firms.

Approved persons

2.206   The FCA intends that approved persons should be able to convert to an equivalent SMF without the need for a firm to reapply. Firms should check the updated Financial Services Register after the commencement of the new regime to ensure they hold the correct approvals after automatic conversion. If a controlled function does not map onto a corresponding SMF, regulatory approval is no longer required and existing approvals will lapse when the new regime begins. These individuals may become certified staff.

2.207   APER continues right up until commencement of the SMCR and the FCA will be dealing with applications for approval up to that point.

Certified staff

2.208   The FCA plans to implement the rules for certification gradually. Some previously approved individuals will become certified staff under the new regime, typically those individuals holding controlled functions 28 and 29 covering systems and controls and significant management respectively. The conduct rules will apply to all certified staff from commencement of the new regime so firms will need to know who their certified staff are by this stage.

2.209 The FCA proposes giving firms (enhanced, limited and core) 12 months from commencement to prepare to apply the conduct rules to 'other conduct rules staff'.

Core and limited scope firms

2.210 As stated at 2.204, individuals at core and limited scope firms will be automatically converted wherever possible, with no action required by firms. This means that no additional checks (eg mandatory criminal records checks) will be required as these will already have been carried out. However, the FCA suggests that firms consider whether any changes to approvals are required before commencement.

2.211 The FCA sets out in CP17/40 how certain controlled functions will map onto equivalent SMFs.

Enhanced firms

2.212 Enhanced firms will need to submit statements of responsibilities and a management responsibilities map to convert existing approved individuals to new SMFs, together with a Form K conversion notification. If a firm fails to submit a Form K it will be in breach of regulatory requirements, APER approvals will lapse and the firm will not have any SMR approvals. Firms in this situation would need to re-apply for approval of individuals through the full SMCR application process, including mandatory criminal records checks and regulatory references.

2.213 Where a firm wants a person to perform a SMF after commencement and it does not hold a mapped APR function it must submit the new SMCR Form A.

2.214 Firms should note that an application submitted to take effect on or after commencement will be subject to the majority of SMCR requirements, including criminal records checks but not regulatory references since these will only come into force on commencement.

Fitness and propriety

2.215 The FCA and the PRA have worked together to revise the fitness and propriety questions. These include adding a new question asking whether the candidate has ever participated in arbitration proceedings (see Chapters 4 and 6).

Banking firms: training staff

2.216 A separate chapter in CP17/40 affects banks, building societies, credit unions and PRA designated investment firms and sets out how the FCA will implement the new prescribed responsibility for training staff in the conduct rules. This new prescribed responsibility means firms have to allocate responsibility to a SM, who must ensure that the firm meets its obligations (including the requirement to train relevant staff) under the conduct rules.

2.217 This prescribed responsibility applies to *all* firms under the extended SMCR but the FCA proposes to implement this new requirement for banking firms *before* commencement of the extended SMCR.

24 GUIDANCE ON THE DUTY OF RESPONSIBILITY FOR INSURERS AND FCA SOLO REGULATED FIRMS: CP17/42, PS18/16

2.218 The FCA has also published guidance on the statutory duty of responsibility as applicable to insurance and reinsurance firms regulated by the FCA (insurers) and FCA solo regulated firms. See 2.173 ff for further details on the duty of responsibility.

2.219 The statutory duty of responsibility is extended to SMs of insurers and will be extended to FCA solo regulated firms on extension of the SMCR. The guidance set out in the Decision Procedure and Penalties Manual in the FCA's Handbook (DEPP 6.2) will be extended to apply to this category of person.

2.220 The FCA points out that when it is considering whether a SM has complied with the duty, it will look at whether they acted in accordance with their statutory, common law and other legal obligations including, but not limited to, the conduct rules and other Handbook rules.

2.221 The FCA also highlights the following:

- It will decide whether to take action based on the duty of responsibility by applying its published criteria in DEPP.

- The FCA will not apply standards retrospectively or with the benefit of hindsight.

- SMs may be responsible for the management of activities at their firm that fall outside their prescribed responsibilities – the duty of responsibility will apply to this.

- All the considerations in DEPP 6.2.9 E–G are potentially relevant to an assessment of the steps reasonably expected of all SMs whatever their role and responsibilities.

2.222   The burden of proof remains upon the regulator to prove all the necessary elements. It is not for the SM to show they took reasonable steps; it is for the regulator to establish that they did not.

2.223   The FCA points out that the guidance already set out in DEPP 6.2.9 already sets out an extensive and non-exhaustive list of considerations that it will take into account when considering whether reasonable steps were taken. This addresses concerns about proportionality and context-specific instances.

2.224   The guidance does highlight the regulator's concern that SMs keep adequate records. Whilst this duty of responsibility lies upon SMs and no additional burden to keep records over and above those obligations exists elsewhere in the rules, it is in a SM's interests to keep records explaining or justifying steps that they did or did not take in case questions are raised, whether by the firm, its auditors, customers, insurers or a regulator. Such records may be relevant not only in compliance with the duty of responsibility but also with COCON which requires senior managers to act with due skill, care and diligence.

2.225   The FCA also points out that any relevant FCA investigation is likely to take into account that each SM is also under a COCON obligation to make sure that the business of the firm complies with the firm's record keeping obligations. A SM's failure in this regard may also amount to misconduct for which the FCA may take action.

CHAPTER 3

Certification Regime

David Saunders, Partner, Alice Heatley, Senior Associate and
Susan Mayne, Consultant

I BACKGROUND

3.01   As detailed above (see Chapter 1), the Financial Conduct Authority (FCA) and the Prudential Regulation Authority (PRA) concluded that the behaviours and poor culture within banks played a major role in the 2008/09 financial crisis and other conduct issues, and that holding individuals to account was key to the effective regulation of the financial services sector.[1]

---

1   FCA CP14/13; PRA CP14/14.

3.02 The regulators therefore proposed changes to the way that individuals worked in the financial services sector, with their focus first on UK banks, building societies, credit unions and PRA designated investment firms.[2] However, it had always been the regulators' intention to extend the Senior Managers and Certification Regime (SMCR) to all regulated financial institutions and insurers and reinsurers (see 3.08 and Chapter 2). This rollout was implemented in December 2018 for insurers and reinsurers (see Chapter 12) and will be in place from 9 December 2019 for the rest of the financial services sector. Appointed representatives will remain outside of the regime and subject to the approved persons regime (APER). Further detail about the extension of the regime and the extent to which it applies to different types of firm is set out in Chapter 2.

3.03 The original proposals for the SMCR reflected the recommendations of the Parliamentary Commission on Banking Standards (PCBS) and implemented changes required by amendments made to the Financial Services and Markets Act 2000 (FSMA) by the Financial Services (Banking Reform) Act 2013. These proposals included a certification regime, which requires relevant firms to assess for themselves the fitness and propriety of certain employees who could pose a risk of significant harm to the firm or any of its customers. From the start, it was always the regulators' aim that behavioural and cultural change would come from individuals themselves.

3.04 The concept of fitness and propriety is not a new one, although it takes on an increased significance under the SMCR. Under APER individuals performing controlled functions had to be assessed as fit and proper by the regulators according to the regulators' standards.

3.05 A key aspect of the certification regime is the importance it places on firms assessing *for themselves* the fitness and propriety of staff performing a role (which is not a senior management function) relating to a relevant firm's regulated activities but which poses *a risk of significant harm* to the firm or any of its customers. Effectively, if an individual performs such a role (a PRA certification function or FCA significant harm function) as defined below at 3.22 and 3.26–3.36 then they must be certified by the firm not the regulator.

Summary of the requirements of the certification regime

The certification regime applies to a broad range of staff who, as a result of their role, could cause harm to the firm or its customers or the market, ensuring that firms assess them as fit and proper to carry out certification functions which are prescribed by the regulators. Firms should note that, in light of their different statutory objectives (see Chapter 1) the FCA and PRA rules and guidance may differ in certain details.

Under the regime, all SMCR firms must:

---

2 Collectively referred to as 'relevant authorised persons' in FSMA, s 71A. The definition is limited to 'UK institutions' defined as institutions 'incorporated in, or formed under the law of any part of, the United Kingdom' and includes UK subsidiaries of overseas firms.

- *Identify* those staff who perform a certification function, as prescribed by the regulators.

- *Assess* whether certification function staff are fit and proper to perform their role. Assessment must take place on recruitment and then on an on-going basis, at least annually (note that assessments can be more regular and, for example, triggered by certain events such as a disciplinary process). When making this assessment firms should take into account whether the individual has obtained a qualification; has undergone or is undergoing training; and possesses a level of competence.

- *Issue a certificate* to the certified person which states that the firm is satisfied the person is fit and proper to carry out the certified function and states what aspect of the firm's affairs the person will be involved in as part of performing their function.

- *Give a notice in writing to the person being assessed,* if a firm decides not to issue a certificate after carrying out a fit and proper assessment. This notice must set out the steps (if any) it proposes to take and the reasons for these steps.

3.06   The certification regime effectively requires financial institutions to regulate their own employees. Individuals under the certification regime are not subject to regulatory approval, unlike senior managers; however, a firm should ensure that no employee carries out a certification function without having first been certified as fit and proper to do so. Responses to the FCA's original consultation on the regime expressed concerns about this additional responsibility for firms, including the loss of comfort that comes from the regulator separately assessing the fitness and propriety of individuals.[3] The regulators responded in terms that it was Parliament's clear intention that the senior managers regime should be narrower than APER, allowing the regulators to focus resources on authorising and supervising the most senior staff in firms.

3.07   Full details of the process of assessing staff as fit and proper are set out in Chapter 4.

2   EXTENDED REGIME: A SUMMARY

3.08   As outlined above (see Chapter 2) it was always the intention that the reforms proposed by the PCBS would be extended across the financial services sector. In October 2015, the government announced the proposals for extension of the SMCR,[4] which will replace APER for those regulated firms not already covered by the SMCR.

3   FCA CP15/9.
4   See   www.gov.uk/government/uploads/system/uploads/attachment_data/file/468328/SMCR_policy_paper_final_15102015.pdf.

3.09   Provision to extend the SMCR to all sectors of the financial services industry, including insurers, investment firms, asset managers, insurance and mortgage brokers and consumer credit firms was made in s 21 of and Sch 4 to the Bank of England and Financial Services Act 2016.

3.10   In July 2018, the regulators published policy statements and near-final rules[5] extending the SMCR across all FCA solo regulated firms, regulated insurers and reinsurers – approximately 47,000 FSMA authorised firms in total.

3.11   The extended regime came into force on 10 December 2018 for insurers and will be extended to FCA solo regulated firms on 9 December 2019 (see Chapters 2 and 12). Firms will need to have identified employees performing certification functions by these dates and to have trained them on the conduct rules (Chapter 6 and 3.14) but they are not required to issue a certificate of fitness and propriety until one year later (see 3.17).

3.12   The FCA's proposals introduce some new concepts, most notably a three-tiered approach to compliance depending on the size, scale and complexity of a firm. Firms coming into the regime will be either enhanced, core or limited scope firms (see 2.30 ff).

3   MOVING TO THE CERTIFICATION REGIME UNDER THE EXTENDED SMCR

3.13   In December 2017 the FCA published a consultation paper setting out how it proposes to transition FCA firms and individuals from APER to the SMCR.[6] Given the disparity in size and nature of affected firms, the FCA suggested a proportionate approach to conversion. The FCA in its July 2018 policy statement clarified that firms will have 12 months from the start of the new regime to complete their fitness and propriety assessments and to get certification paperwork in place.

3.14   Detailed guidance was provided by the FCA on the SMCR and how to convert existing approvals in a guide[7] published at the same time as the final policy statements on extension. This guide brings together the issues consulted on and the changes made in the feedback to consultation; however, where there is conflict with any provisions in the Handbook, the Handbook supersedes the guide.

---

5   FCA PS18/14 (FCA solo regulated firms); FCA PS18/15 (insurance sector); PRA PS15/18 (insurance sector).

6   FCA CP17/40; see also FCA CP17/41 on transferring insurers and individuals to the senior managers and certification regime; and PRA CP28/17 on implementing the extension of the senior managers and certification regime to insurers.

7   https://www.fca.org.uk/publication/policy/guide-for-fca-solo-regulated-firms.pdf.

3.15   The FCA plans to implement the rules for certification gradually so firms will have time to undertake the fitness and propriety assessments for relevant staff. Some previously approved individuals will become certified staff under the new regime. It is also possible that in some very small firms there will no certified staff since no individuals will be performing certification functions.

3.16   The regulators' conduct rules (see Chapter 6) will apply to all certified staff from commencement of the new regime so firms will need to have established by then who their certified staff are.

3.17   This means that while the conduct rules will apply to these individuals from commencement, firms must have completed their fitness and propriety assessments and certified the relevant employees before 9 December 2020 (and, for insurers, before 10 December 2019) at the latest. Firms will not be required to obtain regulatory references for existing employees who will become certified staff provided that they will be performing the same role after the start of the new regime.[8]

Fitness and propriety questions

3.18   The regulators have worked together to revise the fitness and propriety questions and have included a new question asking whether the candidate has ever participated in arbitration proceedings. Full details on the fitness and propriety assessment are set out in Chapter 4.
Further details on the extended regime are set out in Chapters 2 and 4.

Practical guidance

We have seen firms deliberating on the subject of those individuals registered as CF28 or CF29 and whether they migrate to a senior management function (SMF) role or whether they become certified. We have seen both approaches adopted and it generally comes down to whether the individual reports directly to the board or to another SMF. If it is the latter then the certified route is in most circumstances the appropriate option unless a reporting line is going to change.

---

4   THE CERTIFICATION REGIME: FINAL RULES FOR THE BANKING SECTOR

3.19   In July 2015 the regulators published rules[9] for a new accountability framework for individuals working in relevant firms, which came into force for

---

8   Guide to the SMCR for solo regulated firms, chapter 13.
9   FCA CP15/22; PRA PS16/15.

relevant firms on 7 March 2016. These rules were initially set out in SYSC 5.2 of the FCA Handbook and in CRR Firms – Certification of the PRA Rulebook. Under the revised sections of the FCA Handbook following extension of the regime, the certification part will be set out in SYSC 27.[10]

3.20   As stated at 3.06, individuals who perform certification functions are *not* subject to regulatory approval (in contrast to senior managers) although a firm must assess for itself individuals performing certification functions as being fit and proper to do so prior to commencing performance of those functions (with limited exceptions – see 3.47) and on, at least, an annual basis. A relevant firm must take reasonable care to ensure that none of its employees performs a specified function under an arrangement entered into by the firm in relation to the carrying on by it of a regulated activity unless the employee has a valid certificate issued by the firm.[11]

5   WHO IS IN THE CERTIFICATION REGIME?

3.21   The certification regime extended the application of FCA and PRA regulation to a wider population than under the old APER. FSMA gives power to the regulators to specify a set of significant harm functions in order to minimise the risk that an employee at a relevant firm performs such a function without being certified as fit and proper to do so.

3.22   The certification regime therefore applies to employees who perform a FCA or PRA specified significant-harm or certification function. These significant harm or certification functions are set out in the FCA Handbook and PRA Rulebook. The term 'significant harm function' comes from FSMA and describes a person performing these functions as someone 'involved in one or more aspects of the firm's affairs, so far as relating to a regulated activity, and those aspects involve, or might involve, a risk of significant harm to the firm or any of its customers'.

3.23   If a role meets the definition of a certification function, the firm must make sure that anyone doing that role has been certified, in other words assessed as fit and proper to carry out the job and been issued with a certificate. The regime only applies if the firm has individuals performing a certification function, where it relates to a regulated activity.

3.24   Certificates should state that the firm is satisfied that the individual is a fit and proper person to perform the certification function and set out the aspects of the firm's business in which the individual will be involved. If a senior manager is performing a certification function that is not related to their senior manager function (SMF) then they will also need to be certified. An example would be a director of a firm who is also a CF30 (customer function under APER).

10   This can be found in FCA PS18/14.
11   FSMA, ss 63E, 63F.

3.25 The regulators agreed that the certification regime should cover individuals who have the potential to cause significant harm to a firm, even where individuals are not performing a SMF.[12]

FCA definition of certification employee

3.26 The population of individuals who can pose a risk of significant harm to a firm's customers is wider than the population that can harm the firm itself. In addition to certain material risk takers[13] (who can cause harm to the firm and consumers), the FCA's certification regime therefore captures customer-facing roles that are subject to qualification requirements (such as mortgage and retail investment advisors), individuals who supervise or manage a certified person (provided they are not a SMF holder) and any other significant influence function roles under APER not otherwise covered by the senior managers regime (such as benchmark submitters).

3.27 The regulators' rules describe the certified roles and the FCA has stated[14] that it does not expect firms to assess, independently of this, whether or not any staff outside the scope of the certification functions set out in the rules could be in a position to pose significant harm.

3.28 The FCA specifies *significant harm* functions in the FCA Handbook SYSC5.[15]

FCA table of certification functions (extract from PS18/14)

Certification function	Overview
Significant Management Function (current CF29) Proprietary traders (also covered by current CF29) Cass Oversight Function (current CF10a)	These individuals perform functions that would have been Significant Influence Functions under APER. These important roles can seriously affect how the firm conducts its business
Functions subject to qualification requirements	This includes, for example, mortgage advisers, retail investment advisers and pension transfer specialists. The full list is in the FCA's Training and Competence Sourcebook

---

12 FCA CP14/13; PRA CP14/14.
13 The definition of material risk taker is taken from European legislation on remuneration. Firms subject to these rules are already required to identify their material risk takers.
14 FCA CP15/22.
15 SYSC 27 in the updated rules following extension.

Certification function	Overview
The client dealing function	This function has been expanded from the CF30 function under APER to apply to any person dealing with clients, including retail and professional clients and eligible counterparties. This will cover people who: • advise on investments (other than a non-investment insurance contract) and perform other related functions, such as dealing and arranging • deal, as principal or agent, and arrange (bring about) deals in investments • act in the capacity of an investment manager and all functions connected with this • act as a bidder's representative
Anyone who supervises or manages a Certified Function (directly or indirectly) but is not a senior manager	This will ensure that people who supervise certified employees are held to the same standard of accountability. It also ensures a clear chain of accountability between junior certified employees and the senior manager ultimately responsible for that area. For example, if a firm employs a customer-facing financial adviser, every manager above them in the same chain of responsibility will have to be certified (until the senior manager approved under the SMR is reached)
Material Risk Takers	The concept of Material Risk Takers (also known as Remuneration Code staff) already exists for firms under the FCA's remuneration rules (SYSC 19). They are a category of staff that all firms under AIFMD, UCITS, IFPRU and BIPRU are already required to identify under the FCA's remuneration regime. These firms need to consider all types of risk when identifying their Material Risk Takers. This includes prudential, operational, conduct and reputational risks. All of these Material Risk Takers will be covered by this certification function.
Algorithmic trading	This function includes people with responsibility for: • approving the deployment of a trading algorithm or a material part of one • approving the deployment of a material amendment to a trading algorithm or a material part of one, or the combination of trading algorithms • monitoring or deciding whether or not the use or deployment of a trading algorithm is or remains compliant with the firm's obligations

3.29 The certification functions only apply where the firm has people in these roles and many functions will not be relevant to certain firms. It is also possible that in very small firms there will be no one in the certification regime if there is only a handful of senior individuals supported by administrative staff.

Practical guidance

Over the course of the past three years there has been debate as to whether the definitions of 'certified role' need to be extended to better suit other sectors. The regulator has resisted this by including guidance in the consultation papers around roles such as customer service leads, collections, complaints where they would fall in to the definition of significant management function and whether the roles being undertaken could create significant harm for the firm or its customers.

PRA definition of certification employee

3.30   In light of its statutory objective as a prudential regulator, the PRA's certification regime focuses on functions that might involve a risk to safety and soundness of the firm. The PRA specifies certification functions by reference to the concept of a *significant risk taker*. This definition is intended to align the scope of the certification regime with those employees caught by the definition of material risk takers, for remuneration purposes, under the Capital Requirements Regulation (CRR) EU 575/2013 (see Chapter 7).

3.31   Rules relating to certification functions are in the certification part of the PRA Rulebook.

3.32   In its original consultation and policy statement the PRA specified 'significant harm functions' (certification functions) that covered a smaller population of employees than those of the FCA. For firms subject to the CRR the PRA's certification regime comprised certain 'material risk takers' as defined with reference to criteria in Commission Delegated Regulation EU 604/2014. This regulation sets out qualitative and quantitative criteria to identify categories of staff.

3.33   The regulators' joint policy statement on Remuneration (see Chapter 7) included a definition for staff that are 'material risk takers' and therefore subject to remuneration rules.

3.34   In a policy statement in March 2016[16] the PRA amended the definition of 'significant risk taker' in the certification rules to align it with the definition of material risk taker in the Remuneration rules, by reflecting the wording of Article 2 of the Commission Delegated Regulation.[17] Most employees covered by the enlarged definition would in any event have been covered by the FCA certification rules. However, not every individual classified as a material risk

---

16 PRA PS9/16.
17 The PRA definition of 'significant risk taker' is set out at PRA Rulebook CRR firms Certification 1.2.

taker will necessarily fall within the certification regime. For example, senior managers and non-executive directors (NEDs) will not fall within the certification regime (unless they additionally perform a certification function, which would be unusual). There may also be employees who are material risk takers but who are not sufficiently involved in a regulated activity; such employees will not be performing a certified function.

3.35   Credit unions are not subject to the CRR and so do not have an obligation to identify material risk takers. As such, a separate, simplified definition of certification functions was set out for credit unions.[18] The PRA rules define a significant risk taker for credit unions as any employee that is a member of the governing body; or a member of senior management; is responsible for and accountable to the management body for the activities of the independent risk management function, compliance function or internal audit function; or heads a function responsible for legal affairs, finance, human resources, remuneration policy, information technology or economic analysis.

3.36   In a supervisory statement[19] the PRA has helpfully set out its expectations of how firms should act when deciding which roles are certification functions.

6 DEFINITION OF 'EMPLOYEE' FOR CERTIFICATION PURPOSES

3.37   An employee for certification purposes is broadly defined and includes[20] someone who personally provides or is under an obligation personally to provide services to the firm under an arrangement between the firm and that person and who is subject to the supervision, direction and control of the firm.[21]

3.38   The certification regime does not, therefore, for example, apply to a NED.[22]

3.39   Advisers employed by a firm on a contract basis and a person seconded from a contractor may fall within the certification regime.[23] In deciding if a person seconded from a contractor is fit and proper, a firm may take into account information and references from the contractor. In deciding how much reliance to place upon the contractor, a firm should take into account:

- the contractor's familiarity with a firm's regulatory certification obligations;

- whether any reference addresses the firm's required fitness and propriety criteria;

---

18 PRA Rulebook CRR firms Certification 1.2.
19 SS28/15.
20 FSMA, s 63E(9).
21 FCA SYSC 5.2.21G; PRA Rulebook CRR Firms Certification 1.2.
22 FCA SYSC 5.2.26R; PRA Rulebook CRR Firms Certification 1.3.
23 FCA SYSC 5.2.10.G; see also guidance in FCA SYSC 5.2.21G.

- the degree to which a firm believes it can rely on a contractor's judgement about the secondee's fitness and propriety and the grounds for that belief.

Practical guidance

Making sure interim and contracting staff are embedded within the SMCR is a vital requirement. Firms have struggled at times to put in place a fit and proper assessment framework for these individuals who, by their nature, may be temporary but, determined by their role, can be in a position to cause harm. While these individuals may not be subject to the same remuneration structure as permanent employees they do need to be assessed from a FIT perspective and, where appropriate, subject to training and development schemes.

---

7   TERRITORIAL APPLICATION OF THE CERTIFICATION REGIME

3.40   The certification regime for UK firms, EEA and non-EEA branches applies to individuals who carry out regulated activities and who are based in the UK (the territorial limitation).[24]

3.41   Additionally, the FCA specifies that for UK firms the regime is limited to people performing a certification function who are either based in the UK (or spend more than 30 days a year in the UK) or, if based outside the UK, are dealing with UK clients.[25] The 30-day window is aimed at addressing short-term moves within firms and groups in and out of the UK. This means that if a person based overseas does not deal with UK clients but would otherwise have been carrying out one of the FCA certification functions (had they been based in the UK), the certification regime will not apply to them.

3.42   The exception to this is where an individual is a *material risk taker* under one of the FCA's remuneration codes. For these individuals, there is no territorial limitation.[26] This means that if the individual is a material risk taker under a remuneration code, the certification regime will apply even if they are based overseas and do not deal with a UK client.

---

24   FCA feedback statement FS15/3; FCA PS15/30 (which removes the application of the certification regime to individuals who deal with clients in the UK); FCA SYSC 5.2.19R.
25   FCA SYSC 5.2.19R.
26   FCA SYSC 5.2.19(3)R.

Diagram of territoriality and certification[27]

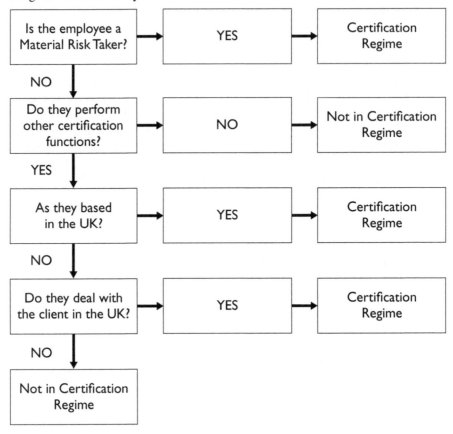

8   CERTIFICATION FUNCTIONS

Holding several significant harm functions

3.43   Several elements of a job may involve a significant harm function or a person may perform several significant harm functions as part of the same job. The regulators do not expect firms to issue multiple certificates to every certification employee. A firm may describe in a certificate the function performed in broad terms without listing all the activities that the function may involve.

3.44   However, if a person performs more than one certification function, the firm must certify that the person is fit and proper to carry out *each* function.[28] There may be different competencies required for the different functions so a firm

---

27 Copied from FCA Guide to SMCR for FCA solo regulated firms.
28 PRA SS28/15; FCA SYSC 5.2.16G; assessment should take into account the factors set out in the Fitness and Propriety Part of the PRA Rulebook CRR Firms; and in FIT in the FCA Handbook.

must assess that the individual is fit and proper to perform each role (although this can be done as part of a single assessment process).

3.45   A job description as part of an employment contract should be consistent with the certification functions and, if the individual takes on additional or different responsibilities, the job description should be updated to reflect this.

Senior manager carrying out certification function

3.46   If a senior manager also performs a certification function that is closely linked to their role as a senior manager, they will not need to be certified under the certification regime. However, if the certification function is very different from what they are doing as a senior manager they will also need to be certified.[29]

Temporary cover for certified staff for up to four weeks

3.47   Where a firm appoints a person to perform a function which would otherwise be a significant harm function, and the appointment is to provide cover for a certified person whose absence was reasonably unforeseen, and the appointment is for less than four weeks, it will not be treated as a certification function. In such instances, the firm will not have to issue a certificate to the employee covering for the certified person. This exclusion does *not* apply to FCA certification functions that require a qualification.[30] In such a case, the firm should take reasonable care to ensure that no employee performs that function without a valid certificate, and the certificate should be issued before the individual starts to perform the function.

3.48   If a firm needs to find cover for a longer period (if an employee, for example, is on secondment or maternity leave) that employee must be certified.

3.49   Where there is an absence of an employee performing a qualification requirement function the firm should take reasonable care to ensure that no employee of that firm performs that function without a valid certificate and a certificate should be obtained before the person starts to perform the function.[31]

New functions and fitness and propriety assessments

3.50   As noted at 3.51, where a certification employee's role changes to involve a new function involving a certification function part way through the 12-month certification period, and that new function may have different requirements relating to personal characteristics, level of competence, knowledge and experience, qualifications or training, then the firm must assess whether the

29 FCA CP17/25.
30 SYSC 5.2.27R and 5.2.28G; PRA Rulebook Certification 2.4.
31 FCA SYSC 5.2.28G.

employee is fit and proper to perform that new function before they start. A new certificate may not be necessary if the existing certificate is drafted broadly enough to cover the new function.

Practical tip: Drafting an offer letter for certified staff

When drafting an offer letter, a firm must ensure that an offer is always subject to the employee obtaining and maintaining certified status.

The offer letter should be made conditional on the receipt of satisfactory regulatory references and satisfactory relevant checks (such as credit, criminal records and other background checks).

A firm may wish to include a warranty that the candidate has made full disclosure of all matters that are or may be relevant to the fitness and propriety assessment.

The offer letter should state that the individual must comply with the relevant regulatory individual conduct rules and associated guidance.

Employment contracts should make clear that if an employee loses certified status then employment may be terminated. It should also be made clear to new employees (whether in the employment contract or another written document, such as the employee handbook) that grounds for summary dismissal include the provision of any false or misleading information at recruitment or for the purposes of any fitness and propriety assessment.

Moving functions during the certification year

3.51   Where a certified employee's role changes to involve a new certification function part way through the 12-month lifespan of a certificate and the new function has different requirements relating to personal characteristics, level of competence, knowledge and experience, qualifications or training, a firm must assess whether the employee is fit and proper to perform that new function before they start, rather than waiting until the annual assessment date.[32]

9   WHEN SHOULD EMPLOYEES BE ASSESSED FOR CERTIFICATION FUNCTIONS?

3.52   Firms should assess certified staff as being fit and proper on the following occasions:

- when a candidate or existing employee takes up a certified role;

- at least annually (for the purpose of reissuing a certificate);

---

32 SYSC 5.2.17G; SS28/15 (updated May 2017); PRA SS28/15 provides information on what should be included on certificates and what happens when a certified employee moves part way through the certification year.

- when disciplinary proceedings raise a certification issue (such as misconduct); and

- where a certification risk or issue has been identified.

3.53 Assessment should always take place prior to appointment. Further detail about the assessment process and timing is set out in Chapter 4.

10   TEMPORARY UK ROLE: THE 30-DAY RULE

3.54 If an individual is based outside the UK and spends no more than 30 days in any 12-month period performing what would be a FCA specified significant harm function, none of the FCA specified significant harm functions will apply to them. This exemption only applies if the individual is appropriately supervised by a senior manager or a certification employee whose certificate covers the FCA specified significant harm function in question.[33]

11   ADDITIONAL FLEXIBILITY IN DRAFTING CERTIFICATES

3.55 A certificate can cover functions that a certification employee is not currently performing, provided the firm has assessed the employee's fitness for these additional functions.

3.56 If this is the case, a certificate should not normally cover an additional function where the firm is required to consider the employee's fitness before allowing them to perform it. In other words, if the new function has different requirements relating to personal characteristics, level of competence, knowledge and experience, qualifications, or training, then a certificate should not be issued until a full fitness and propriety assessment has been undertaken.

12   LENGTH OF CERTIFICATION

3.57 A certificate is valid for 12 months beginning with the date of issue and the employee must be certified both at the point of recruitment and *at least* annually. The FCA states in its guidance to the rules[34] that it believes that FSMA allows a firm to draft a certificate to expire after fewer than 12 months; however, a certificate cannot be drafted to last more than 12 months.

3.58 The regulators envisage that annual certification will normally take place at the same time as annual appraisals.

---

33 SYSC 5.2.28AR. Examples of the 30-day rule are set out in the FCA Handbook at SYSC 5 Annex 1G.
34 SYSC 5.2.12G.

3.59   The ability of a firm to certify an individual for a shorter period will be useful when monitoring an individual's performance, enabling a shorter probationary period of certification pending an improvement in performance.

3.60   Once a person is in a certified role, it is the firm's responsibility to ensure that they are assessed on an on-going basis.

3.61   The frequency and extent of reassessment will vary from firm to firm and in relation to certain issues. Some firms have stated[35] that they require a self-declaration annually and repeated external checks, such as credit checks annually.

13   MAINTAINING A RECORD OF CERTIFIED EMPLOYEES

3.62   A firm must keep a record of every employee who has a valid certificate.[36]

Drafting a contract of employment for a certified employee

A contract of employment for a certified employee should include the following provisions:

- The employment should be made conditional upon obtaining and maintaining certified status.

- Lack or loss of certification may result in the immediate termination of employment. Such a provision will help a firm to defend a claim for wrongful dismissal on the basis that the contractual terms provided for such a termination.

- The employee may be asked to warrant that they have disclosed all and any matters which may have an impact on a fitness and propriety assessment.

- The employment should be made conditional upon the certified employee conducting themselves in a fit and proper manner in accordance with their regulatory obligations.

- The employment must be made conditional upon the receipt of satisfactory regulatory references; there should be a provision stating that in the event that a reference is updated during the course of employment which discloses something which impacts upon the individual's fitness and propriety, the firm reserves the right to terminate employment, with or without notice.

---

35 BSB statement of good practice – certification regime: fitness and propriety assessment principles, 28 February 2017.
36 SYSC 5.2.15G.

- The certified employee should be required to comply with the individual conduct rules.

- The regulators' whistleblowing rules should be referred to and the contract should refer to the firm's compliant whistleblowing policy.

- Any confidentiality provision should not limit a certified employee's rights under the regulatory whistleblowing rules.

14 BANKING STANDARDS BOARD RESPONSE TO CONSULTATION ON EXTENSION OF THE SMCR: POINTS ON CERTIFICATION

3.63 In its response to the FCA's consultation[37] on extending the SMCR, the Banking Standards Board (BSB) highlighted some of its practical insights into the implementation of the regulatory regime so far.

3.64 The BSB notes that the introduction of the regime presents an opportunity for firms to demonstrate that they are taking responsibility for ensuring high standards of competence and conduct among their employees and to learn from approaches that are now becoming established practice in the banking industry. It underlines that regulatory requirements are starting points, not end-points, to support and enable positive cultures.

3.65 The BSB has focused primarily on assessing the fitness and propriety of certified staff and on the regulatory references regime. In developing its good practice guidelines, the BSB has sought to:

- highlight the need for a fair and transparent process from the perspective of individuals;

- give firms a measure of confidence that fitness and propriety assessments being conducted by their peers are to a high standard, taking into account similar types of information;

- highlight the links between the certification regime and organisational culture; and

- use the certification regime as an opportunity to raise standards of behaviour and competence across the industry.

3.66 As noted at 3.55, the regulatory regime provides sufficient flexibility in terms of implementation, which allows firms to tailor and scale the regime to their own business models and organisational cultures.

---

37 FCA CP17/25.

3.67 Some specific areas where firms have sought to share good practice are:

- Where they are required to make difficult subjective judgements about an individual's fitness and propriety without categorical evidence. This is particularly challenging in circumstances where evidence about an event may be incomplete or purely anecdotal.

- When assessing fitness and propriety of individuals based overseas, particularly where local laws prohibit or make difficult accessing information that the firm would typically use to inform fitness and propriety assessments in the UK.

- When providing regulatory references.

- When deciding whether to remove an individual's certificate or keep it in place with remediation or additional controls. This will to some extent depend on firms' individual risk tolerances or practical considerations, but is ultimately a judgement that balances the requirements of the regime, the specific details of the issue and fairness to the individual.

3.68 A common example of an issue that can be remediated is an individual's financial soundness due to an unforeseen change in circumstances. Most firms in the BSB's working group said that they would generally be as supportive as possible in such a case. They focused less on the debt and more on an individual's ability and commitment to making regular payments.

3.69 When determining whether or not to issue a certificate, firms generally took into account how the information had come to light, with individuals encouraged to discuss risks and issues proactively.

3.70 Firms also emphasised the role of the individual in taking ownership of remediating any financial issue and keeping to the agreed plan. Maintaining confidentiality was crucial for the individual. Where relevant and appropriate, firms recommended increasing the frequency of screening of these individuals.

3.71 Firms discussed a number of approaches to issuing a certificate in such cases, including not issuing a certificate until the concerns had gone; issuing a certificate for a role with more controls or for a shorter period; or trusting the individual to manage their own situation subject to routine screening checks.

3.72 In larger firms, firms should consider moving an individual to a different role while the specific issue is remediated; this is likely to be more difficult for smaller firms.

3.73 Ultimately it is a firm's responsibility how to implement the SMCR so inevitably there may be considerable variation across the sector.

CHAPTER 4

Fitness and Propriety

Elizabeth Graves, Partner, David Saunders, Partner, Simon Collins, Managing Director Regulatory ES Consulting, Susan Mayne, Consultant

I ASSESSING FITNESS AND PROPRIETY

Senior managers and certification staff: fitness and propriety assessments

4.01   As detailed elsewhere in this book, firms have a greater responsibility under the SMCR to assess for themselves the suitability of key staff to perform the roles to which they are recruited. Under the Senior Managers Certification Regime (SMCR), senior managers, certified employees and non-executive directors (NEDs) all need to be assessed on recruitment and on an ongoing basis (at least annually) as fit and proper to carry out their roles. Under the extended SMCR regime (see 4.11 and Chapter 2) NEDs who are not senior managers are also subject to fitness and propriety assessments, save in limited scope firms. The FCA has accordingly extended its detailed guidance in the Fit and Proper Test for Approved Persons (FIT) in the FCA Handbook (see 4.14 and Chapter 3) to cover certification staff and non-approved NEDs. To support an assessment firms need to undertake an extensive evidence-gathering exercise, part of which will entail obtaining satisfactory regulatory references in accordance with regulatory requirements (see Chapter 5). This requirement to obtain a regulatory reference will also apply to NEDs whether or not they are senior managers.

4.02   Whilst senior managers must be approved by the regulator before they can undertake their role, it is the still the firm's responsibility to ensure that they are assessed as fit and proper according to the regulators' rules and guidance and to carry out the appropriate checks prior to an application to the regulator for approval. This can of course delay the recruitment process, a matter which should be factored into offer letters and recruitment plans.

4.03   The FCA emphasises that its own approval process is not a substitute for the checks that a firm should carry out on its prospective recruits.[1] Only when the regulator is satisfied that the candidate for a senior manager role is fit and proper to perform the function will it grant approval.[2]

4.04   Given the importance of continued certification or approval for staff, firms should carry out assessments fairly and transparently and should not rely on unfounded allegations or suspicions. An individual could potentially argue that a decision not to certify them, which was reached without proper investigation and on unsubstantiated grounds, constitutes a breach of the implied duty of trust and confidence that exists between employer and employee. The importance of a thorough, fair and properly documented process cannot be underestimated.

---

1   FIT 1.1.3G.
2   FSMA, s 60A.

Practical guidance

What we have seen over the past two and half years is that the on-boarding process for the majority of new staff takes longer than pre the regime. This is due to increased robust procedures around the whole on-boarding process linked to references and due diligence. In particular this has impacted on the recruitment of senior staff and so building an elongated timeframe is probably sensible to manage the expectations of the firm and the individual concerned.

Non-executive directors and fitness and propriety assessments

Pre-extension of the SMCR regime

4.05   Prior to the extension of the SMCR, the rules relating to NEDs are largely laid down by the PRA. A distinction should first be made between NEDs who carry out senior management functions (SMFs) and those who do not.

4.06   The only NEDs who require regulatory pre-approval before the extension of the regime are those who hold the following positions:

- chairman;

- senior independent director;

- chairs of audit, risk, remuneration and nomination committees.

4.07   Other NEDs are known by the PRA as 'notified NEDs' and by the FCA as 'standard NEDs'.

4.08   The PRA requires SMCR firms regulated by it to assess the fitness and propriety of NEDs who carry out SMFs and of notified NEDs, both prior to appointment and periodically thereafter.

4.09   The PRA must also be informed of the identity of notified NEDs and of any information that might affect an assessment of a NED's fitness and propriety.

4.10   All NEDs are subject to the regulatory references regime, irrespective of whether or not they hold a SMF.

Post-extension of the SMCR regime

4.11   Under the rules for the extension of the SMCR regime, all NEDs who are not subject to regulatory approval as a senior manager (sometimes referred to as non-approved NEDs) as well as those NEDs who are senior managers must be assessed as fit and proper by the firm and the regulatory reference regime will apply to all NEDs, as it does now.

4.12   The exception to this rule is for limited scope firms (see Chapter 2). For limited scope firms,[3] sole traders are not required to seek regulatory references or criminal records checks. If any employees meet the definition or perform one of the certification functions, the fit and proper requirements apply. Non-approved executive directors and NEDs in limited scope firms are not subject to the fit and proper requirements, including regulatory references and criminal record checks.

2   CRITERIA FOR FITNESS AND PROPRIETY ASSESSMENTS

4.13   When assessing candidates for senior management or certification functions, the Financial Services and Markets Act 2000 (FSMA) requires firms to have regard to any general rules that the regulator has made concerning the qualifications, training, competence and personal characteristics required by an individual for that role.

4.14   The FIT section in the FCA Handbook sets out detailed guidance about the matters that a firm should consider as part of assessing a person's fitness and propriety. Under these rules, fitness and propriety should be judged by reference to a person's:

- honesty, integrity and reputation;

- competence and capability, including whether the person satisfies any relevant FCA training and competence requirements;

- financial soundness.[4]

These same criteria apply for the PRA assessment of fitness and propriety. Firms should note that the FCA states that these criteria are 'the most important considerations' which suggests that other considerations may be taken into account. Firms should use the FCA and PRA guidance to assess whether not meeting one of the criteria means that someone is not fit and proper; this should always be a question of evaluation and judgement.

4.15   This means that those staff subject to a fitness and propriety assessment should discharge their roles in a way that is consistent with the standards of behaviour and competence outlined in the conduct rules relating to each of these elements of fitness and propriety. The FCA has placed great emphasis on culture and it will expect cultural considerations to be taken into account when firms assess fitness and propriety. For example, in the context of sexual harassment in the workplace, Megan Butler (executive director of the FCA) stated 'when we talk about being fit and proper ... we are not merely talking about financial decision making but also in terms of culture ... we do not compartmentalise what makes individuals fit and proper'.[5]

---

3   FCA Guide for solo regulated firms.
4   FCA Handbook, FIT 1.3.
5   Megan Butler's speech on a panel to the Women's and Equalities Committee May 2018.

4.16   Guidance in the FCA's FIT Handbook and the PRA Rulebook – CRR firms – Fitness and Propriety sets out the factors that should be considered when assessing people as fit and proper. FIT 1.3 provides guidance to firms about the criteria the FCA expects a firm to consider when assessing fitness and propriety. PRA guidance on assessing fitness and propriety can also be found in its supervisory statement SS28/15. Firms can also glean guidance from decisions of the Upper Tribunal (Tax and Chancery). For example, the Upper Tribunal in *Ford & Owen v FCA*[6] has recently provided helpful guidance on the meaning of integrity and the duty to be open and cooperative with the regulators. The Banking Standards Board has also produced helpful guidance for the banking sector which can be applied to other financial services and insurance firms.

4.17   The FCA has made clear that firms should apply the fitness and propriety criteria proportionately[7] – there is no 'one size fits all' approach. This means that the assessment of fitness and propriety may differ from firm to firm. This should be taken into account in the context, say, of a transfer of a business. The individuals transferring may have been assessed as fit and proper in the transferring business but the standards in the transferee firm may be different and require a fresh assessment.

4.18   Under the SMCR, additional evidence should be obtained when assessing candidates for senior manager, certification or non-approved NED roles. These criteria are set out at 4.52 ff.

Regulators' rules and guidance on fitness and propriety

4.19   As noted at 4.13, when assessing the fitness and propriety of a person to perform a senior management function or a certification function, a firm must have regard, in particular, to whether that person:

- has obtained a qualification;

- has undergone, or is undergoing, training;

- possesses a level of competence; or

- has the personal characteristics,

as required by general rules set out by the regulators.

4.20   The FCA did not amend or add to the existing rules relating to qualifications, training, competence and personal characteristics required by individuals in certain roles. However, it did amend the guidance in the existing FIT module of the FCA Handbook.

4.21   Due to its different approach to providing rules and guidance, the PRA did not have as many pre-existing rules relating to fitness and propriety. It

6   [2018] UKUT 0358.
7   FCA CP15/22.

therefore added rules to give effect to FSMA requirements, which are set out in the CRR firms – Fitness and Propriety part of the PRA Rulebook.

4.22 Given its different statutory objectives as a regulator, the test set out in the PRA Rulebook[8] is slightly different and requires an individual to have the personal characteristics, necessary level of competence, knowledge and experience and appropriate training and qualifications to enable the sound and prudent management of the firm. The PRA states that a firm should have regard to all relevant matters that may have arisen whether in the UK or elsewhere. In its supervisory statement[9] the PRA states that when assessing whether an individual is fit and proper, firms should have regard to the characteristics set out in FIT 1.3 (see 4.25 ff).

4.23 We set out in 4.25 ff key points from the FIT guidance and the Banking Standards Board (BSB) guidance on the assessment criteria, which together assist firms in understanding what aspects to focus on when carrying out a fitness and propriety assessment.

Practical guidance

The regulators focus on performance management in the assessment process and in particular the personal characteristics an individual possesses. Where an individual has managerial or supervisory responsibilities the regulator is looking for firms to consider whether the individual's personality suits the role. This development is on the back of poor incentive structures within firms and issues such as a lack of speaking out due to perceived 'bullying'.

Sexual harassment and fitness and propriety

4.24 In response to the House of Commons Women's and Equalities Committee report on workplace sexual harassment, Megan Butler of the FCA has clarified that the SMCR will hold leaders to account and while the fitness and propriety test does not expressly address sexual harassment, aspects of an individual's behaviour are relevant for this assessment. The Committee has urged regulators to make clear that sexual harassment by regulated individuals is a breach of regulatory requirements and should count in the context of a fitness and propriety assessment (see Chapter 11).

8　PRA Rulebook – CRR firms – Fitness and Propriety 2.6; see also European Banking Authority guidelines on the assessment of the suitability of members of the management body and key function holders 2012 (assessment criteria).

9　PRA SS28/15.

3   FIT 1.3 AND FIT 2.1–2.3: FCA GUIDANCE ON ASSESSING FITNESS AND PROPRIETY

General guidance on carrying out assessments

4.25   The FCA suggests that when assessing fitness and propriety a firm should take into account:

- the nature, scale and complexity of the firm's business, the nature and range of financial services and activities undertaken in the course of that business; and

- whether the person has the knowledge, skills and experience to perform the specific role that the person is intended to perform.

4.26   The FCA states that if a matter comes to a firm's attention that suggests an individual might not be fit and proper (for example, through the medium of a regulatory reference) the firm should take into account how relevant and how important that matter is.

4.27   A firm assessing the continuing fitness and propriety of staff should assess the role that the individual is actually performing at the time the assessment is done. For this purpose the assessor should be given an up-to-date job description in advance of the assessment.[10]

4.28   The FCA provides that when assessing an individual to perform a controlled function, it will have regard to the main assessment criteria set out in FIT 2. The FCA requires firms that are required to assess the fitness and propriety of senior managers and certification staff to have regard to substantially the same factors as those outlined in FIT 2.

4.29   When assessing fitness and propriety, the FCA will also take account of the activities of the firm, the permission held by that firm and the markets within which it operates.

4.30   The criteria listed in FIT 2.1–2.3 are given as guidance and firms are advised that it is not intended as a definitive list.

4.31   A firm that is assessing the continuing fitness and propriety of a senior manager must notify the FCA if it believes that there are grounds on which the FCA could withdraw its approval.[11]

Practical guidance

When assessing fitness and propriety firms should be alert to information from all sources including, for example, social media.

---

10   FIT 1.3.4BG.
11   FIT 1.3.4AG; SUP 10C.14.24R.

FIT 2.1: honesty, integrity and reputation

4.32   The FCA sets out matters to which a firm should have regard when considering honesty, [12] integrity[13] and reputation.[14] Any matters that come to light regarding an individual being assessed should be considered only where relevant to the requirements and standards of the regulatory system. So, for example, a conviction for a criminal offence will not automatically mean that an employee cannot be assessed as fit and proper – it must be considered in the overall context of the employee's role and circumstances.

4.33   Under the FCA guidance, firms should inform themselves of all relevant matters which have arisen in the UK or elsewhere, including checking for convictions for a criminal offence (where legally entitled to do so) and contacting previous employers. One issue that needs to be considered here is whether these checks can be processed under the General Data Protection Regulation and Data Protection Act 2018. We address this issue at 4.132.

4.34   With regard to convictions for a criminal offence, the PRA repeats the FCA's position that[15] a conviction for a criminal offence should not automatically mean an application should be rejected. The PRA also suggests that each application should be treated on a case-by-case basis, having regard to a range of factors which may include but are not limited to:

● the seriousness, and circumstances surrounding, the offence;

● the explanation offered;

● the relevance of the offence to the proposed role;

● the passage of time since the offence was committed; and

● evidence of rehabilitation.

4.35   The matters referred to in FIT 2.1.1G to which a firm should have regard, when assessing honesty, integrity and reputation include, but are not limited to:

(1) whether the individual has been convicted of any criminal offence; this *must* include any spent convictions; particular consideration will be given to offences of dishonesty, fraud, financial crime or an offence under legislation relating to companies, building societies, industrial and provident societies, credit unions, friendly societies, banking, other financial services, insolvency, consumer credit companies, insurance, consumer protection, money laundering market manipulation and insider dealing, whether or not in the UK;

(2) whether the individual has been the subject of any adverse finding or any settlement in civil proceedings, particularly in connection with investment or

---

12 See *Hussein v FCA* [2018] UKUT 186.
13 See *Wingate v SRA* [2018] 1 WLR 3969 and *Ford & Owen v FCA* [2018] UKUT 0358.
14 See *Marriott v FSA* (2009) FSMT Case 073.
15 PRA SS28/15, para 4.8.

other financial business, misconduct, fraud or the formation or management of a company;

(3) whether the individual has been the subject of, or interviewed in the course of, any existing or previous investigation or disciplinary proceedings, by the appropriate regulator, by other regulatory authorities clearing houses and exchanges, professional bodies, or government bodies or agencies; [16]

(4) whether the person is or has been the subject of any proceedings of a disciplinary or criminal nature, or has been notified of any potential proceedings or of any investigation which might lead to those proceedings;

(5) whether the person has contravened any of the requirements and standards of the regulatory system or the equivalent standards or requirements of other regulatory authorities clearing houses and exchanges, professional bodies, or government bodies or agencies;

(6) whether the person has been the subject of any justified complaint relating to regulated activities;

(7) whether the person has been involved with another organisation that has been refused registration, authorisation, membership or a licence to carry out a trade, business or profession, or has had that registration, authorisation, membership or licence revoked, withdrawn or terminated, or has been expelled by a regulatory or government body;

(8) whether, as a result of the removal of the relevant licence, registration or other authority, the person has been refused the right to carry on a trade, business or profession requiring a licence, registration or other authority;

(9) whether the person has been a director, partner or concerned in the management, of a business that has gone into insolvency, liquidation or administration while the person has been connected with that organisation or within one year of that connection;

(10) whether the person, or any business with which the person has been involved, has been investigated, disciplined, censured or suspended or criticised by a regulatory or professional body, a court or tribunal, whether publicly or privately;

(11) whether the person has been dismissed, or asked to resign and resigned, from employment or from a position of trust, fiduciary appointment or similar;

(12) whether the person has ever been disqualified from acting as a director or disqualified from acting in any managerial capacity;

(13) whether, in the past, the person has been candid and truthful in all his dealings with any regulatory body and whether the person demonstrates a readiness and willingness to comply with the requirements and standards of the regulatory system and with other legal, regulatory and professional requirements and standards.

16 Firms should also consider individuals' conduct during proceedings, even as witnesses; have they been honest and open? Have they sought to conceal information?

FIT 2.2: competence and capability

4.36   When assessing competence and capability, firms must note that assessing experience is not a tick box exercise; by itself, competence is rarely a ground for failing a fitness and propriety assessment. The matters referred to in FIT 2.2 G to which a firm should have regard when assessing competence and capability include, but are not limited to:

(1) whether the person completes any relevant training and competence requirements in relation to the certified function;

(2) whether the person has demonstrated by experience or training that they are suitable to perform the function they are intended to perform; and

(3) whether the person has adequate time to perform the function in question and meet the responsibilities associated with that function.

4.37   The FCA also states that a firm should consider a person's convictions, dismissals and suspensions from employment for drug or alcohol abuses or other abusive acts only in relation to a person's continuing ability to perform the certified function in question.[17]

FIT 2.3: financial soundness

4.38   The matters referred to in FIT 2.3 G to which a firm should have regard when assessing financial soundness include, but are not limited to:

(1) whether the person has been the subject of any judgment debt or award, in the UK or elsewhere, that remains outstanding or was not satisfied within a reasonable period;

(2) whether in the UK or elsewhere, the person has made any arrangements with his creditors, filed for bankruptcy, had a bankruptcy petition served on him, been adjudged bankrupt, been the subject of a bankruptcy restrictions order (including an interim bankruptcy restrictions order), offered a bankruptcy restrictions undertaking, had assets sequestrated, or been involved in proceedings relating to any of these.

4.39   The FCA would not expect a firm to require a candidate to supply a statement of assets or liabilities. The fact that a person is of limited financial means will not, of itself, affect their suitability for the role.

4.40   When determining a person's financial soundness for the purposes of the fitness and propriety test, the PRA also states[18] that it would not expect a candidate (whether for a senior management or certification function) to supply a statement of assets or liabilities.

---

17   FIT 2.2.2A–G.
18   SS28/15, para 4.9–4.10.

4 BANKING STANDARDS BOARD GUIDANCE ON REGULATORS' FITNESS AND PROPRIETY CRITERIA

4.41   The Banking Standards Board (BSB) has published a Statement of Good Practice: Fitness and Propriety Assessment Principles[19] and two supporting non-mandatory guidance publications aimed at assessment of fitness and propriety.[20] In its guidance the BSB sets out valuable assistance to firms in understanding and evaluating the regulators' criteria for fitness and propriety. While aimed at the banking sector, the BSB guidance has general application across the regulated sector and is outlined below.

Honesty, integrity and reputation

4.42   Honesty and integrity are demonstrated by a person who consistently speaks and acts truthfully and fairly in their dealings with others, and who seeks to recognise and deal with ethical conflicts.

4.43   Reputation in this context is the assessment of how an individual's behaviour has affected the impressions or opinions of others about the firm or industry as a whole. Such impressions and opinions may be influenced by:

- external factors (eg the views of previous employers or peers in other firms);

- factors internal to the firm (eg the views of colleagues); and

- aspects of the individual's public activities outside the workplace or professional sphere.

4.44   The BSB recommends that information to assess this element of fitness and propriety for a new role can be obtained from a regulatory reference and pre-employment checks (such as character references or professional references from a line manager, colleagues or other relevant parties).

4.45   The BSB recommends that information to assess this element of fitness and propriety for an annual assessment can be obtained from a performance appraisal and individual portfolio of achievement.

Competence and capability

4.46   There are two dimensions to competence and capability:

- the professional experience and qualifications that the individual brings to the role; and

---

19 28 February 2017; see https://www.bankingstandardsboard.org.uk/pdf/Assessing-F&P-Statement-of-Good-Practice.pdf.

20 BSB Supporting guidance to Statement of Good Practice: the certification regime: fitness and propriety assessment principles; establishing pass/fail criteria and evidencing the F&P assessment ('BSB Supporting Guidance').

- the performance of the individual in their role, developing and maintaining their knowledge and skills as demonstrated over time.

4.47　The BSB recommends that information to assess this element of fitness and propriety for a new role can be obtained from the recruitment process, pre-employment checks and individual portfolio of evidence. This includes the individual's application form, interview notes, other assessment outcomes, qualifications required for the role, educational attainment and other relevant qualifications.

4.48　The BSB recommends that information to assess this element of fitness and propriety for an annual assessment can also be obtained from a performance appraisal and individual portfolio of achievement.

Financial soundness

4.49　Financial soundness is demonstrated by an individual who behaves in a financially responsible way and whose financial circumstances do not create a risk of compromising their professional and/or ethical conduct.

4.50　The BSB recommends that information to assess this element of fitness and propriety can be obtained for a new role from screening checks. Screening checks are an important part of the pre-employment checks when a person is joining a firm for the first time (particularly with regard to financial soundness).

4.51　Where an individual transfers to a different role internally, as long as screening information on financial soundness remains valid, complete, accurate and up-to-date, then additional screening checks do not need to be performed.

5　ADDITIONAL CHECKS TO BE CARRIED OUT BY THE FIRM

4.52　Before starting a role, due diligence by way of the hiring, transfer or promotion process will generate a significant amount of information. Firms must verify that the individual holds the requisite qualifications.

4.53　Firms must additionally carry out at least the following checks:

- criminal records checks (but see 4.123);

- credit checks;

- obtaining references for the previous six years of service with current and former employers (see 4.60 and Chapter 5).

4.54　The BSB gives examples of the types of checks that might be undertaken (the list is not exhaustive):

Honesty and integrity:

- disclosure and barring service (or overseas equivalent)
- Clearing House (eg LCH.Clearnet)
- Staff fraud checks
- Company searches
- Sanctions check

Reputation:

- Professional Body Registers (where available)

Competence and capability:

- Professional Body Registers (where available)

Financial soundness:

- Credit reference agency
- County court judgment
- Bankruptcy order

4.55   Based on the information disclosed in these checks, firms should consider whether the individual meets the appropriate standard required to carry out their functions.

4.56   The BSB recommends in the Statement of Good Practice[21] that the fitness and propriety assessment of a person new to a certified role should be managed through:

- the recruitment process (such as interview notes, assessment results and rationale for hiring);
- screening checks (eg criminal records checks, credit checks and qualification validation);
- regulatory references (see 4.60);
- training and induction programmes relevant to the requirements of the role;
- self-declaration (retrospective) and a commitment to uphold high standards of behaviour and competence (forward looking) by the individual. These provide an opportunity for disclosing pertinent information (eg financial difficulties or a relevant internal relationship).

---

21 See 4.41.

4.57   The BSB recommends that firms should take into account the time and support needed for an individual who is new or returning to a certified role to attain full competence for that role; this may require an in-year assessment.

4.58   The annual appraisal documentation supported by self-declarations and current screening checks (or vetting) will be a key source of information for firms carrying out assessments of existing certified staff.

4.59   A firm's fitness and propriety assessment processes must be aligned with existing processes so that the outcomes are not inconsistent. The BSB cites the example of an individual receiving a written warning following a disciplinary hearing but the fitness and propriety assessment concluding that they are not fit and proper and their certificate is removed.

Regulatory references

4.60   A firm will need to carry out a thorough due diligence exercise to satisfy itself of the candidate's fitness and propriety for an approved (senior manager) or certified role. A crucial part of this assessment includes obtaining a regulatory reference. The requirements for a regulatory reference are detailed in Chapter 5.

4.61   In line with the Fair and Effective Markets Review recommendations (see 5.05), the FCA requires firms to request a regulatory reference prior to the appointment of any person who applies to carry out a senior manager or certified function (and under the extended rules, for non-approved NEDs).

Key point: Responsibility for ensuring fitness and propriety of staff

Individuals responsible for carrying out the assessment will vary across different firms and may include line managers, or individuals in HR and/or Compliance Departments. However, when deciding who should determine the question of fitness and propriety firms should bear in mind that ultimate responsibility for ensuring staff are fit and proper lies with senior managers and not with the HR department. A firm should identify the individuals who are most appropriate to conduct the assessment and ensure that they are competent and capable to assess each of the fitness and propriety elements. Training may be necessary to ensure the individual carrying out the assessment understands the rules and guidance; some form of monitoring may be necessary to ensure consistency and fairness.

Firms should record the decision-making process in order to justify their conclusions to the regulators. Record keeping should include thought processes which led to an outcome.

The process should be appropriately reviewed, and firms should also ensure that there is an appropriate level of supervision and support for those responsible for the assessment to limit bias and avoid any potential conflicts of interest.

A firm should consider what support and guidance it could offer to those carrying out fitness and propriety assessments, including appropriate training on evaluating fitness and propriety issues and discussing the outcome of an assessment with an individual. The training should be periodically undertaken and refreshed. Line managers should be trained to recognise and understand certification risks and issues as part of performance management.

There may also be a need for wider training to relevant staff and more tailored training for certain business functions such as Compliance, HR and Audit.

4.62   The regulators have stated that they envisage the annual fitness and propriety re-certification process to be conducted in conjunction with annual appraisals. The fitness and propriety process can take account of and reflect information generated by other internal processes such as appraisals, disciplinary procedures and performance management. Firms will need to review the individual's conduct and performance to confirm that the required standard has been met.

Practical guidance

In order to try to achieve consistency of approach throughout a firm, particularly larger firms where different departments may be assessing fitness and propriety, some firms have formed 'people' committees. These committees may have replaced other HR committees but will typically contain representation from HR, Legal and Compliance functions and, where appropriate, input from the business.

4.63   When assessing staff, it is the firm's responsibility to ensure the truth of the information received.

Support for individuals being assessed

4.64   The BSB recommends that firms consider the support required by individuals being assessed for fitness and propriety.[22] Firms may want to make use of induction programmes and/or workshops to introduce staff to the requirements of the certification regime.

4.65   Periodic training might also be used to address the assessment. Firms may wish to offer training, guidance and support to individuals in relation to their own fitness and propriety and what might constitute an appropriate level of self-declaration for the purpose of the assessment (one example is the factors that might need to be taken into account in deciding whether it is relevant to disclose a relationship with a colleague, such as the nature of the relationship, the nature

---

22 BSB statement of good practice – certification regime: fitness and propriety assessment principles, 28 February 2017.

of the role and the proximity of the role to transaction decisions, privileged information or cash and settlement operations).

6   SUMMARY OF THE BANKING STANDARDS BOARD GUIDANCE ON THE CERTIFICATION REGIME: THE FITNESS AND PROPRIETY ASSESSMENT PROCESS

4.66   The BSB's first supporting guidance[23] was directed at helping firms with the options available to them when making certification decisions, especially in cases where issues are not clear-cut. The guidance is intended to provide those assessing fitness and propriety with further information on what each element of fitness and propriety means and how it can be assessed. It contains:

- definitions of each element of fitness and propriety;

- an overview of different types of fitness and propriety assessment and potential sources of information for both; and

- an example of an assessment record template.

4.67   The BSB's second non-mandatory good practice supporting guidance focuses on dealing with the risks and issues that may arise when assessing the fitness and propriety of certified staff.[24] The guidance sets out a 'good practice framework' to help firms and individuals making certification decisions.

4.68   Whilst the guidance contains illustrative examples, the BSB emphasises that the challenges that firms face will be unique to each firm and they will need to exercise their own judgement in each case.

4.69   In this guidance the BSB identifies four instances when fitness and propriety must be assessed:

- when an individual takes up a certified role either on joining the firm or following internal transfer ('new role assessment');

- annually, for the purposes of reissuing a certificate ('annual assessment');

- in response to another event, such as the outcome of a disciplinary proceeding, that generates a certification issue ('triggered assessment'); and

- in-year to monitor the fitness and propriety of an employee at a shorter interval than 12 months where a certification risk or issue has been identified ('in-year assessment').

4.70   The BSB emphasises that demonstrating fitness and propriety is not a one-off annual event but an ongoing commitment on both sides. Equally important

---

23 https://www.bankingstandardsboard.org.uk/pdf/Assessing-F&P-Supporting-Guidance.pdf.
24 https://www.bankingstandardsboard.org.uk/wp-content/uploads/2018/02/BSB-Certification-decision-guidance-draft-incorp-reg-comments-v0.3.pdf.

is the opportunity afforded by the assessment to recognise good behaviours and achievements.

7   ESTABLISHING 'PASS/FAIL' CRITERIA

4.71   The BSB advises[25] that a firm should be clear about the tolerances that are acceptable to its firm when assessing fitness and propriety, including:

- identifying potential individual characteristics or circumstances that may call into question a person's fitness or propriety;

- identifying whether there are certain roles or responsibilities where there is a greater risk of a certification issue arising;

- determining what self-declarations should be required and when; and

- determining what screening checks will be applied and when.

4.72   It recommends that a firm should develop a rounded approach using a range of different sources of information to conduct an assessment in line with the firm's risk tolerance, code of conduct and other employee policies. Assessors should be sufficiently competent to recognise certification risks. Firms should not use the fitness and propriety assessment process as an excuse to discipline individuals for reasons that are not related to their fitness and propriety.

4.73   There should be a clear process for investigating certification issues, so that a fair and reasonable approach is taken to gather all the evidence for a particular case, and deal with the circumstances when a person leaves the firm while under investigation.

4.74   Firms should put a structured framework or policy in place for individuals for whom the assessment highlights a development or remediation need (see 4.88). The BSB cites[26] as an example where an individual's performance is inadequate but their fitness and propriety is not called into question. A firm might first wish to place them on a performance improvement plan (PIP) rather than withdraw the certificate. Where broader organisational issues are identified, a firm may wish to consider addressing policy and process weaknesses.

4.75   The BSB also recommends that where shortcomings in an individual's performance or behaviour are considered non-significant for the purposes of fitness and propriety, a firm should attempt to resolve these through alternative means to formal disciplinary procedures (eg constructive feedback or training).

---

25 BSB statement of good practice – certification regime: fitness and propriety assessment principles, 28 February 2017.
26 BSB statement of good practice – certification regime: fitness and propriety assessment principles, 28 February 2017.

4.76   There should also be a framework in place to evaluate the significance of information that may call a person's fitness and propriety into question.

4.77   Whilst a person is stated to be either certified or not certified, the actual position is more nuanced. A firm may certify an individual but also incorporate measures to remedy any perceived shortfalls by, say, placing the individual on a performance improvement programme and potentially an in-year assessment.

8   BSB GUIDANCE: STRUCTURE OF THE FITNESS AND PROPRIETY ASSESSMENT

4.78   The BSB recommends that the fitness and propriety assessment should follow three stages:

● sourcing and evaluating evidence (via annual assessment or where there is new information);

● deciding whether to issue a certificate and taking action to mitigate risks or remediate an issue where necessary;

● recording the outcome (also of relevance to regulatory references).

Sourcing evidence

4.79   The BSB notes that most of the evidence sourced will result from a firm's other processes such as performance evaluation, disciplinary procedures etc. Any information put forward must be current.

4.80   Importantly, the actions taken as part of one process (eg a disciplinary process) must be consistent with the fitness and propriety assessment. This means that firms should at all times during different processes have in mind the impact on a fitness and propriety assessment.

4.81   While firms assess certified staff's fitness and propriety, it is for individuals to also build and maintain evidence demonstrating their fitness and propriety and for carrying out mitigating or remedial steps. The BSB urges firms to ensure that their culture supports their employees in acting in a way that is fit and proper.

Evaluating evidence

4.82   The key point to bear in mind is that a fitness and propriety assessment is not like a disciplinary process, although there may be some common factors.

4.83   Firms are required to reach a view on the information before them on whether the regulators' requirements for fitness and propriety have been met, namely:

- honesty, integrity and reputation;

- competence and capability; and

- financial soundness.

4.84   When evaluating evidence, a firm must ask: what are the issues? Why are they relevant for the individual's fitness and propriety? Approaches may differ between firms but all firms must articulate the element of fitness and propriety to which any evidence relates and why it is relevant.

4.85   Firms should put in place a framework to help those persons carrying out the assessment to evaluate information consistently. The BSB sets out a non-exhaustive list of relevant factors to consider when assessing the significance of information and examples of how a firm might apply these factors.

Actions following assessment

Maintaining fitness and propriety

4.86   Where there is a newly-certified population, a firm may consider – in addition to mandatory training – investing in additional training or support.

Mitigating a risk

4.87   A firm should consider putting in place steps to mitigate risks. For example, where there is a perceived conflict of interest, a firm should ensure that the individual does not work on matters relating to that client, together with additional controls.

Remediating an issue

4.88   A firm should consider supervision and other actions to ensure that an individual is able to improve to the required standard, where possible. It should consider action plans agreed with the individual and remember that a certificate can be issued for less than a year, allowing for a further in-year assessment.

Where the issue cannot be remediated

4.89   If an issue cannot be remediated – for example, there are serious issues concerning the individual's honesty, which cannot be resolved – the individual cannot be certified as fit and proper.

Practical guidance

The issue of conduct rule breaches is not only sensitive given the potential impact on an individual's career but also critical to ensure consistency of approach. Firms should be defining their conduct rule breach policy in line with their existing breach policy. One of the areas to consider carefully is whether behaviours and activities outside of the individual's day-to-day role are in scope. Where there are matters of integrity firms are including behaviour generally.

---

9   APPEALING THE OUTCOME OF AN ASSESSMENT

4.90   It is good practice[27] to establish a process for the independent review of an outcome of an assessment. This is particularly the case when the individual concerned is already an employee of the firm. The nature of the certification regime does mean it is likely that the assessor will be completely independent of the individual being assessed. Firms could mitigate against this risk by having a policy and procedure to review marginal decisions; auditing a number of fitness and propriety assessments from each division to ensure consistency; and/or establishing a panel or committee to review an individual's appeal, chaired by an independent practitioner (eg NED or a practitioner from a different part of the business).

4.91   There should be a clear appeal process against the conclusion of the assessment, which should be aligned with other relevant processes (such as the appeal against a disciplinary finding or performance management process). The BSB recommends that an individual should be given the opportunity to challenge any decision leading to the withdrawal of a certificate, before the certificate is actually withdrawn.

4.92   Some firms have developed fitness and propriety committees to consider appeals in order to ensure a consistent approach.

10   THE FITNESS AND PROPRIETY CERTIFICATE

4.93   The fitness and propriety certificate must state that the firm is satisfied that the person is fit and proper to perform the function to which the certification relates[28] and the certificate is valid starting with the day on which it was issued.

---

27 BSB statement of good practice – certification regime: fitness and propriety assessment principles, 28 February 2017.
28 FSMA, s 63F.

4.94   Firms applying for approval of senior managers will need to carry out an assessment of whether the proposed senior manager is fit and proper to carry out his or her role prior to making the application.

11   SOLVENCY II FIRMS

4.95   Where an application relates to a function within a Solvency II Directive firm (see 7.256 ff) and is for an FCA controlled function which is also a Solvency II Directive 'key function' as defined in the PRA Rulebook, then the FCA will also have regard to the assessment made by the firm as required in Article 273 of the Solvency II Regulation,[29] rules 2.1 and 2.2 of the PRA Rulebook: Solvency II firms: Insurance – Fitness and Propriety and other factors as set out in EIOPA guidelines on systems of governance.[30]

12   ESTABLISHING FITNESS AND PROPRIETY AS PART OF A GLOBAL GROUP

4.96   The BSB has given guidance[31] on the challenge faced by global groups in the context of employees moving to the UK from overseas and in-scope employees who are based overseas.

4.97   The assessment of any such employees should be as robust as the process undertaken for UK-based staff.

4.98   The challenge for firms comes in the form of legal limitations; in France, for example, credit checks are not permissible. Firms therefore need to be flexible in developing their approach to allow for variations in the information available and permissible in other countries. They should, however, also be consistent in terms of the standards they are trying to attain and outcomes they are trying to achieve.

4.99   It may be necessary to develop or update mobility processes to ensure that fitness and propriety assessments are carried out for internationally mobile individuals prior to their taking up certified roles.

13   EVIDENCING THE FITNESS AND PROPRIETY ASSESSMENT

4.100   A firm should record the sources of information or tools used in an assessment and ensure that the individual carrying out the assessment records

---

29   EU 2015/35 of 10 October 2014.
30   28 January 2015, guideline 16.
31   BSB statement of good practice – certification regime: fitness and propriety assessment principles, 28 February 2017.

their judgement at least annually, including any behaviours that may be relevant to an assessment.[32] Good practice in this regard would include:

- a consolidated record of all sources of information that had been used in the assessment and the frequency of their use in any assessment;

- tracking and monitoring information on an ongoing basis;

- records of any issues that called into question the fitness and propriety of any individual;

- details of the relevant parties who had been consulted (eg Legal, Compliance, Risk); and

- the rationale for the assessor's judgement in reaching the certification decision.

4.101   There should be a system in place to log and track certification issues and a framework established so that issues identified can inform the development of good practice.

14   WHAT IF THE FIRM CANNOT CERTIFY AN EMPLOYEE?

4.102   If a firm decides not to certify an employee after a fitness and propriety assessment, the firm must give that person a notice in writing stating:

(1) what steps, if any, the firm proposes in relation to that person; and

(2) the reasons for proposing to take those steps.[33]

4.103   It should also consider if the circumstances warrant making a notification to the FCA for a breach of the conduct rules.[34] A firm should always remember its duty to be open and cooperative with the regulator and must consider whether the facts upon which a decision not to re-certify an individual trigger a requirement to notify the regulator.

4.104   When a certified employee is suspended for investigation purposes this does not (in contrast to a senior manager) trigger an immediate notification obligation to the regulator. However, if a disciplinary step is taken (see Chapter 6) this must be notified to the regulator as part of the firm's annual notification obligations.

4.105   If a firm is unable to certify an employee who has been holding a certification role or assess a senior manager as fit and proper to undertake their functions, this poses employment issues for the individual and the firm.

---

32 BSB statement of good practice – certification regime: fitness and propriety assessment principles, 28 February 2017.
33 SYSC 5.2.13 G.
34 SYSC 5.2.14 G; SUP 15.3.11R.

4.106 Termination of employment should never be a kneejerk reaction. Firms should first consider whether the loss of certified status is permanent or for a shorter period pending, say, the obtaining of a relevant qualification. In the latter case, the firm should consider whether it is possible to offer the employee alternative work until they regain their certified status. In any event, firms should consider whether alternative employment can be offered before deciding to initiate the process for terminating an individual's employment.

4.107 Sometimes, following an assessment, an employee may be put under remediation or other controls (eg supervision). Such an outcome must be consistent with the conclusion of any disciplinary proceedings and if it is not, a firm should clearly record the reasons for the difference in outcomes. A divergence in outcomes would be unusual and likely to lead to a complaint from the individual and potentially tribunal proceedings.

4.108 The BSB offers the following guidance:

'[H]ow firms link the information they generate about an individual to the elements of fitness and propriety, will reflect their approach to what is relevant to fitness and propriety. Some firms will, for example, link all disciplinary outcomes to the fitness and propriety assessment; others may not consider this necessary, if the disciplinary action they take is consistent with what they would have done as part of a fitness and propriety process. Whatever its approach, a firm needs however to articulate the element of fitness and propriety to which any piece of evidence relates, and why this evidence is relevant'.

4.109 As highlighted at 4.69, the fitness and propriety panel may choose to certify an individual for a shorter period during which the individual's performance is monitored and re-assessed. The disciplinary panel should ensure that the employee understands the consequences for their employment, should they not reach the required standards in the timeframe.

4.110 It is important to always bear in mind the employment consequences of a failure to pass a fitness and propriety assessment: are there alternatives to dismissal? Has a fair process been followed? Have remediation, supervision and controls and other options been considered?

Practical point: Failure to pass the fitness and propriety test

If an individual fails to meet the required fitness and propriety standards and there is no suitable alternative employment or other steps that can be taken (such as supervision or training), the firm will likely want to terminate that individual's employment. Any such dismissal will likely expose a firm to an allegation of unfair dismissal by the individual concerned, provided that the employee has sufficient length of qualifying service.

In response to any such claim, the firm may be able to rely on the grounds stated for lack of certification (eg misconduct) but this may not always be the case. Without clear grounds for dismissal, a firm will have to argue in its defence that the employee was dismissed due to 'some other substantial reason' – a 'catch all' reason which is provided for under the Employment Rights Act 1996 if there is no other clear reason (such as misconduct/ capability) for the dismissal. However, it will still be necessary for the employer to follow a fair procedure and to have considered all options alternative to dismissal before reaching any decision to dismiss an employee. For the same reasons, employment tribunals may have higher expectations of the level of investigation to be undertaken by an employer before deciding to dismiss a senior manager or certified person for misconduct or capability reasons.

Given the (relatively high) risk that an employee who loses their certified or approved status will not be able to find equivalent work in the financial services sector, it is likely that successful employment claims in an employment tribunal will result in significant financial awards to the employee, since the employee will be unlikely to substantially mitigate their loss.

15 DISCIPLINARY PROCEEDINGS AND FITNESS AND PROPRIETY ASSESSMENTS

4.111 Employers should generally combine, so far as possible, any proceedings in respect of non-renewal with disciplinary proceedings.

4.112 If a disciplinary process precedes the fitness and propriety assessment, the findings of the disciplinary panel will need to be taken into account. If the disciplinary panel chooses to dismiss the employee, a fitness and propriety panel may not proceed to an assessment.

4.113 However, the circumstances of the dismissal should be recorded in a regulatory reference. In this context, firms should check their standard disciplinary policies to ensure that for certified (and senior manager) employees there is no clause that states that a written warning will be removed from an employee's personnel file after a period of time. For regulatory reference purposes, this will no longer be possible.

4.114 In the context of a suspected act of misconduct or other issue which triggers an investigation and disciplinary proceedings, a firm must immediately consider the impact on a certified individual's fitness and propriety. It is likely that the individual will be subject to concurrent or consecutive proceedings to consider the issue in a regulatory and a disciplinary context. A delicate balance must therefore be struck between an investigation for regulatory purposes, a fitness and propriety assessment and disciplinary proceedings, in which Compliance, HR and Legal departments must work together cooperatively at all stages (including drafting the disciplinary paperwork) whilst ensuring that the decision-making processes are kept separate.

4.115 The BSB[35] states that the process for assessing fitness and propriety must be aligned with existing processes such as disciplinary proceedings and performance management. Unforeseen events may necessitate reactive assessments such as triggered assessments (in response to another event) or in-year assessments (where a certification risk has been identified).

4.116 Firms have approached the alignment of the two processes in different ways. Some firms have established committees which are responsible for assessing an individual's fitness and propriety for regulatory purposes separately from any disciplinary process. A disciplinary hearing manager's role is limited to considering whether the individual's conduct was acceptable and the appropriate sanction. Any assessment of fitness and propriety which is triggered by the disciplinary process is hived off to the fitness and propriety committee after the disciplinary hearing. Other firms (usually those smaller in size) have left it to the disciplinary hearing manager to consider both conduct issues and to carry out any assessment of fitness and propriety triggered by the disciplinary process.

Key points: Issues arising out of disciplinary hearings and investigations

- Investigations must be carried out *impartially and fairly*. Investigations that are significantly influenced by others (eg HR, Compliance or those carrying out a fitness and propriety assessment) may result in an unfair dismissal finding by an employment tribunal, should the employee bring such a claim.

- Employees and workers have the statutory *right to be accompanied* at disciplinary hearings but not during investigation hearings, subject always to any contractual right that allows this. The right is to be accompanied by a trade union official or a fellow worker. However, a firm may choose to allow an employee to be accompanied by another person of his or her choice, if it deems this appropriate in the circumstances.

- The general rule is that *investigations* should be concluded as quickly as possible and that any suspensions for investigation purposes should be kept to a minimum duration. However, this is often difficult in a regulatory context where investigations can be protracted. Firms should regularly review suspensions to ensure they are still appropriate.

- Firms should take care to observe *internal disciplinary policies*, breach of which may give the individual the right to claim breach of trust and confidence.

---

35 BSB statement of good practice – certification regime: fitness and propriety assessment principles, 28 February 2017.

- A kneejerk *suspension* can be a breach of trust and confidence, as suspension is not a neutral act. Where an employer has failed to consider alternatives to suspension, the courts have held in some cases that there had been a breach of mutual trust and confidence.

- There is no right to *legal representation at disciplinary hearings* under UK legislation. However, employees may in exceptional cases (there has not yet been a successful claim) be able to establish a right to legal representation by virtue of Article 6 of the European Convention on Human Rights as implemented in the UK by the Human Rights Act 1998. Case law has established that this right may only apply where the outcome of disciplinary proceedings would have a 'substantial influence' on subsequent proceedings that determine a civil right (in this case, the right to practise a profession). Given that a loss of regulatory approval for a senior manager will effectively mean the end of their career in financial services, this is likely to be a case where this argument may be run. However, given recent employment case law on this argument, it will be hard for an employee to succeed. A court would need to find that the FCA or PRA would be substantially influenced by an adverse disciplinary finding and not be able to exercise its own independent judgment.

16   FINANCIAL SERVICES REGISTER

4.117   The Financial Services Register[36] is a public register that contains information for all relevant firms and individuals that have been regulated by the SMCR. The Register can be searched to find information about whether a firm is authorised by the FCA or the PRA or is exempt, and on whether an individual is an approved senior manager.

4.118   The FCA has published a consultation[37] on an additional proposed Directory to sit alongside the Register. This Directory would:

- make information public on additional individuals carrying out a wider range of roles (such as certified staff and non-approved NEDs);

- present information on these individuals and the senior managers that the FCA continues to approve in a way that is more accessible and user-friendly; and

- enable users to find information on these individuals in a single public location.

36   https://register.fca.org.uk.
37   FCA CP18/19.

17   CRIMINAL RECORDS CHECKS

Senior managers and certified staff

4.119   There is a distinction in the approach that must be taken with regard to criminal records checks for senior managers as compared with certification regime staff. The regulators' rules provide that firms are not required to arrange or conduct criminal records checks for any staff other than senior managers,[38] PRA notified NEDs (who require regulatory approval to carry out certain SMFs[39]), credit union NEDs and non-SMF board directors subject to competence requirements[40] in FCA solo approved firms (other than those designated as limited scope). In the case of notified and credit union NEDs, a standard Disclosure and Barring Service (DBS) check should be carried out (not covering spent convictions because they are not carrying out controlled functions).

4.120   The rules provide that a firm must 'obtain the fullest information that it is lawfully able to obtain about the candidate under Part V of the Police Act 1997 (certificates of criminal records etc) and related subordinated legislation of the UK' before applying to the regulator for approval as a senior manager or on appointment as a PRA notified NED, credit union NED or non-SMF board director subject to competence requirements

4.121   FCA guidance suggests that in England and Wales a firm should get an application form from the DBS or an umbrella body. It should ask the candidate to complete and return the form to it and then the firm should send the completed form to the DBS or umbrella body. The candidate should then be asked to show the certificate to the firm when it is returned by the DBS. There is an equivalent procedure in Scotland (Disclosure Scotland) and Northern Ireland (AccessNI). The firm should not send a copy of the certificate to the FCA. If a candidate is employed by a contractor, the firm may ask the contractor to obtain the certificate.[41]

4.122   When assessing the fitness and propriety of individuals who are applying for roles that fall within the certification regime, the FCA does not require criminal records checks to be carried out (see 4.123 ff). Firms may still choose to employ such checks for staff who are not applying for positions under the senior managers regime, subject to them being legally able to do so (but see 4.132 regarding potential data protection issues).

---

38 SUP 10C.10.16; para 3.10 FCA CP15/22; PRA Fitness and Propriety Assessments by Firms, para 2.9.

39 Criminal records checks are not required for other NEDs who do not perform SMFs.

40 The term non-SMF board director subject to competence requirements is defined in the Glossary as:

(in relation to an SMCR firm) a board director of the firm who meets the following conditions:

(a) they are not an SMF manager of the firm; and

(b) the firm is required to assess their fitness and propriety under the competent employee rule, SYSC 28 (Insurance distribution: specific knowledge, ability and good repute requirements) any directly applicable EU legislation or any other requirement of the regulatory system.

41 SUP 10C 10.19G.

Requesting a criminal records check

4.123   The starting point for carrying out criminal records checks is that an employer can in certain cases request a standard or an enhanced certificate from the DBS/Disclosure Scotland (a basic certificate may only be obtained by the individual themselves – but see 4.126).

4.124   The key issue arises not with obtaining the certificate but with processing the information (which triggers obligations under the Data Protection Act 2018 – see 4.132):

- A basic certificate does not disclose spent convictions.

- A standard certificate contains details of convictions, spent and unspent; cautions, spent and unspent; police reprimands and warnings.

- An enhanced certificate contains further information such as 'relevant police information'.

4.125   Whilst employers may ask an employee whether they have any convictions, voluntary disclosure is problematic since the individual may not disclose full information to the employer/may refuse to disclose the information etc.

4.126   Further, requiring a person to request their own basic criminal records check by way of subject access request may be a criminal offence (see s 184 of the Data Protection Act 2018 'prohibition of requirement to produce relevant records').[42]

4.127   Generally, if an employer wants to know whether an employer has any unspent convictions, they cannot routinely undertake a DBS check.

4.128   However, financial services and certain other employers may take advantage of the exemption in the Rehabilitation of Offenders Act 1974 (Exceptions) Order 1975 (ROH Order),[43] which allows certain employers to apply to the DBS for a standard certificate which discloses spent convictions and cautions. Where an individual is to be employed in a specific role which is listed in Sch 1 to the ROH Order (eg positions of trust) spent convictions can be disclosed. An approved person under the APER regime is a specific role listed in Sch 1 to the ROH order. However, under the extended regime only senior manager roles are listed and, accordingly, no exemption exists for certification staff who do not perform SMF.

---

42 But see ICO guidance 'the Data Protection Act gives you the right to find out what personal information the UK criminal justice system, including police forces, might hold about you. A request for your personal information is called a "subject access request". It does not cover criminal records checks for employment purposes, known as a DBS check [...]. If a criminal records check is required for your work, then your employer should explain how to apply for this'. This suggests it is not a criminal offence for an employer to ask for a basic check but the employer would still need to satisfy one of the relevant processing conditions (see below).

43 SI 1975/1023.

Carrying out DBS checks for senior managers and certified staff: a summary

4.129   As explained at 4.02, under the SMCR, the obligation is on the employer (rather than the regulator) to ensure the fitness and propriety of senior managers and certified persons.

4.130   The FCA rules make clear that criminal records checks are mandatory for senior managers but not for certified persons. This creates a problem for firms that carry out routine criminal records checks for certified staff and indeed other staff who may pose a risk to the business or customers. While the FCA Handbook makes clear[44] that the obligation to carry out such checks only extends to senior managers and certain NEDs, the FCA's FIT criteria guidance states that fitness and propriety for senior managers and certified persons is assessed taking into account a candidate's honesty, integrity and reputation, which entails whether someone has been convicted of a criminal offence.

4.131   There appears to be an inconsistency in that the FCA retains in its fitness and propriety guidance the recommendation that firms carry out criminal records checks on its certified persons and in its recent policy statement extending the SMCR to state that it is not proportionate to do so given the anticipated high numbers of such staff who will fall within the certification regime.

4.132   The sticking point comes with regard to the processing of the information. Information about criminal offences is personal data and so it cannot be processed unless there is a lawful ground on which to do this under Article 10 of the General Data Protection Regulation (GDPR) and the Data Protection Act 2018. For data protection purposes, the issue is how widely can 'generally accepted principles of good practice relating to a type of body or activity' be interpreted so that carrying out these checks can be valid under the Data Protection Act 2018 and the GDPR? There is no clear answer; however, it remains the case that to assess the fitness and propriety of certified persons (as well as senior managers) the employer must assess (inter alia) their honesty, integrity and financial soundness.

Practical guidance

Ultimately the firm needs to assess its risk appetite as to whether to carry out criminal records checks on certified staff and risk scrutiny by the Information Commissioner's Office (ICO).

4.133   There is very little guidance from the ICO that assists an employer trying to make a judgment call. However, if an employer can show that they have asked the right questions and approached the issue methodically, it is hoped that the ICO will exercise some latitude.

---

44   Annex to PS18/14 – SYSC22.5.19 under extended rules.

CHAPTER 5

Regulatory References

Elizabeth Graves, Partner, Holly Short, Principal Associate and Olivia Toulson, Principal Associate

1 BACKGROUND TO THE INTRODUCTION OF REGULATORY REFERENCES

5.01 In the post mortem that was undertaken following the financial crisis, three key trends in the years prior to the crisis could be identified, all of which contributed to the willingness or ability of firms to uphold strong standards of market conduct:

(1) senior managers became increasingly remote and unaccountable for their traders' behaviours and for upholding standards in day-to-day trading operations. This was considered to be due to a growing trend towards delegation of responsibilities, remote reporting and delegation of responsibility to the regulators who were perceived to have little 'bite'. A particular aspect of the last factor was that firms relied largely on the Financial Conduct Authority's (FCA) predecessor, the Financial Services Authority, to assess the fitness and propriety of individuals to perform their roles under the Approved Persons Regime (APER);

(2) few senior managers actually faced any consequences for failing to ensure that their teams upheld appropriate standards of market practice. That was particularly true in less-regulated markets, where practices were governed by voluntary codes which lacked any element of real sanction for breach;

(3) there was a shift in power within firms towards big-hitting trading staff, reflecting the high profits they generated. There was little personal incentive to uphold market standards, since big profits for firms generated large bonuses for traders.

5.02 These trends were apparent in many enforcement investigations (see Chapter 13). For example, FCA enforcement notices in respect of LIBOR ('London Interbank Offered Rate') manipulation identified weak or non-existent management of trading staff in banks and brokers and a lack of clearly defined responsibilities. Codes were voluntary and evidence of traders colluding with or placing pressure on staff, against the interests of the markets or customers, was a consistent theme of these investigations. Questions were raised about the professionalism of staff across the financial services industry but particularly about those that worked on trading desks.

5.03 The results of these investigations and in particular the large personal incentives on trading staff led to widespread support for tackling these issues through greater individual accountability, strengthened qualifications, stronger governance structures and better aligned incentives.

2 DEVELOPMENT OF THE REGULATORY REFERENCES REGIME

5.04 There has been significant legislative reform in recent years. The Parliamentary Commission on Banking Standards (see Chapter 1) argued that APER had failed to set clear expectations for individuals performing critical roles in banks and recommended strengthening the accountability of traders and their incentives to behave appropriately by shifting governance responsibilities from the regulators to firms, accompanied by stronger and more focused approval and enforcement powers to all the regulators in respect of senior individuals. As detailed elsewhere in this book, the Senior Managers Certification Regime (SMCR) was introduced by the UK through the Banking Reform Act 2013.[1]

5.05   Respondents to the government's consultation on strengthening accountability in banking[2] raised concerns about issues raised by references and criminal record checks, prompting reform. The final report of the Fair and Effective Markets Review (FEMR)[3] in June 2015 noted that respondents to the FEMR's consultation expressed particularly strong views about the need to prevent 'rolling bad apples', a term used to describe individuals within financial institutions with poor conduct records moving between firms.[4] It was felt that the degree to which such activity occurred had enabled such staff to avoid any disciplinary action being taken against them and meant that firms had no way of recovering any of the bonuses previously paid to them in the event their actions were found to have contributed to the firm's poor performance. The FEMR agreed on the importance of tackling the 'rolling bad apples' issue subject to the constraints imposed by employment, data protection and human rights law.

5.06   In particular, firms reported that it had become increasingly difficult to acquire information on individuals' conduct records from previous employers simply through the use of employment references. This was despite the fact that authorised firms subject to the APER regime had a duty to request references about approved persons from previous employers and authorised firms in receipt of such a request had a duty to respond and to provide any information relevant to the fitness and propriety of the relevant individual to the requesting firm.

5.07   The failures of this system were said in part to reflect increasing concerns of firms about the risks of legal challenge from employees who felt they had been unfairly reported on or described in their references. There was also evidence that firms had flouted the rules and reached compromise or settlement agreements as part of negotiated exits with employees under which a firm agreed to limit the scope of information provided in references or, worse still, committed to provide any future employer with a reference confirming the firm had no concerns about the fitness and propriety of the individual (when in fact, the firm may have had concerns about the individual's fitness and propriety but had settled with the employee to avoid any dispute). A standard form of reference was often agreed.

5.08   Finally, individuals quite often resigned prior to investigations relating to disciplinary action being concluded. While Form C (which an authorised firm

---

1   See Chapter 1.
2   FCA CP15/9, chapter 3.
3   http://www.bankofengland.co.uk/markets/Documents/femrjun15.pdf – the FEMR was aimed at restoring and reinforcing confidence in the fixed income etc markets in the wake of serious misconduct in earlier years.
4   See Fair and Effective Markets Review 2015, para 5.1.3.3, 'Tackling 'rolling bad apples''.

was required to submit to the FCA whenever an approved person left the firm) required the firm to disclose if the individual had resigned during an investigation, the writers of this chapter believe that full details of the circumstances of the individual's departure may not always have been communicated in a reference to a new employer. No such disclosure obligation existed under APER in relation to other staff who were not approved persons. An individual's resignation often prevented a firm commencing or completing disciplinary action. Concerns about legal action by former employees meant few firms would provide details in any reference provided to a new employer about question marks over an individual's fitness and propriety prompted by an investigation if the employee's departure meant that the employee had not had a formal opportunity to make representations about his or her conduct.

5.09 The FEMR concluded that there was a strong case for the regulators to agree a form setting out in detail the basic information that firms should include in regulatory references to improve a firm's ability to investigate an individual's past conduct effectively. Such a form would build on information requirements already proposed under the new SMCR rules and help to promote a uniform approach. Firms would be clearly prohibited from using settlement agreements and confidentiality obligations with departing employees to limit disclosure of information required in such regulatory reference forms under the SMCR rules.

5.10 In October 2015 the FCA and Prudential Regulation Authority (PRA) published a joint consultation paper[5] 'Strengthening accountability in banking and insurance: regulatory references', which proposed requirements relating to the content and format of employment references for individuals subject to the SMCR or the Senior Insurance Managers Regime (SIMR). The proposals applied to relevant authorised persons (RAPs),[6] Solvency II Directive insurers and large non-directive firms. The consultation proposals received 30 responses, most of which supported the objectives but some raised concerns. For this reason, interim rules[7] were introduced pending the finalisation of final regulatory reference rules.

5.11 Final rules[8] were published in the regulators' policy statements in September 2016 and applied from March 2017 (see further 5.43 ff).[9]

5.12 The extension of the SMCR will for the first time extend the regulatory reference regime to senior managers, certified staff and also to non-executive directors (NEDs) working for all other Financial Services and Markets Act 2000 (FSMA) regulated firms (excluding appointed representatives) from 9 December

---

5   FCA CP15/31; PRA CP36/15.
6   As defined in FSMA, s 71A, namely: (i) deposit takers (banks, building societies and credit unions); (ii) certain PRA regulated investment banks; (iii) branches of foreign banks operating in the UK.
7   FCA PS16/3; PRA PS5/16.
8   FCA PS16/22; PRA PS27/16.
9   The final rules are contained in: www.handbook.fca.org.uk/handbook/SYSC/22/?view=chapter; www.prarulebook.co.uk/rulebook/Content/Chapter/302352/02-05-2017#302352.

2019.[10] The regime also applied to all senior managers and certified staff working for insurers and reinsurers under the extended regime from 10 December 2018.[11] All such firms (with the exception of appointed representatives) will become 'full scope' firms (see 5.56).

3   COMMON LAW DUTIES WHEN PREPARING A REFERENCE

5.13   Despite the introduction of a template for regulatory references (see 5.127 ff) with the requirement for the disclosure of prescribed information under the regulatory reference rules,[12] common law duties should not be overlooked when preparing a reference. Under common law, the starting point is that there is no duty to request or provide a reference. However, if a reference is provided it must be true, accurate and fair and not give a misleading impression. The requirement under common law to exercise due skill and care is noted in the FCA regulatory reference rules.[13]

5.14   When providing a reference for a current employee the employer must take care not to breach the implied term of trust and confidence. In *TSB v Harris*,[14] the employer provided a reference that referred to complaints made about its former employee of which she had not been informed and to which she had therefore not been able to respond. The Employment Appeal Tribunal (EAT) upheld the employment tribunal's finding that this breached the mutual implied duty of trust and confidence. A reference must not give an unfair or misleading impression overall or be unfairly selective when providing information or by including facts or opinions in such a manner as to give rise to a false or mistaken inference in the mind of a reasonable recipient.[15]

5.15   When giving a reference to an ex-employee, there are still obligations to provide an honest and fair reference. If a firm goes beyond what it should put in a reference for an existing or ex-employee, there are potential areas of tortious liability. These can be summarised as follows:

10 FCA CP17/25 (See Glossary of terms 'regulatory references' and section 6.12).
11 FCA CP17/26 (See 'Guide to the regime' 2.1, chapter 5, paragraph 5.12); PRA CP14/17. Solvency II insurers subject to the SIMR have been required to obtain and provide to other fully scope firms regulatory references in respect of senior insurance managers and NEDs since March 2017 when regulatory references were first introduced for banks. However, those individuals at insurers who became certified persons and had not previously performed controlled functions became subject to regulatory references for the first time when the SMCR was extended to insurers in December 2018. The FCA has confirmed that firms did not need to apply for regulatory references for senior managers or approved persons who were automatically converted to SMCR on 10 December 2018 or for certified staff doing the same job before and after the SMCR came into force, FCA PS18/15 (See 'Transitional arrangements', 9.8 and 9.13).
12 The template can be found in: FCA Handbook SYSC Annex 1, PRA Rulebook – CRR firms – fitness and propriety 7.1.
13 SYSC 22.5.4G.
14 [2000] IRLR 157.
15 *Kidd v Axa Equity & Law* [1999] EWHC QB 184; see also *Bartholomew v London Borough of Hackney* [1999] IRLR 246.

- *Negligent misstatement* An employer must take all reasonable care when providing a reference.[16] This duty is owed both to the employee and to the recipient of the reference. A clear disclaimer can mitigate this risk.

- *Breach of statutory duty: FSMA, s 138D* FSMA, s 138D provides: 'The contravention by an authorised person of a rule made by the FCA is actionable at the suit of a private person who suffers loss as a result of the contravention, subject to the defences and other incidents applying to actions for breach of statutory duty'. This section provides that a person who suffers loss as a result of the breach of a FCA or PRA rule by an authorised person has a right of action for damages for loss.

- *Deceit* If false information is intentionally and knowingly given to a firm that asks for a reference, the supplier of the reference could be sued for deceit. The employee would need to show that the giver of the reference made a factual representation knowing or being reckless as to whether it was true, intending the future employer to rely on it and the future employer then relies on it, to the employee's detriment.

- *Defamation* The reference must be capable of justification to avoid the risk of a defamation action if an employee fails to secure a new job because their reputation is damaged. To prove defamation, a statement must generally be false and made to someone other than the person being defamed. To contest an allegation of defamation, the reference giver must be able to support any comments evidentially and show that the views expressed were honestly held.

- *Malicious falsehood* An employee may have an action for damages if a reference contains untrue comments, which have been made maliciously (including recklessly). Since firms will now have to decide for themselves who is 'fit and proper' (instead of relying on the regulator's assessment) there may be an increase in claims, particularly given that employees who receive poor references will likely be frozen out of the financial services industry. A knock-on effect of this will be that employees will be less likely to be able to mitigate their loss and so financial exposure will be greater.

- *Discrimination/victimisation* It is important to ensure that references given do not discriminate on any protected ground and in particular references must not be tainted by the fact that the employee has previously complained about or brought a claim based on alleged discrimination.

Spring v Guardian Assurance plc[17]

5.16   In this leading case on the duty to give a reference, the House of Lords held that the defendant, Guardian Assurance plc, was liable in damages to Mr Spring for negligent misstatement because it had given him a bad reference. Mr Spring had left Guardian to join a competitor, Scottish Amicable. Both companies were members of LAUTRO (Life Assurance and Unit Trust Regulatory Organisation)

16   *Spring v Guardian Assurance* [1995] 2 AC 296.
17   [1995] 2 AC 296.

which meant that if Mr Spring wanted to work for another LAUTRO member he would have had to obtain a reference from Guardian Assurance. The reference had to be given in the context of the then applicable rules of LAUTRO which provided:

> '1. A person shall not be appointed as a company representative or a member unless that member has first taken reasonable steps to satisfy itself that he is of good character and the requisite aptitude and competence, and those steps shall include taking up of references relating to character and experience.
>
> 2. A member which receives an enquiry for a reference in respect of a person whom another member or appointed representative is proposing to appoint shall make full and frank disclosure of all relevant matters which are believed to be true to the other member or representative.'

The reference provided by Guardian stated that Mr Spring 'was seen by some of the sales staff as a person who consistently kept the best deals to himself' and that 'he is a man of little or no integrity and could not be regarded as honest'. As a result of the reference, Scottish Amicable refused to employ Mr Spring who subsequently brought a claim for negligent misstatement and malicious falsehood.

5.17   The House of Lords found that Guardian had been negligent in providing the reference to Scottish Amicable and had failed to exercise reasonable care in respect of the allegations made regarding Mr Spring's competency. In order to have fulfilled its duty to provide an accurate and fair reference, the employer should have made reasonable enquiries as to the factual basis of any statements made; had Guardian made such investigations they would have found that Mr Spring had not acted dishonestly.

5.18   The court heard that there was a duty of care owed by the employer in providing a reference, knowing that a bad one might damage Mr Spring's prospects of employment and that they were in breach of that duty.

5.19   It should also be noted that the duty owed by the giver of a reference does not solely lie towards the individual but also towards the recipient of the reference (new employer) who could also bring a claim based on a negligent reference.

5.20   In *Cox v Sun Alliance*[18] the Court of Appeal held that the defendant employer was negligent when, after entering into agreed settlement terms which had included an agreed reference stating that Mr Cox had resigned and that any further enquiry would be responded to with a summary of Mr Cox's career, it sent to Mr Cox's new employer a reference suggesting that he had resigned while investigations were underway regarding his honesty. The Court of Appeal said that a reasonable inquiry into the factual basis of the statements in the reference

18 [2001] IRLR 448.

should have been carried out to discharge the duty of care and suggested that an employer is not obliged to continue an investigation into misconduct after an employee's resignation. This decision sits uneasily with an employer's obligations under the regulatory reference rules. Consistent with the judgment, the FCA has confirmed that the regulatory reference obligations do not create a duty on any firm to investigate alleged misconduct of an employee or former employee.[19] But this does not accord with the FCA's guidance that a firm should give as complete a picture as possible of an employee's conduct and should also afford to an employee the opportunity to comment on the underlying matters in relation to which disclosure is given in any reference.[20]

5.21   More recently, in *Hincks v Sense Network Ltd,*[21] Mr Hincks, an independent financial advisor employed by Cooperative Independent Financial Solutions (CIFS), was required to obtain pre-approval for advice and sales. CIFS had authority to conduct activities regulated by the FCA by acting as an appointed representative for Sense Network Ltd (Sense). Mr Hincks breached the pre-approval and another administrative requirement and was suspended. Mr Hincks again sold an investment in breach of the pre-approval process and his authority was terminated. Sense referred to these and related matters in a reference. Mr Hincks brought a claim against Sense for negligent misstatement on the basis that where negative opinions were based on an investigation and its conclusions, the reference giver had to be satisfied that the investigation had been reasonably conducted and procedurally fair. Mr Hincks argued that the reference gave a misleading impression. The High Court disagreed that the reference writer should be expected to assess the fairness of an earlier investigation.

5.22   The standard of care that should be exercised would vary from case to case but should comprise the following:

- to conduct an objective and rigorous appraisal of facts and opinion;

- to take reasonable care to be satisfied that the facts set out in the reference were accurate and true and there was a proper and legitimate basis for any opinion expressed;

- to take reasonable care that the reference was fair by not misleading either by reason of what is not included or by implication, nuance or innuendo.

5.23   The case suggests that, at the very least, the reference writer should have reviewed the investigation report (which is often a lengthy document) before providing any reference.

5.24   There may be cases when the duty must go beyond the guidance in *Hincks*: for example, if there were clear errors on the material available to the reference writer or if information casts doubt on the reliability or integrity of the facts or opinions in the material. The guidance in this case is helpful for employers

---

19 SYSC 22.5.18(2)G.
20 SYSC 22.5.3G and SYSC 22.5.5G.
21 [2018] EWHC 533.

who may have to provide regulatory references years after an individual has left employment. It underlines the importance of keeping proper records and documentation (see 5.146).

5.25   In particular, regulated firms should ensure that where an opinion in a reference is derived from an earlier investigation, a reference provider should take reasonable care in considering and reviewing the underlying material so that the reference writer is able to understand the basis for the opinion and be satisfied that there is a proper and legitimate basis for the opinion.

Liability of a prospective employer

5.26   There are some cases where a prospective new employer could be at risk of a claim being made against it as a result of a reference they have received from a former employer of an individual. In *Bullimore v Pothecary Witham Weld Solicitors*[22] the actions of Sebastian's, a firm of solicitors, as a prospective new employer (as well as those of the previous employer, Witham Weld (WW)) amounted to unlawful victimisation.

5.27   Ms Bullimore was made redundant from her role at WW but was offered, subject to satisfactory references, employment with Sebastian's. A partner at WW had provided Sebastian's with a damaging reference which referred to a sex discrimination claim that Ms Bullimore had brought against it, her 'poor relationship' with the firm's partners and that she could be 'inflexible as to her opinions', ultimately labelling her as troublesome. As a result of the reference, Sebastian's altered its terms and conditions, adding a probationary period to the contract which Ms Bullimore refused to accept. As a result, the employment offer was withdrawn.

5.28   The employment tribunal found the actions of both the past and prospective new employer to be unlawful victimisation. Prior to the tribunal hearing, Ms Bullimore and Sebastian's reached a settlement so that the hearing was limited to a consideration of the compensation. An award of £7,500 for injury to feelings was made against WW. However, no award was made against WW in respect of loss of earnings, as the tribunal found that Sebastian's actions of withdrawing the job offer broke the chain of causation and WW was therefore not liable.

5.29   On appeal to the EAT, it was held that it was 'evidently foreseeable' that the prospective new employer would react to the poor reference as it did and therefore, WW, as a matter of policy and fairness, ought plainly to be liable for the direct consequences of its actions and remitted the matter to the same tribunal to consider Ms Bullimore's loss of earnings claim.

22   UK/EAT/0189/10.

Accuracy, truth and fairness

5.30   The case of *Jackson v Liverpool City Council*[23] is a rare example of where the court found in favour of the employer. In 2007 Mr Jackson had left employment at Liverpool City Council (Liverpool) with a favourable reference to take up employment with Sefton Borough Council (Sefton). One year later, Mr Jackson applied for another role within Sefton which itself was also subject to satisfactory references. However, this time, the reference provided by Liverpool referred to the fact that serious allegations had been raised against Mr Jackson in respect of recording and record keeping. However, a decision had been made that the allegations could not be investigated as he was no longer employed.

5.31   Liverpool had not suggested that any investigation had taken place nor had they suggested any belief in Mr Jackson's guilt of the allegations. The general rule is that an employer is under no duty to provide a reference for an employee or ex-employee, but if they do, care should be exercised so as to provide a reference which is true, accurate and fair (see 5.13), otherwise the employer may incur liability. The trial judge concluded that the reference was true and accurate but that it was not fair.

5.32   However, the Court of Appeal felt that the trial judge had erred in his application of the correct approach and of the test of whether a reference was accurate and fair when there were unresolved disciplinary issues relating to an ex-employee for three reasons:

(1) An investigation would have been difficult and would have taken some time to resolve which was probably unrealistic within the timeframe of a job reference. Alternatively, no reference at all would have put Mr Jackson in a worse position as Sefton would have had no mechanism to assess his adequacy for the job.

(2) The reference made it clear that Mr Jackson left employment prior to any investigation and that, had the allegations been found to be true, it would have resulted in a performance plan rather than disciplinary action. A telephone call between Liverpool and Sefton was found to be an integral part of the reference as the referee had underlined the fact that there had been no investigation, meaning that it could not answer the questions either positively or negatively; ultimately leaving it up to Sefton to decide whether to raise the issue with Mr Jackson.

(3) Considering *Spring* (see 5.16 ff), accuracy and truth went to the facts forming the basis of the reference; fairness went to the overall balance of the reference and any opinion contained within it. According to the decision in *Bartholomew v London Borough of Hackney*,[24] fairness related to the nuances or innuendo which might be drawn from factual assertions; that was

---

23   [2011] EWCA Civ 1068.
24   [1998] EWCA Civ 1604. In this case a reference only mentioned one side of a dispute between the employer and employee (in circumstances where a settlement was reached between the parties).

different from requiring fairness in the form of some procedural mechanism which might permit the ex-employee to challenge an adverse opinion, as the trial judge had done in this case. Taking both cases into consideration, the reference and the conversation between Liverpool and Sefton had been careful and fair.

4 DATA PROTECTION

5.33   Providing a reference will generally mean that personal data will be processed and so be subject to the Data Protection Act 2018 (DPA 2018) which implements the General Data Protection Regulation (GDPR),[25] and the Information Commissioner's Employment Practices Code (the Code). Part two of the Code includes recommendations for employers when giving references.

5.34   The provider of a reference must ensure that the requirements of the data protection principles and the Code are met, including the maintaining and retaining of employment records requirements. Under the DPA 2018 the giving of a reference is more complicated than under the Data Protection Act 1998 (DPA 1998). It will not be possible to rely on implied consent or consent in a generic clause in order to process personal data. For the purposes of giving a reference, the data subject must give explicit and unambiguous consent. Confidential references should not therefore be given unless the employee explicitly consents to this. A particular issue arises in relation to the disclosure of information about health absences (which was sensitive personal data under the DPA 1998 and is still a special category of personal data under the DPA 2018). For this disclosure, explicit consent is necessary.

5.35   The FCA and the Information Commissioner's Office (ICO) published a joint update on the GDPR, which has applied in the UK by way of the DPA 2018 from 25 May 2018.

5.36   The FCA does not believe that the GDPR imposes requirements which are incompatible with the rules in the FCA Handbook. Compliance with the GDPR is a board responsibility and firms must be able to demonstrate the steps they have taken to comply.

5.37   The FCA and the ICO worked closely together in order to prepare for the GDPR. The FCA has considered compliance with the GDPR under their rules, eg the requirements in SYSC.[26] Under part of their obligations under SYSC firms should maintain and improve appropriate technology and cyber resilience systems and controls. It is important that firms comply with the DPA 2018 to avoid the risk of ICO fines and FCA sanctions. Firms will need to test their systems and processes to ensure compliance with enhanced data subject rights and the requirements under the GDPR/DPA 2018. Staff should understand what

---

25   EU 2016/679.
26   https://www.fca.org.uk/news/statements/fca-and-ico-publish-joint-update-gdpr.

their obligations are in this respect and training should be provided, for example, on compliance with data subject access requests. Firms should also carry out regular data audits to ensure compliance, eg assessing what time of information is being held, for how long and how it is being stored.

Regulatory references and data subject access requests

5.38   Individuals have the right under the DPA 2018 to obtain a copy of personal data which a current, former or prospective employer holds about them as well as other supplementary information. It helps individuals to understand how and why an organisation is using their data, and to check it is being done lawfully. However, an exemption exists for confidential references processed for the purpose of deciding whether to employ an individual or appoint an individual to an office.[27] The ICO has provided the following guidance about the exemption:

'Example

Company A provides an employment reference in confidence for one of its employees to company B. If the employee makes a subject access request to company A or company B, the reference will be exempt from disclosure. This is because the exemption applies to the reference regardless of whether it is in the hands of the company that gives it or receives it.'[28]

Impact of common law on financial services firms

5.39   *Jackson* (see 5.30 ff) provides useful guidance on how to deal with situations where an employee has left prior to concerns about their performance or conduct being investigated. Employers can disclose the allegations so long as they make it clear that investigations have not taken place and that, therefore, no assumptions should be drawn from them. However, as noted at 5.30, the requirement for full disclosure under the regulatory reference rules may mean that in many cases where an employee leaves prior to the conclusion of an investigation there remains a tension between the requirement for an ex-employer's full disclosure and the requirement not to mislead or breach the duty of care under common law.

> ### Practical guidance
>
> In most cases, when an employee leaves, it will be very difficult to pursue any unresolved issues or matters which subsequently come to light in respect of the former employee. However, in the financial services industry former

---

27 DPA 2018, Sch 2, Part 2, para 24 and GDPR, Articles 5, 13(1)–(3), 14(1)–(4) and 15(1)–(3).
28 ICO Guide to the General Data Protection Regulation, Exemptions (https://ico.org.uk/for-organisations/guide-to-the-general-data-protection-regulation-gdpr/exemptions/).

> employers may well be required to resolve such issues in order to determine whether they have grounds to withhold or to claw back pay in accordance with regulatory rules and their own policies and rules. See Chapter 8.

5.40   Employers may also wish to resolve such issues in order that they can disclose matters relevant to an individual's fitness and propriety of which they consider the future employer should be aware. To assist them in doing so, they may therefore wish to put contractual mechanisms in place requiring former employees to provide assistance where issues arise post-employment. Without an incentive, such provisions are likely to be hard to enforce.

5.41   There may, however, be difficulty in enforcing such contractual provisions against an employee who alleges constructive dismissal.[29]

5.42   Regulated employers will always need to balance their common law obligations to ex-employees and their duties under the regulatory reference rules. Treading this path will not always be easy, particularly in cases where misconduct is suspected but not proven (perhaps because the employee has resigned before an investigation has taken place). A regulatory reference policy should be in place, which outlines the rules and draws together the separate interests of Compliance and Human Resources departments. Indeed, SYSC 22.8 states that a firm should establish, implement and maintain policies and procedures that are adequate to comply with regulatory reference obligations.

5   ORIGINAL CONSULTATION ON REGULATORY REFERENCES

5.43   On 7 October 2015, the FCA and PRA issued a joint consultation paper[30] proposing changes to the way that banks sought and provided references for individuals subject to the SMCR or the SIMR, key function holders and notified NEDs.

5.44   In summary, the main proposals put forward by the FCA and PRA in the consultation paper included:

- a requirement for firms to request regulatory references going back for a period of six years;

- modifying certain prescribed responsibilities for senior managers to include compliance with the regulatory reference rules;

---

29 *Rock Refrigeration Ltd v Jones* [1996] IRLR 675 (CA) (post-termination restrictions in a contract of employment rendered unenforceable due to the employer's wrongful dismissal of the employee in breach of contract).

30 FCA CP15/31 and PRA CP36/15, 'Strengthening accountability in banking and insurance: regulatory references'.

- a requirement for firms to include reference to conduct rules breaches in the previous six years where the firm has concluded that a breach occurred and the facts which led the firm to that conclusion;

- a requirement for firms to include reference to any conclusion reached in the previous six years that the individual was not fit and proper and the facts which led to that conclusion;

- requiring disclosures in a standard format including the requirement to confirm when there is no relevant information to disclose;

- requiring firms to update references given in the previous six years in particular circumstances; and

- confirming that firms must not enter into any arrangements that limit their ability to disclose relevant information in the future.

5.45 In addition to these changes, the consultation paper also included a proposed standard template reference for firms to use, which was to help ensure that each of the disclosure requirements would be met going forwards.

5.46 Consultation on the FCA and PRA proposals closed on 7 December 2015 and, while the majority of those who responded supported the objective of preventing 'bad apples' rolling between firms unchecked, a number of those responding expressed concern about certain elements of the proposals. In February 2016, the FCA published its initial feedback on the consultation document[31] and noted that a full policy statement would be forthcoming after further consideration had taken place over the concerns raised.

5.47 In February 2016, the PRA separately published its initial feedback on the consultation document[32] and noted several issues that had been raised which the PRA and FCA wanted to consider further before publishing final rules.

5.48 The FCA and PRA both confirmed that they would implement provisional arrangements between 7 March 2016 and 6 March 2017 to enable further time to address the concerns raised in the consultation and to publish final rules. These interim rules remained in force until the final rules were implemented.

---

31 FCA PS16/3, 'Strengthening accountability in banking'.
32 PRA PS5/16, 'Strengthening accountability in banking and insurance: Implementation of SM&CR and SIMR; and PRA requirements on regulatory references'.

6 REGULATORY REFERENCES: FINAL RULES

5.49   The final rules on regulatory references were published by the FCA[33] and the PRA[34] in September 2016 with an implementation date of 7 March 2017. The implementation date coincided with the implementation of the full SMCR and the application of Conduct Rules to 'other Conduct Rules staff' (see Chapter 6). Regulatory references are intended to form a key part of the fitness and propriety assessment for senior managers and certified staff.

5.50   The FCA's policy statement noted that key areas of feedback on the proposed regulatory reference regime included:

- practical difficulties in updating references where new information came to light after an employee had left employment, including data protection concerns;

- requests for clarification about whether firms were under a duty to investigate suspected misconduct or a duty to offer employees a right to reply as part of the disciplinary process;

- requests for clarification about the information firms were expected to provide within the 'all relevant information' catch all and what type of information firms were expected to disclose beyond the six-year period for mandatory disclosures; and

- the need for a standard market template that reflected the current regulatory requirements regarding Conduct Rule breaches.

5.51   In addition, the PRA's policy statement noted further areas of feedback on the regulatory reference regime as follows:

- the potential difficulties of obtaining information on individuals' conduct and fitness and propriety from overseas employers and those firms in the UK who fall outside the scope of the regime;

- the rationale for requiring regulatory references for individuals who are to be appointed to a position internally or from entities within the same group; and

- potential issues caused by requiring certain full scope regulatory reference firms to obtain regulatory references before applying for pre-approval of a senior manager or controlled function.

---

33 FCA PS16/22, 'Strengthening accountability in banking and insurance: regulatory references final rules'.
34 PRA PS27/16, 'Strengthening accountability in banking and insurance: PRA requirements on regulatory references (part II)'.

7 APPLICATION OF THE REGULATORY REFERENCE REGIME

Application of the regulatory reference rules to individuals

5.52   From 7 March 2017, the regulatory reference regime applied to individuals being recruited into:

- senior management and senior insurance management functions;

- certification functions;

- FCA controlled functions and significant harm functions and PRA notified NEDs[35]

within deposit takers[36] and PRA investment firms (generally banks), Solvency II firms and large non-Directive insurers.

5.53   In their consultation papers on extending the SMCR regime, the FCA and PRA proposed that the regime would apply to *all* FSMA-regulated firms and insurers under the extended SMCR. This was confirmed in the regulators' policy statements.[37] The regulatory reference rules are set out in SYSC 22 in the FCA Handbook and in the Fitness and Propriety section in the PRA Rulebook.

Territorial application

5.54   There is no territorial limitation on the application of the regulatory reference rules although the rules do not apply to an overseas firm that does not have an establishment in the UK.[38] This means that the obligation to provide a reference applies even if the employee worked in an overseas office of the employer.

5.55   For an overseas firm the obligation to give a regulatory reference only applies if the individual is or was an employee of its branch in the UK and only relates to their activities as such.[39]

8 REGULATORY REFERENCES: EXTENSION OF THE SMCR

5.56   The FCA and the PRA have each published policy statements on extending the SMCR to all FCA regulated firms from 9 December 2019 and to all insurers and reinsurers from 10 December 2018. From implementation,

---

35 A notified NED is a non-executive director whose appointment is notified to the regulator after it has taken place. Under the extension of the SMCR, the rules will also apply to NEDs working in all FCA regulated firms and insurers/ reinsurers.
36 Banks, building societies, credit unions.
37 FCA PS18/14; PS18/15; PRA PS15/18.
38 SYSC 22.1.3R.
39 SYSC 22.1.6.

the regulatory references regime will apply to these firms in respect of their senior managers, certified staff and NEDs. For these purposes, all firms will be 'full scope' regulatory reference firms. References to 'other firms' in the FCA's Handbook is to appointed representatives, to which the full SMCR regime does not apply.[40] Appointed representatives will not be full scope firms under the extended regime as they fall outside the SMCR but are under an obligation to provide a regulatory reference when requested.

5.57 The FCA has confirmed that there is no requirement to obtain regulatory references for those individuals automatically converted to senior manager roles or approved person roles when the firm first becomes subject to the SMCR.

5.58 The FCA has clarified that a firm need only respond to a request for a regulatory reference from another regulated firm. Firms do not need to respond to speculative references submitted before an individual has been proposed for a function – for example, a recruitment agency vetting a candidate before a firm has considered appointing that person to a specific function.

9   WHO IS COVERED BY THE REGIME?

5.59 A full scope firm must obtain regulatory references for employees being recruited or appointed for the first time to perform the following roles:

● senior management functions under the SMCR;

● significant harm functions under the SMCR;

● notified NEDs.[41]

5.60 Until they became subject to the full SMCR, insurance firms subject to SIMR had to obtain regulatory references for employees being recruited or appointed for the first time to perform the following roles:

● senior insurance management functions under the SIMR;

● key function holders;

● FCA controlled functions;

● notified non-executive directors (see 5.56 – notified NEDs in FCA regulated firms that are not CRR firms or Solvency II insurers will also be covered).

From 10 December 2018 all regulated insurers and reinsurers were subject to the SMCR and became full scope firms.

5.61 For the purposes of a regulatory reference the definition of 'employee' is wide. The FCA rules provide that 'employee' includes a reference to a person who:

40 SYSC 22.1.1A.
41 SYSC 22.2.1R and 22.1.3R.

(a) personally provides, or is under an obligation personally to provide, services to the employer under an arrangement made between the employer and the person providing the services or another person; and

(b) is subject to (or to the right of) supervision, direction or control by the employer as to the manner in which those services are provided.[42]

5.62   The definition also includes a person who is an approved person or director who performs a function under an arrangement entered into by the employer or a contractor of the employer or performs any service or function for the employer in their capacity as an employee of another member of the employer's group.

5.63   Concerns had been raised in consultation about workers undertaking certification functions who may be employed by their own limited company or seconded from a professional services firm and who are not subject to the disciplinary procedures to the entity to which they provide services. Any reference generated by an individual's own limited company could create obvious problems. The FCA's position is that there is a duty on firms to ensure that staff in these roles meet the regulatory standards of being fit and proper and references are a key tool in achieving this.

Volunteers and contingent workers

5.64   The obligation to obtain regulatory references extends to obtaining references for individuals who are volunteers or contingent workers if they will be performing a senior management function, a FCA controlled function or a significant harm function.[43]

10   REQUIREMENTS OF THE REGULATORY REFERENCE RULES

5.65   The FCA and PRA regulatory reference rules should be read in conjunction with each other.

5.66   The first distinction that must be made is between a *full scope regulatory reference firm* ('full scope firm') and other firms authorised by the FCA/PRA ('regulated firms'). From implementation of the extension of the SMCR across all regulated firms, insurers and reinsurers all firms subject to the extended regime will be full scope firms and there will be no distinction, other than in relation to appointed representatives (which are subject to more limited obligations). Until this date, the distinction between full scope and other regulatory reference firms applies.

---

42 See FCA Glossary definition of 'employee' (3) and (4)(a).
43 FCA PS16/22.

5.67   A full scope firm is covered by all the requirements of the regulatory reference regime. Other firms regulated by the FCA/PRA have more limited obligations under the regime, although these firms will be covered by the full regime after the extension of the SMCR. All regulated firms will then be full scope firms.

5.68   Until implementation of the extended SMCR,[44] full scope firms include all firms that are regulated by the PRA with the exception of small non-Directive[45] firms (although such firms will fall into scope following the extension of the SMCR). A full scope firm will therefore include every firm that is a Capital Requirements Regulation[46] (CRR) firm; a credit union or a third country CRR firm in relation to the activities of its establishment in the UK.

5.69   A CRR firm is a UK bank, building society or a PRA designated investment firm. A third country CRR firm is an overseas firm that is not an EEA firm. In short, a full scope firm will include:

● banks, building societies and PRA designated investment firms;

● credit unions;

● Solvency II insurers and reinsurers;

● Lloyd's of London and Lloyd's managing agents;

● insurance special purpose vehicles.

Responsibility for compliance with regulatory reference rules

5.70   The responsibility for complying with the regime will lie with the senior manager for that function so implementation and compliance become part of senior management duties, in tandem with the human resources department. It is therefore important that senior managers understand the requirements of the regime and ensure that line managers and other reference-givers are compliant when requesting and giving regulatory references and complying with other aspects of the regime.

5.71   A firm must establish, implement and maintain policies and procedures that are adequate to comply with the regulatory reference obligations.[47]

11   THE REQUIREMENT TO OBTAIN REGULATORY REFERENCES BEFORE REGULATORY APPROVAL OR CERTIFICATION

5.72   In practice, this rule requires a full scope firm (A) to take reasonable steps to obtain regulatory references before an application is made for regulatory

---

44   10 December 2018 for insurers and reinsurers; 9 December 2019 for other FCA regulated firms.
45   Solvency II Directive.
46   Capital Requirements Regulation 575/2013 (EU).
47   SYSC 22.8.

approval to perform a senior manager function (SMF) or controlled function or before a certificate can be issued (or renewed) for a certified employee.[48]

5.73   From implementation of the SMCR on 10 December 2018 to the insurance sector (see Chapter 12) insurers and reinsurers became full scope firms and subject to all the regulatory reference rules. When the SMCR is extended across the rest of the financial services sector on 9 December 2019, all regulated financial services firms (other than appointed representatives) will also become full scope firms.

5.74   An appropriate reference should be obtained from the current employer of the prospective employee (P) and anyone who has been P's employer in the last six years (see 5.95). The full scope firm must take reasonable steps to obtain the reference before the prescribed time limits (see 5.110 ff).

5.75   A regulated firm (that is not a full scope firm) is not required to request a regulatory reference but if it does ask for a regulatory reference from a full scope firm, the full scope firm providing the reference must provide all the information in the mandatory template (see 5.127 ff).

5.76   Equally, if a regulated firm is asked for a reference by a full scope firm it must respond to the request as far as possible, given the records it has retained.

5.77   The obligation of a full scope firm applies even where the employer already has a reference. For example, a RAP should obtain a reference whenever it renews the certificate of a certification employee. Changing jobs within the same full scope firm may require a reference.[49] However, a full scope firm does not necessarily need to obtain a new reference each time; sometimes an existing reference will still be appropriate for the purpose.

5.78   For example, if a full scope firm appoints a person to a certified or approved role and later wants to appoint the individual to another certified or approved position or make a change in their role, the full scope firm (A) should consider whether to ask the firm giving the reference (B) to reissue or amend its reference.

What information should be requested?

5.79   If the firm from which A (a full scope firm) is requesting a reference (B) is also a full scope firm, A must request the following information from B:

(i)   all information of which B is aware that B reasonably considers to be relevant to A's assessment of whether B is fit and proper;

---

48   SYSC 22.2.2R; Fitness and Propriety 2.7.1; PRA Rulebook, Fitness and Propriety 2.7.4.
49   SYSC 22.7.5G.

(ii) this information need only be disclosed in relation to something that occurred or existed in the six years before the reference request up to the date of giving the reference and in the case of serious misconduct, at any time;

(iii) the information requested in questions A–G of part one of the mandatory template (see 5.127 ff).

5.80   Where B is not a full scope firm, A must request the information in (i) and (ii) above but the questions in (iii) need not be asked. A regulated firm that is not a full scope firm *must* disclose this information; an employer outside the sector cannot be obliged to provide this information.

5.81   Where B is a full scope firm, it must disclose the information in questions A–F of the mandatory template, whether or not A, the firm requesting the reference, is a full scope firm.[50]

5.82   When deciding what information to request, A must have regard to the factors set out SYSC 22 Annex 2R. These are:

(a) any outstanding liabilities of that person from commission payments;

(b) any relevant outstanding or upheld complaint against the prospective employee (P);

(c) section 5 of the relevant Form A in SUP 10A Annex 4 (application to perform controlled functions under APER) or SUP 10C Annex 2 (application to perform senior management functions);

(d) FIT 2 (main assessment criteria);

(e) the persistency of any life policies sold by P.[51]

5.83   For the purposes of assessing what is relevant for the fitness and propriety assessment, the individual's employment record and the role they intend to move into are relevant rather than the role they previously held.

When should the reference be obtained?

5.84   A reference should be obtained for certified staff before a certificate can be issued in respect of them. A reference for senior management applications must be obtained no later than one month before the end of the application process.[52] When the SMCR is extended across all FCA regulated firms, a regulatory reference should be obtained before the appointment of a non-SMF NED.[53]

---

50 SYSC 22.2.2(4)R.
51 This only applies if SUP 16.8.1G(1) (persistency reports from insurers) applies to B.
52 FSMA, s 61; the Form A application period is three months from the date of receipt of application.
53 SYSC 22.2.3R.

5.85 The regulators recognise that for senior managers this deadline may not be possible in all cases. In circumstances where any of the recruiting firm, the firm providing the reference (B) or any other person/body would have to make a public announcement, references can be obtained before the end of the application period.[54]

5.86 The PRA states that in cases where obtaining the necessary references for approval as an SMF would trigger a market-sensitive notification requirement a firm must require such references before the PRA will approve the candidate.[55]

5.87 The FCA notes that there are circumstances in which it would be reasonable for a firm to delay getting a reference for a senior manager. These include where asking for a reference earlier would create a serious risk of:

- breaching the confidentiality of a wider commercial or corporate transaction;

- prematurely triggering the need for a public announcement; or

- the candidate not applying for the position in the first place because it would reveal to the candidate's current employer the proposed move too soon.[56]

SYSC 22.2.3R – Table: Summary of what positions need a reference and when (table copied from FCA Handbook)

Position	When to obtain reference	Comments
(A) Permitting or appointing someone to perform an FCA controlled function or a PRA controlled function	One month before the end of the application period Where a request for a reference would require: (a) the firm requesting the reference; (b) the employer giving the reference; or (c) any other person; to make a mandatory disclosure prior to P disclosing to its current employer that such application has been made, the date is the end of the application period.	
(B) Issuing a certificate under section 63F of FSMA (Certification of employees by relevant authorised persons).	Before the certificate is issued	This includes renewing an existing certificate.

54 SYSC 22.2.3R; see also PRA SS28/15 (updated May 2017) para 6.21.
55 PRA SS28/15 (updated May 2017) paras. 6.21–6.23.
56 SYSC 22.7.11G.

Position	When to obtain reference	Comments
(C) Appointing someone to any of the following positions (as defined in the PRA Rulebook): (a) a notified non-executive director; (b) a credit union non-executive director; or (c) a key function holder.	Not applicable	SYSC 22.2.2.1R (obligation to obtain a reference) does not apply to a firm appointing someone to the position in column (1). However SYSC 22.2.2R does apply to a firm asked to give a reference to a firm appointing someone to the position in column (1).

Regulatory references and fitness and propriety approval/ certification

5.88   A firm does not need to submit copies of regulatory references received when making an application to the FCA for approval of a senior manager. However, the FCA may consider that it needs to see the information in a reference before it reaches a decision. If so, it may formally ask for that information and extend the time limit in which it has to make its decision until it gets the reference.[57]

5.89   If a full scope firm cannot obtain a reference in the required timescale it should still try to obtain the reference as soon as possible afterwards.[58] If regulatory approval cannot be obtained pending receipt of a regulatory reference, the full scope firm should consider whether the employee can carry out an alternative role pending approval. Clearly, in such a case the employment documentation should reflect this temporary role and make provision for termination in the event that approval is not forthcoming.

5.90   Where a full scope firm needs to fill a vacancy for a certified employee which could not have been reasonably foreseen, the FCA recognises that it may not be reasonable to expect the full scope firm to obtain a regulatory reference prior to obtaining the certificate. However, it must do so as soon as reasonably possible and if a reference obtained later raises concerns about the person's fitness and propriety the firm should revisit its decision to issue the person with a certificate.[59]

5.91   As with a senior manager, the offer letter, employment contract and other employment documentation should make clear that the employment is summarily terminable on receipt of a reference which means that the firm cannot certify the individual as fit and proper.

---

57 SYSC 22.7.11G; SUP 10C.28G provides additional details about requests for further information and the effect they have on the time the FCA has to make a decision about an application.
58 SYSC 22.7.9G.
59 SYSC 22.7.10G.

5.92   The PRA will treat an application without a reference as incomplete and will not approve candidates until the firm confirms it has obtained all necessary references. As noted at 5.59, a regulatory reference should also be obtained when appointing someone to be a notified NED.

5.93   The PRA in its supervisory statement[60] notes that s 60A of the FSMA which requires firms to satisfy themselves that candidates for a SMF are fit and proper before applying to the PRA for approval applies irrespective of the circumstances. Therefore where a firm cannot obtain all necessary references before applying to the PRA for approval in relation to a SMF the PRA expects the firm to explain in the application why it was not possible to obtain the required reference(s); confirm that it is satisfied the candidate is fit and proper and list the evidence; and commit to obtaining all necessary references as soon as reasonably practicable.

5.94   Firms should note the 12-week rule for senior managers in the event of unforeseen absences (see Chapter 2) in which case a temporary appointment may be made without regulatory approval and the receipt of regulatory references subject to the relevant conditions being satisfied.

12   COLLECTING REGULATORY REFERENCES FOR REGULATED ROLES FOR THE PREVIOUS SIX YEARS OF EMPLOYMENT

5.95   The regulators expect full scope firms to take reasonable steps to collect regulated references from all former employers of the prospective employee, including those based overseas or outside of the financial services sector for the previous six years of the individual's employment.

5.96   The full scope firm must in particular request all information of which the other firm is aware that it reasonably considers to be relevant to its assessment of whether the individual is fit and proper. Other non-full scope regulated firms and other firms outside the sector are not required to answer questions A–F of the mandatory template (see 5.127 ff) but will be asked to provide all information relevant to the hiring firm's assessment of fitness and propriety. As stated at 5.56 ff, the distinction between full scope and other regulated firms will largely disappear (other than for appointed representatives) following the extension of the SMCR across all regulated firms, insurers and reinsurers.

5.97   It is important that a full scope firm makes all reasonable efforts to obtain such a reference. The regulator will expect to see several attempts to get the information and a full scope firm will need to maintain adequate records to evidence its attempts. If a reference simply cannot be obtained (whether from the previous employer or another source if a reference cannot be obtained), the full scope firm must ensure that it obtains as much information as possible on

60 PRA SS28/15.

the individual to satisfy itself of their fitness and propriety. The full scope firm may wish to consider notifying the regulator that it has been unable to obtain a regulatory reference.

Making and drafting the request for a reference

5.98   A full scope firm providing a reference must provide the information in the mandatory template; however, there are no requirements about the form in which other regulated firms should provide a reference.

5.99   When making a regulatory reference request a regulated firm A (this includes full scope firms) should give another regulated firm B sufficient information to let B know that the requirements apply to the reference it is being asked to give and which requirements apply.[61] This may include, for example, the job title of the role, whether it involves SMFs or certified functions and it may be helpful to provide the recipient with the job description for the role. As long as it complies with this requirement, A does not have to set out specifically the information it wants to obtain.[62] This is because B should include that information even though B is not specifically asked to include it.

5.100   However, a regulated firm (including full scope firms) asking for a reference from a current or former employer outside the sector will normally need to specify the information it would like.[63]

5.101   A full scope firm A that is requesting a reference from a current or former employer that is not a full scope firm will normally need to specify what information it would like.[64]

5.102   Full scope firms providing a reference have more detailed requirements. When giving a reference to a regulated firm a full scope firm must use the mandatory template.[65] A regulated (full scope or other) firm may make minor changes to the format of the template when giving a reference provided it includes the required information. A full scope firm may include additional material in the template document provided this does not alter the scope of any of the questions in the template.[66]

5.103   A full scope should use the template even if a regulated firm requesting the reference does not ask it to.

---

61   SYSC 22.3.3G.
62   SYSC 22.3.3G.
63   SYSC 22.3.4G.
64   SYSC 22.3.4G.
65   SYSC 22.4.2R.
66   SYSC 22.4.3G.

5.104   Firms should remember that the regime sets out minimum requirements for a reference; a regulated firm may ask for more than is required under the rules.

5.105   A regulated firm need not include information in a regulatory reference from a criminal records check under the Police Act 1997. The recruiting firm should carry out a criminal records check itself if necessary.[67]

References for the last six years of employment

5.106   Regulatory references must cover the previous six years of employment (there is no limit on time in the case of disclosing serious misconduct) and be sought from a firm in its capacity as the employee's current or former employer and, *if different*, any firms at which the candidate has performed the following roles:

- a SMF;

- another controlled function;

- a certification function;

- a notified NED function or credit union NED function;

- a senior insurance management function;

- any other key function holder in a Solvency II insurer.

5.107   A regulated (including full scope) firm (B) must disclose to another regulated firm (A) all information of which B is aware that B reasonably considers to be relevant to A's assessment of the individual is fit and proper. This relates to something that occurred or existed in the six years before the request for a reference or between the date of the request and the date B gives the references or (in the case of serious misconduct) at any time.[68] As noted at 5.99, if B is full scope it must also disclose information in questions A–F of the mandatory template, irrespective of whether A is a full scope firm.

5.108   Employers should note the FCA's guidance[69] that where there is a course of conduct such as market manipulation individual events connected to it that occurred more than six years ago may still be within the six-year look-back period. This applies to updating references as well.

5.109   Additionally, where there is a serious matter the six-year time limit does not apply. The FCA sets out[70] the kind of circumstances in which it envisages that an employer should disclose old misconduct. The length of time that has

---

67   SYSC 22.5.19G.
68   SYSC 22.2.2R.
69   SYSC 22.5.9G.
70   SYSC 22.5.11.

elapsed is relevant to deciding whether the matter is serious. The key question is how important the information still is for the requesting firm's assessment of the candidate's fitness for the function that they are going to perform.

Practical guidance

Many firms already subject to the regulatory reference regime have found that having to revisit an historic case involving a complex disciplinary or regulatory investigation some years later to comply with its duty under the regulatory reference regime is resource-intensive. Where those involved at the firm in the original investigation process have moved on, the risk of getting it wrong increases. A practice has therefore developed in many larger institutions of preparing draft regulatory references whenever an individual leaves or following any complex investigation and 'mothballing' these ready for any future request. A firm that follows such a practice must of course ensure that any 'mothballed' regulatory reference is refreshed based on any new facts known to the firm at the time the reference is given.

---

13   PROVIDING A REGULATED REFERENCE WITHIN SIX WEEKS OF A REQUEST

Reference within six weeks

5.110   A regulated firm (B) must provide a reference to another regulated firm (A) as soon as reasonably practicable where A is considering appointing someone to a senior management or other controlled role or issuing a certificate for an individual.[71]

5.111   A full scope firm that currently or formerly employed the prospective employee within the last six years preceding the request must provide a regulatory reference in the form of the mandatory template and answer all the questions in the template as soon as reasonably practicable[72] and it is expected that this should normally be within six weeks of a request.[73] A regulated firm should also provide all information relevant to the hiring firm's fitness and propriety assessment within six weeks of being asked.[74] Other firms outside the sector will also be asked to provide this information but cannot be obliged to provide it. Firms may also include mitigating information.

5.112   The writers of this chapter understand that, in practice, it may take some firms between 8 and 12 weeks to provide regulatory references, especially where the issues to be addressed in the regulatory reference are not straightforward and

---

71   SYSC 22.2.1(R).
72   SYSC 22.2.2(1)R, PRA Fitness and Propriety – Regulatory References.
73   SYSC 22.5.17G.
74   SYSC 22.5.17G.

so the firm wishes to obtain legal advice about these (eg firm wishes to disclose concerns about an individual's conduct record in the reference).

Information in the reference

5.113   Importantly, a full scope regulatory reference firm must disclose all the information in questions A–F of part one of the mandatory template *whether or not* the firm requesting the reference is a full scope or other regulated firm.[75] A full scope firm may make minor amendments to the form of the template provided that the reference includes all the information required.[76] See 5.79 for the information in the template.

5.114   This obligation does not extend to those companies that sit outside of the financial services sector and so full scope firms should be aware that they may not receive a response from all previous employers that are outside the sector within this six-week timescale, or at all. The only real concession offered[77] concerns intra-group moves (see 5.149–5.151).

5.115   B is only required to disclose something that occurred or existed in the six years before the reference request up to the date B gives the reference, or at any time in relation to serious misconduct.[78]

Criminal records checks

5.116   A full scope or regulated firm giving a reference need not include information from a criminal records check under the Police Act 1997.[79] The recruiting firm should carry out a criminal records check itself if necessary,[80] subject always to complying with the requirements of the DPA 2018 (see Chapter 4).

Disclosure of information that has not been verified

5.117   A full scope or regulated firm is not required to include in a reference the fact that an ex-employee left while disciplinary proceedings were pending or had started although it may do so if it wishes.[81] The writers have observed that many firms already subject to the regulatory regime choose to provide this information voluntarily. The FCA notes that including such information might suggest there

---

75   SYSC 22.2.2(4).
76   SYSC 22.4.2 R.
77   PS16/22.
78   SYSC 22.5.10G and SYSC 22.5.11G provide guidance on the meaning of serious misconduct.
79   FCA PS16/22.
80   SYSC 22.5.19G; SUP 10C.10.16R requires a firm to carry out such a check when appointing a SMF manager.
81   SYSC 22.5.2G.

is cause for concern even though the firm may not have established that the ex-employee was actually responsible for misconduct. However, all regulated firms should provide as complete a picture of the employee's conduct record as possible to new employers.[82]

5.118   The FCA does not expect a firm to disclose information that has not been properly verified and it should not include unproven allegations or mere suspicions.[83] It cites as an example a situation where an employee leaves while disciplinary proceedings are pending or have started. In circumstances where an ex-employer has not established the facts a firm may choose to include such information subject always to its duties to the ex-employee and recipient of the reference.

Is there a conduct rule breach?

5.119   If a regulated firm has taken disciplinary action of the type described in question F of the mandatory template against the employee for whom it has been asked to provide a reference, the firm should consider whether the basis on which it took that action amounts to a breach of any individual conduct requirements. If it does, it should include that disciplinary action has been taken in the response box to question F.[84] This applies even if the grounds of the disciplinary action did not include such a breach of individual conduct requirements. This only applies to disciplinary action taken after 7 March 2017 or in the case of a full scope firm, where its records do not record whether previous conduct subject to disciplinary action amounted to a breach. There is no wider obligation to investigate whether there are facts that show that there has been a conduct breach.

All relevant information

5.120   This section goes beyond the mandatory information required in part one of the template. This leaves employers providing the reference with a difficult decision as to what information to disclose and what to withhold (see 5.131 ff).

Right to comment: fairness in a reference

5.121   The FCA points out the common law duties (as outlined at 5.31 ff) owed to the employee. In this light, for example, it notes that fairness will normally require a regulated firm to have given an employee an opportunity to comment on information in a reference (this would be the right to comment on the allegations to which the reference relates rather than the reference itself). A firm could do this

---

82   SYSC 22.5.3G.
83   SYSC 22.5.1R; PRA PS27/16.
84   SYSC 22.6.3G.

in the context of disciplinary proceedings. The PRA states that giving individuals the right to comment on allegations does not equate to giving them a right to edit or veto the contents of a regulatory reference.[85]

5.122 A regulated firm can still include an allegation if an employee has unreasonably declined the invitation to comment on it.[86] The FCA guidance suggests that where a regulated firm should have given an employee an opportunity to comment on an allegation at the time it arose it must give the employee the opportunity when the firm is preparing the reference.

5.123 Any right to comment does not mean that there is a wider duty to investigate whether there are facts that show that there has been a conduct breach.[87] In any event, there is no obligation to include the employee's views in the reference, but the firm should take those views into account so far as appropriate when deciding whether something should be disclosed and how the disclosure is drafted.[88]

5.124 The FCA states that where a regulated firm should have given an employee an opportunity to comment on an allegation if the allegation is to be included in a reference, the firm should give the employee that opportunity rather than merely leave the allegation out of the reference.[89] This may mean that where a regulated firm has not given its employee an opportunity to comment on a matter when it first arose, it should do so when the firm is preparing the reference. This may apply, for example, where an investigation is conducted which touches on an employee's conduct after the employee left the firm in question.

5.125 The FCA also states that when giving a reference, a regulated firm may give frank and honest views but only after taking reasonable care as to factual content and as to the opinions expressed. References should be true, accurate, fair and based on documented fact.[90] See also 5.170.

What if records are incomplete?

5.126 The FCA provides that if a firm's records do not cover the maximum period required in the template, this should be noted in the reference[91] – but this must only be done when there is a genuine need. It should not be a routine disclosure.

---

85 PRA SS28/15.
86 SYSC 22.5.5G.
87 SYSC 22.5.5.
88 SYSC 22.5.5(8)G.
89 SYSC 22.5.5G.
90 SYSC 22.5.4(3).
91 SYSC 22.5.8G.

14 THE MANDATORY TEMPLATE

5.127 This requirement to provide information in the mandatory template (see Appendix 1) applies to full scope firms even if only to state that there is no relevant information to disclose. A different format may be used provided the information is as set out in the mandatory template. The purpose of this is to ensure consistency across firms. Full scope firms must answer each question even if to state that there is nothing to disclose.

5.128 The mandatory template is the same for both regulators and focuses on the disclosure of information relevant to a hiring firm's assessment of an individual's fitness and propriety. A full scope firm can also include matters in the reference that are not required by the template.

5.129 However, for firms that are not full scope firms there are no requirements about the form in which they provide a reference.[92] Other regulated firms and firms outside the sector need only provide all information relevant to the hiring firm's fit and proper assessment of the individual). In its supervisory statement[93] the PRA states that where a regulated firm is requesting a reference from a firm that is not full scope (or where it does not know whether the firm is full scope) it should clearly specify the information it requires to be provided as a minimum.

5.130 For further details, see 5.131 ff.

15 INFORMATION TO BE DISCLOSED IN A REGULATORY REFERENCE

5.131 The regime focuses on the provision of information in a reference that is relevant to regulatory matters only and, in particular, information that is relevant to a hiring firm's assessment of fitness and propriety and confirmed misconduct.[94]

5.132 What is relevant will depend on both the individual's employment record and the role they intend to move into. This leaves considerable uncertainty for a firm regarding matters which are not strictly regulatory, for example bullying or harassment of colleagues. A firm which decides to disclose concerns around this type of conduct should explain why it considers it to be relevant to an individual's fitness and propriety and take particular care to ensure that the disclosure provides a fair and accurate picture overall. Another example is sexual harassment. The FCA has suggested[95] following a House of Commons select committee report that firms should take such actions into account when considering fitness and propriety assessments (see Chapter 11).

---

92 SYSC 22.3.1G.
93 SS28/15.
94 See PRA Fitness and Propriety 5.1. See also FCA CP15/31; PRA CP36/15.
95 See House of Commons Women's and Equalities Report 2017/19: https://publications. parliament.uk/pa/cm201719/cmselect/cmwomeq/725/725.pdf.

5.133   In its supervisory statement[96] the PRA stated that where a firm A is requesting a regulatory reference from another firm subject to the regulatory reference rules, firm A should make it sufficiently clear that the request is subject to the requirements in Fitness and Propriety in the PRA Rulebook by attaching or referring to the regulatory template.

5.134   Under the regulatory reference regime, full scope firms are required to disclose the following information in the prescribed template:

- details of any certification or controlled function or of any notified NED or credit union NED or key function holder role held and a summary of what the role involved;

- details of any other roles performed while an employee of the firm or an employee of any firms within the same group in the preceding six years;

- where the firm has concluded that the employee was in breach of the FCA's conduct rules or the approved persons requirements or the PRA's conduct rules or conduct standards in the six years before the request for a reference, that conclusion and the facts that led to that conclusion;

- where the firm has concluded that the employee was not fit and proper to perform a function in the six years before the request for a reference, that conclusion and the facts that led to that conclusion;

- details of the basis and outcome of any disciplinary action (limited to issuing a formal written warning, suspension[97] or dismissal and/or adjustment to the individual's remuneration) arising from the two points above. A firm must disclose the details of the basis and outcome of any disciplinary action as a result of the concluded breaches/conclusion of 'not fit and proper' status above (including details such as whether formal warnings were issued or any adjustment to the individual's remuneration was made *as part* of the disciplinary action/ breach of an individual conduct requirement). Reductions in remuneration would not be disclosable if it was triggered by, say, a downturn in financial performance as opposed to malus or clawback applied in response to a Conduct Rules breach; and

- Section 'G': 'Any other information' that would reasonably be considered to be relevant to a firm's assessment of whether an individual is fit and proper. On the one hand the FCA provides that a firm is not required to disclose information that has not been properly verified;[98] on the other, a firm is supposed to provide as complete a picture of the employee's conduct as possible.[99] The requirement to provide 'all relevant information' generated considerable feedback during consultation, especially with regard to the need to ensure consistency of approach.

---

96 SS28/15, 6.
97 Firms are not required to disclose suspensions imposed pending an internal investigation as these do not fall within the meaning of disciplinary action in FSMA, s 64C.
98 SYSC 22.5.1R.
99 SYSC 22.5.3G.

Firms are left to make a judgment on a case-by-case basis, having regard to their general duty to give fair and accurate references, with obligations to both the ex-employee and recipient of the reference. SYSC 22.5.2G states:

> 'for example, this chapter does not necessarily require a firm to include in a reference the fact that an ex-employee left while disciplinary proceedings were pending or had started. Including such information is likely to imply that there is cause for concern about the ex-employee but the firm may not have established that the ex-employee was actually responsible for misconduct. However a firm may include such information in a reference if it wishes to.'

Key point

Section G throws up the most issues in practice. It is a question of judgement as to what other information may be relevant to this assessment. Firms should also remember that section G can be used to record mitigating circumstances as well as details of any breach. For example, it may state that an individual's conduct and performance has in all other respects been exemplary and that this breach was a one-off.

5.135　The PRA states that this section may also include information on events that did not culminate in formal disciplinary action.[100]

5.136　The requirement to disclose 'all relevant information' is limited to the same limit as required for mandatory disclosures (ie six years from the date of the reference request). The FCA reminds firms to consider other relevant legislation, such as those relating to the rehabilitation of offenders and spent convictions.

5.137　The FCA makes clear that when providing a reference, a firm may give 'frank and honest views but only after taking reasonable care as to factual content, and as to the opinions expressed' whilst ensuring that references should be true, accurate fair and based on documented fact.[101]

5.138　Outside of the mandatory disclosure requirements, the regulators expect firms to exercise judgement, bearing in mind the importance of disclosing information relevant to the hiring firm alongside the need to be fair to former employees and comply with any relevant legal obligations.

Practical guidance

In order to ensure a consistent approach to issues relevant to fitness and propriety which are included in regulatory references, some firms have chosen to establish a Fitness & Propriety Committee composed of representatives

---

100 PRA SS28/15.
101 SYSC 22.5.4G.

from their compliance, human resources and legal departments to consider such issues.

16   UPDATING REGULATORY REFERENCES PROVIDED OVER THE PREVIOUS SIX YEARS WHERE MATTERS ARISE THAT WOULD CAUSE A REFERENCE TO BE DRAFTED DIFFERENTLY

5.139   The obligation to update a regulatory reference does not apply to references provided before 7 March 2017. The obligation to revise references applies to full scope firms only and arises when:

- the full scope firm B is aware of matters or circumstances that mean that if B had been aware of them when giving the reference, it would have drafted the reference differently;

- B has since giving the reference reached conclusions described in question E of the template or taken disciplinary action of the type described in question F; *and*

- if B had reached those conclusions within the six-year period, B would have drafted the reference differently.

Additionally, it must be reasonable to consider the differences to be significant for an assessment by the recipient of the reference of the fitness and propriety of the individual.

5.140   B must have been a full scope firm when it gave the reference for the duty to update to apply.[102]

5.141   The obligation is limited to updating the employee's current employer where that employer is a regulated firm.[103] This avoids data protection concerns about sharing information with firms that may not have a legitimate reason for receiving such information. The FCA has added a requirement on the updating firm to enquire whether the firms to which it has provided a reference in the past six years currently employ the individual concerned. The rules provide that B must make reasonable enquiries as to the identity of the prospective employee's (P) current employer.

5.142   The obligation to update applies to any notice period served between providing a reference and the individual leaving the firm and, for ex-employees, for a period of six years from the date the individual left the firm. In circumstances where a firm discovers serious misconduct that occurred more than six years prior to the individual leaving the firm but which only came to light within six years of the individual leaving, details of the serious misconduct may have to

---

102 SYSC 22.2.4(3)R.
103 SYSC 22.2.5R.

be disclosed. The regulators have provided guidance on the meaning of serious misconduct and the factors to be taken into consideration when deciding whether disclosure is required.[104]

5.143   B does not need to update A (the recipient company) if P is not yet or is no longer employed by A or if, despite making reasonable enquiries, B does not know whether P is still employed by A.[105] If a full scope firm has given a regulatory reference within the previous six years to a regulated firm and it asks that firm whether the individual is still an employee of the regulated firm, the regulated firm must answer that question as soon as reasonably practicable.[106]

5.144   In practice, the obligation to update a regulatory reference is likely to arise where a firm discovers historic misconduct and the firm concludes that misconduct and a breach of the relevant rules or behavioural standards has occurred. As a result, whenever a firm takes disciplinary action, consideration should be given as to whether a breach of an individual conduct requirement has occurred. In practice, firms will need to do this as part of the notification process to regulators. See also 5.170–5.171.

17   NOT ENTERING INTO AN ARRANGEMENT OR AGREEMENT THAT CONFLICTS WITH REGULATORY REFERENCE OBLIGATIONS

5.145   The regulators were cognisant of the fact that some employers may reach agreement with employees on termination or resignation about the terms of a reference to be provided. The regulatory reference regime prohibits regulated firms from entering into any form of arrangement or agreement that may inhibit their ability to provide and update a regulatory reference.[107] In particular, settlement agreements and COT3 agreements should not fetter a regulated firm's ability to provide and update a regulatory reference in the future although this rule is not limited to agreements or arrangements entered into when the employee leaves. The FCA specifies that a regulated firm must not give any undertakings to suppress or omit relevant information in order to secure a negotiated release.

Practical guidance: Can a firm show an employee or ex-employee a draft reference?

As a firm is prohibited from entering into any form of arrangement that inhibits its ability to provide a regulatory reference, care is needed. The firm can, in principle, share with an employee or ex-employee the form of the reference it intends to give to the new employer. However, if the individual asks for changes to be made the firm must ensure that it only incorporates

---

104 See FCA SYSC 22.5.10G and SYSC 22.5.11G.
105 SYSC 22.2.5R.
106 SYSC 22.2.7R.
107 SYSC 22.5.13–16R; Fitness and Propriety 5.3.

those changes if it is satisfied that doing so would not compromise the firm's regulatory obligations to disclose the matters it is bound to disclose by the regulatory rules and would not create a misleading impression of the employee's conduct. Despite the strengthened rules on regulatory references, it remains common for exiting employees to seek to negotiate the terms of their regulatory reference – after all, the content will affect the individual's opportunity to pursue a career in financial services. Those practitioners advising employees need to ensure that the individual understands that while a dialogue about the content of the reference may be appropriate in certain circumstances, ultimately if the firm disagrees with the employee's view of what it should say, it cannot fetter in any way its obligation to comply with the regulatory requirements.

18 RETAINING RELEVANT EMPLOYMENT RECORDS FOR A PERIOD OF SIX YEARS AND IMPLEMENTING APPROPRIATE POLICIES AND PROCEDURES

5.146   In order to enable firms to comply with the obligation to update a regulatory reference, firms are required to retain records relating to ex-employee's conduct and fitness and propriety for a period of six years following resignation or termination.[108] Firms are also required to establish and maintain adequate policies and procedures to ensure compliance with the regulatory reference requirements.[109]

5.147   Where the record keeping requirements do not apply (because the firm giving the reference is not a full scope regulatory reference firm) a firm must still give a reference based on the records that it has.[110] A full scope regulatory reference firm is also not in breach if it fails to include something relevant in a regulatory reference because it destroyed the records before the rules came into force.[111]

19 REQUIREMENT TO CONSIDER WHETHER THERE HAS BEEN A CONDUCT BREACH

5.148   If a regulated firm has taken disciplinary action of the type set out in question F in part one of the mandatory template against an employee and that regulated firm is asked to give a regulatory reference, it should consider whether the basis on which it took that action amounts to a breach of any individual conduct requirements. If the firm decides that the basis on which it took action

---

108 SYSC 22.9.
109 SYSC 22.8.1R; Fitness and Propriety 5.5.
110 SYSC 22.9.4G.
111 SYSC 22.9.5G.

does amount to a breach of those requirements, it should include that disciplinary action under question F, even if the grounds of the disciplinary action did not include such a breach of individual conduct requirements. This requirement does not apply to disciplinary action taken before 7 March 2017.[112]

20   RECRUITING INTERNALLY OR WITHIN A GROUP

5.149   A full scope firm need not ask for a reference from another firm that is within the same group if there are adequate arrangements in place under which the requesting firm has access to the same information sources as the firm employing the individual.[113]

5.150   This exception applies where the group has 'centralised records or alternative means of sharing information as part of the fit and proper assessment of candidates'. The onus is on the recruiting firm, within the group, to obtain the necessary information to satisfy its obligations to ensure that the individual is fit and proper. The FCA has also made changes to the template to allow regulatory references to be provided on a group basis. A group reference must still provide the necessary information on a legal entity basis, regardless of how many times the individual has changed roles or moved between firms within the group in the six-year period. The aim of this rule is to give full scope regulatory reference firms that are part of a group flexibility to rely on centralised records, but internal mechanisms must adequately enable firms to meet their obligations.[114]

5.151   The PRA clarifies that it expects firms to implement appropriate policies to ensure that if an individual leaves the group a complete regulatory reference can be provided covering the previous six years of employment.

21   PRACTICAL CONSIDERATIONS ARISING FROM THE NEW REGIME

References from overseas and non-financial services employers

5.152   As set out at 5.95 ff, the regulatory reference regime requires firms to take reasonable steps to obtain references from all former employers, including those based overseas or who are not subject to the regulatory reference regime.[115]

5.153   Following concerns expressed during the consultation period, the regulators confirmed that the obligation is for a firm to take *reasonable steps* to obtain references and it will be for individual firms to satisfy themselves that those steps have been taken even if, ultimately, they are unable to obtain a reference.

---

112 SYSC 22.6.3G.
113 SYSC 22.7.1R; PRA Rulebook Fitness and Propriety 2.7.2; PRA SS28/15, paras 6.14–6.17.
114 PRA SS28/15.
115 SYSC 22.1.4G.

The PRA has confirmed that, if there are any relevant legal impediments to obtaining references, these will be taken into consideration.[116] For example, local law in a jurisdiction outside the UK may prohibit the disclosure of certain types of information regarding a former employee to a potential new employer.

5.154 The PRA suggests that when recruiting a candidate who was based overseas, the steps may include:

- approaching all relevant current and former overseas employers;

- explaining that UK regulation requires them to request certain information and to specify the information they require; and

- collecting as much of this information as the overseas employers are legally able and willing to provide.

5.155 Employers should therefore retain records of all efforts made to obtain references and to gather as much information as possible about the prospective employee. The PRA also notes that several jurisdictions have registers containing information relevant to the conduct and/or fitness and propriety of certain categories of financial services professionals. These registers may be a valuable source of information to help firms meet their obligations.

What about where an executive search firm is used?

5.156 The PRA in its supervisory statement requires a firm to give information to another full scope firm where the hiring firm has outsourced the collection of information on a candidate to an unregulated third party, such as an executive search firm. In such a case, the firm requesting the reference should make clear that the unregulated third party is acting on its behalf.

Regulatory and common law requirements

5.157 As noted at the beginning of this chapter, when providing references in respect of former employees, the provider of a reference owes various common law duties to its current or former employee and to the recipient of a reference. These duties co-exist alongside a firm's regulatory obligations under the regulatory reference regime.

5.158 In the guidance accompanying the final rules, the regulators make clear that whilst firms may give frank and honest views about former employees, care should be taken as to factual content and the opinions expressed in a reference.[117] The FCA suggests in its guidance[118] that an example of the general duty of care under common law will normally require a firm to give an employee an

---

116 PRA SS28/15.
117 SYSC 22.5.4G.
118 SYSC 22.5.5G.

opportunity to comment on *information* in a reference; it makes clear, however, that there is no obligation upon the employer to allow the employee to comment on the reference itself, just the allegations contained in it. This obligation to give an employee an opportunity to comment does not mean that there is a wider duty to investigate whether there are facts that show that there has been a conduct breach. It is not necessary to include the employee's comments in the reference; simply the employer should be able to show that the employee's views have genuinely been taken into account when deciding what information should be disclosed and how to disclose it.

5.159   Ideally, employers should ensure that any opinions expressed in regulatory references are tested with the individual before the reference is shared with prospective employers. If no factual basis for the opinions can be established, action should be taken to amend the reference.

Record keeping

5.160   The requirement to provide a regulatory reference means that full scope firms will need to ensure that adequate records of employees' and ex-employees' conduct and fitness and propriety assessments are retained for up to six years after they have left the firm's employment.[119] The senior manager responsible for regulatory references will need to ensure that all relevant individuals understand this obligation and that their retention policies and processes are in place and running effectively.

Expired warnings

5.161   If a warning for a conduct issue has expired for internal purposes, it must still be disclosed for the purposes of a regulatory reference if the warning was given in the six years prior to the giving of the reference. Firms should ensure that their policies reflect this; warnings may expire for the purposes of internal escalation but disciplinary policies, procedures and template warning letters should explain that warnings and/or other expired sanctions may still be disclosed in a regulatory reference. It is the responsibility of firms to develop internal policies and processes that ensure compliance with their legal and regulatory obligations.[120]

5.162   However, firms are not required to revisit disciplinary action that took place before the new rules came into force; in such cases disclosure should be based on the records as they stand.[121]

---

119 SYSC 22.9.2; PRA Fitness and Propriety 5.5.
120 PRA PS27/16.
121 FCA PS16/22.

Misconduct investigations – past misconduct and employee resignations

5.163 During the consultation process, a number of organisations responded to a question asking whether the new regulatory reference regime was, in fact, placing them under a positive obligation to investigate all instances of historic misconduct if they had arisen within six years of an employee leaving or if the misconduct was serious.

5.164 The FCA[122] suggests that a firm should, where feasible, conclude investigations before an employee leaves although there is no duty to do so and often this will not be possible.

5.165 Organisations were also unclear on whether the new regime placed them under an obligation to disclose information about allegations of misconduct when an employee had resigned during the course of the investigation and the employer had been unable to complete its investigation.

5.166 While the guidance accompanying the final rules makes clear that firms are not *necessarily* required to include information in a reference that an employee left mid-way through an investigation, it also states that a firm may include such information if it wishes to subject to the duties outlined in this chapter.[123]

5.167 Employers have questioned whether ex-employees should therefore be afforded a right of reply to investigation conclusions or new allegations of misconduct of which they were not previously aware in line with the FCA's guidance outlined at 5.164. In order to demonstrate fairness to former employees, employers would be advised to offer ex-employees either a right to reply to conclusions where the employee has resigned mid-way through an investigation or an opportunity to participate in new investigations if they are to be undertaken post termination.[124]

5.168 The FCA also clarifies that if a firm has taken disciplinary action against an employee as set out in question F in part one of the regulatory reference template a firm giving a reference should consider whether the basis on which it took such action amounts to a breach of any individual conduct rule.[125] This requirement does not apply to disciplinary action taken before 7 March 2017.

122 SYSC 22.5.18G.
123 SYSC 22.5.2G.
124 SYSC 22.5.5G.
125 SYSC 22.6.3G.

Can a firm disclose matters which may not amount to serious misconduct which occurred outside the six-year period?

5.169   Despite the FCA's published guidance regarding the type of conduct that amounts to serious misconduct, it is often quite difficult to determine whether historic conduct amounts to 'serious misconduct'. In these circumstances, the firm faces a difficult decision: to disclose or not to disclose? While the rules do not appear to require disclosure of matters which occurred more than six years ago unless those matters amount to serious misconduct, the firm is required to disclose any matters of which it considers the recipient firm should be aware for the purpose of determining an individual's propriety and to give the fullest possible picture of an employee's conduct. The FCA's guidance makes clear that the firm may choose to disclose matters which are not strictly required to be disclosed by the rules if considered relevant to fitness and propriety. The dilemma is most acute where a firm discovers only after an employee has left historic matters which give cause for concern (see 5.170).

What should a firm do if it receives a regulatory request for an ex-employee whose conduct has been called into question after leaving?

5.170   In such circumstances unless the ex-employee has participated in the firm's investigation of the conduct issues, he or she may be entirely unaware that an issue has arisen.

5.171   The firm should contact the ex-employee to inform him or her of the matters that have come to the employer's attention after the individual left the firm and which the firm believes may need to be addressed in the regulatory reference. To ensure fairness, the ex-employee should be invited to review underlying evidence of the matters giving rise to concerns and to make any representations that the firm should take into account in deciding what should be disclosed in the regulatory reference. This affords to the ex-employee similar rights to any current employees who have the opportunity to make representations during a disciplinary process. Some firms may choose to invite the employee to make representations in person (similar to a disciplinary hearing) and others may prefer to simply offer the right to make written representations. Those responsible for drafting the reference must consider the representations from the ex-employee in determining what disclosures should be made in the regulatory reference.

Legal representation

5.172   Given the significance of a regulatory reference which could be career-ending, individuals are increasingly likely to press for legal representation in disciplinary hearings. While there is generally no legal right to representation in a misconduct disciplinary hearing,[126] firms may wish to consider allowing limited legal representation in certain, more complex cases, where there is a risk of challenge from a former employee or significant career impact. Some firms have policies which provide for a financial contribution by the firm towards the costs of a senior manager or certification function employee obtaining independent legal advice in appropriate circumstances.

Suspension pending disciplinary action

5.173   In its policy statement[127] the FCA has confirmed that there is no requirement to disclose in a reference that an employee has been suspended pending an internal investigation.[128] This confirms that the focus of the regulatory reference regime is on 'concluded breaches' of conduct rules or requirements.

5.174   If an employee resigns after being suspended but before an investigation is concluded, employers should again consider the question of whether the employee should be afforded the right to reply to the outcome of the investigation, particularly if the employer considers that information about its investigation will need to be disclosed as part of a regulatory reference (with particular regard to section G of the mandatory template).

Obtaining references

5.175   When recruiting a prospective employee an employer will not necessarily know who employed the employee for the previous six years. The FCA suggests that the firm should ask the candidate for details of their past employers and how to contact them.[129] Sometimes a previous employer will not be a regulated firm. As outlined at 5.95 ff, a full scope firm will still need to take all reasonable steps to obtain the required information. The FCA states that it accepts that the previous employer may not be willing to provide the information[130] but there is still an expectation that a full scope firm will make every reasonable attempt to obtain a reference, possibly from another source.

5.176   A problem may arise where a firm from which a regulatory reference is being sought has previously agreed a reference in settlement terms/COT3. If that other firm is a full scope or other regulated firm it will have to balance its duties to the regulator against breaching the settlement terms agreed with the ex-employee. If the firm providing the reference is a firm outside the sector it

---

126 Firms should note that there could be a challenge under human rights law where disciplinary proceedings could substantially influence any subsequent decision of a regulatory body.

127 PS16/22.

128 PS16/610: suspensions imposed pending an internal investigation do not constitute 'disciplinary action' under FSMA, s 64C.

129 SYSC 22.7.3G.

130 SYSC 22.7.4G.

is unlikely to provide the information requested if it might breach the terms in a settlement agreement.

Data protection

5.177   General data protection issues are highlighted at 5.33 ff. Additionally, with particular respect to the regulatory reference regime, the FCA and the ICO have together discussed the impact of the General Data Protection Regulation which applied in the UK from 25 May 2018, resulting in a joint update.[131] The update notes that complying with the FCA's rules requires regulated firms to process personal data. The ICO states that it does not believe that the GDPR imposes requirements which are incompatible with the rules in the FCA Handbook. Indeed there are a number of requirements that are common to the GDPR and the financial regulatory regime. The FCA notes that compliance with GDPR is now a board level responsibility, and firms must be able to produce evidence to demonstrate the steps that they have taken to comply. The requirement to treat customers fairly is also central to both data protection law and the current financial services regulatory framework. The FCA and the ICO are working together to establish guidance on regulatory references and the GDPR.

What happens if disclosing required information requires the disclosure of confidential information?

5.178   The FCA stated in its policy statement[132] that a reference should provide description of the breach and its outcome; such disclosures would not normally include commercially sensitive information. However, if such a scenario arose, the FCA suggests that a firm could apply to the regulators for a waiver.

Findings after a reference has been given

5.179   As detailed at 5.139 ff a full scope firm has an obligation to update a reference when it becomes aware of matters that would have caused it to draft the reference differently.[133] The most obvious scenario is misconduct that comes to light after the employee has left. However, it is possible that other circumstances may come to light that exonerate the employee. In such circumstances it seems that the full scope regulatory reference firm that provided the reference should also make reasonable inquiries as to the identity of the ex-employee's current employer and give details of those differences as soon as reasonably practicable.

5.180   What if the employee dismissed for a conduct rule breach brings an employment tribunal claim and wins a claim for unfair dismissal? If the

---

131 https://www.fca.org.uk/news/statements/fca-and-ico-publish-joint-update-gdpr, February 2018.
132 FCA PS16/22.
133 SYSC 22.2.4R.

reference-giver has no cause to change their mind about the facts in the original reference (for example, the claim may have succeeded for a variety of reasons, including simply procedural) then the best approach may be to add a note to the reference as originally drafted indicating the tribunal's findings.

TUPE transfers

5.181   Concerns have been voiced that in the event of a transfer subject to the Transfer of Undertakings (Protection of Employment) Regulations 2006[134] a full scope firm which inherits such employees should obtain regulatory references in respect of them. To date, the FCA and PRA have not provided guidance on this issue but a wary transferee may wish to undertake due diligence as to the steps that the transferor firm has taken to assess individuals' fitness and propriety.

---

134 SI 2006/246.

CHAPTER 6

The SMCR Conduct Rules

Gregory Brandman, Partner and Daniel Allan, Senior Associate

I INTRODUCTION

6.01   The focus of this chapter is principally on the conduct rules as we would expect them to be enforced by the FCA and on the guidance published by the Financial Conduct Authority (FCA) in respect of compliance with the conduct rules and its approach to enforcement. This is for various reasons. First, the range of conduct rules staff that is within the disciplinary jurisdiction of the FCA is much wider than that within the Prudential Regulatory Authority's (PRA) jurisdiction (and will only continue to grow). Second, the FCA has considerably more enforcement resources at its disposal than the PRA and can consequently be expected to take the lead in the vast majority of conduct rule-based enforcement actions. Third, the PRA's guidance about compliance with the conduct rules is, generally speaking, either the same as, or consistent with, the FCA's. We have, however, also referred to PRA guidance where we think it is helpful to do so.

6.02   As detailed elsewhere in this book, a key driver for the introduction of the Senior Managers And Certification Regime (SMCR) was the aim to strengthen individual accountability in financial services and to create a system that enables firms and regulators to hold senior managers, in particular those holding the most important roles within a firm, to account for individual misconduct, poor governance and poor culture.

6.03   Accordingly, on 7 March 2016, the SMCR, including new conduct rules, replaced the Statements of Principle and Code of Practice for Approved Persons (APER) for 'relevant authorised persons' (RAPs), namely banks, building societies, credit unions and PRA designated investment firms. It has subsequently been decided to extend the SMCR to all firms authorised to provide financial services under the Financial Services and Markets Act 2000 (FSMA), with effect from December 2019 (December 2018 for insurers and reinsurers). The effect of this extension of the SMCR will be, inter alia, to bring most staff working in financial services in FCA solo regulated firms[1] within the scope of the FCA's conduct rules. More general detail about the extension of the regime is set out in Chapter 2.

6.04   Section 64A of FSMA gives to the FCA and the PRA the power to make rules about the conduct of employees in RAPs[2] (see Chapter 2) and approved persons. Using this power, the regulators have published new conduct rules under the SMCR which apply to certain individuals within RAPs. The new conduct rules issued under the SMCR have a much wider application than the rules under APER in that a number of them will apply to most members of staff working for RAPs in a 'non-ancillary'[3] role, whereas APER applied to a much smaller body of individuals, who were approved by the FCA to hold controlled functions.

---

1   This is the expression used by the FCA to describe firms regulated only by the FCA, rather than also by the PRA.
2   FSMA, s 71A contains the definition of RAPs.
3   See 6.31 ff for an explanation of this term.

6.05   The SMCR conduct rules are high level statements of principle which reflect the core standards expected of staff that work within the combined scope of the regime. There are two tiers of conduct rules under the SMCR:

- The first tier, which currently applies to all staff at RAPs working in a non-ancillary role (this is defined at 6.31 ff) focuses on the concepts of acting with integrity; skill, care and diligence; and regard to the interests of customers – as well as being open and cooperative with the regulators; and observing proper standards of market conduct.

- The second, which applies only to those individuals at RAPs who have been approved by the PRA and the FCA to hold a senior management function (or 'senior managers' as we will call them in this chapter), focuses on the need for senior managers to take reasonable steps to ensure that the part of the business for which they are responsible is controlled effectively and that it complies with the relevant requirements and standards of the regulatory system.

6.06   Under the proposed extension of the SMCR to all FCA solo regulated firms in December 2019 (see Chapter 2) the conduct rules will apply to relevant employees in all authorised firms,[4] replacing APER in its entirety. As stated at 6.03, the conduct rules were extended to insurers in December 2018.

6.07   The SMCR conduct rules articulate the minimum standards of acceptable behaviour that must be observed by those falling within their scope. Contracts of employment should specifically refer to the conduct rules as being binding on staff, with the consequence that breach may result in disciplinary action, including, where appropriate, dismissal. The PRA specifically requires the conduct rules to be contractually enforceable against senior managers (the FCA does not expressly require this) but, irrespective of this requirement, it is good practice to ensure that all staff are contractually bound by the regulators' conduct rules, as applicable to them. This will mean that breaching the conduct rules will also mean a breach of a contractual term of employment. Together with the regulatory reference regime (see Chapter 5) the impact of the conduct rules and the related rules around certification, reporting and notification will mean that the conduct of all relevant staff employed by authorised firms, not just senior managers and certification staff, will be subject to greater scrutiny than ever before, both by their employers and the regulators.

6.08   It follows then, given the focus on individual accountability, that one of the key aspects of the SMCR for anybody working in an authorised firm is the FCA and PRA's rules and guidance on the standards of conduct to which individuals are expected to adhere in the performance of their roles. This chapter looks specifically at these conduct rules and at the potential consequences for individuals and their employers of breaching them, both in the way of internal disciplinary process; and notification and reporting to the regulators and possible regulatory sanction.

---

4   And to insurers and reinsurers from 10 December 2018.

Practical guidance

When drafting offer letters of employment or contracts of employment, ensure that the offer or continued employment is expressly conditional on the individual complying with the regulators' conduct rules. Breach of the rules will be treated as a disciplinary issue as well as being a regulatory breach and may be subject to both internal processes.

2 BACKGROUND

6.09 Final SMCR conduct rules were published in July 2015[5] and applied from commencement of the SMCR for RAPs from March 2016. They apply to most staff working for RAPs, other than ancillary staff such as receptionists, post room, print room and security personnel (see 6.33).

6.10 Firms initially covered by the SMCR and the conduct rules (ie RAPs) included:

(1) UK banks and building societies.

(2) PRA designated investment firms.

(3) Credit unions.

(4) Branches of overseas banks operating in the UK.[6]

However, as highlighted at 6.03, insurers and reinsurers became subject to the SMCR (including conduct rules) on 10 December 2018 (see Chapter 12) and the SMCR is being extended to the rest of the financial services sector on 9 December 2019.

6.11 For the insurance sector, the PRA's senior insurance managers regime (SIMR) initially implemented similar conduct standards. The SMCR has replaced the SIMR and the SMCR (including the new conduct rules) has been extended to apply to the insurance sector with effect from 10 December 2018 (see Chapter 12).

6.12 The conduct rules will also apply to the non-ancillary staff of all FCA solo regulated firms, when the SMCR is extended to them in December 2019 and the conduct rules will apply to all such firms' regulated and unregulated financial services activities[7] (including any related ancillary[8] activities).

---

5 FCA CP15/22; PRA PS16/15.
6 FSMA, s 71A(4); Financial Services and Markets Act 2000 (Relevant Authorised Persons) Order 2015 (SI 2015/1865).
7 Note that this is a narrower scope of application than under the banking regime, see 6.22.
8 For example, an activity carried out in connection with a regulated activity.

6.13 Consequently, following the extension of the SMCR to FCA solo regulated firms, the senior manager and individual conduct rules will apply to all authorised firms, including insurers and reinsurers (see Chapter 12).

6.14 Where an individual's conduct fails to comply with an individual conduct rule, the FCA may take enforcement action against that individual.

Practical guidance

It remains to be seen to what extent the FCA will have either the appetite or the resources to take enforcement action against non-senior manager personnel who breach individual conduct rules. It is likely that the FCA will leave it to authorised firms who employ such individuals to investigate and take disciplinary action for breaches of individual conduct rules by such employees while the FCA uses its limited resources to investigate and take enforcement action against senior managers for breaching the individual and senior manager conduct rules.

Individual conduct rules and senior manager conduct rules

6.15 There are two tiers of conduct rules. The first is a general set of rules that applies to most employees in a RAP (*'the individual conduct rules'*)[9]. The second tier consists of rules that only apply to senior managers at RAPs (*'the senior manager conduct rules'*)[10]. The same set of rules is enforced by both the FCA and the PRA, except that the PRA will only enforce the senior manager conduct rules against those individuals at the RAPs which it regulates and the FCA (not the PRA) is responsible for enforcing individual conduct rules 4 and 5 against all relevant staff. Staff at FCA solo regulated firms will only be subject to the disciplinary jurisdiction of the FCA; whereas at dual regulated firms, PRA designated senior managers and certification staff will be subject to the disciplinary jurisdiction of the PRA and all non-ancillary staff will be subject to the disciplinary jurisdiction of the FCA. The rules are set out in more detail below.

6.16 Senior managers in dual regulated firms must therefore comply with both FCA and PRA conduct rules irrespective of whether they are FCA or PRA approved senior managers.[11]

---

9   FCA COCON 2.1.
10   FCA COCON 2.2.
11   FCA COCON 1.1.3R, 1.1.4R; PRA conduct rules 1.1.

3 KEY SOURCES

6.17   The conduct rules (and the majority of the guidance pertaining thereto) which apply to authorised firms are found within the Code of Conduct (COCON) section of the FCA Handbook ('the Handbook') and (for PRA designated firms) under the heading 'conduct rules' in the PRA Rulebook[12] (for insurers see Chapter 12). The guidance provided by each regulator in respect of compliance with the conduct rules is broadly similar. FCA guidance (which is issued subject to statutory provision)[13] is set out in chapter 3 of COCON; whereas PRA guidance on compliance with the conduct rules (which does not have the same statutory basis) is set out in Supervisory Statement SS28/15. Firms and individuals should be aware that the FCA and PRA guidance is not legally binding.[14] The process and penalties which govern what happens when a conduct rule is breached are explained in various sections of the FCA Handbook, including the Supervision manual (SUP), the Enforcement Guide (EG), and the Decisions Procedure and Penalties manual (DEPP).

4 TERRITORIALITY

6.18   FCA rules state that COCON applies to the conduct of FCA senior managers and certified staff who are material risk takers[15] for a UK RAP, wherever that conduct is performed.[16]

6.19   COCON applies to the conduct of all other conduct rules staff if that conduct is performed from an establishment maintained in the UK by, for a RAP – that person's employer; or, for an insurer – the firm in relation to which the individual carries out controlled functions. Additionally, in the case of a UK RAP, the conduct rules apply to conduct which involves dealing with[17] a client of the firm in the UK[18] from an establishment overseas.[19] For a Solvency II firm (see 7.256) or a small non-Directive insurer COCON applies to the conduct of persons if the conduct is performed from an establishment maintained in the UK by the firm in relation to whom that person carries out controlled functions.[20]

---

12 PRA Rulebook 2.1–2.3, 3.1–3.4; see also PRA guidance in supervisory statement PRA SS28/15.
13 FSMA, s 139A.
14 Although note that the FCA has stated that compliance with its guidance will be treated as compliance with the rule in question.
15 SYSC 5.2.30R.
16 COCON 1.1.9R.
17 In this context, the FCA interprets the phrase 'dealing with' as including having contact with customers and as extending beyond 'dealing' as used in the phrase 'dealing in investments'. See COCON 1.1.11G.
18 See COCON 1.1.11A G for further explanation of what this means.
19 COCON 1.1.10(2)(b)R.
20 COCON 1.1.10R(2)(a)(ii).

5 EXTENSION OF THE SMCR TO ALL AUTHORISED FIRMS – CONDUCT RULES

6.20   The FCA in its Policy Statement PS18/14[21] confirmed its intention to replace the APER section of the FCA Handbook and apply its conduct rules to all FCA solo regulated firms so that a single standard will apply across the market. The two tiers of conduct rules – individual and senior manager – will therefore apply to all regulated firms from 9 December 2019 (insurers, as explained at 6.03, became subject to the conduct rules following the extension of the SMCR on 10 December 2018 – see Chapter 12). This means that the same rules that have applied to non-ancillary staff at RAPs will now apply across the whole UK financial services and insurance sectors. The conduct rules now apply to all senior managers, certified persons, directors and all other employees (other than ancillary staff) in regulated insurers in relation to a firm's regulated and unregulated financial services activities. The FCA has specified[22] that this includes any related ancillary activities carried on in connection with a regulated activity (see 6.22). The scope of activities is the same for all insurers whether they are Solvency II firms, small non-Directive firms, small run-off firms or insurance special purpose vehicles.

6.21   Senior managers and certification staff at FCA solo regulated firms will need to have been trained and to abide by the conduct rules in time for the commencement of the new regime. Firms will have 12 months from commencement of the new regime to put in place processes to comply with the training and reporting requirements and to train their other staff on the conduct rules.

Practical guidance

Senior managers should be aware of their key role in preventing and dealing with misconduct. The senior manager conduct rules, fitness and propriety and other requirements require senior managers to ensure they are properly managing those staff for which they are responsible. The FCA emphasises that senior managers are responsible for setting the culture and conduct in their organisation and establishing appropriate systems and controls. Indeed, senior managers are under a statutory duty of responsibility to take reasonable steps to prevent the occurrence of regulatory breaches in their business unit (see 6.145 ff).

6.22   Following the commencement of the new regime for FCA solo regulated firms, the conduct rules will apply to such firms' regulated and unregulated financial services activities (including any related ancillary activities), for example an activity carried on in connection with a regulated activity. Specifically, the scope of activities covered for authorised firms other than banking firms (RAPs) covers:[23]

---

21   See also FCA CP17/25.
22   FCA PS18/15.
23   COCON 1.1.7A; FCA PS18/14.

- A firm's regulated activities.

- An activity carried on in connection with a regulated activity, or held out as being for the purposes of a regulated activity, or an activity listed in points 2 to 15 of Annex 1 to the Capital Requirements Directive.

- Any activities (regulated or unregulated):
  - that could affect the integrity of the UK financial system;
  - that could affect the ability of a firm to meet the fit and proper threshold conditions; or
  - that could affect the ability of a firm to meet requirements relating to the firm's financial resources.

6.23   This will apply to all FCA solo regulated firms, whether they are limited scope, core or enhanced firms on commencement of the extended regime (see Chapter 2) and also applies to insurers.

6.24   The scope of activities for FCA solo regulated firms is narrower than the FCA's requirements under the SMCR as it applies to RAPs, where the conduct rules apply to everything done by a person on behalf of such firms, whether it is regulated or unregulated or linked to financial services. The FCA has applied a narrower approach to solo regulated firms because it considers that there is less evidence of potential harm to consumers or market integrity arising from the activities of those businesses.

6.25   Some firms conduct a mixture of financial and non-financial activities. When determining whether the conduct rules apply, the firm must assess whether the activity meets the definition of activities covered by the conduct rules. Generally, this will only be the case where there is a connection between the non-financial activity and financial activity.

6.26   Under the extended SMCR regime, the conduct rules will apply to the following staff at all authorised firms:

- all senior managers;

- all non-executive directors (NEDs) who are not senior managers[24] (to whom, in addition to the individual conduct rules, senior manager conduct rule 4 (see 6.86 ff) will also apply);[25]

- all holders of certified functions; and

- all other employees of authorised firms who carry out a 'non-ancillary' role. A list of the ancillary staff who are excluded from the application of the conduct rules is set out in the FCA's Code of Conduct sourcebook.[26]

---

24 The FCA has specified that the conduct rules will also apply to SMFs and board directors, whether or not they come within the definition of 'employee'.
25 This provides that a senior manager must disclose appropriately any information of which the FCA or PRA would reasonably expect notice.
26 COCON 1.1.2 R and see 6.33.

6.27   The FCA has reminded firms that they can apply the conduct rules to all of their staff (ie including those in ancillary roles) if they wish (and many firms do this). But the training obligations, the requirement to report to the FCA conduct rules breaches giving rise to disciplinary action and the FCA's powers of investigation and enforcement in relation to the conduct rules will only apply to those individuals who fall within the scope of the FCA's conduct rules.

6.28   As detailed at 6.29, FSMA also requires firms to make relevant individuals aware that they are subject to the conduct rules where this is the case and to train them in how the rules apply to them in the performance of their roles. Firms must also notify the regulators when disciplinary action has been taken against a person for a conduct rule breach. For senior managers, notification should be made within seven days of the firm becoming aware of the matter. Notification for other individuals should be made annually.[27]

6   TO WHOM DO THE INDIVIDUAL CONDUCT RULES APPLY?

6.29   Individuals who are subject to the conduct rules must fall within the wide definition of an 'employee' as set out in FSMA, s 64A(6). The definition is similar to the definition of 'worker' in the Employment Rights Act 1996:

'[...] a person who –

(a) personally provides, or is under an obligation personally to provide, services to [a firm] under an arrangement made between [the firm] and the person providing the services or another person, and

(b) is subject to (or to the right of) supervision, direction or control by [the firm] as to the manner in which those services are provided [...]'.

6.30   The rules will therefore apply to, for example, contractors, temporary staff and secondees.

Practical guidance

Many firms will apply their conduct rules to all their staff, including ancillary staff. However, the additional requirements under the regulators' rules to train staff and report breaches etc will not apply to these staff. Breach of these rules will in such cases simply be treated under the usual disciplinary procedure.

---

27 There exist separate obligations to report concerns to the FCA about an individual's conduct under existing FCA rules, including under Principle 11 of the FCA's Principles for Businesses.

Staff who are excluded from the application of the new conduct rules

6.31   A key consideration, when analysing the conduct rules, is to understand to which employees they apply. This is explained by the FCA at COCON 1.1.2R. The FCA explains[28] that 'any employee of a relevant authorised person' is covered except for a limited number of 'ancillary staff' whose roles would be the same whether or not they are performed at a financial services firm or a non-financial services firm.

6.32   Ancillary staff include receptionists, switchboard operators, post room staff and security guards. Interestingly, one role that is excluded from the application of the conduct rules is a 'personal assistant or secretary' irrespective of the person (who could be a senior manager) for whom that individual performs that role. Clearly, however, the title of someone's role is not determinative of the issue and the FCA will look at what role the individual was performing in practice.

6.33   The FCA's list of staff which it considers to be 'ancillary' and therefore out of scope of the conduct rules is as follows:

(a) receptionists;

(b) switchboard operators;

(c) post room staff;

(d) reprographics/print room staff;

(e) property/facilities management;

(f) events management;

(g) security guards;

(h) invoice processing;

(i) audio visual technicians;

(j) vending machine staff;

(k) medical staff;

(l) archive records management;

(m) drivers;

(n) corporate social responsibility staff;

(o) data controllers or processors under the Data Protection Act 1998;

(p) cleaners;

(q) catering staff;

28 COCON 1.1.2(6)

(r)   personal assistant or secretary;

(s)   information technology support (ie, helpdesk); and

(t)   human resources administrators /processors.

PRA conduct rules

6.34   The PRA conduct rules are the same as the FCA's (except that they do not include individual conduct rules 4 and 5) and they have a narrower scope of application, ultimately depending on which section of the PRA Rulebook the firm falls under, as set out at 6.39 ff.

6.35   For CRR and non-CRR firms (see Chapter 8), the PRA conduct rules only apply to individuals who are either:[29]

● approved to perform a senior management function;

● an employee of the firm that should have been so approved;

● temporarily performing a senior management function;

● performing a certification function; or

● a conduct rules NED.[30]

Senior managers

6.36   The conduct rules will apply to those who should have been approved to perform a senior management function (but have not been so approved) if they are an employee of the firm.[31] Similarly, if a person is carrying out a certification function, the conduct rules will apply to that person regardless of whether the firm has issued a certificate to them or not and regardless of whether the employee has been notified that COCON applies to them or that the conduct rules apply to them.[32]

Application of conduct rules to temporary absence replacements

6.37   There is an exception to the general application of the rules. If an employee is performing a function that would have been a senior management function but for the 12-week grace period to cover absences which are temporary

---

29   See the PRA Rulebook, CRR Firms – Conduct Rules; and Non-CRR Firms – Conduct Rules.

30   These are defined by the PRA as members of the board who are not approved by the PRA or FCA under FSMA, s 59 to perform a controlled function and do not perform an executive function in relation to the firm.

31   COCON 1.1.2(2) R.

32   COCON 1.1.2(4) R; PRA SS28/15 para 5.3.

or reasonably unforeseen (see Chapter 2), the individual conduct rules (but not the senior manager conduct rules) will apply to that employee (unless of course the employee has otherwise been approved as a senior manager).[33]

6.38   Where an employee is performing a function which would have been a certification function but for the grace period to cover the absence of a certified employee which is reasonably unforeseen, the performance of that function will not cause any of the conduct rules to apply to that employee (see Chapter 3). Firms should note that the periods for which this exception applies differ for each regulator (up to four weeks for the FCA; up to two weeks for the PRA).[34]

7   THE SMCR CONDUCT RULES

6.39   There are two tiers of conduct rules. Like APER, which they have replaced for RAPs, these rules are deliberately written as high-level statements of principle because they cover a large group of employees performing a wide range of different roles.

6.40   Tier 1 is the *individual conduct rules* which currently apply to all non-ancillary staff at RAPs and will apply to such staff at all other authorised firms with effect from 9 December 2019.

6.41   Tier 2 is the *senior manager conduct rules*, which currently apply to those performing senior management functions at RAPs and will apply to senior managers at all other authorised firms with effect from 9 December 2019.

6.42   Importantly, each of the conduct rules applies only to a person's conduct relating to the activities which that person performs in their capacity as an employee or senior manager of the firm.[35] However, behaviour unrelated to such activities could nevertheless be relevant to an assessment of an individual's fitness and propriety.[36] The PRA states that the way in which a person behaves in their private life may be relevant to any assessment, by the regulator or by the firm itself, of whether that person is or remains fit and proper to carry out a senior management function or a certified function.[37]

---

33   SUP 10C.3.13R; PRA Rulebook – Senior Management Functions 2.3; SS28/15 para 5.4.

34   PRA Rulebook – Certification 2.4; SYSC 5.2.27R, although note the FCA rule does not apply to FCA specified significant-harm function (5) (functions requiring qualifications), in which case the firm should take reasonable care to ensure that no employee performs that function without a valid certificate, which should be issued before the person starts to perform the function (SYSC 5.2.28G).

35   FSMA, s 64A(4)–(5) – 'qualifying functions'.

36   SS 28/15, para 5.6 and the FIT section of the FCA Handbook for further details.

37   PRA SS28/15.

Practical guidance

A practical example of such a situation is an employee of an FCA regulated firm who is caught shoplifting. The individual would not be subject to FCA enforcement action for breaching a conduct rule because the act of shoplifting does not relate to his employment by an authorised firm. But the act of shoplifting would clearly be relevant to an assessment of that individual's fitness and propriety to hold a certified or senior management function. Further, if the firm took disciplinary action against the individual, it might not be reportable to the FCA under the SMCR reporting and notification requirements because it would not have been disciplinary action that was taken because of a breach of a conduct rule (although if the individual were a senior manager and were suspended or dismissed as a consequence of the internal disciplinary process, the suspension or dismissal and the reasons therefor would be reportable to the regulators under other rules; see for example SUP10C.14.7R).[38]

First tier – individual conduct rules[39]

6.43   There are five individual conduct rules[40] which provide that an individual must:

(1) act with integrity (rule 1);

(2) act with due skill, care and diligence (rule 2);

(3) be open and cooperative with the FCA, the PRA and other regulators (rule 3);

(4) pay due regard to the interests of customers and treat them fairly (enforceable by the FCA only) (rule 4); and

(5) observe proper standards of market conduct (enforceable by the FCA only) (rule 5).

---

38 See the Final Notice issued by the FCA to Jonathan Burrows for an example of dishonest behaviour in everyday life being used by the FCA as grounds for prohibiting an approved person from holding a controlled function for lacking fitness and propriety. Mr Burrows had been caught deliberately evading paying his full railway fare on his journey to work.

39 These conduct rules broadly reiterate the requirements of APER Statements of Principle 1–4. But individual conduct rule 4 is new in that it places a positive obligation on the employees of a regulated firm to treat customers fairly. This was always an obligation to which authorised firms were subject (see Principle 6 of the FCA's Principles for Businesses), but it is now a conduct rule applying directly to the employees of such firms as well.

40 COCON 2.1; the PRA only applies the first three individual conduct rules to staff within its disciplinary jurisdiction.

Second tier – senior manager conduct rules[41]

6.44   In contrast, the senior manager conduct rules ('SM conduct rules')[42] are focused on the management of the firm. These provide that senior managers:

(1) must take reasonable steps to ensure that the business of the firm for which they are responsible is controlled effectively (SM conduct rule 1);

(2) must take reasonable steps to ensure that the business of the firm for which they are responsible complies with the relevant requirements and standards of the regulatory system (SM conduct rule 2);

(3) must take reasonable steps to ensure that any delegation of their responsibilities is to an appropriate person and that they oversee the discharge of the delegated responsibility effectively (SM conduct rule 3); and

(4) must disclose appropriately any information of which the FCA or PRA would reasonably expect notice (SM conduct rule 4).

6.45   The FCA provides detailed guidance[43] on compliance with the conduct rules, including a non-exhaustive list of examples of conduct that may be in breach of the rules.[44] The PRA also provides helpful guidance in its supervisory statement[45] although, unlike the FCA, it should be noted that the PRA does not have the same statutory power to issue guidance. The FCA states that if an individual has acted in accordance with its guidance it will treat that individual as having complied with the relevant rule or requirement.[46]

Key point

At first sight, the reader could be forgiven for thinking that there is significant overlap between SM conduct rule 4 and individual conduct rule 3. There is indeed some overlap, but they have different scopes of application. Individual conduct rule 3 is largely intended to address scenarios of *reactive* disclosure, for example where an employee of a regulated firm is responding to requests for information from the regulators. On the other hand, SM conduct rule 4 imposes a *proactive* duty on a senior manager to bring to the attention of the regulators any information of which they would reasonably expect notice.

---

41 These rules broadly reiterate the requirements of APER Statements of Principle 5–7, which apply to holders of accountable higher management functions under the APER regime. But senior management conduct rule 3 is new in imposing a mandatory rule about appropriate delegation and effective oversight of delegated responsibilities. There was always clear guidance under APER to the effect that inappropriate delegation was likely to constitute a breach of APER Statement of Principle 6 (see APER 4.6.5G), but appropriate delegation is now a mandatory rule.

42 COCON 2.2; the PRA also applies all four SM conduct rules to staff within its disciplinary jurisdiction.

43 COCON 4.1–4.2.

44 COCON 4.1 and 4.2.

45 PRA SS28/15.

46 FCA Reader's guide to the Handbook (2017): https://www.fca.org.uk/publication/handbook/readers-guide.pdf.

The broader scope of application of the senior manager rule is intended to reflect the fact that, by virtue of their more senior roles, senior managers are likely to have access to greater amounts of information of potential regulatory importance and to have the expertise to recognise when such information may be something requiring to be notified to the regulators (see COCON 4.2.26G–4.2.29G).

Relevance of a senior manager's statement of responsibilities

6.46   When seeking to determine the scope of a senior manager's role and responsibilities for the purpose of assessing whether that individual has breached a senior manager conduct rule or the Duty of Responsibility (see 6.145 ff), the senior manager's statement of responsibilities will usually be the regulators' point of departure. The statement of responsibilities is therefore a critical document which the senior manager must have personally approved and fully understood before accepting their role because it is, potentially, the road map which the regulators will use to establish personal culpability or knowing concern against that individual in the event of a regulatory breach by the firm. There may, however, be cases where all of the senior manager's responsibilities have not been fully articulated in their statement of responsibilities (for example, where the document has not been updated to reflect an individual's revised responsibilities). In such cases, the regulators will look beyond the statement of responsibilities to ascertain the full scope of the senior manager's responsibility in practice. It is very important to keep such documents up to date so as to ensure that they accurately reflect the responsibilities which the senior manager has accepted.[47]

Practical guidance

Firms should also ensure that statements of responsibilities are consistent with job descriptions in employment contracts. If the statement is updated, so too should the job description be updated. Any inconsistency will blur the lines of responsibility and give scope for argument to a senior manager that they are not responsible for any regulatory breach 'in their patch'.

General factors for assessing compliance with the conduct rules[48]

6.47   In addition to the specific guidance cited by the FCA in respect of each conduct rule,[49] the FCA will, when assessing compliance with, or a breach of, a rule in COCON, have regard to the context in which a course of conduct was

---

47   Also, see para 5.13 of SS 28/15.
48   See generally COCON 3.1 and SS 28/15 para 5.7.
49   See COCON 4 and 6.48.

undertaken, including the precise circumstances of the individual case; the characteristics of the particular function performed by the individual in question; and the behaviour expected in that function.

Specific guidance on compliance with individual conduct rules[50]

6.48   In COCON 4.1, by way of guidance, the FCA provides a non-exhaustive list of examples of behaviour which would constitute a breach of each of the five individual conduct rules.

Individual conduct rule 1: integrity

6.49   The list of examples provided by the FCA of conduct that would be in breach of individual conduct rule 1 demonstrates that, in the view of the FCA, the spectrum of behaviour constituting a lack of integrity ranges from deliberate dishonesty to serious incompetence amounting to recklessness. Such examples include misleading a client, an employer (or its auditors) or the regulators. The concept of integrity was discussed in the recent case of *Ford & Owen v FCA*.[51]

6.50   Misleading can be by act or omission and examples of misleading behaviour towards clients that would breach this rule include misleading customers about the risks of an investment, product charges and product performance. Other misleading behaviours include the provision of false or misleading information to the client or one's employer or the regulators, inappropriately destroying evidence of misleading behaviours, falsifying records or returns, misusing confidential information or clients' assets and not paying due regard to the interests of customers, including by recommending investments when it is known that their suitability for the customer in question cannot be justified.

Individual conduct rule 2: due skill, care and diligence

6.51   The non-exhaustive list of examples provided by the FCA of conduct that would be in breach of individual conduct rule 2 includes failing to inform a customer or one's employer of material information in circumstances where the individual was, or ought to have been, aware of such information; or the fact that they should provide it. Such behaviour is expressed to include failing to explain the risks of an investment to a customer and failing to disclose details of product charges and penalties to a customer.

6.52   Further examples of behaviour in breach of this conduct rule are (i) recommending an investment to a customer without having reasonable grounds to believe that it is suitable for that customer; and (ii) undertaking transactions

---

50 COCON 4.1.
51 [2018] UKUT 0358.

without a reasonable understanding of the risk exposure of the transaction either to the customer or to one's firm.

6.53   Further specific guidance is provided in respect of acting with due skill, care and diligence as a manager and examples of behaviours by managers that would breach conduct rule 2 appear at COCON 4.1.8G. (The term 'manager' is not defined and would seem to have a very broad application.) These are all expressed as failures 'to take reasonable steps' and refer to the manager's responsibility to ensure the relevant area of the business is controlled effectively, to inform themselves about the affairs of the business and to delegate with appropriate ongoing oversight.

6.54   The FCA clarifies that individual conduct rule 2 also applies to directors (whether executive or non-executive) when taking part in the activities of the board, other governing body or its committees, including board reporting and participating in meetings.

6.55   PRA guidance regarding compliance with this rule is contained in paras 5.9 and 5.10 of SS 28/15.

Individual conduct rule 3: openness and cooperation with regulators

6.56   The requirement of openness and cooperation under this rule does not just relate to the FCA and the PRA, but also to any other regulators which have recognised jurisdiction in relation to activities to which COCON applies and have a power to call for information from the firm or from individuals performing certain functions in connection with those regulated activities. This may include an investment exchange or an overseas regulator.[52]

6.57   The FCA guidance clarifies that this rule imposes no duty on an individual to report matters directly to a regulator unless they are one of the persons responsible within the firm for reporting matters to the regulator concerned.[53]

6.58   Examples of behaviour amounting to a breach of this conduct rule include failing without good reason to respond promptly or appropriately to requests for information and/or documents from the FCA and/or PRA; and, for approved persons, failing to inform a regulator of information of which the approved person was aware in response to questions from that regulator.

6.59   PRA guidance regarding compliance with this rule is contained in para 5.11 of SS 28/15.

---

52 COCON 4.1.9G.
53 COCON 4.1.10G.

Individual conduct rule 4: paying due regard to the interests of customers and treating them fairly

6.60   This rule applies to all conduct rules staff, regardless of whether they have direct contact or dealings with customers of the firm. This is intended to ensure that, at whatever level actions are being taken, those actions are taken with due consideration of how they can affect the interests of customers or result in customers being treated unfairly.

6.61   The non-exhaustive list of examples provided by the FCA of conduct that would be in breach of individual conduct rule 4 includes failing to inform a customer of material information in circumstances where the individual was, or ought to have been, aware of such information and of the fact that they should provide it to the customer and includes failing to explain the risks of an investment to a customer and providing inaccurate or inadequate information to a customer about a product or service. A number of the examples given here duplicate the examples given in respect of non-compliance with individual conduct rule 2 (due skill, care and diligence). But further examples are given, such as providing a customer with a product that is different to the one applied for by that customer and failing to acknowledge or to seek to resolve mistakes in dealing with customers.

Individual conduct rule 5: observing proper standards of market conduct

6.62   In striking contrast to the other four individual conduct rules, very limited guidance is provided by the FCA as to what behaviours would constitute a breach of this rule. All the FCA states at COCON 4.1.15G is that it will generally be considered that, where an individual's conduct complies with relevant market codes and exchange rules, this will tend to show compliance with individual conduct rule 5. The only further guidance provided is that 'manipulating or attempting to manipulate a benchmark or a market, such as a foreign exchange market, is an example of failing to observe proper standards of market conduct' which is not particularly enlightening.

6.63   The reader may wonder why such limited guidance is provided by the FCA about compliance with individual conduct rule 5. It is, however, clear from the historic enforcement outcomes which have been achieved by the FCA and its predecessor, the Financial Services Authority, in respect of the equivalent rule which applies to approved persons under the APER regime (APER Statement of Principle 3), that compliance with this conduct rule is, above all, a question of regulatory judgement for the FCA (admittedly informed to some extent by relevant codes of market conduct and exchange rules, where these are available.) There are, however, regularly enforcement cases in respect of alleged failures to observe proper standards of market conduct where there are no relevant codes, rules or other guidance available. In such circumstances, the reality is often that 'proper standards of market conduct' end up being whatever the FCA decides such standards should be.

6.64   In response to a recent consultation[54] over a more formal recognition of market codes, some firms noted their concern that current rules, including individual conduct rule 5, mean that compliance with market codes is seen as compulsory rather than voluntary and that mandating codes would competitively disadvantage authorised firms and create an unequal playing field compared with non-authorised firms in the same markets. The FCA responded to these concerns by stating that while its policy encourages FSMA authorised firms to follow market codes through the obligation to observe proper standards of market conduct in the SMCR, in practice many of the codes will also be followed by non-authorised firms. The FCA feels that complying with high standards can in any event be a competitive advantage. See 6.159 ff for more detail concerning the FCA's approach to market codes of practice.

6.65   The FCA confirmed in its response to the consultation that the individual conduct rules are relevant for both regulated and unregulated activities of firms covered by the SMCR; whether a person's conduct complies with individual conduct rule 5 may be evidenced by whether they or their firm comply with relevant market codes when these set out the relevant requirements and standards of the market. In regulated markets, this is in addition to FCA rules and principles.

6.66   The FCA states that compliance with rule 5 can be achieved by following a recognised code but that this is not the only way to discharge that obligation. The FCA does not propose to directly supervise compliance with market codes, even if recognised, in unregulated markets. Further, failure to follow a code that has been formally recognised by the FCA will not in itself be a breach of conduct rule 5; however, action may be taken if an individual deliberately chooses not to observe proper standards and there is harm to consumers or markets. If an individual chooses to comply with the provisions of a recognised market code, this is likely to be helpful evidence that they are observing proper standards of market conduct for the purposes of individual conduct rule 5.

General factors for assessing compliance with the senior manager conduct rules

6.67   It is further explained at COCON 3.1.5G that, when determining whether or not the conduct of a senior manager complies with the SM conduct rules, factors which the FCA would expect to take into account include:[55]

- whether they exercised reasonable care when considering the information available to them;

- whether they reached a reasonable conclusion upon which to act;

- the nature, scale and complexity of the firm's business;

---

54 FCA CP17/37.
55 This guidance is duplicative of that provided by the PRA at para 5.12 of SS 28/15.

- their role and responsibility as determined by reference to the relevant statement of responsibility; and

- the knowledge they had, or should have had, of regulatory concerns, if any, relating to their role and responsibilities.

6.68   It is also explained by the FCA that when assessing compliance by senior managers with the SM conduct rules, the nature, scale and complexity of the business and the role and responsibility of the individual undertaking the activity in question within the firm will be relevant in assessing whether that senior manager's conduct was reasonable.[56]

Specific guidance on senior manager conduct rules (COCON 4.2)

Senior manager conduct rule 1

6.69   This rule requires a senior manager to take reasonable steps to ensure that the business of the firm for which they are responsible is controlled effectively. This essentially reiterates the requirements of APER Statement of Principle 5.

6.70   Specific guidance on compliance with SM conduct rule 1 is provided by the FCA at COCON 4.2.1G–4.2.10G. In particular, the FCA indicates that, in order to comply with the rule, senior managers may find it helpful to review whether each area of the business for which they are responsible has been clearly assigned to a particular individual or individuals. Reporting lines should be clear to all staff as should their respective levels of authorisation.

6.71   Further, senior managers should take reasonable steps to satisfy themselves, on reasonable grounds, that each area of the business for which they are responsible has appropriate policies and procedures for reviewing the competence, knowledge, skills and performance of each individual member of staff.[57] There is further guidance to senior managers on how to deal with unsatisfactory performance by their line reports.[58]

6.72   The FCA also addresses the issue of senior manager handovers in SM conduct rule 1.[59] As part of organising the business, a senior manager should ensure that there is an orderly transition when another senior manager under their oversight or responsibility ceases to perform that function and someone else takes up that function. The FCA has indicated that it would be appropriate for the individual vacating such a position to prepare a comprehensive set of handover notes for their successor. The FCA has stated that those notes should, at a minimum, specify any ongoing matter which the successor would reasonably expect to be aware of in order to (i) perform their function effectively; (ii) ensure

---

56 COCON 3.1.6G.
57 COCON 4.2.6G.
58 COCON 4.2.7G.
59 COCON 4.2.8G.

compliance with the requirements of the regulatory system; and (iii) ensure that the individual with overall responsibility for that part of the business maintains effective control.

Practical guidance

Many firms require senior managers to maintain a 'living handover' document which is regularly kept updated. The requirement to maintain a handover document and to ensure handover obligations are met on termination of employment should be set out in the employment contract or other contractual documentation and variable remuneration may be made conditional on satisfactory compliance with these obligations.

6.73   A non-exhaustive list of examples of conduct that would be in breach of SM rule 1 is set out at COCON 4.2.10G.

6.74   PRA guidance regarding compliance with this rule is contained in paras 5.14 and 5.15 of SS 28/15.

Senior manager conduct rule 2

6.75   This rule requires senior managers to take reasonable steps to ensure that the business of the firm for which they are responsible complies with the relevant requirements and standards of the regulatory system.[60] This essentially reiterates the requirements of APER Statement of Principle 7.

6.76   The guidance issued by the FCA regarding compliance with this rule[61] includes ensuring that all staff within the part of the business for which the senior manager is responsible are aware of the need for compliance; and taking reasonable steps to ensure that the business for which they are responsible has operating procedures and systems with well-defined steps for complying with the detail of relevant requirements and standards of the regulatory system and for ensuring that the business is run prudently.

6.77   There is further guidance around the steps that should be taken by senior managers where they become aware of actual or suspected problems. They must take reasonable steps to ensure that such problems are dealt with in a timely and appropriate manner, which may include engaging third party expert consultants or advisers to assess the adequacy and effectiveness of systems and procedures. The FCA has also indicated that where such advisers make reasonable[62]

---

60   This is defined in the FCA Handbook as being 'the arrangements for regulating the firm or other person in or under the Act [ie FSMA], including the threshold conditions, the Principles and other rules, the Statements of Principle, codes and guidance etc...'.

61   COCON 4.2.11G–4.2.16G.

62   The reasonableness of such recommendations may be subject to a cost benefit analysis.

recommendations for improvements to systems and procedures, they should be implemented by the responsible senior manager in a timely manner unless there is good reason not to do so.

6.78   A non-exhaustive list of examples of conduct which would be in breach of SM conduct rule 2 appears at COCON 4.2.16G. These are generally expressed as failures to take reasonable steps and/or reasonable care and they include failing to respond appropriately when information comes to the attention of the senior manager about significant failings in systems and procedures, such as failing to carry out a full investigation and root cause analysis to understand the reasons for the deficiencies and failing to take reasonable steps to implement recommendations for improvements and remediation. There is further specific guidance around the expectations of senior managers with responsibility for the firm's compliance function.

6.79   PRA guidance regarding compliance with this rule is contained in paras 5.16 and 5.17 of SS 28/15.

Senior manager conduct rule 3

6.80   This rule requires senior managers to take reasonable steps to ensure that any delegation of their responsibilities is to an appropriate person and that they oversee the discharge of the delegated responsibility effectively.

6.81   The FCA explains in the guidance issued under this rule[63] that, before delegating authority for dealing with an issue to a third party, senior managers should have reasonable grounds for believing that the delegate has the necessary capacity, competence, knowledge, seniority and/or skill to deal with the issue. Delegating without having such reasonable grounds will constitute a breach of SM conduct rule 3. By way of example, the guidance indicates that, if the compliance department only has sufficient resources to deal with day-to-day issues, it would be unreasonable to delegate to it the resolution of a complex or unusual issue without ensuring that it had sufficient capacity to deal with the matter adequately.

6.82   The FCA recognises that senior managers will be required to exercise judgement in deciding how issues are dealt with and that sometimes their judgement will be shown, with the benefit of hindsight, to have been wrong. In such circumstances, senior managers will not breach this conduct rule unless, in exercising their judgement about what steps should be taken, or not taken, in response to a particular issue, they have failed to exercise due and reasonable consideration before they delegate or have failed to reach a reasonable conclusion. Where, having considered the position, a senior manager remains in doubt as to how to proceed, it is suggested that they may contact the regulator to discuss their approach.

63 COCON 4.2.17G–4.2.24G

6.83 Crucially, the FCA guidance makes clear that while senior managers may delegate the resolution of an issue, or authority for dealing with a part of the business, they cannot delegate responsibility for it. It is the senior manager's responsibility to ensure that they receive reports on progress and question those reports, where appropriate. Where there are significant concerns about the progress of the delegated task, senior managers should act clearly and decisively. If appropriate, this may require suspending members of staff or relieving them of all or part of their responsibilities.

6.84 Accordingly, failure by a senior manager to supervise and monitor adequately the person to whom responsibility for dealing with an issue or authority for dealing with a part of the business has been delegated will constitute a breach of this SM conduct rule.

6.85 PRA guidance regarding compliance with this rule is contained in paras 5.18 and 5.19 of SS 28/15.

Senior manager conduct rule 4

6.86 This rule requires senior managers to disclose appropriately any information of which the FCA or PRA would expect notice.

6.87 It is explained by the FCA in the guidance attaching to this rule that the disclosure obligation also applies to regulators in addition to the FCA and PRA, which have recognised jurisdiction in relation to activities to which COCON applies and have a power to call for information from the relevant person in connection with their function or the business for which they are responsible. This may include an exchange or an overseas regulator.

6.88 SM rule 4 imposes on senior managers and notified NEDs a broader duty of disclosure than that imposed by individual conduct rule 3. It is explained that individual conduct rule 3 normally applies to responses to specific requests made by the regulators, whereas SM conduct rule 4 applies in the absence of any regulatory request and imposes a proactive duty on senior managers to disclose any information which the regulators would reasonably expect to receive.

6.89 Further guidance is provided to the effect that where a senior manager is responsible for reporting matters to the regulator, failing promptly to inform the regulator concerned of information of which they are aware and which it would be reasonable to assume would be of material significance to the regulator concerned, whether in response to questions or otherwise, will constitute a breach of this rule.[64]

6.90 Where senior managers who do not have specific responsibility for reporting matters to the regulators become aware of information of which they

64 COCON 4.2.27G.

think the FCA or PRA would reasonably expect notice, they should determine whether that information falls within the scope of their responsibilities and, if it does, they should ensure that it is disclosed to the appropriate regulator, where appropriate.[65] However, the PRA has indicated that it would not expect a senior manager to disclose information which they know the firm or another senior manager has already disclosed to the PRA.[66]

6.91 In disclosing appropriately, the person will need to disclose sufficient information for the regulator to understand the full implications in a timely manner. The requirements to be open and cooperative and to disclose information appropriately are considered by the PRA to be particularly important for NEDs.[67] The PRA Approach documents[68] explain that 'if any director has concerns about the firm or its management or governance, the PRA will expect them to press for action to remedy the matter and, if those concerns are not addressed, to alert the PRA'.

6.92 The FCA provides that when assessing whether or not a senior manager's conduct complies with SM conduct rule 4, the FCA will take into account the following factors:[69]

- whether it would be reasonable for the individual to assume that the information would be of material significance to the regulator;

- whether the information relates to the individual themselves or their firm; and

- whether any decision not to report the matter was taken after reasonable enquiry and analysis of the situation.

6.93 PRA guidance regarding compliance with this rule is contained in paras 5.20 to 5.23 of SS 28/15.

Senior managers at listed companies

6.94 The FCA states that regulated firms which are listed on the London Stock Exchange are subject to the provisions of the UK Corporate Governance Code as well as the rules in COCON. Consequently, when forming an opinion as to whether senior managers at such firms have complied with the rules in COCON, the FCA will give due credit if they followed corresponding provisions in the UK Corporate Governance Code and related guidance.[70]

---

65 COCON 4.2.28G.
66 SS 28/15, para 5.22.
67 SS 28/15, para 5.28.
68 The PRA's approach to banking supervision (April 2013) at para 78 and the PRA's approach to insurance supervision (June 2014) at para 88.
69 COCON 4.2.29G.
70 COCON 3.1.7G.

8 CONTRACTUAL ENFORCEABILITY

6.95   The PRA provides that PRA designated firms must contractually require PRA approved persons (senior managers), notified NEDs and credit union NEDs to comply with individual conduct rules 1–3 and SM conduct rule 4. Further, the PRA provides that PRA designated firms must contractually require senior managers to comply with SM conduct rules 1–3.[71] Firms should therefore ensure that senior managers and notified NEDs/credit union NEDs are contractually bound by the conduct rules in the employment contract or other contractual employment documentation.

9 APPLYING CONDUCT RULES TO NEDS[72]

6.96   Only certain NEDs with specific responsibilities (eg chair of a committee) are designated senior managers for the purposes of the conduct rules. Consequently, the regulators initially did not have the ability to take enforcement action against NEDs who were not also designated senior managers for breach of the senior manager conduct rules. It was also doubtful whether NEDs were subject to the individual conduct rules because, in many cases, they were not strictly 'employees' of RAPs.

6.97   However, the Bank of England and Financial Services Act 2016 made provision for the FCA and the PRA to extend the new rules of conduct to apply to all directors at RAPs, including NEDs, whether or not they are senior managers. The regulators have since published rules which apply some (but not all) of the conduct rules to all NEDs in the banking and insurance sectors.[73] On 3 July 2017 these conduct rules were extended to standard non-executive directors[74] (also referred to as 'notified NEDs' by the PRA) in banks, building societies, credit unions and dual regulated investment firms and insurance firms covered by the Senior Insurance Managers Regime (SIMR).

6.98   Standard NEDs are now subject to the five FCA individual conduct rules (including the three PRA individual conduct rules) and SM rule 4, which requires individuals to disclose appropriately any information of which the regulators would reasonably expect notice. SM rules 1, 2 and 3 do not apply to NEDs unless they are also designated senior managers. The FCA has also published additional guidance to individual conduct rule 2 (the requirement to act with due skill, care and diligence) to clarify that this rule applies to an executive director

---

71 PRA Rulebook, Fitness and Propriety 3.1 and 3.2.
72 Guidance on the PRA's approach to applying the conduct rules to NEDs is contained at paras 5.24–5.28 of SS 28/15.
73 See PRA SS28/15; FCA PS17/8; see also Annex 1 of COCON 1, which provides extensive guidance on the role and responsibilities of NEDs subject to COCON.
74 Standard NEDs are defined in the FCA Handbook as those NEDs who do not hold senior management functions and are therefore not subject to regulatory pre-approval.

or NED when acting as a member of the board or other governing body or of its committees.

6.99   There is an issue about NEDs not being employees and therefore not being subject to the same form of disciplinary action that triggers the reporting of breaches (as based on s 64C of FSMA which defines disciplinary action as the issuing of a formal written warning, the suspension or dismissal of the person or the reduction or recovery of remuneration as a disciplinary sanction). The regulators recognise that for NEDs who are not employees, the usual employment law processes may not apply. For example, as NEDs in banks cannot be awarded variable remuneration, they cannot have such remuneration reduced or recovered. The PRA states[75] that for standard (notified) NEDs 'suspension or dismissal' should be interpreted as including the suspension or termination of a directorship and 'formal written warning' should include any equivalent formal written warning or caution issued to a NED.

6.100   However, regardless of employment status, directors may face the equivalent of disciplinary action in respect of breaches of obligations under statute (eg the Companies Act 2006) or provisions set out in other documents or arrangements. Such breaches may lead to action being taken against the director, up to and including their dismissal from office. The FCA states that, in such a case, firms should notify it if any disciplinary action is taken against a NED as a result of a breach of the conduct rules, whether or not those NEDs are employees of the firm. Notification of any breaches of the conduct rules by standard NEDs that result in disciplinary action must be made to the regulators using Form H.

10   PRACTICAL ISSUE

6.101   An act of suspected misconduct that may breach the conduct rules may trigger an internal disciplinary investigation within the firm and a subsequent regulatory notification (see 6.106 ff) which in turn may prompt the regulators to open an enforcement investigation either into the individual responsible for the conduct rule breach, or the firm, or both. The potential impact that such investigations can have on the assessment of an individual's fitness and propriety to hold a senior management function (SMF) or carry out a certified function is considered in Chapter 4.

6.102   This means that various departments will need to work closely in tandem. HR, legal and compliance departments will all need to be involved and each should communicate with the others to ensure all aspects of a breach are covered.

---

75   PRA SS28/15, para 5.35.

11   TRAINING AND OTHER INITIATIVES

6.103   Firms whose staff are subject to the conduct rules must ensure that relevant staff understand that the conduct rules apply to them and take all reasonable steps to ensure such staff understand how those rules apply to them.[76] The FCA sets out guidance on the training that should be provided to staff.[77] Suitable training should ensure that those who are subject to the rules have an awareness and broad understanding of all the rules and a deeper understanding of the practical application of the specific rules which are relevant to their work. This means that firms should ensure that training materials, employee handbooks and other employment documentation all take the conduct rules into account. Record keeping in respect of the training that has been carried out and who has attended it must be adequately maintained.

6.104   SUP 15.3 and 15.11 of the FCA Handbook set out the rules dealing with reporting by RAPs of COCON breaches and related disciplinary action to the FCA.

6.105   Senior managers and certification staff must have been trained and must abide by the conduct rules by commencement of the extended SMCR; however, firms have been given 12 months to put in place processes to comply with the training and reporting requirements and train their other staff on the conduct rules.

12   NOTIFICATION OF CONDUCT RULE BREACHES AND RELATED DISCIPLINARY ACTION TO THE FCA – WHAT SHOULD BE NOTIFIED AND WHEN?

6.106   Regulated firms are subject to the general obligation under Principle 11 of the FCA's Principles for Businesses to notify the FCA and, where appropriate, the PRA of information of which they would reasonably expect to be made aware. Principle 11 is underpinned by a number of specific rules in the FCA Handbook requiring the timely notification by firms of specific information in specific circumstances. One such rule requires firms to notify the regulators if they have information which reasonably suggests that a significant[78] breach of a rule or principle (including the conduct rules) may have occurred.[79]

Practical guidance

When considering suspension, firms must check employment contracts, handbooks etc to ensure that there is a contractual right to suspend to avoid a breach of contract. Further, a firm should ask itself whether suspension is

---

76   FSMA, s 64B(2) and (3) and COCON 2.3.1G.
77   COCON 2.3.
78   Guidance as to what would be 'significant' for these purposes is provided at SUP 15.3.12G.
79   SUP 15.3.11R(1).

a proportionate approach? Firms should consider the consequences for staff of suspension whilst balancing the risks to customers and the expectations of the regulator.

6.107   There is a further requirement under FSMA and a related FCA rule[80] which provides that, where disciplinary action has been taken against a member of conduct rules staff in respect of behaviour amounting to a breach of a conduct rule, the disciplinary action must be notified to the regulators. Disciplinary action for these purposes is defined as the issuing of a formal written warning, the suspension or dismissal of that person or the reduction or recovery of any of such person's remuneration.[81]

Reporting to the regulator

6.108   The FCA has clarified[82] that firms should only report disciplinary action taken in respect of conduct rule breaches once the relevant disciplinary process has been completed and a disciplinary sanction has been applied. This suggests that if an individual leaves the firm during the disciplinary process and the process cannot therefore be completed the firm should not submit a report.[83] The FCA also notes[84] that breaches of professional body codes should not be included in notifications to the regulator unless the individual has also breached FCA conduct rules and the firm has disciplined the employee for that breach.

6.109   Where disciplinary action has been taken by a firm against a senior manager for breach of a conduct rule, this fact must be notified by the firm to the regulators within seven business days.[85] Notifications of disciplinary action taken against other conduct rules staff (including certified staff) for behaviour amounting to a breach of the conduct rules are required to be made in accordance with SUP 15.11.13R to SUP 15.11.15R.[86]

6.110   Essentially, these non-senior manager notifications must be done by way of an annual report using REP008 on the FCA's electronic reporting system GABRIEL, the reporting period for which runs from 1 September to 31 August each year. Such notifications should be made annually to the FCA, within two months of the end of the reporting period.[87]

---

80 FSMA, s 64C and SUP 15.11.6R.
81 SUP 15.11.5 G.
82 FCA PS18/14.
83 Note, however, that where a senior manager resigns while under investigation, this will require notification to the regulators in a qualified Form C under SUP 10C.14.7R.
84 FCA PS18/14, para 5.17.
85 SUP 10C.14.18R; also see SUP 15.11.12 G.
86 SUP 15.11.13R.
87 See SUP 15.11.13R for further details of the annual notification requirements.

6.111   Where a firm has reported a significant breach of a conduct rule and then subsequently takes disciplinary action against a member of conduct rules staff in respect of the same matter, a separate notification of the disciplinary action should be made.[88]

6.112   If, after a firm has notified disciplinary action against an individual for a conduct rule breach, it becomes aware of facts or matters which cause it to change its view that the individual has breached a conduct rule or cause it to determine that the individual has breached a rule other than that to which the notification related, the firm should inform the FCA of those facts and matters and its revised conclusion in line with the firm's obligation to comply with Principle 11, SUP 15.6.4R[89] and, if applicable, SUP 10C or SUP 15.11.13R(4).[90]

6.113   If a firm takes disciplinary action as a result of a conduct breach against an employee but the employee has appealed or plans to appeal, the firm should still report the disciplinary action under s 64C of FSMA but should include the appeal in the notification. The firm should update the FCA on the outcome of any appeal.[91] Where an appeal is successful firms should update the FCA in the following REP008 submission. In the case of a senior manager, a firm should report the result of a successful appeal as soon as reasonably practicable after the appeal.

Settlement or other agreements or arrangements

6.114   The obligation to make a notification under s 64C of FSMA applies notwithstanding any agreement such as a COT3 Acas agreement or any other arrangements entered into by a firm and an employee on termination of the employee's employment. A firm must not enter into any arrangements or agreements that could conflict with its obligations under FCA or PRA rules to make notifications in respect of the conduct rules and its employees' fitness and propriety.[92]

6.115   It should be noted in respect of notifications under FCA rules that knowingly or recklessly providing false or misleading information to a regulator in purported compliance with any requirement imposed under FSMA may be a criminal offence.[93]

---

88   SUP 15.11.7G.
89   This rule requires a firm to notify the FCA immediately if it becomes aware that it may have provided false or misleading information to the FCA.
90   SUP 15.11.8G.
91   SUP 15.11.9G.
92   SS 28/15, para 5.29; SUP 10C.14.26 G; and SUP 10A.15.4 G.
93   FSMA, s 398.

Notifications to the FCA in respect of the suspension of staff

6.116   A firm must always remember its primary obligation under FCA and PRA rules and principles to deal with the regulators in an open and cooperative way and to disclose anything relating to the firm of which the regulators would reasonably expect notice.[94] This duty overrides any other requirements and includes a duty to update the regulator should further information subsequently come to light that is materially different from information previously given to the regulator.[95]

6.117   When considering whether to suspend a member of conduct rules staff pending investigation into a possible conduct rule breach (and it will often be appropriate, or indeed necessary, to suspend an employee from their position pending the outcome of such an investigation) firms should first check their contractual documentation to ensure that they have a contractual right to suspend. If there is no such right, firms should seek to agree a suspension with the individual in order to mitigate the risk of committing a breach of contract.

6.118   Decisions to suspend staff should not be taken lightly, particularly in respect of senior managers, suspensions of whom and the reasons for them are required to be notified to the regulators.[96] Further, case law suggests that suspension should not be a kneejerk reaction since the repercussions may be serious for an individual.[97] While firms should consider whether there is an alternative to suspending the employee, suspension may often be the only viable option in a regulatory context, mindful of the risk arising from an individual remaining in a customer-facing role when there are concerns about their conduct or their fitness and propriety that require to be investigated and the regulators' legitimate expectations in this regard. Internal investigations into misconduct can, however, take time and a lengthy suspension should be kept under regular review to ensure that it remains appropriate, mindful of the employer's duty to treat its employees fairly and reasonably.

13   NOTIFICATION OF CONDUCT RULE BREACHES AND RELATED DISCIPLINARY ACTION TO THE PRA – WHAT SHOULD BE NOTIFIED AND WHEN?

6.119   The FCA requires that, when considering what notifications need to be made to the FCA and when, authorised firms must also consider their notification obligations under PRA rules, where appropriate. These are contained in the Notifications section of the PRA Rulebook.[98]

---

94   FCA Principle 11; PRA Fundamental Rule 7.
95   There is a specific FCA rule dealing with this. See SUP 15.6.4R.
96   SUP 10C.14.7R.
97   See *Agoreyo v London Borough of Lambeth* [2017] EWHC 2019 (QB).
98   General rules regarding the form and method of notifications to the PRA are set out in Notifications 7 and SS28/15. The rules relating to notification of conduct rule breaches to the PRA are set out in the PRA Rulebook at Notifications 11.

6.120   PRA rules state that 'If a firm takes disciplinary action against a person relating to any action, failure to act, or circumstance that amounts to a breach of any conduct rule it must notify the PRA'.[99] In respect of senior managers, notifications under this rule need to be made within seven business days.[100] The PRA imposes the same period for notification where disciplinary action has been taken in respect of persons performing certification functions who are subject to the PRA's conduct rules[101] and also in respect of conduct rules NEDs.[102] (It should be noted that there is no requirement to notify the FCA within seven business days of disciplinary action being taken against persons performing certification functions for a breach of COCON. For the FCA, the requirement is to include such reports in the annual notification that is made under SUP 15.11.13R.)

6.121   There is a separate requirement for a PRA regulated firm to notify the PRA where it becomes aware of information which would reasonably be material to the assessment of the fitness and propriety of a PRA approved person or a person in respect of whom an application for approval to perform a PRA senior management function has been made.[103] The equivalent FCA rules are contained at SUP 10A.14.17R (for FCA approved persons or candidates to be such) and SUP10C.14.18R (for FCA approved senior managers, or candidates to be such).

6.122   Paragraph 5.36 of SS 28/15 notes that, notwithstanding the absence of any internal disciplinary action, the following PRA rules will continue to require misconduct involving notified NEDs to be notified to the regulators as soon as reasonably practicable:

- PRA Fundamental Rule 7, which states that 'a firm must deal with its regulators in an open and cooperative way and must disclose to the PRA appropriately anything relating to the firm of which the PRA would reasonably expect notice';

- Rule 4.4 in the Fitness and Propriety part of the PRA Rulebook, which states that 'if a firm becomes aware of information which would reasonably be material to the assessment of a current or former notified non-executive director's fitness and propriety … it must inform the PRA in writing as soon as practicable'; and

---

99 PRA Rulebook, Notifications 11.2.
100 PRA Rulebook, Notifications 11.4. This rule also explains the form that such notifications should take.
101 PRA Rulebook, Notifications 11.3. This rule also explains the form that such notifications should take.
102 These are defined by the PRA as members of the board who are not approved by the PRA or FCA under FSMA, s 59 to perform a controlled function and do not perform an executive function in relation to the firm.
103 PRA Rulebook, Notifications 11.5. Such notifications must be made on Form D, or (if it is more practical to do so and with the prior agreement of the PRA) by fax or email, as soon as practicable.

- General Organisational Requirements 5.2, which requires CRR firms to ensure that 'members of the management body [are] at all times … of sufficiently good repute and possess sufficient knowledge, skills and experience to perform their duties'.[104]

Practical guidance

It should be noted that in addition to providing formal written notification of breaches of the senior manager conduct rules in accordance with the rules referred to above, firms would also be well advised to notify their usual PRA/FCA supervisory contacts (if they have them) of the issue, either by telephone or by other more prompt means of communication, pending completion of the written notification.

---

14 THE TEST FOR LIABILITY FOR BREACH OF A CONDUCT RULE: PERSONAL CULPABILITY

6.123 It is important to note that at the heart of the conduct rules is the principle that individuals will be in breach of a conduct rule only if there is personal culpability. Accordingly, a senior manager or other member of staff to whom the conduct rules apply will only be liable for breaching a conduct rule where they are deemed by the FCA or the PRA to have been personally culpable for that breach.

6.124 The test for personal culpability is set out at COCON 3.1.3G.[105] It arises where the individual's conduct was either deliberate or where the person's standard of conduct fell below that which would be reasonable in all the circumstances. The burden of proving whether the test for personal culpability is satisfied is on the regulators. Accordingly, in all cases, where the regulators cannot prove on the balance of probabilities that an individual has failed to act reasonably, the individual will not be liable for having breached a conduct rule.

---

104 See also Article 91(1) of CRD IV.
105 See also *John Pottage v FSA* FS/2010/33 for further consideration of the principle of personal culpability as it is applied to holders of significant influence functions (or holders of accountable higher management functions as they are now called under the APER regime). The findings in *Pottage* are also relevant to the question of the personal culpability of senior managers for breaching the SM conduct rules under the SMCR.

15 CONDUCT RULE BREACHES AND ENFORCEMENT ACTION BY THE FCA[106]

6.125   Section 66 of FSMA provides that a regulator may take action against an individual if it appears to the regulator that he is guilty of misconduct, including for breaching the conduct rules, and the regulator is satisfied that it is appropriate in all the circumstances to take action against him.

6.126   There are three bases on which the FCA[107] may take enforcement action against an individual for regulatory misconduct:[108]

(1) breach of the conduct rules;[109]

(2) being knowingly concerned[110] in a firm's contravention of a relevant requirement (such as an FCA rule or one of the FCA's Principles for Businesses); and

(3) breaching the duty of responsibility for senior managers.[111]

Practical guidance

It is unlikely that the FCA would elect to expend its resources in investigating staff below senior manager level for a breach of the individual conduct rules. This is likely to be left by the FCA for the employer to investigate and take disciplinary action, where appropriate. It is even less likely that the FCA

---

106 The PRA's approach to enforcement is set out in its statement of policy dated August 2018, 'The Prudential Regulation Authority's approach to enforcement: statutory statements of policy and procedure'. The procedures for the PRA's Enforcement Decision Making Committee (the EDMC) are contained in the statement of policy PS/EDMC2018 dated August 2018: 'Enforcement Decision Making Committee'.
107 The PRA has equivalent jurisdiction to enforce the conduct rules (except individual conduct rules 4 and 5) against individuals within its disciplinary jurisdiction, namely senior managers, certification staff and conduct rules NEDs at PRA regulated firms.
108 This does not include market abuse under FSMA, s 118, the Market Abuse Regulation (EU) No 596/2014, or the criminal offences of insider dealing, encouraging and disclosing inside information under the Criminal Justice Act 1993; or breaches of any other requirements imposed under FSMA.
109 In respect of staff at RAPs, these are the individual conduct rules and the senior manager conduct rules set out at COCON 2.1 and 2.2 of the FCA Handbook and the equivalent PRA rules in the Conduct Rules section of the PRA Rulebook. For approved persons at FCA solo regulated firms, these are the APER Statements of Principle set out at APER 2 of the FCA Handbook – that is until 9 December 2019, when the SMCR comes into force for FCA solo regulated firms and COCON will thereafter apply to their senior managers and non-ancillary staff.
110 In order to be 'knowingly concerned' in a regulatory breach by the firm, the individual must be aware of the facts giving rise to the breach, but need not know that a breach has actually occurred.
111 This duty currently only applies to statutory directors and individuals performing a senior management function at RAPs. The duty will be extended to such personnel at insurers with effect from 10 December 2018 and to such personnel at FCA solo regulated firms with effect from 9 December 2019, when the SMCR comes into force for those firms. For further details about the scope and extent of this duty, see 6.145 ff.

or the PRA would seek to investigate staff below senior manager level for being knowingly concerned in a contravention by their employer of a relevant requirement under FSMA, although technically the regulators do have such jurisdiction.

6.127   The FCA's approach to enforcement is set out in the Enforcement Guide (EG) within the FCA Handbook and its approach to imposing regulatory sanctions arising from its enforcement work is described in its Decisions Procedure and Penalties manual (DEPP).[112]

6.128   The regulatory sanctions which can be imposed for conduct rule breaches include unlimited fines, the withdrawal of approval to carry out controlled functions and SMF functions and public censure, which may entail the publication of the regulators' findings of misconduct on the PRA and/or FCA websites.[113] The effect of such sanctions can be career limiting, particularly where a prohibition order is also imposed as will generally be the case where the regulators determine as a consequence of their investigation that the individual lacks fitness and propriety to carry out a controlled function or senior management function in the future.

6.129   The regulators can take disciplinary action against an individual for breaching the conduct rules for a period of up to six years after the date on which the regulator knew[114] of the misconduct.[115]

6.130   The FCA makes clear that not all breaches of its rules or requirements constitute serious misconduct.[116] Many breaches can be addressed and remedied without the need for enforcement action. Where the FCA suspects that serious misconduct has occurred, it will usually open an enforcement investigation. Once the FCA has investigated sufficiently to form an accurate understanding of any misconduct that may have occurred and its impact on the firm, consumers and/ or market integrity, it will contact the subject of the investigation in order to try to agree what kind of disciplinary sanction(s) should be imposed. The FCA will only agree to impose a sanction which, in its opinion, constitutes an appropriate regulatory outcome in respect of such misconduct as has occurred. Where the FCA does not find sufficient evidence to support a finding of misconduct, it will discontinue its investigation; or if the misconduct is insufficiently serious to warrant a public outcome, it may issue a private warning.

---

112 See also the FCA Mission: Our Approach to Enforcement, March 2018.
113 FSMA, s 66; see also FCA Handbook – Glossary.
114 The regulator is deemed to know if it has information from which the misconduct can reasonably be inferred –FSMA, s 66(5)(a).
115 FSMA, s 66(4). So far as the FCA is concerned, in practice this means that a warning notice must be issued within six years of the FCA coming into possession of information from which individual misconduct can reasonably be inferred. Otherwise the enforcement action will be out-of-time and the FCA will lose the ability to impose a disciplinary sanction.
116 FCA Mission: Our Approach to Enforcement, March 2018.

6.131   The DEPP sets out a list of circumstances[117] to be taken into account by the FCA when deciding whether it is appropriate to take disciplinary action against a firm or an individual.

6.132   Senior management accountability is a priority item on the credible deterrence agenda of the FCA's Enforcement and Market Oversight Division and holding senior managers to account for misconduct is considered to be one of the regulators' key objectives for establishing good culture and governance within the firms that they regulate.[118] Consequently, the regulators are committed to ensuring that senior managers adhere to their responsibilities and they will bring appropriate enforcement action against senior managers, wherever appropriate. The FCA has for some time now been opening more investigations into individuals than into firms, according to its annual Enforcement Performance Report.

6.133   Where an individual has been placed under investigation, the FCA will usually serve written notice of that fact on the subject of the investigation in the form of a Memorandum and Notice of Appointment of Investigators, provided that such notification will not, in the FCA's view, prejudice the FCA's investigation. The EG makes it clear that it is the FCA's expectation that such investigations will be kept confidential, although this will not of course prevent the subject of the investigation from seeking legal advice. In exceptional circumstances, the FCA may make a public announcement that its Enforcement Division is investigating certain matters.

6.134   The regulators have statutory powers under FSMA to compel the production of documents and information from firms and their employees and, in some respects, from third parties, where such material is relevant for the purposes of an ongoing investigation or, more broadly, where it is reasonably required for the effective discharge of their regulatory objectives.

6.135   These statutory powers include the power to compel individuals to attend interviews with enforcement staff to answer questions for the purposes of an enforcement investigation. Where an interview is carried out by the FCA under compulsion, the interviewee may not unreasonably refuse to answer the FCA's questions. Failing without reasonable excuse to provide information to the FCA in compliance with a requirement under FSMA, including in an enforcement interview, may be treated as a contempt of court.[119] Further, knowingly or recklessly providing false or misleading information to the FCA in response to a regulatory requirement imposed during an enforcement investigation is a criminal offence under FSMA, s 177(4).

6.136   If the FCA decides as a consequence of its investigation to take enforcement action against a firm or an individual, the investigation team will first explain its preliminary findings to the subject of the investigation in order to see

---

117 DEPP 6.2.1G.
118 EG 2.11.
119 FSMA, s 177(2).

whether a 'without prejudice' settlement can be reached. There is no obligation to accept the preliminary findings of the FCA investigators, but there is typically a 28-day window during which a 30% discount may be awarded by the FCA in respect of any penalty or other regulatory sanction (such as a restriction or a limitation) for early settlement of the case.

6.137 If the subject of the investigation does not agree with some or all of the FCA's preliminary findings, it has a number of options. It can settle the case in part, for example by agreeing certain facts and/or whether such facts also amount to breaches of any rules and/or principles;[120] or it can reject the FCA's settlement offer in its entirety and either make written (and if it so wishes oral) representations to the FCA's Regulatory Decisions Committee (RDC),[121] following which, if it does not agree with the FCA's decision it can refer the matter to the Upper Tribunal (Tax and Chancery Chamber).

6.138 The Upper Tribunal is entirely independent of the FCA and will consider the entire case afresh. Alternatively, the subject of the investigation can elect to bypass the RDC altogether and make an expedited reference to the Upper Tribunal.

6.139 As summarised at 6.125, the formal sanctions[122] that the FCA can impose under s 66 of FSMA for regulatory misconduct by individuals include:

● publishing a statement against an approved person or conduct rules staff;

● a financial penalty on an approved person or conduct rules staff;[123]

● a suspension, condition or limitation on an approved person; and

● a disciplinary prohibition under FSMA, s 123A.[124]

---

120 This is achieved by entering into what is known as a 'focused resolution agreement', which allows the subject of the investigation to retain at least some element of the discount for early settlement, even though it is contesting some part of the FCA's findings before the Regulatory Decisions Committee – see DEPP 6.7.3A for further details.

121 The RDC is part of the FCA but is separate from its executive management structure and none of the members of the RDC (except the Chairman) is employed by the FCA. Its function, inter alia, is to decide on behalf of the FCA what disciplinary sanctions should be imposed for regulatory misconduct and market abuse.

122 EG 7.1.2.

123 The FCA has published its penalty calculation methodology at DEPP 6. This varies as between firms and individuals and depending on whether the misconduct is a breach of FCA rules and principles or market abuse. The methodology has been in effect since 2010 and is expected to be reviewed in 2018/19.

124 This is not to be confused with a prohibition order imposed under FSMA, s 56. A section 56 prohibition order is not a sanction imposed for disciplinary purposes, but is a protective measure. It will be imposed on an individual where the FCA determines as a consequence of its investigation into their conduct that they lack fitness and propriety to perform a controlled or senior management function. Due to the protective, rather than disciplinary, nature of this sanction, it can be imposed by the FCA even where a disciplinary sanction is statute-barred because regulatory action was commenced outside the six-year limitation period for individuals. The criteria against which the FCA assesses fitness and propriety are set out in the FIT section of the FCA Handbook and include honesty and integrity, competence and capability and financial soundness.

6.140 The amount of the financial penalty that is imposed as a consequence of regulatory misconduct or market abuse is at the FCA's discretion[125] subject to applying the criteria and guidance set out in DEPP[126] which is based on three principles: disgorgement (to ensure that the individual does not benefit from his misconduct), discipline and deterrence.[127] Firms should note that financial penalties imposed by the regulator must be paid by the person on whom they are imposed and a firm cannot arrange insurance to indemnify any member of staff against the payment of such a penalty.[128]

6.141 The FCA makes clear that it aims to make sure that the sanctions which it imposes for regulatory misconduct are sufficient to deter the firm or individual from re-offending and to deter others from offending. Where it takes disciplinary action against a firm or individual it will consider using all of its sanctioning powers. When assessing the nature of the sanction, the FCA will take into account all relevant circumstances, including what steps the individual or firm has taken to address the harm and to cooperate with the FCA. If an individual or firm fails to take steps to address harm or refuses to cooperate fully with the FCA this will be taken into account and may justify heavier sanctions. At all events, the FCA must act reasonably and any sanction imposed must be proportionate both to the seriousness of the misconduct and the individual or firm's ability to pay.[129]

6.142 Where conditions are placed upon regulatory approval to carry out a controlled function or a senior management function, the employment practitioner will need to consider whether these limitations impact upon the individual's ability to carry out their job. Considerations include amending the statement of responsibilities and job description as well as more fundamental issues about whether a senior manager is so limited in their ability to perform the functions for which they were recruited that the firm must consider alternative employment and even termination. Similarly, a suspension (where approval has been temporarily withdrawn) may impact on the individual's ability to perform their functions. Suspensions and restrictions on carrying out controlled or senior management functions may remain in force for up to two years.[130]

6.143 For misconduct which the FCA does not consider sufficiently serious to warrant the publication of a formal regulatory sanction, it has the power to issue a private warning. The FCA has a wide discretion[131] about when to issue private warnings and makes it clear that they are a non-statutory tool; nor are

125 FSMA, s 66(3)(a) states that the amount should be such as the regulator 'considers appropriate'.
126 DEPP 6.5 and DEPP 6.5B in particular.
127 DEPP 6.5.2 G.
128 GEN 6.1.3–6.1.5.
129 DEPP 6.5.3 G(3). Further, where an individual or a firm can produce verifiable evidence that the imposition of the FCA's proposed sanction would cause serious financial hardship, the FCA may be persuaded to reduce the sanction, or suspend it altogether.
130 FSMA, s 66(3A).
131 EG 7.6.

they a formal determination about whether conduct rules have been breached. However, it does make it clear that private warnings are a more serious form of reprimand than would usually be made in the course of business-as-usual supervisory correspondence.

6.144   Private warnings will sit on the individual's or the firm's compliance file and may be taken into account by the FCA and/or PRA in the event of subsequent misconduct and even aggravate the level of a financial penalty or other regulatory sanction that is imposed in respect of later misconduct. There is, consequently, an obligation on the FCA to identify and explain its concerns to the subject of the private warning about the misconduct in question before issuing the private warning itself. The FCA might be expected to issue a private warning where the matter that is giving cause for concern would not warrant a public outcome and/ or where full remedial action has already been taken.

16   THE DUTY OF RESPONSIBILITY FOR SENIOR MANAGERS

6.145   The statutory Duty of Responsibility was introduced under the Bank of England and Financial Services Act 2016 and came into force for senior managers of RAPs on 10 May 2016. The duty will also apply to senior managers of insurers with effect from 10 December 2018 and to senior managers at FCA solo regulated firms with effect from 9 December 2019, when the SMCR is extended to those firms.[132]

6.146   The Duty of Responsibility specifies that the FCA and the PRA can take action against a senior manager of an RAP where:

- there has been a contravention of a relevant requirement by the senior manager's firm;[133]

- at the time of the contravention or during any part of it, the senior manager was responsible for the management of any of the firm's activities in relation to which the contravention occurred;[134] and

---

132 CP17/42 and PS18/16, The Duty of Responsibility for insurers and FCA solo regulated firms.
133 Consequently, even if a senior manager has not taken reasonable steps, no liability can arise under the Duty of Responsibility without associated misconduct by the firm.
134 The FCA and PRA accept that this will be a question of fact in each case and they have reserved the right to 'look beyond' individuals' statements of responsibilities to ascertain the true position, if appropriate. So while statements of responsibilities will be relevant considerations in this regard, there will be other relevant considerations, according to the regulators. Some of these are set out by the FCA at DEPP 6.2.9-C G.

- the senior manager did not take such steps as a person in their position could reasonably have been expected to take[135] to avoid the contravention occurring or continuing.[136]

6.147 The burden lies on the FCA and the PRA to prove, on the balance of probabilities, that there was a contravention by the firm, that the senior manager was responsible for managing the activities in relation to which the contravention occurred and that the senior manager did not take reasonable steps to avoid the firm's contravention occurring or continuing. As to the third limb of the test, it is not necessary for the senior manager to show that they took reasonable steps; rather it is for the PRA and the FCA to prove that they did not.

6.148 The FCA and PRA have confirmed that in proceedings for enforcement of the Duty of Responsibility, a senior manager will not be bound by any finding of the RDC, a court or tribunal to which they were not privy or a party. This includes any prior admissions made by the firm, eg for settlement purposes, as to whether a contravention of a relevant requirement has in fact occurred.

6.149 Guidance as to the circumstances in which the FCA will apply the Duty of Responsibility is set out in DEPP 6.2.9-A G to 6.2.9-F G. The guidance includes a non-exhaustive list of considerations that may be relevant when determining whether (i) a senior manager was responsible for the management of the firm's activities in relation to which the contravention occurred; and (ii) a senior manager took the steps such a person in their position could reasonably have been expected to take to avoid the contravention occurring or continuing.

6.150 Decisions about whether to take enforcement action based on the Duty of Responsibility will be made by the FCA by reference to its published criteria in DEPP. The FCA will look at all the circumstances of the case, including the seriousness of the breach, the relevant individual's position, responsibilities and seniority and the need to use enforcement powers effectively and proportionately.

6.151 The FCA and the PRA have stated that they will not apply standards retrospectively or with the benefit of hindsight.[137] Both regulators have stated that when they apply the Duty of Responsibility, they will consider what steps a competent senior manager would have taken at that time, in that specific

---

135 DEPP 6.2.9-E sets out a lengthy, but non-exhaustive list of considerations the FCA will take into account in assessing whether a senior manager's actions were reasonable in all the circumstances. The PRA's guidance as to its own expectations in this regard is contained at paras 2.76 and 2.77 of SS28/15. The PRA and FCA both accept that the steps a senior manager in a non-executive role could reasonably have been expected to take may differ from those reasonably expected of a senior manager in an executive role.

136 There is a considerable amount of guidance in DEPP and COCON and SS28/15 regarding reasonable steps by senior managers. In determining whether a senior manager has complied with the duty, the PRA and the FCA will consider their respective guidance, and whether the senior manager has acted in accordance with their statutory, common law and other legal obligations, including but not limited to the conduct rules and other relevant PRA and FCA rules.

137 DEPP 6.2.9-D G.

individual's position, with that individual's role and responsibilities in all the circumstances.

6.152   The FCA and the PRA have both clarified that the Duty of Responsibility will apply to senior managers' individual contributions to collective decisions and their implementation insofar as those contributions are in scope of their senior manager responsibilities.[138]

PRA guidance on the Duty of Responsibility

6.153   The guidance provided by the PRA on the Duty of Responsibility[139] is generally consistent and aligned with the FCA's guidance and the steps reasonably expected of a senior manager under both sets of guidance are essentially the same. Neither set of guidance is prescriptive, however, and the steps that should be taken to comply with the duty will vary from case to case.

6.154   The PRA proposed in its CP14/17 that its guidance for the application of the Duty of Responsibility to insurers would reflect its existing guidance for the application of the duty to deposit takers and PRA designated investment firms. This approach appears to be confirmed by the PRA's Policy Statement 15/18 and the July 2018 update to Supervisory Statement SS35/15.[140]

Commentary

6.155   It remains to be seen how much the ability to take action for breach of the Duty of Responsibility will add to the regulators' enforcement toolkit for dealing with regulatory misconduct by senior managers. The duty only came into effect in 2016 and it is unlikely that any enforcement outcomes for breach of the duty will be seen for some time to come.

6.156   The duty was brought in at the instigation of HM Treasury to replace the original proposal to impose a 'presumption of responsibility' on senior managers, which would (very controversially) have placed the burden of proof on senior managers to satisfy the regulators that they had taken reasonable steps to prevent a contravention of a FSMA requirement occurring or continuing in a part of the business for which they were responsible.

6.157   By confirming under the Duty of Responsibility that the burden of proof remains on the regulators to demonstrate a failure to act reasonably by a senior manager, HM Treasury has considerably watered down the original proposal, which will have come as a considerable relief to all those who would have been subject to the duty.

---

138 DEPP 6.2.9-E G (15); SS28/15, para 2.67.
139 This is set out at paras 2.59 ff of PRA Supervisory Statement SS28/15 dated May 2017.
140 See para 1.15 of FCA PS18/16.

6.158   There is consequently a sense of 'as you were' in relation to the effect of the SM conduct rules and the Duty of Responsibility. This is because the SM conduct rules are largely re-statements of the requirements of the APER Statements of Principle 5–7 as they apply to holders of accountable higher management functions at FCA solo regulated firms. Further, the test for liability remains the same under APER and the SM conduct rules: failing to act reasonably.

Practical guidance

While it is fair to say that the Duty of Responsibility imposes a broader responsibility on senior managers than merely to comply with the SM conduct rules, the reality is that, in most cases, a failure to comply with the Duty of Responsibility would probably constitute a breach of one or more of the SM conduct rules in any event. The standard of conduct (reasonableness) remains the same under the both the duty and the SM conduct rules. Further, for both categories of misconduct, the burden of proof rests with the regulators. As you were, then.

---

17   UNREGULATED FINANCIAL MARKETS AND INDUSTRY CODES

6.159   In a consultation paper[141] the FCA put forward proposals to address concerns that for markets and activities not covered by regulatory rules and principles, the FCA's expectations for good conduct in authorised firms are less clear, and signalled its intention to formally recognise certain market codes. The proposals take into account the development of voluntary industry-written codes of conduct for unregulated financial markets[142] (which do not have any formal FCA recognition status) and the SMCR. The FCA noted that market codes are helpful to articulate clear conduct expectations in unregulated markets and activities. Indeed, the FCA's Mission Statement supports industry standards as a useful way for the industry to police itself. The FCA's proposals are aimed at supporting and encouraging such industry codes but, crucially, are not intended to give them equivalent standing to the FCA's rules and principles.

6.160   The proposals were taken forward by the FCA in its policy statement in July 2018.[143] Industry, firms and responsible senior managers should together ensure that the codes they follow are adhered to. As the FCA notes, all of the individual conduct rules apply to both regulated and unregulated activities. For regulated activities, regulatory rules and requirements determine proper standards of market conduct; in respect of unregulated activities, firms and individuals must

---

141 FCA CP17/37.
142 An unregulated activity is one which is not 'regulated' as defined in the FCA Handbook (specified in Part II of the Financial Services and Markets Act (Regulated Activities) Order 2001 (SI 2001/544).
143 FCA PS18/18.

use their judgement to determine what proper standards of market conduct are. FCA guidance[144] provides that the FCA will look at market codes and whether an individual's conduct complies with these together with exchange rules and other standards in the market in order to determine whether proper standards of market conduct have been observed.

6.161   As noted by the FCA, market codes may take many forms and names (for example, code of conduct/practice/ethics, best practice etc). The FCA states that its own definition is similar to that of the International Federation of Accountants, namely:

> 'Principles, values, standards or rules of behaviour that guide the decisions, procedures and systems of an organisation in a way that (a) contributes to the welfare of its key stakeholders and (b) respects the rights of all constituents affected by its operations'.

6.162   To encourage individuals to abide by applicable market codes the FCA will formally recognise certain market codes[145] and publish a list on its website, subject to certain criteria being met. The FCA emphasises that the codes remain voluntary; rather, the FCA supports and encourages the adoption of such voluntary market codes. Their use is encouraged not mandated. Separately, the FCA declined to take forward the proposed extension of Principle 5 of the FCA's Principles for Businesses to wholly unregulated activities since there were concerns that this would bring in regulation by the back door. However, it will keep this under review.

6.163   There were concerns raised that by listing codes on the FCA website they would gain quasi-regulatory status and move from being voluntary to expected. This is complicated by the fact that some codes are aspirational and high level, lacking sufficient clarity. The FCA responded that recognition does not imply that an individual must follow a particular code and that such a code will not have the mandatory status of a FCA rule.

6.164   Codes that are submitted for recognition should be focused on standards of market conduct, given the link with individual conduct rule 5. The FCA will focus on recognising codes that are related to unregulated activities in financial markets. Non-recognised industry codes are still helpful for individuals subject to the SMCR in determining proper standards of market conduct. In such cases, an individual's own judgement should be exercised. The FCA will consult publicly on a proposed recognition decision, most likely through its quarterly consultation papers. The FCA does not propose to provide interpretive guidance on code provisions and a code will be recognised for a period of three years with the possibility of renewal if recognised codes remain relevant.

---

144 COCON 4.1.5G.

145 Only a small number of codes in priority areas will be recognised to avoid onerous obligations on firms and the FCA.

6.165   Code recognition is linked to the SMCR requirements and the individual conduct rules and territorial application is defined by these rules.[146] Individual conduct rules for senior managers and material risk takers apply wherever their activities are carried out. For all other individuals covered by the SMCR the individual conduct rules apply in relation to their activities performed from an establishment maintained in the UK by their employer or when dealing with clients in the UK from an overseas establishment of a UK authorised firm (see 6.18–6.19).

6.166   The FCA does not intend to directly supervise compliance with market codes; however, market codes may be relevant for firms when considering whether their staff are meeting their SMCR obligations. The FCA expects firms currently subject to the SMCR to train and monitor their staff.[147] The FCA will ensure that firms meet their governance and systems and control obligations, including under the SMCR and named senior managers will have responsibility for taking reasonable steps to ensure compliance with relevant regulatory requirements. Compliance with market codes may be one way to evidence that appropriate training has been provided and that the right behaviours and culture are being encouraged.

6.167   The FCA also highlights the limited circumstances in which it may take enforcement action against individuals in relation to unregulated activities. Market codes can be evidence for determining what proper standards are although the FCA will not take action based solely on a breach of a market code. In other words, recognising a code will not necessarily change the FCA's approach to enforcing its conduct rules.

6.168   Further, the FCA reassures firms that being a signatory to a code does not mean that parties are more likely to be held accountable if they fail to follow it.[148]

18   FINANCIAL STABILITY BOARD TOOLKIT

6.169   The Financial Stability Board (FSB) has published a toolkit[149] to mitigate misconduct risk, including guidance on preventing 'rolling bad apples'. While aimed at systemic risks, there are some useful points to be gleaned from the guidance. The FSB advises that firms should:

- *Communicate conduct expectations early and consistently in recruitment and hiring processes.* Firms should communicate clear and consistent messages about conduct expectations; silence about expected employee conduct could imply that the firm does not take this seriously.

146 COCON 1.1.9 and 1.1.10.
147 COCON 2.3.
148 COCON 3.1.2 provides that the FCA will have regard to the precise circumstances when deciding whether the individual conduct rules have been complied with; see also FSMA, s 64B.
149 FSB 'Strengthening Governance Frameworks to mitigate misconduct risk: a toolkit for firms and supervisors'.

- *Enhance interviewing techniques.* The recruitment process could consider behavioural competency and conduct history and assess the candidate's potential for adhering to the firm's values.

- *Leverage multiple sources of available information before hiring.* Firms could search publicly available and proprietary data sources for available information about candidates. Current employees may have personal knowledge about a candidate's conduct at a previous employer (although this should be treated with caution).

- *Reassess employee conduct regularly.* Firms could update or renew background checks on regular schedules (and provide for such checks in employee documentation) eg after an initial period of employment or at career milestones, including promotions or lateral moves.

- *Conduct 'exit interviews'.*

19   CULTURE

6.170   The FCA has repeatedly stated that its focus going forward will be on the need for regulated firms to foster an appropriate culture which places achieving good outcomes in the interests of their customers at the heart of their business models. To this end, it has published a discussion paper[150] 'Transforming culture in financial services'.

6.171   The FCA believes that there should not be a 'one-size-fits-all' approach to culture and does not attempt to prescribe what any individual firm's culture should be. This is considered to be a matter for the firm's board of directors and senior management to decide. However, the FCA points out that it has set out minimum standards of behaviour in the form of the conduct rules. The discussion paper contains a series of essays which address how to promote good culture within firms.

6.172   The FCA asks in the discussion paper how regulation can promote healthy culture. Two fundamental concepts underpin the FCA's thinking about culture and regulation. The first is that regulation must hold the individual as well as the firm to account and the conduct rules are considered to be a means of achieving this. The second concept is that leaders can manage culture even if they cannot measure it.

---

150 FCA DP18/2.

CHAPTER 7

Remuneration

Paul Fontes, Partner and Susan Mayne, Consultant

I THE REMUNERATION CODES: INTRODUCTION

7.01 Prior to 2009 the remuneration of employees in banks, building societies and other employers in the financial services sector was almost wholly unregulated. This position changed following the 2008 financial crisis when the then Financial Services Authority (FSA) introduced the first remuneration code in August 2009. This code applied to 26 of the larger banks, building societies and broker dealers from 1 January 2010. There are now seven codes applying to different types of financial services firms.

7.02 The original remuneration code arose from the belief that the behaviour and culture within banks played a major role in generating the conditions which led to the financial crisis. In particular, there was a view that the structure of remuneration packages within the industry (typically with an emphasis on substantial annual discretionary bonuses and comparatively low base salaries) incentivised misconduct and encouraged employees to seek to maximise profits in the short-term by taking excessive risks.

7.03 The primary stated purpose of the remuneration codes is to ensure greater alignment between risk and individual reward, to discourage excessive risk taking and short-termism and encourage more effective risk management.

7.04 With the original remuneration code, the UK was the first jurisdiction to introduce specific rules regulating remuneration in the industry in response to the financial crisis. The UK's approach reflected the Financial Stability Board's

Principles and Standards on Sound Compensation Practices published in 2009[1] and was later adapted to implement subsequent European legislation, including the Capital Requirements Directive IV (CRD IV), the Alternative Investment Fund Managers Directive (AIFMD), the Undertakings for Collective Investment in Transferable Securities Directive V (UCITS V) and the revised Markets in Financial Instruments Directive (MiFID II).

7.05   The seven remuneration codes are as follows:

- the Remuneration Part of the PRA Rulebook which applies to CRR firms (ie banks, building societies and PRA designated investment firms). (The Remuneration Part, together with SYSC 19A and SYSC 19D referred to below, implements the remuneration requirements of CRD IV);

- the IFPRU Remuneration Code in SYSC 19A of the FCA Handbook which applies to IFPRU investment firms and relevant overseas firms. This includes firms that deal on their own account or underwrite issues of financial instruments or engage in the safekeeping or administration of financial instruments for the account of clients;

- the AIFM Remuneration Code in SYSC 19B of the FCA Handbook which applies to authorised alternative investment fund managers (AIFMs). (SYSC 19B implements the remuneration requirements of AIFMD);

- the BIPRU Remuneration Code in SYSC 19C of the FCA Handbook which applies to BIPRU investment firms such as brokers, investment managers and advisers who are not dealing in financial instruments on their own account or underwriting issues of financial instruments and who do not engage in the safekeeping or administration of financial instruments for the account of clients;

- the Dual-regulated firms Remuneration Code in SYSC 19D of the FCA Handbook which applies to CRR firms (ie banks, building societies and PRA designated investment firms);

- the UCITS Remuneration Code in SYSC 19E of the FCA Handbook which applies to UK UCITS management companies. (SYSC 19E implements the remuneration requirements of UCITS V); and

- the MiFID Remuneration Incentives Code in SYSC 19F of the FCA Handbook which applies to MiFID investment firms and financial advisers and relates to the remuneration and performance management of sales staff. (SYSC 19F implements the remuneration requirements of MiFID II.) The MiFID Remuneration Incentives Code is dealt with in Chapter 9.

7.06   The key principle of the first six of the remuneration codes referred to in the previous paragraph is that firms must ensure that their remuneration policies and practices are consistent with, and promote, sound and effective risk management.

---

1   Supplementary guidance to the Principles and Standards of Sound Compensation Practices was issued in March 2018.

7.07   Each remuneration code is accessible online.[2] Separately, insurers and reinsurers are bound by the remuneration rules contained in the Solvency II Regulation,[3] which is dealt with at 7.256 ff.

7.08   A firm should first establish which of the remuneration codes applies to them and ensure that they comply with the rules under the relevant code. A firm may have to comply with more than one of the remuneration codes. For example, CRR firms (banks, building societies and PRA designated investment firms) are subject to both the PRA's Remuneration Part and the FCA's Dual-regulated firms Remuneration Code. Firms may also be subject to (say) both the AIFM Remuneration Code and the IFPRU or BIPRU Remuneration Codes.

7.09   Firms should also take into account the guidance and policy statements issued at an EU and domestic level.

7.10   At an EU level, the following guidelines issued by the European Banking Authority (EBA) and the European Securities and Markets Authority (ESMA) respectively are of particular importance:

- the EBA published its final guidelines on sound remuneration policies in December 2015 ('the EBA Guidelines'). The EBA Guidelines have applied since 1 January 2017. Although these guidelines are not strictly binding on firms, they set out the EBA's interpretation of the remuneration provisions of CRD IV and are therefore relevant to those firms subject to the PRA's Remuneration Part, SYSC 19A and SYSC 19D. Regulators in each EU jurisdiction were required to confirm whether they intended to comply with the EBA Guidelines or explain why they did not propose to do so. In February 2016 the PRA and the FCA notified the EBA that they would comply with all aspects of the EBA Guidelines except for the provision that the limit on awarding variable remuneration to 100% of fixed remuneration, or 200% with shareholder approval, (known as 'the bonus cap') must be applied to all firms subject to CRD IV (see 7.12 ff);

- ESMA published equivalent guidelines on sound remuneration policies under AIFMD in July 2013 and under UCITS in March 2016 (together referred to in this chapter as 'the ESMA Guidelines'). The FCA notified ESMA of compliance with all aspects of the ESMA Guidelines.

7.11   At a domestic level both the PRA and the FCA have issued extensive guidance on the application and interpretation of the remuneration codes. The PRA's guidance is contained in a number of supervisory and policy statements, in particular SS2/17. Much of the FCA's guidance is contained within the

---

2   The FCA codes can be accessed at: https://www.fca.org.uk/firms/remuneration; the Remuneration Part of the PRA Rulebook can be accessed at: http://www.prarulebook.co.uk/rulebook/Content/Part/292166/15-08-2017.

3   Regulation EU 2015/35.

text of the remuneration codes themselves, although this is supplemented by separate publications.[4]

The remuneration codes: key principle

Remuneration policies and practices must be consistent with and promote sound and effective risk management.

---

2 THE CRD IV REMUNERATION CODES

7.12   As stated at 7.05, the remuneration requirements of CRD IV are implemented by the PRA's Remuneration Part, SYSC 19A and SYSC 19D (together 'the CRD IV Codes'). The CRD IV Codes all contain similar provisions.

Scope of the CRD IV Codes

7.13   The territorial scope of the CRD IV Codes differs depending on whether a firm is a UK firm or an overseas, non-EEA firm.

7.14   For UK firms, the CRD IV Codes apply to all of their activities, whether they are carried on in the UK, in the EEA or elsewhere. For overseas, non-EEA firms the CRD IV Codes only apply to their activities carried on from an establishment in the UK.

7.15   EEA firms (and their UK branches) are subject to the equivalent rules on remuneration in their home state and the CRD IV Codes do not therefore apply to them.

7.16   A UK firm must apply the requirements of the CRD IV Codes to all entities within its group. UK subsidiaries of overseas, non-EEA firms must apply them to their sub-group.

Application to individuals

7.17   The CRD IV Codes apply to remuneration that is paid in connection with 'employment' by a firm. For this purpose, 'employment' means not only employment under a contract of service but also a contract for services. It also

---

4   In the FCA's remuneration codes, those provisions which constitute legally binding rules are indicated by the letter 'R' in the left-hand margin, those provisions which constitute guidance are indicated by the letter 'G' and those provisions compliance with which tends to evidence compliance with a particular rule are indicated by the letter 'E'.

applies to individuals whose services are provided to a firm by a third party. The CRD IV Codes therefore apply not only to employees, but also to consultants, agency workers and secondees.

7.18　　There are certain provisions which firms are expected to apply on a firm-wide basis including, for example, the obligations to ensure that:

- the firm's remuneration policy is consistent with and promotes sound and effective risk management and does not encourage risk taking that exceeds the level of tolerated risk of the firm; and

- payments relating to the early termination of a contract reflect performance achieved over time and are designed in a way that does not reward failure or misconduct.

7.19　　However, other obligations only apply to those members of staff designated as 'material risk takers' in the PRA's Remuneration Part or 'Remuneration Code staff' in SYSC 19A and SYSC 19D (such staff are referred to in this chapter as 'MRTs' or 'Code staff'). Furthermore, some of these obligations can be disapplied for Code staff who satisfy the criteria for the *de minimis* concession (see 7.25).

Who is a 'material risk taker'?

7.20　　The EBA Guidelines provide that firms should carry out an annual assessment to identify all staff whose professional activities have or may have a material impact on the firm's risk profile. This assessment should be based on the qualitative and quantitative criteria set out in Commission Delegated Regulation 604/2014 (Regulatory technical standards to identify staff who are material risk takers) ('the RTS').

7.21　　The RTS provide that an individual is a MRT if he satisfies one or more of a number of criteria. These include:

- qualitative criteria relating to the individual's seniority, role and decision-making power (whether, for example, the individual is a member of senior management, head of a material business unit or responsible for the firm's risk management, compliance or internal audit function); and

- quantitative criteria based on the individual's remuneration. The quantitative criteria apply to individuals who:
  - were awarded total remuneration of €500,000 or more in the preceding financial year;
  - are within the top 0.3% of staff who have been awarded the highest total remuneration in the preceding financial year; or
  - were awarded remuneration in the preceding financial year which was at least equal to the lowest total remuneration awarded to a member of senior management or to any other MRTs.

7.22   Guidance on identifying MRTs is contained in the PRA's Supervisory Statement SS2/17 and in the FCA's Frequently Asked Questions on remuneration (FG17/5). SS2/17 makes it clear that all firms are required to identify MRTs in accordance with the RTS regardless of their size or remuneration proportionality level (see 7.28 ff). This includes UK-headquartered firms, subsidiaries and branches of non-EEA firms. According to SS2/17, the PRA's view is that all staff members carrying out activities which enable them to expose the firm to a material level of risk should be identified as MRTs even where those staff members do not fall within the criteria set out in the RTS. In FG17/5 the FCA also confirms that MRTs include, but are not limited to, those employees identified under the criteria in the RTS.

7.23   Where an individual meets the quantitative, but not any of the qualitative criteria, it is possible for them to be excluded from identification as MRTs. Where their total remuneration in the preceding financial year was between €500,000 and €750,000, this can be done by notification to the PRA or FCA as appropriate. Where their remuneration in the preceding financial year was more than €750,000 or they were in the top 0.3% of high earners, prior approval is required from the PRA or FCA as appropriate. Where their remuneration in the preceding financial year was more than €1m, approval will only be given in exceptional circumstances and the PRA or FCA (as appropriate) must inform the EBA beforehand.

7.24   Firms must maintain a record of their Code staff and take reasonable steps to ensure that they understand the implications of their status as Code staff, including the potential for remuneration which does not comply with certain requirements of the CRD IV Codes to be rendered void and recoverable by their firms.[5]

De minimis concession

7.25   The *de minimis* concession enables a firm to disapply the rules in the CRD IV Codes in relation to:

- guaranteed variable remuneration;

- retained shares or other instruments;

- deferral; and

- performance adjustment;

where an individual satisfies both of the following conditions:

- his variable remuneration is no more than 33% of his total remuneration; and

- his total remuneration is no more than £500,000.

---

5   PRA's Remuneration Part 3.4; SYSC 19A.3.5R; SYSC 19D.3.6.

7.26 This rule is subject to the overall requirement that the firm's remuneration policy is consistent with and promotes sound and effective risk management and does not encourage excessive risk taking.

Part-year Code staff

7.27 The PRA in SS2/17 and the FCA in FG17/6 and FG17/8 have issued detailed guidance on the approach to be taken where an individual has, in relation to a given performance year, only been Code staff for part of the year. Unless an exceptional or irregular payment has been made in relation to their appointment, the rules relating to retained shares and other instruments, deferral and performance adjustment do not need to be applied to individuals who have been Code staff for less than three months in the relevant performance year. Where the individual has been Code staff for more than three months, then those rules will need to be applied to a proportion of the individual's remuneration, unless the *de minimis* concession applies.

Proportionality: level one, two and three firms

7.28 Article 92(2) of CRD IV provides that the rules relating to remuneration should be applied by firms in a manner and to the extent that is appropriate to their size, internal organisation and the nature, scope and complexity of their activities. This is known as the *principle of proportionality*.

7.29 In the UK this principle has been applied by the PRA and FCA by categorising firms into one of three proportionality levels based on their total assets. A firm's level then dictates the extent to which it is required to comply with the CRD IV Codes. Proportionality level one is the highest level requiring the greatest degree of compliance and proportionality level three is the lowest.

The PRA Rulebook: proportionality

7.30 Rule 5.1 of the PRA's Remuneration Part reflects Article 92(2) and requires a relevant firm, when establishing and applying the total remuneration policies for MRTs, to comply with the Remuneration Part in a way and to the extent that is appropriate to its size, internal organisation and the nature, scope and complexity of its activities.

7.31 The PRA's expectations on how firms should comply with Rule 5.1 are set out in its supervisory statement SS2/17. SS2/17 provides guidance on the process for dividing firms into proportionality levels and the extent to which firms in particular proportionality levels are required to comply with the CRD IV Codes.

7.32   The table below, which is reproduced from SS2/17, sets out how firms are divided into the proportionality levels.

Proportionality level	Type of firm	Relevant total assets on relevant date of firm[6]
Proportionality level one	Bank, building society or full scope investment firm	Exceeding £50bn
Proportionality level two	Bank, building society or full scope investment firm	Exceeding £15 bn, but not exceeding £50 bn
Proportionality level three	Bank or building society	Not exceeding £15 bn
	Full scope investment firm	Not exceeding £15 bn
	Limited licence investment firm or limited licence investment firm	Not applicable

7.33   Where a firm is part of a group which contains other firms which are also subject to the PRA's Remuneration Part then it will be allocated to the proportionality level of the firm in the group with the highest proportionality level. As a result, all firms in a group should be subject to the same remuneration rules.

7.34   However, the PRA may consider providing individual guidance to vary a firm's proportionality level. This may be either up or down. SS2/17 gives a number of examples of circumstances where such guidance may be given. These include where a firm is just below the threshold for a particular proportionality level but its business model or growth strategy suggest that it should fall within a higher level, or where a firm falls into a higher proportionality level than would otherwise be the case because it is a member of a group containing a firm with a higher proportionality level.

7.35   The PRA considers it may be appropriate for firms in proportionality level three to disapply the rules relating to:

- retained shares or other instruments;
- deferral;
- performance adjustment including the rules relating to clawback; and
- buy-outs.

7.36   The PRA also takes the view that, while proportionality level three firms must maintain an appropriate balance between fixed and variable remuneration, the 'bonus cap' in Rule 15.9(3), which limits variable remuneration to 100% of fixed remuneration (or 200% with shareholder approval) applies to proportionality level one and two firms only.

---

6   Broadly, this means the average of the firm's total assets on the firm's last three accounting reference dates or, for overseas (non-EEA) firms, the average of the firm's total assets that covered the activities of the UK branch as at 31 December for the last three years.

7.37 In addition, the PRA considers that, whilst firms in proportionality levels one and two should establish remuneration committees, it may be appropriate for the governing body of level three firms to act as the remuneration committee.

FCA general guidance on proportionality

7.38 The FCA has published its own general guidance on proportionality on the IFPRU Remuneration Code in SYSC19A[7] and on the Dual-regulated firms Remuneration Code in SYSC 19D.[8] To all intents and purposes, this reflects the guidance issued by the PRA in SS2/17.

7.39 The FCA's guidance makes it clear that the disapplication of the rules on retained shares and other instruments, deferral, performance adjustment and the bonus cap for proportionality level three firms is not automatic. In all cases the relevant firm should assess whether the requirements may be disapplied under the proportionality rule. The FCA expects a firm's senior management to be able to demonstrate why the firm believes it is reasonable to disapply the relevant rule.

EBA Guidelines and proportionality

7.40 It is important to note that the guidance issued by the PRA and the FCA is not entirely consistent with what the EBA Guidelines say about proportionality. The EBA's view is that CRD IV sets out minimum requirements with which all relevant firms should comply. In particular, the EBA Guidelines state that the limitation on the maximum ratio between fixed and variable remuneration to 100% (or 200% with shareholders' approval) should be applied to all MRTs in firms subject to CRD IV and their subsidiaries even if those subsidiaries are not themselves subject to CRD IV.

7.41 In February 2016 the PRA and the FCA notified the EBA that they did not intend to comply with this aspect of the EBA Guidelines. As the EBA Guidelines do not have the force of law in the UK, proportionality level three firms in the UK may continue to disapply the bonus cap.

7.42 In November 2016 the European Commission published proposals to amend CRD IV. These included a proposed amendment to clarify that the rules on remuneration applied to all firms and their MRTs except for those below certain thresholds. However, under the proposal the exception would only allow for the disapplication of the rules on deferral and payment in instruments for:

- a firm with average assets less than or equal to €5bn in the preceding four years; and

7   FG17/6.
8   FG17/8.

- staff members whose annual variable remuneration does not exceed €50,000 and does not represent more than 25% of the staff member's annual total remuneration.

7.43   The proposed amendment (which is contained in the latest draft of the new CRD V Directive presented to the Council of the European Union on 25 May 2018) does not therefore provide for any relaxation of the bonus cap for smaller firms and still represents a much stricter position on proportionality than that currently adopted by the PRA and the FCA.

Fixed and variable remuneration

7.44   Before considering the detailed requirements of the CRD IV Codes, it is worth exploring the distinction between fixed and variable remuneration.

7.45   Under the CRD IV Codes:

- fixed remuneration primarily reflects an employee's professional experience and organisational responsibility as set out in the employee's job description and terms of employment; and

- variable remuneration reflects performance in excess of that required to fulfil the employee's job description and terms of employment.

7.46   It is variable remuneration, rather than fixed remuneration, that is subject to performance adjustment under the CRD IV Codes.

7.47   For guidance on the distinction it is necessary to refer to the EBA Guidelines. The EBA Guidelines make it clear that under CRD IV remuneration is either fixed or variable; there is no third category. Unless a remuneration component can clearly be designated as fixed remuneration in accordance with the criteria in the EBA Guidelines, then it should be considered as variable remuneration. To determine what is variable remuneration, it is therefore necessary first to work out which elements of remuneration will be regarded as fixed.

7.48   The EBA states that remuneration is *fixed* where the conditions for its award and its amount:

- are based on predetermined criteria;

- are non-discretionary reflecting the level of professional experience and seniority of staff;

- are transparent with respect to the individual amount awarded to the individual staff member;

- are permanent, ie maintained over a period tied to the specific role and organisational responsibilities;

- are non-revocable; the permanent amount is only changed via collective bargaining or following renegotiation in line with national criteria on wage setting;

- cannot be reduced, suspended or cancelled by the firm;

- do not provide incentives for risk assumption; and

- do not depend on performance.[9]

7.49 Fixed pay is often easy to recognise, the most obvious examples being an employee's base salary and typical benefits such as monthly pension contributions, private medical insurance and life insurance. The EBA Guidelines also provide that the following remuneration components should be considered as fixed, where all similar situations are treated in a consistent way: (a) remuneration paid to expatriate staff to address additional costs of living and higher tax rates in a different country; and (b) subject to certain conditions being met, allowances used to increase the basic fixed salary for staff working abroad and receiving less remuneration than would be paid on the local employment market for a comparable position.

Role-based allowances

7.50 The most controversial issue in relation to the distinction between fixed and variable remuneration has been the use of role-based allowances (RBAs). Following the introduction of the bonus cap, many firms recognised that they needed to substantially increase fixed pay for their Code staff in order to be able to maintain the amount of their total remuneration. Rather than doing this by increasing base salary (which would have an impact on the calculation of other benefits and be difficult to reduce), they sought to do this by the introduction of 'fixed' or 'role-based' allowances. These RBAs initially took a number of different forms, but in many cases they were drafted in such a way that the firm could vary, withdraw or suspend them in certain circumstances. They were therefore seen by the EBA as a means by which firms were evading the bonus cap by paying additional amounts to staff which, whilst appearing to be fixed, were in fact variable.

7.51 The EBA Guidelines specifically address the issue of allowances. In order for them to be categorised as fixed remuneration, they must meet the requirements of fixed remuneration referred to at 7.48. In addition, the following factors should be taken into account:

- the allowance should be tied to a role or organisational responsibility and awarded as long as no material changes happen regarding the responsibilities and authorities of the role so that in fact the staff would have a different role or organisational responsibility;

9   EBA Guidelines, para 117.

- the amount of the allowance should not depend on any factors other than fulfilling a certain role or having a certain organisational responsibility and reflecting criteria such as their professional experience; and

- any other staff member fulfilling the same role or having the same organisational responsibility and who is in a comparable situation would be entitled to a comparable allowance.

7.52   In practice, the use of RBAs remains widespread, although as a result of the EBA Guidelines, they now tend to be structured so that:

- they are granted and paid for the period of time that the individual undertakes the relevant role;

- they are non-forfeitable; and

- they may only be varied with the individual's consent.

Ratio of fixed remuneration to variable remuneration and the bonus cap

7.53   Article 94(f) of CRD IV provides that the fixed and variable components of total remuneration must be appropriately balanced and that the fixed component must represent a sufficiently high proportion of the total remuneration to allow the operation of a fully flexible policy on variable remuneration components, including the possibility to pay no variable remuneration component.

7.54   Furthermore, Article 94(g) provides that firms must set appropriate ratios between the fixed and the variable component of the total remuneration and the variable component must not exceed 100% of the fixed component of the total remuneration for each individual. Member states may set a lower percentage and may allow a firm's shareholders to approve a higher maximum ratio provided that the variable remuneration component does not exceed 200% of the fixed remuneration component.

7.55   The PRA and FCA have implemented these provisions in the PRA's Remuneration Part 15.11, SYSC 19A.3.44 and SYSC 19D.3.48R to SYSC 19D.3.49R.

7.56   With very limited exceptions,[10] firms in all three proportionality levels (see 7.28 ff) are required to comply with the requirement to maintain an appropriate balance between fixed and variable remuneration and to ensure that fixed remuneration is sufficiently high to allow them to apply a fully flexible policy on variable remuneration. In practice, this means that the proportion of fixed remuneration should not be so low that firms consider that they have to

---

10   The FCA has stated in FG17/6 and FG17/8 that it may be appropriate for limited licence firms and limited activity firms to disapply the ratios between fixed and variable components of total remuneration in SYSC 19D.3.48R.

award some element of variable remuneration even when this is not justified by the firm's financial performance and profitability. This is reinforced by the EBA Guidelines which state that staff should not be dependent on the award of variable remuneration as this might otherwise create incentives for short-term-oriented excessive risk taking.[11]

7.57   However, as explained at 7.36, the PRA and the FCA take the view that the rule that variable remuneration should not exceed 100% of fixed remuneration (or up to 200% with shareholder approval) may be disapplied by firms in proportionality level three.

7.58   The procedure for firms obtaining approval to increase the ratio from 100% to up to 200% is set out in PRA's Remuneration Part 15.11, SYSC 19A.3.44A to SYSC 19A.3.44C and SYSC 19D.3.49 to SYSC 19D.3.51R.

7.59   In summary, to increase the ratio from 100% to up to 200%, firms must obtain the approval of at least 66% of the firm's shareholders (although this threshold rises to 75% if less than 50% of the shares or equivalent ownership rights are represented). For this purpose the PRA considers that these percentage thresholds should be calculated by reference to the shares or other ownership rights in the firm which, in turn, means the voting rights capable of being cast on the relevant resolution and which attach to the shares or ownership rights.[12]

7.60   Firms must notify the PRA and/or the FCA (as appropriate) without delay of any recommendations to shareholders to increase the ratio and the reasons for it. They must also demonstrate that the proposed higher ratio does not conflict with the firm's obligations under CRD IV and the CRR.

7.61   One question that has arisen is who the firm's shareholders are for this purpose. This is particularly relevant in a group context where a firm's only shareholder is its parent company. In its policy statement PS7/13 the PRA said that it expected firms wishing to increase the ratio to obtain the approval by seeking a resolution of the shareholders of the ultimate EEA parent. For UK-headquartered banking groups or subsidiaries of EEA-headquartered groups, this would require shareholders of the ultimate EEA parent to increase the ratio for the group as a whole. For UK subsidiaries of non-EEA firms, the PRA said that it would accept a resolution of the immediate non-EEA parent company. Branches of non-EEA firms are expected to obtain approval from the shareholders of the relevant non-EEA firm.

---

11 EBA Guidelines, para 183.
12 SS2/17, para 5.40.

Variable pay in shares, share-linked or equivalent non-cash instruments

7.62   The CRD IV Codes provide that at least 50% of variable remuneration must consist of an appropriate balance of:

* shares or equivalent ownership interests, share-linked instruments or for non-listed firms equivalent non-cash instruments; and

* where possible, other instruments that adequately reflect the credit quality of the firm as a going concern and are appropriate for use as variable remuneration.[13]

7.63   The instruments must be subject to an appropriate retention period which is designed to align incentives with the longer-term interests of the firm.[14]

7.64   These rules apply both to the portion of the remuneration component that is deferred and the portion that is not deferred. Provided that at least 50% of each portion is paid in instruments, it is not necessary for each portion to have the same split between cash and instruments. The EBA Guidelines state that, where firms award a higher portion than 50% of variable remuneration in instruments, they should prioritise a higher share of instruments within the deferred portion of the variable remuneration component. The FCA has also stated in FG17/5 that it considers it good practice for the deferred portion of variable remuneration to contain a higher proportion of instruments.

7.65   The EBA Guidelines state that instruments paid as variable remuneration should be subject to a retention period of at least one year, although where the deferral period is at least five years, a retention period of at least six months for the deferred portion may be imposed for Code staff who are not members of the management body or senior management.[15]

7.66   The EBA Guidelines also provide that firms should not pay any interest or dividends on instruments which have been awarded as variable remuneration under deferral arrangements either during or at the end of the deferral period.[16]

7.67   As stated at 7.35, the rules on paying variable remuneration instruments may be disapplied by proportionality level three firms and in the case of Code staff who satisfy the *de minimis* criteria.

---

13 Regulation 527/2014 sets out the type of instruments that are considered appropriate.
14 PRA's Remuneration Part 15.15; SYSC 19A.3.47R; SYSC19D.3.56R.
15 EBA Guidelines, para 267.
16 EBA Guidelines, para 258.

Establishing the bonus pool and *ex-ante* adjustments

7.68   When measuring financial performance for the purpose of establishing a bonus pool or components of variable remuneration, firms must ensure that their assessments:

- take into account the cost and quantity of the capital and the liquidity required;

- include adjustments for all types of current and future risks; and

- take into account the need for consistency with the timing and likelihood of the firm receiving potential future revenues incorporated into current earnings.[17]

7.69   Firms must base their assessments of financial performance principally on profits.[18] To determine profits, the PRA's Remuneration Part states that firms must adjust their fair value accounting model profit figure by the incremental change in its regulatory prudent valuation adjustment figure across the relevant performance period.

7.70   Firms must ensure that total variable remuneration is generally considerably contracted where subdued or negative financial performance occurs, taking into account both current remuneration and reductions in remuneration previously awarded through malus or clawback arrangements.[19]

7.71   Firms must apply both ex-ante adjustment and ex-post adjustment. Ex-post adjustment (which adjusts remuneration after it has been awarded on the occurrence of specific events) is considered at 7.85 ff. Ex-ante adjustment adjusts remuneration before it has been awarded to take account of the intrinsic risks that are inherent in a firm's business activities.[20]

7.72   Ex-ante adjustment should take into account not only financial risks but also non-financial risks. In FG17/5 the FCA gave the following examples of non-financial risks that should be taken into account notwithstanding that they may be difficult to measure:

- building and maintaining positive customer relationships;

- reputation;

- achieving in line with the firm's strategy and values; and

- effectiveness and operation of the risk and control environment.

7.73   Although the PRA and the FCA do not prescribe the process that firms should follow when risk-adjusting their bonus pools, they do say that firms

17   PRA's Remuneration Part 11.1; SYSC 19A.3.22R; SYSC 19D.3.23R.
18   PRA's Remuneration Part 11.3; SYSC 19A.3.25R; SYSC 19D.3.27R.
19   PRA's Remuneration Part 11.6; SYSC 19A.3.27R; SYSC 19D.3.29R.
20   PRA's Remuneration Part 11.4; SYSC 19D.3.29R.

should have a risk adjustment framework that provides a clear and verifiable mechanism for measuring performance which leads to risk adjustments being made in a clear and transparent manner.[21]

7.74   Firms should be able to provide the PRA and/or the FCA as appropriate with details of all the adjustments that have been made whether through the application of formulae or the exercise of discretion.[22] The FCA suggests that this can be done by setting out the stages involved in determining the final bonus pool, with adjustments separately distinguishable for major risk and performance considerations, and any collective adjustments in relation to ex-post risk adjustment made at the end of the process.[23]

Awards of variable remuneration

7.75   Firms must ensure that performance-related remuneration is based on a combination of the assessment of the performance of the individual, the business unit concerned and the overall results of the firm. When assessing individual performance, financial and non-financial criteria must be taken into account.[24] For these purposes, the non-financial criteria should include the extent of the individual's adherence to effective risk management and compliance with applicable regulatory requirements. In appropriate circumstances, non-financial criteria should override financial criteria.[25]

7.76   Performance should be assessed in a multi-year framework to ensure that the assessment process is based on longer-term performance and that the payment of performance-based components of remuneration is spread over a period which takes account of the underlying business cycle of the firm and its business risks.[26]

Deferral

7.77   The deferral of a proportion of variable remuneration is a key tool for aligning incentives with risk in that:

●   the value of deferred variable remuneration which is awarded in the form of instruments should (at least in theory) go up or down in accordance with the overall performance of the firm thereby incentivising individuals not to take excessive risks; and

●   through the application of malus (see 7.85 ff) it gives the firm an opportunity to adjust the amount of the deferred variable remuneration to take into

---

21   SS2/17, para 5.16; SYSC 19D.3.25R.
22   SS2/17, para 5.17; SYSC 19A.3.23G; SYSC 19D.3.24G.
23   FG17/5, para 6.7.
24   PRA's Remuneration Part 15.4; SYSC 19A.3.36R; SYSC 19D.3.39R.
25   SYSC 19A.3.37G; SYSC 19D.3.41G.
26   PRA's Remuneration Part, 15.6; SYSC 19A.3.38R; SYSC 19D.3.43R.

account any risks that have crystallised during the deferral period, instances of individual misconduct uncovered, any failures of risk management and the subsequent performance of the firm and/or relevant business.

7.78   In order to ensure effective risk management, the deferral period should reflect the timeframe during which risks are likely to crystallise and the results of poor performance, poor risk management or misconduct come to light.

7.79   Under PRA's Remuneration Part 15.17, SYSC 19A.3.49R and SYSC 19D.3.59R, firms must defer at least 40% of variable pay awarded to Code staff who do not satisfy the *de minimis* exemption. Where the variable remuneration component is £500,000 or more, or is payable to a director of a firm that is significant in terms of its size, internal organisation and the nature, scope and complexity of its activities (ie a proportionality level one firm), then at least 60% of the variable remuneration award must be deferred.[27] However, the PRA states in SS2/17 that firms should also consider whether this deferral ratio should be applied in cases of variable remuneration awarded below £500,000.[28]

7.80   The period of deferral varies depending on the role being undertaken by the relevant individual. For firms subject to the PRA Remuneration Part then:

- for Code staff who are performing a PRA designated senior management function, the deferral period is no less than seven years with no vesting taking place until three years after the award and vesting no faster than on a pro rata basis;

- for Code staff who do not perform a PRA designated senior management function, but who satisfy certain of the qualitative criteria in the RTS[29] (often referred to as 'risk managers') the deferral period is no less than five years with vesting no faster than on a pro rata basis; and

- for all other Code staff, no less than three years with vesting no faster than on a pro rata basis.

7.81   For firms that are not subject to the PRA Remuneration Part and are authorised and regulated by the FCA only, then the deferral period must not be less than three to five years with vesting no faster than on a pro rata basis.[30]

---

27 PRA's Remuneration Part, 15.8; SYSC 19A.3.49R; SYSC 19D.3.59R.
28 SS2/17, para 5.44.
29 For example, they are members of the firm's management body or senior management; are responsible for the risk management, compliance or internal audit functions; head (or report directly to the head of) a material business unit; or head a function such as legal affairs, finance, human resources or information technology.
30 SYSC 19A.3.49R.

Policy on deferral

7.82   Whilst the requirements strictly only apply to Code staff who do not satisfy the *de minimis* exemption, the PRA states in SS2/17 that it expects firms to have a firm-wide policy (and a group-wide policy where appropriate) on deferral and that the proportion of variable remuneration deferred should generally rise with the ratio of variable remuneration to fixed remuneration and with the quantum of variable remuneration awarded.[31] See also 7.85 ff on performance adjustment.

7.83   Guidance in SYSC 19A and SYSC 19D states that the FCA expects firms to apply at least the principles relating to deferral 'on a firm-wide basis'.[32] This suggests that, when applying deferral to staff who are not caught by the strict requirements in the CRD IV Codes, it is not necessary for firms to apply the same percentages and deferral periods and they may consider it appropriate to defer a lower percentage of variable remuneration and/or apply shorter deferral periods.

Proportionality level three firms

7.84   As stated at 7.35, proportionality level three firms may consider it appropriate to disapply the strict requirements relating to deferral altogether, although they should be prepared to justify their approach to the PRA or the FCA as appropriate. They should also consider having a firm-wide policy on deferral as a matter of best practice and in accordance with the general requirement to ensure that their remuneration policies are consistent with, and promote, sound and effective risk management.

Performance adjustment: malus and clawback

7.85   CRD IV states that variable remuneration, including the deferred portion, should only be paid or vest if it is sustainable according to the financial situation of the firm as a whole and is justified on the basis of the performance of the firm, the business unit and the individual concerned. Up to 100% of total variable remuneration should be subject to malus or clawback arrangements.

What is malus and clawback?

7.86   Malus is defined in the EBA Guidelines as an arrangement that permits the firm to reduce the value of all or part of deferred variable remuneration based on ex-post risk adjustments before it has vested. Clawback is defined as an arrangement under which the individual has to return ownership of an amount

---

31   SS2/17, para 5.44.
32   SYSC 19A.2.3G; SYSC 19D.2.2G.

of variable remuneration paid in the past or which has already vested to the firm under certain conditions.

7.87 As the PRA explains in SS2/17, performance adjustment (ie the use of malus and clawback) allows firms to adjust remuneration to take account of risks that have subsequently crystallised. This includes instances of employee misbehaviour or material error, material downturn in performance or a material failure of risk management.[33]

The rules on performance adjustment

7.88 The general requirement in CRD IV that variable remuneration must only be paid or vest if it is sustainable according to the financial situation of the firm as a whole and justified on the basis of the performance of the firm, the business unit and the individual concerned is reflected in the CRD IV Codes.[34]

7.89 The CRD IV Codes also require firms to set specific criteria for the application of malus and clawback and to ensure that they cover situations where the employee:

- participated in or was responsible for conduct which resulted in significant losses to the firm; or

- failed to meet appropriate standards of fitness and propriety.[35]

7.90 The CRD IV Codes go on to provide that, as a minimum, a firm should reduce unvested deferred variable remuneration when:

- there is reasonable evidence of employee misbehaviour or material error;

- the firm or relevant business unit suffers a material downturn in its financial performance; or

- the firm or the relevant business unit suffers a material failure of risk management.[36]

7.91 Although what is stated is an evidential requirement rather than a rule, contravention of this provision tends to establish contravention of the general requirement in the PRA's Remuneration Part 15.20(1), SYSC 19A.3.51 and SYSC 19D.3.61(1).

7.92 Furthermore, PRA authorised firms must make all reasonable efforts to recover an appropriate amount corresponding to some or all vested variable

---

33 Paragraph 4.4 of SS2/17 makes it clear that firms should not only rely on malus and clawback in these circumstances. They should also consider making reductions to in-year variable remuneration awards.
34 PRA's Remuneration Part 15.20(1); SYSC 19A.3.51R; SYSC 19D.3.61(1)R.
35 PRA's Remuneration Part 15.21; SYSC 19A.3.51AR; SYSC 19D.3.62R.
36 PRA's Remuneration Part 15.22; SYSC 19A.3.52E; SYSC 19D.3.63E.

remuneration when either of the following circumstances arise during the period in which clawback applies (which may be after the employee's employment has ended):

- there is reasonable evidence of employee misbehaviour or material error; or

- the firm or the relevant business unit has suffered a material failure of risk management.[37]

7.93   In deciding whether and to what extent it is reasonable to seek recovery of any or all of an employee's vested variable remuneration, a firm must take into account all relevant factors including, in the case of a material failure of risk management, the proximity of the employee to the failure and their level of responsibility.[38]

7.94   As for the period in which variable remuneration should potentially be subject to performance adjustment, PRA authorised firms must ensure that:

- any variable remuneration is subject to clawback for a period of at least seven years from the date on which it was awarded; and

- in the case of an MRT who performs a PRA senior management function, the firm can within that seven-year period give a notice to the employee to extend it to at least ten years from the date on which it was awarded where:
  - the firm has commenced an investigation into facts or events which it considers could potentially lead to the application of clawback; or
  - the firm has been notified by a regulatory authority (including an overseas regulatory authority) that an investigation has been commenced into facts or events which the firm considers could potentially lead to the application of clawback by the firm.[39]

7.95   The prescriptive rules relating to performance adjustment only apply to Code staff who do not satisfy the *de minimis* exemption. However, as with deferral, the PRA states in SS2/17 that it generally expects PRA authorised firms to have a firm-wide policy (and a group-wide policy where appropriate) on performance adjustment.[40]

7.96   As stated at 7.35, proportionality level three firms may consider it appropriate to disapply the strict requirements relating to performance adjustment altogether, although they should be prepared to justify their approach to the PRA or the FCA as appropriate. They should also consider having a firm-wide policy on performance adjustment as a matter of best practice and in accordance with the general requirement to ensure that their remuneration policies are consistent with, and promote, sound and effective risk management.

---

37 PRA's Remuneration Part 15.23; SYSC 19D.3.64(1)R.
38 PRA's Remuneration Part 15.23; SYSC 19D.3.64(2)R.
39 PRA's Remuneration Part 15.20; SYSC 19D.3.61R.
40 SS2/17, para 4.10.

PRA guidance on performance adjustment

7.97   Detailed guidance on the PRA's expectations in relation to performance adjustment and the application of malus and clawback is contained in SS2/17.[41] Key points to note from this guidance are as follows:

- A firm's remuneration policies and employment contracts should make it clear that, among other things, variable remuneration awards are conditional, discretionary and contingent upon a sustainable and risk-adjusted performance and may be subject to forfeiture or reduction at the employer's discretion. Firms should maintain adequate records of remuneration awards made to both current and former employees should recovery of vested remuneration be required in the future.

- The use of performance adjustment should not be limited to employees directly culpable of malfeasance. For example, in cases involving a material failure of risk management or misconduct, firms should consider applying performance adjustment to those employees who:
  - were aware (or could reasonably have been expected to be aware) of the failure or misconduct but failed to take adequate steps to address it;
  - by virtue of their role or seniority could be deemed indirectly responsible or accountable for the failure or misconduct including senior staff responsible for setting the firm's culture or strategy; and
  - by virtue of their seniority within control functions could be considered responsible for weaknesses and failings in control functions relevant to the failure or misconduct.

- Firms can apply performance adjustment to variable remuneration even where the variable remuneration being adjusted does not relate to performance in the year in which the misconduct or risk management failure occurred or came to light.

- Firms should develop adequate procedures for deciding cases that could result in reductions to in-year variable remuneration or in the use of malus and clawback. These procedures could either be part of, or sit alongside, a firm's disciplinary procedures. Among other things, the performance adjustment procedure should:
  - promote consistency, fairness and robustness in the application of performance adjustment;
  - set specific, indicative criteria on the kinds of cases that may trigger the use of performance adjustment; and
  - set out a clear process for determining culpability, responsibility or accountability, including allowing individuals under investigation to make representations.

- Where an individual is subject to an internal or external investigation which could result in performance adjustment, a firm should freeze the vesting of

---

41   To a large extent this guidance reflects the guidance given by the FCA in its general guidance on the application of ex-post risk adjustment to variable remuneration under SYSC 19D which was published in July 2015.

their awards until the investigation has concluded and the firm has made and communicated its decision.

Practical guidance

Firms should ensure that they have the contractual right to freeze variable pay pending investigations to avoid the risk of a breach of contract claim.

- Firms should ensure that the value of, and reasons for, performance adjustments are clearly communicated in writing to affected individuals. Where reductions are made to in-year remuneration awards, there should be a clear process for determining the amount of variable remuneration that would have been awarded had the adjustment not been made.

- When deciding on the amount of any performance adjustment, the criteria that firms should take into account include:
  - the cost of fines and other regulatory actions;
  - direct and indirect financial losses attributable to the relevant failure;
  - reputational damage;
  - the impact on the firm's relationships with its stakeholders including shareholders, customers, employees, counterparties and regulators;
  - the impact on profitability;
  - the timeframe during which the event occurred and whether losses or costs are still accumulating;
  - the extent of customer detriment; and
  - redress costs.

7.98   Firms should be able to clearly quantify and articulate the impact of any performance adjustment on bonus pools and record the methodology used so that the value of each adjustment can be determined.

Introducing malus and clawback provisions

7.99   The CRD IV Codes do not themselves confer a right on firms to apply performance adjustment. Rather, firms are under an obligation to ensure that they have introduced appropriate provisions into their employees' employment contracts, incentive plan rules or other contractual documentation. In practice, many firms have introduced performance adjustment (or malus and clawback) policies and ensured that awards of variable remuneration are made subject to their terms.

7.100   In the absence of consent from the employee or a clear right to make a unilateral variation, malus and clawback provisions cannot generally be retrospectively introduced so that they apply to existing awards. This problem was highlighted in *Daniels v Lloyds Bank Plc*[42] in which it was held that Lloyds

---

42   [2018] EWHC 660 (Comm).

Bank had unlawfully sought to introduce and apply a malus provision to existing awards under a long-term incentive plan without the consent of the relevant individuals.

Malus and clawback: other employment law considerations

7.101   Exercising clawback and requiring employees to repay amounts of variable remuneration potentially falls foul of s 15 of the Employment Rights Act 1996 which provides that an employer may not receive a payment from a worker it employs unless:

- the payment is required or authorised to be made by virtue of a statutory provision or a relevant provision of the worker's contract; or

- the worker has previously signified in writing their agreement or consent to the making of the payment.

7.102   As the CRD IV Codes do not constitute statutory provisions which authorise such payments, it is important that firms have appropriate provisions in their contracts with their employees authorising deductions.

7.103   A firm exercising its discretion to apply malus or clawback will be subject to the same rules that apply to the exercise of a discretion when making an initial award of a bonus. These rules are dealt with in Chapter 8. When applying malus or clawback rights, a firm must therefore exercise its discretion in good faith and, following *Braganza v BP Shipping Ltd*,[43] should ensure that it takes into account all relevant factors and disregards irrelevant factors.

7.104   It has also been suggested that clawback provisions may in certain circumstances be open to challenge on the grounds that they amount to an unenforceable penalty. In practice, such challenges are unlikely to be successful following the Supreme Court's decision in *Cavendish Square Holdings BV v Makdessi*.[44]

Clawback on a gross or net of tax basis?

7.105   Firms also need to consider whether the drafting of their clawback provisions should allow for repayment of the gross amount of the variable remuneration which is subject to the adjustment or the amount that the employee received net of tax. Indeed, it may be advisable to draft the provision in such a way that the firm has the discretion to choose the basis on which clawback is effected.

43   [2015] ICR 449.
44   [2015] UKSC 67, [2016] AC 1172.

7.106   If repayment is made on a gross basis, then the employee will not be entitled to repayment from HMRC of the income tax and national insurance contributions that were originally deducted from the gross amount. However, based on the Upper Tribunal's decision in *HMRC v Julian Martin*[45] and the guidance published by HMRC in paras EIM00800 to 00845 of the HMRC Employment Income Manual, the amounts repaid may be treated as negative taxable earnings enabling the employee to claim tax relief.

Practical guidance

Ensure that contractual provisions on clawback specify whether clawback is made on a gross or net of tax basis. Alternatively, give the firm discretion to choose which basis to apply.

Guaranteed variable pay

7.107   Prior to the introduction of the remuneration codes, it was common practice for banks and other financial institutions to provide guaranteed bonuses to members of staff and, in particular, senior members of staff. Such bonuses were typically (but by no means exclusively) offered to new recruits and often applied not only to the current bonus year but for a number of subsequent years as well.

7.108   Such bonuses are now generally considered to be inconsistent with sound risk management. This is reflected in Article 94(1)(d) of CRD IV which states that 'guaranteed variable remuneration is not consistent with sound risk management or the pay-for-performance principle and shall not be a part of prospective remuneration plans'. The circumstances in which guaranteed variable remuneration may be acceptable are now very limited and are prescribed in Article 94(1)(e).

7.109   The EBA Guidelines recognise that guaranteed variable remuneration can take several forms such as a guaranteed bonus, a sign-on bonus or a minimum bonus and that they can be awarded in either cash or in instruments.[46] Typically, a bonus is regarded as 'guaranteed' if it will be paid to the employee regardless of the performance of the firm, the relevant business unit or the employee. Such bonuses are often only conditional on the employee not resigning or being dismissed for misconduct before the payment is made or the award vests.

7.110   The rules in the CRD IV Codes regarding guaranteed variable remuneration reflect the requirements of Article 94(1)(e) of CRD IV and provide that firms must not award guaranteed variable remuneration unless:

---

45 [2014] UKUT 429 (TCC).
46 EBA Guidelines, para 137.

- it is exceptional;

- it occurs in the context of hiring new Code staff;

- the firm has a strong and sound capital base; and

- it is limited to the first year of service.[47]

7.111 What is meant by 'exceptional' in this context? The guidance on this from the PRA and the FCA states that guaranteed variable awards should not be the norm or common practice and should be limited to rare, infrequent occurrences.[48]

7.112 Do these rules only apply to the hiring of Code staff? Although there was previously some uncertainty as to whether the rules on guaranteed variable remuneration applied more widely, it is now clear that they only apply to Code staff who do not fall within the *de minimis* exemption. Firms are not required to apply the rules on a firm-wide basis.

7.113 Should guaranteed variable remuneration be subject to the rules on instruments, deferral and performance adjustment? The PRA and FCA guidance make it clear that guaranteed remuneration should be subject to the same rules that apply to other forms of variable remuneration awarded by the firm.[49] These include the rules relating to payment in instruments, deferral and performance adjustment. For the purposes of the bonus cap, the PRA's guidance also confirms that guaranteed variable remuneration should be included in the variable component of the fixed to variable ratio for the relevant performance period in which the award is made.

7.114 Firms are not required to give prior notification to the PRA or FCA of awards of guaranteed variable remuneration awards. However, the PRA guidance states that all guaranteed variable remuneration awards should be documented and included in a firm's annual remuneration policy statement.[50]

Retention awards

7.115 Retention awards (ie awards which are contingent on an individual remaining in employment with the firm for a period of time) differ from guaranteed variable remuneration.[51]

7.116 The EBA Guidelines confirm that they may be used in in the context of restructurings, in wind-downs of a business or following a change of control.[52]

47 PRA's Remuneration Part 15.7; SYSC 19A.3.40R; SYSC 19.D.3.44R.
48 SS2/17, para 5.31; SYSC 19A.3.43G; SYSC 19D.3.46G.
49 SS2/17, para 5.33; SYSC 19A.3.42G; SYSC 19D.3.46G.
50 SS2/17, para 5.34.
51 SS2/17, para 5.38; PS17/10.
52 EBA Guidelines paragraph 128

However, as with guaranteed variable remuneration, the FCA expects that retention awards should not be common practice for Code staff and should be limited to rare, infrequent occurrences.[53]

7.117   PRA authorised firms should notify the PRA and FCA as appropriate before they award any retention bonuses[54] and provide justification when a retention award is offered to an MRT. In such cases the PRA will consider whether the award is appropriate.[55]

7.118   Furthermore, retention payments must comply with the requirements on variable pay, including ex-post risk adjustment, payment in instruments, deferral, retention, malus and clawback[56] and form part of variable remuneration for the purpose of the ratio between fixed and variable components of remuneration.[57]

7.119   The EBA Guidelines make it clear that retention bonuses should not be awarded to compensate for the fact that performance-related remuneration has not been paid due to insufficient performance or a firm's financial situation.[58]

Buy-outs of variable remuneration

7.120   It is common practice in the financial services industry that, when an employee moves to a new firm, the new firm will make an award to the employee to 'buy out' the deferred remuneration that the employee will forfeit on leaving his current firm.

7.121   For PRA authorised firms detailed rules relating to buy-outs agreed on or after 1 January 2017 are set out in the PRA's Remuneration Part 15A.

7.122   These rules provide that before agreeing to provide a buy-out a firm must obtain a 'remuneration statement' from the employee.[59] The remuneration statement is a statement that must be provided to the employee by his previous firm within 14 working days of the employee's request. The remuneration statement must contain the following information:

● all periods during which the employee was a MRT;

● the amount of unvested variable remuneration available to be bought out applicable to the periods during which the employee was a MRT ('available unvested variable remuneration'); and

---

53   SYSC 19A.3.43G; SYSC 19D.3.46G.
54   SYSC 2/17, para 5.39; SYSC 19D.3.46G.
55   SS2/17.
56   EBA Guidelines, para 129.
57   SS2/17, para 5.39; SYSC 19D.3.47G.
58   EBA Guidelines, para 130.
59   PRA's Remuneration Part 15A.4.

- the duration of retention, deferral, performance and clawback arrangements that the previous firm would apply to each amount or part of an amount of available unvested variable remuneration.[60]

7.123   The amount of the buy-out provided by the new employer must not be greater than the aggregate amount of unvested variable remuneration referred to in the remuneration statement provided to the firm by the employee.[61] Further, the firm providing the buy-out must ensure that the buy-out aligns with the long-term interests of the firm, including appropriate retention, deferral, performance and clawback arrangements.

7.124   The duration of the retention, deferral, performance and clawback arrangements applied to a buy-out (or part of a buy-out) must be no shorter than the outstanding duration relating to the unvested variable remuneration that is being bought out.[62] The PRA expects firms to structure buy-outs so that they vest no faster than the awards they replace.[63]

7.125   Once a buy-out has been provided to an employee, the firm must send a buy-out notice in writing to the employee's previous firm to inform it of the amount of the unvested variable remuneration that has been 'bought out' and of the duration of the retention, deferral, performance and clawback arrangements that apply.[64]

7.126   A firm may only award, pay or provide a buy-out if it is subject to terms which give the firm a contractual right to reduce all or part of the buy-out by way of malus and clawback if it receives a 'reduction notice' from the previous firm.[65]

7.127   A reduction notice must be sent by the previous firm if it considers that it would have applied malus or clawback to the employee's variable remuneration had the employee remained in its employment.[66] If so, it must determine the amount of unvested variable remuneration it would have reduced or the amount of vested remuneration it would have clawed back. The previous firm must make such determinations fairly and reasonably and must:

- provide the employee with details and the proposed reasons for the proposed determination;

---

60 PRA's Remuneration Part 15A.7.
61 PRA's Remuneration Part 15A.4.
62 PRA's Remuneration Part 15A.3.
63 SS2/17, para 5.35.
64 PRA's Remuneration Part 15A.5.
65 PRA's Remuneration Part 15A.2.
66 PRA's Remuneration Part 15A.8 provides that for these purposes consideration should only be given to malus adjustments of unvested variable remuneration where there is reasonable evidence of employee misbehaviour or material error or the previous firm or relevant business unit suffers a material failure of risk management (ie potential malus adjustments for a material downturn in the financial performance of the previous firm or the relevant business unit should not be taken into consideration).

- allow the employee to make representations as to why the proposed determination should not be made; and

- take account of those representations in making the determination.[67]

7.128   Once the final determination has been made, the reduction notice should be sent to the new firm and to the employee within 14 working days.[68]

7.129   On receipt of a reduction notice from a previous firm, the firm must reduce the buy-out by, or make all reasonable efforts to recover from the employee an amount corresponding to, the amounts notified to it by the previous firm. Any such reduction should take place before the next vesting date or, in the case of clawback, within a reasonable period and no later than the end of the applicable clawback period.[69]

7.130   The PRA has confirmed that in applying malus or clawback to the buy-out the firm should act solely as an executor in relation to the determination made by the previous employer.[70]

7.131   As stated at 7.35, the PRA in SS2/17 confirms that it may be appropriate for a firm in proportionality level three to disapply the rules on buy-outs.[71]

7.132   The rules as described on buy-outs do not apply to firms that are regulated *only* by the FCA. However, such firms must still ensure that any buy-outs they provide are aligned with the long-term interests of the firm and are subject to appropriate retention, deferral and performance and clawback arrangements.[72]

Variable remuneration based on future performance and long-term incentive plans

7.133   The EBA Guidelines provide that where an award of variable remuneration, including an award made under a LTIP, is based on past performance of at least one year, but also depends on future performance conditions, the following should apply:[73]

- firms should clearly set out to staff the additional performance conditions that have to be met after the award for the variable remuneration to vest;

- firms should assess before the vesting of variable remuneration that the conditions for its vesting have been met;

---

67 PRA' Remuneration Part 15A.11 makes it clear that a contravention of these rules is actionable and renders the previous firm liable to the employee for any loss they suffer as a result.
68 PRA's Remuneration Part 15A.9.
69 PRA's Remuneration Part 15A.6.
70 SS2/17, para 5.37.
71 SS2/17, para 2.16.
72 SYSC 19A.3.40AR.
73 EBA Guidelines, para 8.2.

- the additional forward-looking performance conditions should be set for a predefined performance period of at least one year;

- when the additional forward-looking performance conditions have not been met, up to 100% of the variable remuneration awarded under those conditions should be subject to malus arrangements;

- the deferral period should end at the earliest one year after the last performance condition has been assessed; and

- for the calculation of the ratio between the variable and the fixed component of the total remuneration, the total amount of the variable remuneration awarded should be taken into account in the financial year for which the variable remuneration, including any LTIP award, was awarded. This should also apply when the past performance was assessed in a multi-year accrual period.

7.134   Guidance from the PRA and FCA states that awards should be based on both financial and non-financial criteria and the performance of the individual, the business unit and the firm.[74] Whatever non-financial criteria are used firms should be able to justify how they are appropriate for the business model and strategy of the firm and the process for measuring them should be transparent and robust.[75]

7.135   Non-financial criteria could include measures relating to building and maintaining positive customer relationships, reputation, achievement in line with the firm's strategy or values and the effectiveness and operation of the risk control environment.[76] Quantitative criteria should be appropriately risk adjusted and should include economic efficiency measures such as risk-adjusted return on capital, economic profit and internal economic risk capital.[77]

7.136   The PRA guidance in SS2/17 recognises that to capture all risk components a combination of quantitative metrics and discretionary approaches may be required. As a result of this guidance, the EBA Guidelines referred to at 7.133 and the provisions of the CRD IV Codes themselves, malus and clawback provisions should be included in the LTIP rules.

Pensions

7.137   The CRD IV Codes provide that a firm must ensure that its pension policy is in line with its business strategy, objectives, values and long-term interests.[78] This rule does not generally cause any difficulty. The structure of most

---

74   SS2/17, para 5.25; FG17/5.
75   SS2/17, para 5.25.
76   FG17/5.
77   SS2/17, para 5.26.
78   PRA's Remuneration Part 12.1; SYSC 19A.3.29R; SYSC 19D.3.31R.

firms' pensions arrangements cannot be said to incentivise excessive risk taking as the benefits are not based on performance.

7.138   Where the pension benefits are not based on performance and are consistently granted to a category of staff, they will be regarded as fixed pay.

7.139   The particular focus of the CRD IV Codes and the EBA Guidelines is on discretionary pension benefits which are regarded as a form of variable pay.[79] The EBA Guidelines state that a firm should ensure that where an employee leaves the firm (including on retirement), discretionary pension benefits should not be paid without consideration of the economic situation of the firm or the risks that have been taken by the employee which may affect the firm in the long term.[80]

7.140   Under the CRD IV Codes (which reflect the EBA Guidance):

(1) where the employee leaves the firm before retirement, any discretionary pension benefits must be held by the firm for a period of five years in the form of instruments; and

(2) where the employee reaches retirement, discretionary pension benefits must only be paid to the employee in the form of instruments and subject to a five-year retention period.[81]

Severance pay

7.141   The CRD IV Codes provide that a firm must ensure that 'payments relating to the early termination of a contract reflect performance achieved over time and are designed in a way that does not reward failure or misconduct'.[82] The PRA and FCA expect firms to apply this rule on a firm-wide basis.[83]

7.142   Although the PRA and the FCA have not provided much guidance on the application of this rule, it is thought that it is not intended to prevent firms from honouring contractual notice payments or from compromising genuine statutory employment claims that an employee may have on termination. Rather, the rule is intended to prevent firms from including generous 'golden parachute' payments in contracts of employment which may be triggered even where the employee's performance has been poor or the employee has been guilty of misconduct.

7.143   Firms should also avoid making generous ex gratia severance payments on termination where they are not justified by performance or the employee's conduct.

---

79 EBA Guidelines, para 8.5.
80 EBA Guidelines, para 8.5.
81 PRA's Remuneration Part 12.1; SYSC 19A.3.29R; SYSC 19D.3.29R.
82 PRA's Remuneration Part 15.14; SYSC 19A.3.45R; SYSC 19D.3.54.
83 SS2/17, para 5.47; SYSC 19A.2.3G; SYSC 19D.2.2G.

7.144   Much more detailed guidance on severance payments is included in the EBA Guidelines.[84] The EBA Guidelines provide that severance payments should be considered to be variable remuneration and should therefore be taken into account for the purpose of calculating the ratio between fixed and variable pay and should be subject to the rules on deferral, payment in instruments and, presumably performance adjustment (although performance adjustment is not specifically mentioned in the EBA Guidelines).[85]

7.145   There are, however, some exceptions to this which are as follows:

• severance payments which are mandatory under national law or following a court decision. This would include a statutory redundancy payment or an award of compensation for unfair dismissal or discrimination;

• severance payments which are calculated through a predefined generic formula set within the remuneration policy. This may include, for example, payments under a firm's enhanced redundancy policy;

• payments which are paid to the employee in the future where the settlement agreement contains a non-competition clause. This is provided that the payments do not exceed the amount of fixed remuneration that the employee would have earned had they remained employed up to the end of the non-competition period; and

• other severance payments paid on redundancy or to compromise an actual or potential dispute where the firm has demonstrated to the regulator the reasons and appropriateness of the amount of the severance payment.

7.146   Payments falling into these categories do not need to be regarded as variable pay for the purposes of calculating the ratio between fixed and variable remuneration and do not need to be subject to the rules on deferral, payment in instruments and performance adjustment.[86]

7.147   The EBA Guidelines state that severance payments should not provide for a disproportionate reward but for appropriate compensation in the case of early termination of the contract. As the CRD IV Codes also make clear, severance payments must reflect performance achieved over time and not reward failure or misconduct. Severance pay should not be awarded where there is an obvious failure which allows for the contract to be terminated immediately (eg in cases of gross misconduct). Nor should it be awarded where a staff member resigns voluntarily in order to take up a position in a different legal entity, unless a severance payment is required by national labour law.

7.148   Where severance pay is awarded, a firm must be able to demonstrate to the regulator the reasons for the severance payment, the appropriateness of the amount awarded and the criteria used to determine the amount, including that it

---

84 EBA Guidelines, para 9.3.
85 EBA Guidelines, para 154.
86 EBA Guidelines, para 154.

is linked to the performance achieved over time and that it does not reward failure or misconduct.

Personal investment strategies

7.149   The CRD IV Codes place an obligation on firms to ensure that their employees undertake not to use personal hedging strategies or insurance contracts to undermine the risk alignment effects embedded in their remuneration arrangements (ie employees should not be allowed to hedge or insure against the risk of a malus adjustment to, or clawback of, their remuneration). Firms must also maintain effective arrangements to ensure that employees comply with their undertakings.[87] The PRA and FCA expect these rules to be applied on a firm-wide basis.[88]

7.150   The EBA Guidelines provide that firms should at least obtain from Code staff a commitment that they will refrain from using such personal hedging strategies or contracts of insurance and that firms' human resources or internal control functions should at least perform 'spot-check inspections' of compliance with these declarations on internal custodianship accounts. Firms should also require Code staff to notify them of any other custodial accounts that they hold.[89]

Non-executive directors and variable pay

7.151   PRA authorised firms are prohibited from awarding variable remuneration to non-executive directors in relation to their roles as non-executive directors.[90] This is consistent with the EBA Guidelines which state that members of the firm's supervisory function should be compensated with fixed remuneration only.[91]

Record keeping and compliance

7.152   The CRD IV Codes require firms to ensure that their remuneration policies, practices and procedures (including performance appraisals, processes and decisions) are clear and documented.[92]

7.153   A firm that maintains a website must explain on its website how it complies with the CRD IV Codes.[93]

---

87   PRA's Remuneration Part 13; SYSC 19A.3.30R; SYSC 19D.3.32R.
88   SS2/17 5.47; SYSC 19A.2.3G; SYSC 19D.2.2G.
89   EBA Guidelines, para 10.1.
90   PRA's Remuneration Part 15.3; SYSC 19D.3.38R.
91   EBA Guidelines, para 171.
92   PRA's Remuneration Part 6.5; SYSC 19A.2.4G; SYSC 19D.2.3R.
93   PRA's Remuneration Part 7.5; SYSC 19A.3.12AR; SYSC 19D.3.13R.

7.154 The CRD IV Codes provide that firms must ensure that variable remuneration is not paid through vehicles or methods that facilitate non-compliance with their obligations under the CRD IV Codes.[94]

Breaches of the CRD IV Codes – voiding and recovery

7.155 The CRD IV Codes contain provisions which render void any provision of an agreement that contravenes the prohibitions on Code staff being remunerated in the ways specified in the rules relating to:

- guaranteed variable remuneration;
- deferred variable remuneration;
- clawback; and
- buy-outs.[95]

7.156 However, these voiding provisions only apply to proportionality level one firms (and credit institutions and UK-designated investment firms/ IFPRU 730K firms or relevant third country IFPRU 730K firms that are part of a group containing a proportionality level one firm).[96] They may also be disapplied in respect of Code staff who satisfy the *de minimis* criteria.[97]

7.157 Where a firm has made a payment (or transferred property) pursuant to a provision which is void, then it must take reasonable steps to recover it.[98] Furthermore, the firm must not award, pay or provide variable remuneration for the same performance year to a person who has received remuneration pursuant to a void provision unless the firm has obtained a legal opinion stating that the award, payment or provision complies with the relevant CRD IV Code.[99] A payment made in breach of this rule is itself void and the relevant firm should take reasonable steps to recover it.[100]

7.158 The voiding provisions do not apply to provisions that were entered into before the voiding rules were made[101] or to provisions that were agreed at a time when the rules did not apply either to the firm or in respect of the individual because the individual fell within the *de minimis* exemption.[102]

7.159 The PRA and FCA expect to be notified of any breach of the rules to which the voiding provisions apply. Such notification should include information

---

94 PRA's Remuneration Part 14.1; SYSC 19A.3.32R; SYSC 19D.3.34R.
95 PRA's Remuneration Part 16.9 to 16.6; SYSC 19A Annex 1; SYSC 19D Annex 1.
96 PRA's Remuneration Part 16.3 and 16.4; SYSC 19.3.54R; SYSC 19D.67R.
97 SS2/17 2.21; SYSC 19A.3.54R; SYSC 19D.3.67R.
98 PRA's Remuneration Part 16.14; SYSC 19A Annex 1.5R; SYSC 19D Annex 1.7R.
99 PRA's Remuneration Part 16.16; SYSC 19A Annex 1.7; SYSC 19D Annex 1.10R.
100 PRA's Remuneration Part 16.1 and 16.16; SYSC 19A.3.54R; SYSC 19D.3.67R.
101 PRA's Remuneration Part 16.11; SYSC 19A Annex 1.2AR; SYSC 19D Annex 1.3R.
102 PRA's Remuneration Part 16.12; SYSC 19A Annex 1.3AR; SYSC 19D Annex 1.5R.

on the steps that the firm has taken or intends to take to recover the relevant payment or property.[103]

3   BIPRU REMUNERATION CODE

Introduction

7.160   The BIPRU Remuneration Code is contained in SYSC 19C of the FCA Handbook. As stated at 7.05, it applies to BIPRU investment firms such as brokers, investment managers and advisers who are not dealing in financial instruments on their own account or underwriting issues of financial instruments and who do not engage in the safekeeping or administration of financial instruments for the account of clients.

7.161   In addition to UK BIPRU firms, the BIPRU Remuneration Code applies to the UK activities of third country BIPRU firms, ie firms that that have their head office outside the EEA. The BIPRU Remuneration Code does not apply to firms that have their head office in the EEA.[104]

7.162   Unlike the CRD IV Codes and the AIFM and UCITS Remuneration Codes, the guidance on remuneration policies contained in the EBA and ESMA Guidelines is not strictly relevant to the interpretation of the BIPRU Code.

7.163   Where a BIPRU firm is also subject to the AIFM Remuneration Code (SYSC 19B) or the UCITS Remuneration Code (SYSC 19E), then the firm is deemed to have met its obligations under the BIPRU Remuneration Code by complying with the AIFM Remuneration Code or the UCITS Remuneration Code as the case may be.[105]

Purpose and general requirement

7.164   The purpose of the BIPRU Remuneration Code is to ensure that firms have risk-focused remuneration policies which are consistent with and promote effective risk management and do not expose them to excessive risk.[106] To that end the general requirement in SYSC 19C.2.1 is for firms to establish, implement and maintain remuneration policies, procedures and practices that are consistent with and promote sound and effective risk management.[107]

---

103 SS2/17, para 5.45; SYSC 19A Annex 1.8G; SYSC 19D Annex 1.11G.
104 SYSC 19C.1.1R.
105 SYSC 19C.1.1AG; SYSC 19C1.1BG.
106 SYSC 19C.1.6G.
107 SYSC 19C. 2.1R.

BIPRU Remuneration Code staff

7.165   As with the CRD IV Codes, certain provisions of the BIPRU Remuneration Code only apply to certain categories of staff. In the BIPRU Remuneration Code they are known as 'BIPRU Remuneration Code staff'.

7.166   BIPRU Remuneration Code staff include senior management, risk takers, staff engaged in control functions and any employee receiving total remuneration that takes them into the same remuneration bracket as senior management and risk takers whose professional activities have a material impact on the firm's risk profile.[108] The guidance in SYSC 19C.3.6G states that the following persons should normally be part of the firm's BIPRU Remuneration Code staff:

- persons performing a significant influence function or who are senior managers;

- heads of significant business lines (such as fixed income, foreign exchange, commodities, securitisation, sales areas, investment banking, commercial banking, equities, structured finance, lending quality, trading areas and research) and any individuals or groups within their control who have a material impact on the firm's risk profile; and

- heads of support and control functions (such as credit/market/operational risk, legal, treasury controls, human resources, compliance and internal audit) and any other individuals within their control who have a material impact on the firm's risk profile.

Proportionality

7.167   The BIPRU Remuneration Code provides that a firm, when establishing and applying the total remuneration policies for BIPRU Remuneration Code staff, should comply with the relevant requirements in a way and to an extent which is appropriate to its size, internal organisation and the nature, scope and complexity of its activities.[109]

7.168   General guidance on the application of the principle of proportionality to the BIPRU Remuneration Code is given in FG17/7. This provides that it may not be necessary for firms to apply the remuneration principles set out in the BIPRU Remuneration Code at all.[110] These are the remuneration Principles 1 to 12 which are set out in SYSC 19C.3.7R to SYSC 19C.3.53G and which are summarised at 7.171 ff. It goes on to state that it will normally be appropriate for a firm to disapply the pay-out process rules under the BIPRU Remuneration Code which relate to the following:

- retained shares or other instruments;

---

108 SYSC 19C.3.4R.
109 SYSC 19C.3.3R.
110 FG17/7, para 2.3.

- deferral;

- performance adjustment; and

- the ratios between fixed and variable components of total remuneration.[111]

7.169   As a result, unless they are also subject to the AIFM Code or the UCITS Code or they are part of a group which contains a firm subject to the CRD IV Codes, BIPRU firms may not be subject to any stringent requirements in relation to the way in which they reward their staff.

Key remuneration principles of the BIPRU Remuneration Code

7.170   The key principles of the BIPRU Remuneration Code are summarised in the following paragraphs.

7.171   These principles strictly only apply to BIPRU Remuneration Code staff,[112] although the FCA considers that firms should apply a number of the rules on a firm-wide basis (including those relating to guaranteed variable remuneration, deferral and payments related to early termination).[113] However, as stated at 7.168, it may not be necessary for firms to apply the remuneration principles set out in the BIPRU Remuneration Code at all under the proportionality principle.

7.172   As with the CRD IV Codes, there is a *de minimis* exemption. Firms do not have to apply the rules relating to guaranteed variable remuneration, payment in instruments, deferral and performance adjustment to BIPRU Remuneration Code staff whose:

- total remuneration does not exceed £500,000; and

- variable remuneration is no more than 33% of their total remuneration.[114]

General requirements

7.173   A firm must ensure that:

- its remuneration policy is consistent with and promotes sound and effective risk management and does not encourage risk taking that exceeds the level of tolerated risk at the firm.[115] This reflects the general requirement of the BIPRU Remuneration Code referred to at 7.164;

---

111 FG17/7, para 2.4.
112 SYSC 19C.3.3R.
113 SYSC 19C.2.3G.
114 SYSC 19C.3.34G.
115 SYSC 19C.3.7.

- its remuneration policy is in line with the business strategy, objectives, values and long-term interests of the firm;[116]

- its remuneration policy includes measures to avoid conflicts of interests;[117] and

- its governing body adopts and periodically reviews the general principles of the firm's remuneration policy and is responsible for its implementation.[118] Reviews should take place at least annually.[119] Firms that are significant in terms of size, internal organisation and the nature, scope and complexity of their activities must establish a remuneration committee.[120] The FCA accepts that it may be possible for such firms to justify not establishing a remuneration committee on proportionality grounds, although in such cases they should be able to demonstrate that the functions which would otherwise have been performed by the remuneration committee would be discharged with sufficient authority and independence from those performing executive functions within the firm.[121]

Control functions

7.174 A firm must ensure that employees engaged in control functions (ie functions such as risk, legal, human resources, compliance and internal audit) are independent from the business units they oversee, have appropriate authority and are remunerated:

- adequately to attract qualified and experienced staff; and

- in line with the achievement of their objectives, independent of the performance of the business areas they control.[122]

Profit-based measurement and risk adjustment

7.175 A firm must ensure that the calculation of variable remuneration components or pools includes adjustment for all types of current and future risks.[123] Assessments of financial performance used to calculate variable remuneration components or pools must be based principally on profits.[124] Firms must ensure that total variable remuneration is generally considerably contracted when subdued or negative financial performance of the firm occurs.[125]

---

116 SYSC 19C.3.8.
117 SYSC 19C.3.9.
118 SYSC 19C.3.10.
119 SYSC 19C.3.11.
120 SYSC 19C.3.12.
121 FG 17/7, para 4.2.
122 SYSC 19C.3.14R.
123 SYSC 19C.3.22R.
124 SYSC 19C.25R.
125 SYSC 19C.3.27R.

7.176 Where a firm makes a loss the FCA generally expects no variable remuneration to be awarded, although it recognises that variable remuneration awards may nonetheless be justified in certain circumstances such as where it is necessary to incentivise employees working in a new business venture which is loss-making in its early stages.[126]

Pension policy

7.177 A firm's pension policy must be in line with its business strategy, objectives, values and long-term interests. Where discretionary pension benefits are given to an employee before retirement, the firm must hold them for a period of five years in the form of instruments. When employees reach retirement any discretionary pension benefits must be paid in the form of instruments and subject to a five-year retention period.[127]

Personal investment strategies

7.178 Firms must ensure that employees undertake not to use personal hedging strategies or contracts of insurance to undermine the risk-alignment effects embedded in their remuneration arrangements and that they maintain effective arrangements for ensuring that employees comply with their undertakings.[128]

Performance assessment

7.179 Where remuneration is performance-related, the total amount of the remuneration must be based on a combination of the assessment of the performance of the individual, the relevant business unit and the overall results of the firm. When assessing individual performance financial and non-financial criteria should be taken into account.[129] Non-financial criteria should include adherence to risk management and compliance with applicable regulatory obligations.[130] The assessment of performance should be set in a multi-year framework.[131]

---

126 SYCS 19C.3.28G.
127 SYSC 19C.3.29R.
128 SYSC 19C.3.30R.
129 SYSC 19C.3.36R.
130 SYSC 19C.3.37G.
131 SYSC 10C.3.39G.

Guaranteed variable remuneration, buy-outs and retention payments

7.180   Firms must not award, pay or provide guaranteed variable remuneration unless it:

- is exceptional;

- occurs in the context of hiring new BIPRU Remuneration Code staff; and

- is limited to the first year of service.[132]

7.181   Guaranteed variable remuneration should be subject to the same deferral criteria as other forms of variable remuneration awarded by the firm.[133]

7.182   Buy-outs of variable remuneration should not be more generous in their amounts or their terms (including any deferral or retention periods) than the variable remuneration that is being bought out and should be subject to appropriate performance adjustment requirements.[134]

7.183   Retention awards should generally only be awarded where a firm is undergoing a major restructuring and a good case can be made for retention of particular key staff members on prudential grounds. Proposals to give retention awards should be notified to the FCA.[135]

Ratios between fixed and variable remuneration

7.184   There is no bonus cap under the BIPRU Remuneration Code. However, firms must set appropriate ratios between the fixed and variable components of total remuneration and ensure that they are appropriately balanced. The fixed component should represent a sufficiently high proportion of total remuneration to allow the operation of a fully flexible policy on variable remuneration including the possibility to pay no variable remuneration component.[136]

Severance payments

7.185   Firms must ensure that payments related to the early termination of a contract reflect performance achieved over time and are designed in a way that does not reward failure.[137] Firms should review existing contractual termination payments to ensure that they are consistent with this principle.[138]

---

132 SYSC 19C.3.40R.
133 SYSC 19C.3.42G.
134 SYSC 19C.3.41E.
135 SYSC 19C.3.43G.
136 SYSC 19C.3.44R.
137 SYSC 19C.3.45R.
138 SYSC 19C.3.46G.

Payment in instruments

7.186   At least 50% of variable remuneration (both deferred and non-deferred) must be paid in shares or other instruments. Such shares or other instruments must be subject to an appropriate retention policy designed to align incentives with the longer-term interests of the firm.[139]

Deferral

7.187   At least 40% of variable remuneration should be deferred over a period of not less than three to five years with vesting on no faster than a pro rata basis. At least 60% of variable remuneration must be deferred for directors of firms that are significant in terms of their size, internal organisation and the nature, scope and complexity of their activities or if the award of variable remuneration is more than £500,000.[140]

Performance adjustment

7.188   The BIPRU Remuneration Code provides that firms should make malus adjustments in certain circumstances, but not does contain obligations relating to clawback.

7.189   It states that variable remuneration should only be paid or vest if it is sustainable according to the financial situation of the firm and justified according to the performance of the firm, the relevant business unit and the individual.[141]

7.190   Unvested deferred variable remuneration should be reduced where:

- there is reasonable evidence of employee misbehaviour or material error;

- the firm or the relevant business unit suffers a material downturn in its financial performance; or

- the firm or the relevant business unit suffers a material failure of risk management.[142]

7.191   The governing body (or remuneration committee) should approve performance adjustment policies including the triggers under which adjustment would take place. Firms are expected to maintain adequate records of material performance adjustment decisions.[143]

---

139 SYSC 19C.3.47R.
140 SYSC 19C.3.49R.
141 SYSC 19C.3.51R.
142 SYSC 19C.3.52E.
143 SYSC 19C.3.53G.

4 AIFM AND UCITS REMUNERATION CODES

Introduction

7.192   As the AIFM Remuneration Code and the UCITS Remuneration Code both apply to asset management firms (albeit different types of asset management firms) and contain similar provisions, it makes sense to consider them together. They are referred to collectively in this section as 'the AIFM/UCITS Codes'.

7.193   The AIFM Remuneration Code is contained in SYSC 19B of the FCA Handbook and is intended to implement the remuneration provisions of AIFMD. It applies to full scope UK alternative investment fund managers (AIFMs) such as hedge funds, private equity funds and real estate funds, whether they manage funds in the UK, the EEA or elsewhere.[144] It does not apply to 'small AIFs' which are those with assets under management of: (a) €500m or less for funds that are unleveraged and have no redemption rights exercisable during the period of five years from the initial investment; or (b) €100m in other cases including where assets have been acquired through the use of leverage.[145]

7.194   The UCITS Remuneration Code is contained in SYSC 19E of the FCA Handbook and is intended to implement the remuneration provisions of UCITS V. UCITS V sets out a harmonised framework for UCITS (undertakings for collective investment in transferable securities), ie investment funds that can be sold to retail investors throughout the EU. The UCITS Remuneration Code applies to a UK UCITS management company that manages a UCITS scheme or an EEA UCITS scheme. It does not apply to an EEA UCITS management company as such a company will be subject to the rules of its home jurisdiction.[146]

ESMA Guidelines on sound remuneration policies

7.195   The AIFM/UCITS Remuneration Codes need to be read in conjunction with the ESMA Guidelines. ESMA published:

● guidelines on sound remuneration policies under the AIFMD on 3 July 2013 ('the AIFMD Guidelines'); and

● guidelines on sound remuneration policies under the UCITS Directive on 31 March 2016 ('the UCITS Guidelines').

7.196   As stated at 7.195, the AIFMD Guidelines and the UCITS Guidelines are referred to collectively in this chapter as 'the ESMA Guidelines'.

7.197   The ESMA Guidelines are intended to ensure that the remuneration principles are applied consistently across the EU and, among other things, provide

---

144 SYSC 19B.1.1.
145 SYSC 19E.1.1R; Alternative Investment Fund Managers Regulations 2013 (SI 2013/1773), reg 9.
146 SYSC 19E.1.1R.

guidance on proportionality, governance of remuneration and requirements on risk alignment and disclosure.

7.198   As stated at 7.10, the FCA has notified ESMA of compliance with all aspects of the ESMA Guidelines.

Purpose and general requirement

7.199   The AIFM/UCITS Codes require the AIFM or management company to establish remuneration policies and practices for their AIFM/UCITS Code staff that are consistent with, and promote, sound and effective risk management and do not encourage risk taking which is inconsistent with the risk profile of the funds it manages.[147]

AIFM and UCITS Remuneration Code staff

7.200   As with the CRD IV Codes and the BIPRU Remuneration Code, certain provisions of the AIFM/UCTIS Codes only apply to certain categories of staff, known in the AIFM Code as 'AIFM Remuneration Code staff' and in the UCITS Remuneration Code as 'UCITS Remuneration Code staff'. In the ESMA Guidelines they are referred to as 'identified staff'. They are referred to collectively in this chapter as 'AIFM/UCITS Remuneration Code staff'.

7.201   AIFM/UCITS Remuneration Code staff comprise those categories of staff whose professional activities have a material impact on the risk profiles of the firm[148] or the funds[149] it manages. Such staff include:

- senior management;

- risk takers;

- staff engaged in control functions; and

- any employees whose total remuneration takes them into the same remuneration bracket as senior management and risk takers.[150]

7.202   As with the CRD IV Codes and the BIPRU Remuneration Code, there is a *de minimis* exemption. Firms do not have to apply the rules relating to payment in retained units, shares or other instruments, deferral and performance adjustment to AIFM/UCITS Remuneration Code staff whose:

- total remuneration does not exceed £500,000; and

- variable remuneration is no more than 33% of their total remuneration.[151]

147 SYSC19B.1.2R; SYSC 19E.2.1R.
148 The term 'firm' is used to denote an AIFM or UCITS management company.
149 The term 'fund' is used to denote an AIF or a UCITS fund.
150 SYSC 19B.1.3R; SYSC 19E.2.2R.
151 SYSC 19B.1.13AG; SYSC 19E.2.17G.

7.203 The AIFM Remuneration Code also provides that the rules relating to guaranteed remuneration do not have to be applied to AIFM Remuneration Code staff meeting the *de minimis* exemption.[152] However, there is no equivalent provision in the UCITS Remuneration Code.

Proportionality

7.204 As with the CRD IV Codes and the BIPRU Remuneration Code, the AIFM/UCITS Remuneration Codes provide that firms should comply with the principles of the Codes in a way and to the extent that is appropriate according to their size, internal organisation and the nature, scope and complexity of their activities.[153]

7.205 The FCA has published guidance on applying the proportionality principle under the AIFM Remuneration Code.[154] In summary, the guidance states that certain AIFMs may be able to disapply the rules relating to:

- retained units, shares or other instruments;

- deferral; and

- performance adjustment (together known as 'the pay-out process rules').

7.206 Whether an AIFM may be able to disapply these rules depends on its size, internal organisation and the nature, scope and complexity of its activities. In terms of size, the key issue is the AIFM's assets under management. The presumption is that AIFMs whose assets under management fall below the thresholds set out in the table below will be able to disapply the pay-out process rules. Conversely, AIFMs whose assets under management are above the thresholds should apply the pay-out process rules.

Type of firm	AuM threshold
AIFMs which manage portfolios of AIFs that are unleveraged and have no redemption rights exercisable during a period of five years following the date of the initial investment in each AIF	£5bn
AIFMs which manage portfolios of AIFs in other cases, including any assets acquired through use of leverage	£1bn

7.207 AIFMs should then consider other proportionality elements referred to in the guidance before determining whether the presumption derived from the table should apply to them.

152 SYSC 19B1.13AG.
153 SYSC 19B.1.4R; SYSC 19E.2.4R.
154 FCA's General guidance on the AIFM Remuneration Code (January 2014).

7.208 Factors which may favour the disapplication of the pay-out process rules include the following:

- the AIFM is not listed and traded on a regulated market;

- the AIFM's senior management own a majority stake in the AIFM;

- the AIF's strategies or scope of investment is limited by regulation in such a way that investor risk is mitigated;

- the discretion of the AIFM or its delegated portfolio manager is strictly controlled with pre-defined narrow parameters or investment decisions are made according to prescribed rules (eg there is a mandate to track an index);

- the AIFM is associated with a low level of risk; and

- the AIFM's fee structure avoids incentives for inappropriate risk taking.

7.209 The FCA has declined to publish equivalent guidance on proportionality in respect of the UCITS Remuneration Code. Rather, it has suggested that firms review the UCITS Guidance and consider the guidance they have given on the AIFM Remuneration Code to understand their expectations in relation to the requirements under the UCITS Remuneration Code.

Key remuneration principles of the AIFM/UCITS Remuneration Codes

7.210 The AIFM/UCITS Remuneration Codes apply to remuneration or benefits of any type paid by the firm, any amounts paid by the fund itself (including carried interest or performance fees) and to the transfer of units or shares.[155]

General requirements

7.211 A firm must ensure that:

- its remuneration policy is consistent with, and promotes, sound and effective risk management and does not encourage risk taking which is inconsistent with the risk profiles of the funds it manages;[156]

- its remuneration policy is line with the business strategy, objectives, values and interests of the firm, the funds it manages and their respective investors;[157]

- its remuneration policy contains measures to avoid conflicts of interest;[158] and

---

155 SYSC 19B.1.4R; SYSC 19E.2.4R.
156 SYSC 19B.1.5R; SYSC 19E.2.5R.
157 SYSC 19B.1.6R; SYSC 19E.2.6R.
158 SYSC 19B.1.6R; SYSC 19E.2.6R.

- its governing or management body adopts and reviews at least annually the general principles of the remuneration policy and is responsible for its implementation.[159]

7.212 Firms that are significant in terms of their size, the complexity of their internal organisation and the nature, scope and complexity of their activities should establish a remuneration committee.[160] Guidance on which firms should establish a remuneration committee is contained in the ESMA Guidelines.[161]

Control functions

7.213 A firm must ensure that employees engaged in control functions are compensated according to the achievement of the objectives linked to their functions and independent of the performance of the business areas that are within their remit.[162] The remuneration of the senior officers in the risk management and compliance functions must be directly overseen by the remuneration committee, or, in the absence of a remuneration committee, the firm's management body.[163]

Performance assessment and risk adjustment

7.214 A firm must ensure that performance related remuneration is based on a combination of an assessment of the performance of the individual and of the business unit or funds concerned and the overall results of the firm. When assessing individual performance financial and non-financial criteria should be taken into account.[164] Performance should also be assessed in a multi-year framework appropriate to the life-cycle of the AIFs managed by the AIFM or any holding period recommended to investors of the UCITS managed by the UCITS management company.[165]

7.215 Furthermore, a firm must ensure that the measurement of performance used to calculate variable remuneration components, or pools of variable remuneration components, includes a comprehensive adjustment mechanism to integrate all relevant types of current and future risks.[166]

7.216 The ESMA Guidelines confirm that these obligations only apply to AIFM/UCITS Remuneration Code staff, although it is strongly recommended that they be applied firm-wide.[167]

---

159 SYSC 19B.1.7R; SYSC 19E.2.7R.
160 SYSC 19B.1.9R; SYSC 19E.2.9R.
161 See UCITS Guidelines, paras 54–59; AIFMD Guidelines, paras 52–57.
162 SYSC 19B.1.10R; SYSC 19E.2.10R.
163 SYSC 19B.1.11R; SYSC 19E.2.11R.
164 SYSC 19B.1.12R; SYSC 19E.2.12R.
165 SYSC 19B.1.13R; SYSC 19E.2.13R.
166 SYSC 19B.1.21R; SYSC 19E.2.24R.
167 UCITS Guidelines, Annex II; the AIFMD Guidelines, Annex II.

Guaranteed variable remuneration

7.217   A firm must not award, pay or provide guaranteed variable remuneration unless it:

- is exceptional;

- occurs only in the context of hiring new staff; and

- is limited to the first year of engagement.[168]

7.218   As stated at 7.205, the AIFM Remuneration Code provides that this rule can be disapplied in respect of AIFM Remuneration Code staff who fall within the *de minimis* exemption. However, there is no equivalent provision in the UCITS Remuneration Code. Furthermore, the ESMA Guidelines suggest that this obligation should be applied on a firm-wide basis.[169]

7.219   The AIFM/UCITS Remuneration Codes do not expressly refer to retention payments. However, the ESMA Guidelines state that retention bonuses represent variable remuneration and can only be awarded to the extent that risk alignment provisions are properly applied.[170]

Ratios between fixed and variable remuneration

7.220   There is no bonus cap under the AIFM/UCITS Remuneration Codes. However, a firm must ensure that:

- fixed and variable components of total remuneration are appropriately balanced; and

- the fixed component represents a sufficiently high proportion of the total remuneration to allow the operation of a fully flexible policy on variable remuneration components, including the possibility to pay no variable remuneration component.[171]

7.221   The ESMA Guidelines provide that this obligation only applies to AIFM/UCITS Remuneration Code staff, although it strongly recommends that it be applied on a firm-wide basis.[172]

Severance payments

7.222   A firm must ensure that payments related to the early termination of a contract:

---

168 SYSC 19B.1.14R; SYSC 19E.2.14R.
169 UCITS Guidelines, Annex II; the AIFM Guidelines, Annex II.
170 UCITS Guidelines, para 13; AIFMD Guidelines, para 14.
171 SYSC 19B.1.15R; SYSC 19E2.15R.
172 UCITS Guidelines, Annex II; AIFMD Guidelines, Annex II.

- reflect performance achieved over time; and

- are designed in a way that does not reward failure.[173]

7.223 Although this obligation only applies to AIFM/UCITS Remuneration Code staff, the ESMA Guidelines strongly recommend that it be applied firm-wide and, if it is not, that firms should be able to demonstrate why they did not apply it more widely.[174]

Retained units, shares or other instruments

7.224 A firm must ensure that a substantial portion, and in any event at least 50%,[175] of any variable remuneration component consists of units or shares, or equivalent ownership interests, in the relevant fund or equivalent non-cash interests or instruments. This rule applies to both deferred and non-deferred portions of the variable remuneration component and the interests or instruments must be subject to an appropriate retention policy designed to align incentives with the long-term interests of the firm, the funds it manages and the relevant investors in the funds.[176] The FCA considers that a retention period of six months should normally be sufficient.[177]

7.225 This obligation is subject to the legal structure of the relevant fund. The FCA's general guidance on the AIFM Remuneration Code recognises that the legal structure of the AIF may make the application of the rule impracticable. In these circumstances, the AIFM has the option of using shares or other instruments linked to the firm or its parent company or shares or other instruments linked to the performance of the funds or other portfolios managed by the firm or its affiliates.

7.226 In other circumstances, for example where the AIFM manages a lot of AIFs or in respect of the remuneration of senior management or staff in compliance or audit functions, it may be appropriate for the AIFM to pay staff in shares or other instruments linked to the AIFM or its parent company or in shares or instruments linked to the performance of a weighted average of the AIFs managed by the AIFM.[178]

7.227 The ESMA Guidelines provide that the obligation to make payment in retained units, shares or other instruments only applies in respect of AIFM/UCITS Remuneration Code staff.[179] As stated, this rule can be disapplied

---

173 SYSC 19B.1.16R; SYSC 19E.2.16R.
174 UCITS Guidelines, Annex II; AIFMD Guidelines, Annex II.
175 This minimum does not apply if the management of AIFs/UCITS accounts for less than 50% of the total portfolio managed by the AIFM/UCITS management company (SYSC 19B.1.17R; SYSC 19E.2.18R).
176 SYSC 19B.1.17R; SYSC 19E.2.18R.
177 FCA's General guidance on the AIFM Remuneration Code.
178 FCA's General guidance on the AIFM Remuneration Code.
179 UCITS Guidelines, Annex II; AIFMD Guidelines, Annex II.

for AIFM/UCITS Remuneration Code staff who fall within the *de minimis* exemption.[180]

Deferral

7.228 A firm must not award, pay or provide a variable remuneration component unless a substantial portion, and in any event at least 40%, of the variable remuneration component, is deferred.[181] For a variable remuneration component of a particularly high amount, at least 60% of the amount must be deferred. £500,000 should be considered a particularly high amount for these purposes although firms should consider whether lesser amounts should be considered to be particularly high, taking into account, for example, significant differences in pay among staff.[182]

7.229 The deferral period should be appropriate to the life cycle and redemption policy of the AIF or the holding period recommended to investors in the relevant UCITS and in both cases should be aligned to the nature of the risks of the relevant AIF or UCITS. Under the AIFM Remuneration Code the deferral period must be at least three to five years unless the life cycle of the relevant AIF is shorter. Under the UCITS Remuneration Code the deferral period must be at least three years. Under both codes vesting must be no faster than on a pro rata basis.[183]

7.230 The ESMA Guidelines provide that the deferral obligation only applies in respect of AIFM/UCITS Remuneration Code staff.[184] As stated at 7.25, this rule can be disapplied for AIFM/UCITS Remuneration Code staff who fall within the *de minimis* exemption.[185]

Performance adjustment

7.231 A firm must ensure that any variable remuneration, including a deferred portion, is paid or vests only if it is:

● sustainable according to the financial situation of the firm as a whole; and

● justified according to the performance of the fund, the business unit and the individual concerned.[186]

7.232 The total variable remuneration should generally be considerably contracted where subdued or negative financial performance of the firm or

---

180 SYSC 19B.1.13AG; SYSC 19E.2.17G.
181 SYSC 19B.1.18R; SYSC 19E.1.20R.
182 SYSC 19B.1.18G; SYSC 19E.2.21G.
183 SYSC 19B.1.18R; SYSC 19E.2.20R.
184 UCITS Guidelines, Annex II; AIFMD Guidelines, Annex II.
185 SYSC 19B.1.13AG; SYSC 19E.2.17G.
186 SYSC 19B.1.19R; SYSC 19E2.22R.

the relevant fund occurs. When considering reducing remuneration in these circumstances, firms should take into account both current compensation and reductions in payouts of amounts previously earned, including through malus or clawback arrangements.[187]

7.233 The ESMA Guidelines provide that the obligation to make performance adjustments (including through application of malus and clawback) only applies in respect of AIFM/UCITS Remuneration Code staff.[188] As stated, this rule can be disapplied for AIFM/UCITS Remuneration Code staff who fall within the *de minimis* exemption.[189]

Pension policy

7.234 A firm must ensure that its pension policy is in line with the business strategy, objectives, values and long-term interests of the firm itself and the funds it manages. Where discretionary pension benefits are given to an employee before retirement, the firm must hold them for a period of five years in the form of instruments. When employees reach retirement any discretionary pension benefits must be paid in the form of instruments and subject to a five-year retention period.[190]

7.235 The ESMA Guidelines state that this obligation only applies to AIFM/UCITS Code staff, but the strong recommendation is that it is applied firm-wide.[191]

Personal investment strategies

7.236 Firms must ensure that employees undertake not to use personal hedging strategies or contracts of insurance to undermine the risk-alignment effects embedded in their remuneration arrangements.[192]

7.237 The ESMA Guidelines state that this obligation only applies to AIFM/UCITS Remuneration Code staff, but the strong recommendation is that it is applied firm-wide.[193]

Partners and LLP members

7.238 Many AIFMs and UCITS management companies are structured as partnerships or limited liability partnerships (LLPs). Partners or members of

---

187 SYSC 19E2.23G.
188 UCITS Guidelines, Annex II; AIFMD Guidelines, Annex II.
189 SYSC 19B.1.13AG; SYSC 19E.2.17G.
190 SYSC 19B.1.22R; SYSC 19E.2.25R.
191 UCITS Guidelines, Annex II; AIFMD Guidelines, Annex II.
192 SYSC 19B.1.23R; SYSC 19E.2.26R.
193 UCITS Guidelines, Annex II; AIFMD Guidelines, Annex II.

LLPs (referred to collectively as 'partners' in this section) are remunerated through payments of profit share, rather than through a combination of fixed remuneration (such as a salary) and variable remuneration (such as an annual discretionary bonus). Profit share payments are not expressly dealt with in the AIFM/UCITS Remuneration Codes and there is therefore a question as to how the rules should be applied to them.

7.239   The ESMA Guidelines state that dividends and distributions that partners receive as owners of a firm are not covered by the remuneration provisions of AIFMD or UCITS V (unless they result in the circumvention of the relevant rules).[194]

7.240   The FCA's general guidance on the AIFM Remuneration Code provides that it is first necessary for firms to determine:

- the portion of profit share payments received by partners that represents a return on equity in the relevant firm. This portion is not subject to the remuneration requirements ('the out-of-scope remuneration'); and

- the portion of profit share payments received by partners that represents remuneration within the scope of the AIFMD ('the in-scope remuneration').

7.241   Once this determination has been made, it is then necessary to determine which components of the in-scope remuneration represent fixed remuneration and which represent variable remuneration.

7.242   The FCA's general guidance states that one approach would be to consider how the partnership or LLP pays its partners. It suggests that:

- an amount of additional profit share paid to senior or founding partners (particularly if structured as an automatic allocation without adjustment for performance) is likely to constitute out-of-scope remuneration;

- drawings taken as an advance of profit share will be in-scope remuneration and may be considered as fixed remuneration; and

- discretionary profit share payments will be in-scope remuneration and may be considered as variable remuneration, especially if the amount depends on performance.

7.243   An alternative approach would be to benchmark the partner's profit share against:

- the remuneration structures of others in similar roles or businesses; and

- the return on equity or return on capital expected in a similar investment context to that of the partner.

---

194 UCITS Guidelines, para 15; AIFMD Guidelines, para 17.

7.244 Another factor which may influence the determination of in-scope/out-of-scope remuneration is whether the partner devotes his or her full time and attention to the firm. A larger percentage of the partner's profit share should be considered out-of-scope remuneration where the partner works less than full-time in an executive position.

7.245 Although the FCA has not issued equivalent guidance on the UCITS Remuneration Code, the same principles presumably should apply to UCITS Remuneration Code staff who are engaged as partners rather than employees.

7.246 One difficulty that arises for partners who are subject to the rules on deferral is the way in which they are taxed. A partner is subject to income tax on his share of the partnership's or LLP's profits in the tax year in which they arise, even if the relevant profits are not actually paid to the partner in that year. This could result in a dry tax charge for partners on any deferred remuneration.

7.247 However, this issue is dealt with by specific legislation in the context of AIFM partnerships (there being no equivalent legislation for UCITS management partnerships or LLPs). Broadly, this legislation applies to partnerships or LLPs the regular business of which is managing one or more AIFs (or which carries out one or more functions of managing one or more AIFs as the delegate of (or as the sub-delegate of a delegate of) a person whose regular business is managing one or more AIFs) and which elect to come within the rules.

7.248 This election must be made within six months after the end of the first period of account for which the election is to have effect. Under the rules, broadly, an individual partner can allocate to the relevant LLP or partnership all or part of his profit share (from the partnership's or LLP's AIF management trade) consisting of upfront remuneration taking the form of instruments with a retention period of at least six months or of deferred remuneration.

7.249 The effect of this is that the partnership or LLP (rather than the partner) is subject, in the tax year in which its relevant period of account ends, to income tax at the additional rate on the profit allocated to it. Broadly, if all or part of the relevant remuneration vests in the partner he is subject to income tax in the tax year of (in the case of deferred remuneration) vesting or (in the case of upfront remuneration) in which the profit would normally have been allocated to the partner, but will receive a credit for the income tax paid by the partnership or LLP.

Delegates

7.250 It is common in the investment management industry for firms to delegate some of their investment management functions (such as portfolio or risk management) to a third party. The ESMA Guidelines provide that, when delegating investment management functions, firms should ensure that:

- the entities to which the functions are delegated are subject to regulatory requirements on remuneration that are equally effective as those applicable under the ESMA Guidelines; and

- appropriate contractual arrangements are put in place with the delegates in order to ensure that there is no circumvention of the remuneration rules in the ESMA Guidelines. These contractual arrangements should cover any payments made to the delegates' AIFM/UCITS Remuneration Code staff as compensation for the performance of investment management activities on behalf of the firm.[195]

7.251   The UCITS Guidelines make it clear that the remuneration rules under CRD IV are considered to be equally effective as those under UCITS V.[196] The FCA's general guidance on the AIFM Remuneration Code suggests that the FCA would consider the requirements of the BIPRU Remuneration Code (as well as the IFPRU and Dual-regulated firms Remuneration Codes) to be equally effective.

Individuals performing non-AIFMD business

7.252   The FCA's general guidance on the AIFM Remuneration Code recognises that AIFM Remuneration Code staff may not be involved in the management of AIFs or may spend some of their time performing AIFMD business and some of their time performing non-AIFMD business.

7.253   To the extent that AIFMD Remuneration Code staff are not involved in the management of AIFs, this can be taken into account when applying the proportionality principle and may justify the disapplication of the pay-out process rules. Some staff performing non-AIFMD business may also not be considered AIFM Remuneration Code staff because of their limited impact on the risk profiles of the AIFM or the AIFs it manages.

7.254   For individuals whose work is a mixture of AIFMD and non-AIFMD business a firm may apportion their remuneration according to the type of business performed and treat each portion under the relevant remuneration regime. The apportionment may be on the basis of time, funds under management or another appropriate benchmark.

7.255   Although the FCA has not issued equivalent guidance on the UCITS Remuneration Code, the same principles presumably should apply to UCITS Remuneration Code staff.

195 UCITS Guidelines, para 16; AIFMD Guidelines, para 18.
196 UCITS Guidelines, para 17.

5 INSURERS, REINSURERS AND SOLVENCY II

Background

7.256 The Solvency II Directive 2009/138/EC (Solvency II), which came into force on 1 January 2016, sets out regulatory requirements for insurance and reinsurance firms. Solvency II is a single supervisory regime for all of the EU and has proportionate application, depending on the nature, scale and complexity of risks posed to the firm's business. The European Insurance and Occupational Pensions Authority (EIOPA), which contributed to the development of the regulatory framework, monitors and ensures the consistent application of Solvency II.

7.257 Solvency II applies to most EU insurers and reinsurers,[197] with very small firms excluded from scope.[198]

7.258 The Solvency II remuneration requirements are contained in Article 275 of the Commission Delegated Regulation (EU) 2015/35 (Solvency II Regulation) which is directly applicable to Solvency II firms.[199] In 2016 the PRA published policy statement PS22/16 together with supervisory statement SS10/16 (which was updated in July 2018). PS22/16 and SS10/16 set out the PRA's expectations of how compliance with the remuneration requirements of the Solvency II Regulation may be achieved particularly by 'significant insurers' (PRA category 1 and 2 firms).

Text of Article 275 of Solvency II Regulation

7.259 The text of Article 275 of the Solvency II Regulation is set out in full below:

'1. When establishing and applying the remuneration policy referred to in Article 258(1)(l), insurance and reinsurance undertakings shall comply with all of the following principles:

(a) the remuneration policy and remuneration practices shall be established, implemented and maintained in line with the undertaking's business and risk management strategy, its risk profile, objectives, risk management practices and the long-term interests and performance of the undertaking as a whole and shall incorporate measures aimed at avoiding conflicts of interest;

(b) the remuneration policy promotes sound and effective risk management and shall not encourage risk-taking that exceeds the risk tolerance limits of the undertaking;

---

197 Solvency II, Article 2.
198 Solvency II, section 2, Articles 3–12.
199 EIOPA also published 'Guidelines on systems of governance' 2015, SS10/16.

(c) the remuneration policy applies to the undertaking as a whole, and contains specific arrangements that take into account the tasks and performance of the administrative, management or supervisory body, persons who effectively run the undertaking or have other key functions and other categories of staff whose professional activities have a material impact on the undertaking's risk profile;

(d) the administrative, management or supervisory body of the undertaking which establishes the general principles of the remuneration policy for those categories of staff whose professional activities have a material impact on the undertaking's risk profile is responsible for the oversight of its implementation;

(e) there shall be clear, transparent and effective governance with regard to remuneration, including the oversight of the remuneration policy;

(f) an independent remuneration committee shall be created, if appropriate in relation to the significance of the insurance or reinsurance undertakings in terms of size and internal organisation, in order to periodically support the administrative, management or supervisory body in overseeing the design of the remuneration policy and remuneration practices, their implementation and operation;

(g) the remuneration policy shall be disclosed to each member of the undertaking's staff.

2. The specific arrangements referred to in point (c) of paragraph 1c shall comply with all of the following principles:

(a) where remuneration schemes include both fixed and variable components, such components shall be balanced so that the fixed or guaranteed component represents a sufficiently high proportion of the total remuneration to avoid employees being overly dependent on the variable components and to allow the undertaking to operate a fully flexible bonus policy, including the possibility of paying no variable component;

(b) where variable remuneration is performance-related, the total amount of the variable remuneration is based on a combination of the assessment of the performance of the individual and of the business unit concerned and of the overall result of the undertaking or the group to which the undertaking belongs;

(c) the payment of a substantial portion of the variable remuneration component, irrespective of the form in which it is to be paid, shall contain a flexible, deferred component that takes account of the nature and time horizon of the undertaking's business: that deferral period shall not be less than three years and the period shall be correctly aligned with the nature of the business, its risks, and the activities of the employees in question;

    (d) financial and also non-financial criteria shall be taken into account when assessing an individual's performance;

    (e) the measurement of performance, as a basis for variable remuneration, shall include a downwards adjustment for exposure to current and future risks, taking into account the undertaking's risk profile and the cost of capital;

    (f) termination payments shall be related to performance achieved over the whole period of activity and be designed in a way that does not reward failure;

    (g) persons subject to the remuneration policy shall commit to not using any personal hedging strategies or remuneration and liability-related insurance which would undermine the risk alignment effects embedded in their remuneration arrangement;

    (h) the variable part of remuneration of the staff engaged in the functions referred to in Articles 269 to 272 shall be independent from the performance of the operational units and areas that are submitted to their control.

    3.   The remuneration policy shall be designed in such a way as to take into account the internal organisation of the insurance or reinsurance undertaking, and the nature, scale and complexity of the risks inherent in its business.'

Supervisory statement SS10/16: applying Article 275

7.260   The PRA expects all Solvency II firms to comply with the remuneration requirements of Article 275 and with the EIOPA 'Guidelines on systems of governance'.[200] SS 10/16 is aimed at significant[201] insurance firms but the PRA suggests that it may be read as a guide for smaller firms when reviewing their remuneration policies and practices. Indeed, the PRA states[202] that it expects smaller firms[203] to comply appropriately with the Solvency II Regulation when setting their remuneration policies.

7.261   The application of proportionality does not mean that a smaller firm may disapply the requirements. Rather, appropriate judgement should be exercised to ensure the requirements are applied proportionately and modified where required to fit the nature and size of the business.

7.262   SS10/16 does not set out absolute requirements as these are contained in the directly applicable Solvency II Regulation. The PRA suggests that Category

---

200 SS10/16, para 2.1.
201 Category 1 and 2 PRA regulated firms.
202 SS10/16, para 6.3.
203 Category 3–5 PRA regulated firms.

1 and 2 firms which cannot meet the PRA's expectations as set out in SS10/16 should contact the PRA.

Remuneration policy

7.263 All entities within the scope of a Solvency II group should have a consistent remuneration policy that is in line with the group's risk management and internal control system. Material risks at group level should also be reflected appropriately in the design of remuneration arrangements across all group entities.[204]

7.264 This does not mean that the same remuneration policy with identical variable remuneration structures and pay practices must apply to every group entity. Whilst the PRA expects non-EEA entities in the group to comply with their obligations under Solvency II, it recognises that it may be necessary to deviate from the group remuneration policy for staff identified in accordance with Article 275(1)(c) ('Solvency II staff') who are employed by non-EEA entities located in jurisdictions with conflicting local regulatory, legal, operational or taxation requirements. Significant deviations from the group's remuneration policy should be reported to the PRA.[205]

Application to non-Solvency II entities

7.265 Many insurance groups contain banking and asset management entities which are subject to other regulatory regimes such as CRD IV, AIFMD and UCITS V, and so different remuneration requirements may need to be applied within the group. However, the PRA stipulates that there should still be a high degree of consistency across individual firm policies to enable the remuneration policy to be controlled at group level.

Proportionality

7.266 Article 275(3) provides for the application of the proportionality principle when designing the remuneration policy. The remuneration policy should therefore take into account the internal organisation of the insurance or reinsurance undertaking, and the nature, scale and complexity of the risks inherent in its business.

7.267 The PRA's view is that it is appropriate to limit the application of the expectations set out in SS10/16 to significant firms only (Category 1 and 2 PRA regulated firms),[206] although smaller firms[207] should still comply appropriately

---

204 SS10/16, para 2.3.
205 SS10/16, para 2.4.
206 See 'PRA's approach to insurance supervision', March 2016.
207 Category 3–5 PRA regulated firms.

with the Solvency II Regulation when setting their remuneration policies. The application of the proportionality principle does not mean that smaller firms can simply disapply the requirements altogether. Rather, they should apply and modify them in a way which reflects their size and the nature of their businesses.[208]

7.268   As stated at 7.25, under the CRD IV Codes, the BIPRU Remuneration Code and the AIFMD/UCITS Remuneration Codes there is a *de minimis* exemption which allows firms to disapply certain rules (including those relating to payments in instruments, deferral and performance adjustment) in respect of individuals whose:

- total remuneration is no more than £500,000; and

- variable remuneration is no more than 33% of their total remuneration.

7.269   There is no equivalent *de minimis* exemption that applies under Solvency II. However, the PRA states in SS10/16 that it will take this indicator of proportionality into account when assessing the arrangements that firms have put in place to comply with the remuneration requirements under Solvency II. The implication of this seems to be that the PRA will generally not take any issue with a firm that does not apply the rules relating to payments in instruments, deferral and performance adjustment to individuals who meet these criteria.[209]

Solvency II staff

7.270   The specific remuneration arrangements set out in Article 275(2) only apply to:

- the administrative, management or supervisory body;

- persons who effectively run the undertaking or have other key functions; and

- other categories of staff whose professional activities have a material impact on the firm's risk profile.

7.271   Individuals falling within these categories are referred to as 'Solvency II staff'.

7.272   The PRA expects the following individuals to be identified by firms as Solvency II staff:

- board members;

- executive committee members;

208 SS10/16, para 6.3.
209 SS10/16, para 6.4.

- senior management function (SMF) holders with PRA or FCA supervisory pre-approval and significant influence functions (SIF) holders with FCA supervisory pre-approval;

- key function holders (KFHs) reported to the PRA; and

- material risk takers (MRTs).[210]

7.273   KFHs will include those individuals with significant responsibility for the risk management, compliance, actuarial and internal audit functions and, in the PRA's view, possibly also the investment, IT and claims management functions. This extends not just to those with significant responsibility for such functions at group level, but also those who have such responsibility at the level of the regulated entity.[211]

7.274   The PRA does not mandate any specific arrangements that should be put in place to identify MRTs. However, the expectation is that MRTs would include underwriters with significant underwriting limits relative to the firm's overall risk tolerance and investment managers able to commit to significant credit risk exposures and market risk transactions above a certain material threshold.[212]

7.275   Firms are expected to keep a record of the assessment criteria applied to determine their Solvency II staff and the final list of Solvency II staff for each performance year.[213]

Deferral

7.276   Article 275(2)(c) requires firms to defer 'a substantial portion' of any variable remuneration component paid to Solvency II staff for a period of no less than three years. Deferred variable remuneration must vest no faster than pro rata from year one.

7.277   The variable remuneration component means the aggregate amount awarded in a given performance year under bonus plans, LTIPs and/or any other variable remuneration plans in which the individual participates. For these purposes, LTIP awards should be valued at the grant date as the maximum potential value that could be paid out if 100% of the performance conditions are met with the deferral period commencing on grant.[214]

7.278   Article 275(2)(c) does not specify what percentage of any variable remuneration component is regarded as being 'a substantial portion'. However,

---

210 SS10/16, para 3.2.
211 SS10/16, para 3.4.
212 SS10/16, para 3.5.
213 SS10/16, para 3.8.
214 SS10/16, para 4.2.

the PRA's view is that this is very unlikely to be less than 40%.[215] This reflects the deferral obligations under CRD IV, AIFMD and UCITS V.

Malus and clawback

7.279   Article 275 does not specifically refer to malus adjustments. However, the PRA considers that, in order to comply with Article 275, firms must consider whether or not to apply malus during the deferral period and to be able to apply it where appropriate (eg where there has been a specific risk management failure).[216]

7.280   Firms should therefore ensure that their deferred remuneration plans (including their LTIPs) give them the right to make malus adjustments during the deferral period in appropriate circumstances.

7.281   There is no obligation under Article 275 to apply clawback and no expectation under SS10/16 that firms should build clawback rights into their remuneration arrangements for Solvency II staff.

Performance measurement

7.282   Under Article 275(2)(b), where variable remuneration is performance-related, the total amount of variable remuneration paid to Solvency II staff must be based on an assessment of the performance of the individual, the business unit concerned and the overall results of the firm or group. Assessments of performance should be based on financial and non-financial criteria.[217] According to the PRA's guidance in SS10/16 the non-financial criteria should include the extent of the employee's adherence to effective risk management and compliance with relevant regulatory requirements.[218]

7.283   As for the obligation in Article 257(2)(e) to include in the measurement of performance a downwards adjustment for exposure to current and future risks, taking into account the undertaking's risk profile and the cost of capital, the PRA expects firms to be able to demonstrate how they have taken into account the risks they face in the short to long term and the cost of capital when determining variable remuneration at aggregate and individual level.[219]

7.284   The PRA notes that particular care should be taken to ensure that variable remuneration awarded to Solvency II staff in risk management, compliance, internal audit and actuarial functions is not determined using criteria which

---

215 SS10/16, para 4.3.
216 SS10/16, para 4.4.
217 Article 275(2)(d).
218 SS10/16, para 5.1.
219 SS10/16, para 5.2.

measure the performance of the operational units or business areas under those individuals' control.[220]

Termination payments

7.285   As noted, Article 275(2)(f) provides that 'termination payments shall be related to performance achieved over the whole period of activity and be designed in a way that does not reward failure'. The PRA's view is that termination payments for Solvency II staff should be 'fair and proportionate relative to prior performance'.[221]

7.286   As with the rules relating to termination payments under the CRD IV Codes, this is not intended to prevent firms from honouring reasonable contractual notice payments or from compromising genuine statutory employment claims that an employee may have on termination. Rather, the rule is intended to prevent firms from including generous 'golden parachute' payments in contracts of employment which may be triggered even where the employee's performance has been poor or the employee has been guilty of misconduct. Firms should also avoid making generous ex gratia severance payments on termination where they are not justified by performance or the employee's conduct.

6   BREXIT AND FINANCIAL SERVICES REMUNERATION

7.287   What, if any, developments there may be in the regulation of remuneration in the financial services sector in light of Brexit is unclear at the time of writing. What is certain is that immediately following the UK's departure from the EU (due to take place on 29 March 2019) the existing regimes will continue in force.

7.288   Depending on the future relationship that exists between the UK and the EU after 29 March 2019, it may be that the UK will no longer be bound to comply with the remuneration rules in the relevant directives (ie CRD IV, AIFMD, UCITS V and Solvency II) that underpin the current remuneration regimes described in this chapter.

7.289   The FCA has, however, made it clear that Brexit will not necessarily lead to de-regulation. In a speech in July 2016, shortly after his appointment as Chief Executive of the FCA, Andrew Bailey commented that Brexit was not going to lead to a 'bonfire of regulation'. More recently, in a speech in October 2018, Mr Bailey stated that there were good reasons for the UK regulatory regime to stay closely aligned to the EU; these reasons included the close integration of UK and EU markets and the fact that much of the body of EU law and regulation in the sector had been developed by the UK together with other member states.

220 SS10/16, para 5.4.
221 SS10/16, para 5.5.

7.290   It is also worth noting that in certain respects (for example in relation to the rules on buy-outs and the application of clawback in the PRA's Remuneration Part and the Dual-regulated firms Remuneration Code) the UK has chosen to go beyond simply implementing the strict obligations contained in CRD IV.

7.291   The most likely area for reform in the regulation of remuneration (subject always to the nature of the relationship between the UK and EU following 29 March 2019) is the bonus cap. The removal of the bonus cap was identified by Mark Carney, the Governor of the Bank of England, as a possibility in November 2017. His position was supported by Mr Bailey who confirmed in the same month that this was one element of regulation that the UK may seek to dispense with following its departure from the EU.

7.292   The comments from Mr Carney and Mr Bailey came as no surprise as the UK government had always opposed the introduction of the bonus cap (principally on the grounds that it would result in significant increases in fixed pay which would not be subject to performance adjustment) and had initiated a legal challenge to it in September 2013. (This was subsequently abandoned after the Advocate General issued his opinion that the cap was lawful in November 2014.[222]) However, at the time of writing, there are no firm proposals to remove the bonus cap.

222 Opinion in Case C-507/13

CHAPTER 8

Bonuses and Employment Law Considerations

Elizabeth Graves, Partner and Susan Mayne, Consultant

I VARIABLE PAY – BACKGROUND

8.01   In financial institutions, bonuses (or variable – as opposed to fixed – remuneration) form a significant portion of senior employees' remuneration packages. The advantages of awarding variable remuneration are clear: such payments incentivise staff and encourage strong performance. However, the Parliamentary Commission on Banking Standards (PCBS) highlighted the negative side of over-incentivisation, which could result in excessive and dangerous risk taking. For a more detailed discussion of what constitutes fixed and variable pay see 7.65–7.73.

8.02   The restraints on variable remuneration under EU and domestic laws and regulation are set out in Chapter 7. However, employers also need to comply with the duties owed to employees or former employees according to both express and implied terms of their employment.

2 EXPRESS TERMS

8.03   The first place to start in determining an employer's bonus obligations is the express terms of the employment contract together with any collateral documents. Clearly, if the employment contract confers an express right to a bonus calculated according to a defined formula (a guaranteed bonus), it will be difficult for the employer to avoid paying a bonus according to those terms unless overridden by a statutory or regulatory requirement (for example, under companies legislation or a requirement of a remuneration code; see Chapter 7).[1]

8.04   Express terms may be found in handbooks, governing documents of a plan (or rules) or in a separate award letter. Express terms may also be oral.

Dresdner Kleinwort Limited and Commerzbank AG v Attrill[2]

8.05   In *Dresdner Kleinwort Limited and Commerzbank AG v Attrill*, the claimant and 104 others were employed subject to contracts of employment which provided that they would be eligible for consideration of such discretionary awards as in the employer's absolute discretion it saw fit to award. An employment handbook stated that the employer could vary the terms and conditions in the handbook and of employment generally, but such changes could only be made by a member of human resources and had to be communicated in writing, unless the change affected a group, in which case notification could be by display on notice boards or company intranet.

8.06   In an attempt to retain staff in connection with the sale of Dresdner Kleinwort to Commerzbank, the employees were promised the payment of a bonus from a guaranteed minimum bonus pool (a 'retention pool'). The creation of a minimum retention pool was announced live to staff at a town hall and via the company's intranet with allocation of bonuses to be made 'in the usual way'.

8.07   The employees successfully argued that letters sent to them subsequently setting out details of the payments but subject to a material adverse change (MAC) clause amounted to a breach of contract. The Court of Appeal accepted that the town hall announcement followed by the intranet announcement were sufficient to create a binding unilateral variation of the contract entitling the employees to a bonus payment from the retention pool. The introduction of the MAC clause was a breach of the implied duty of trust and confidence.

Brogden v Investec[3]

8.08   In *Brogden* the High Court set out the basic legal principles on contractual interpretation in relation to express terms:

---

1   There may be exceptional occasions when a term will be implied into a contract to deprive an employee of the benefit of an express term (for example, in *Tesco Stores Ltd v Pook* [2003] EWHC 823 (Ch) a term was implied that an employee may not exercise a share option in accordance with the express rules of the plan because to do so would allow the employee to take advantage of his own wrongdoing, which, had the employer known of it at the time, would have entitled the employer to summarily dismiss the employee).
2   [2013] EWCA Civ 394.
3   [2014] IRLR 924.

- the aim is to ascertain what a reasonable person having all the background knowledge which would reasonably have been available to the parties in the situation they were in at the time of the contract would have understood the parties to have meant by the words they used;

- the court identifies the meaning of contractual language not simply by adopting the point of view of a reasonable bystander but by assuming the parties themselves were reasonable people using the language of the contract to express a common intention;

- if contractual language is capable of more than one interpretation the court generally should prefer the interpretation which is most consistent with business common sense;

- the law excludes from admissible background information previous negotiations of the parties. However, the law does not exclude the use of such evidence for the purpose of establishing that a fact that may be relevant as background was known to the parties. This includes facts communicated by one party to the other in the course of the negotiations.

3   DISCRETIONARY BONUSES AND IMPLIED TERMS

8.09   The Court of Appeal in *Khatri v Co-operatieve Raiffeisen-Boerenleenbank BA*[4] noted that 'if banks decide to reward their employees by means of purely discretionary bonuses then they should say so openly and not seek to dress up such a bonus with the language of entitlement qualified by a slight phrase which does not make it absolutely clear that there is in fact no entitlement at all'.

8.10   Mr Khatri claimed that he should have received a guaranteed bonus under the terms of his contract of employment despite the employer having changed the terms of the bonus scheme (Mr Khatri refused to sign an acceptance to the change). The Court of Appeal held that as there were no other changes to his terms of employment and Mr Khatri had not signed the new bonus terms, it would be quite wrong to infer that he had accepted changes to his contract.[5]

Partial discretion

8.11   Express terms may confer an entitlement to participate in a bonus scheme, but that payment depends on the exercise of the employer's discretion as to the amount of bonus, if any ('partial discretion').

8.12   An employer must take care not to make representations as to an expected level of bonus since this may give rise to a contractual entitlement despite the express language that the amount is at the employer's discretion.

---

4   [2010] EWCA Civ 397.
5   *Solectron Scotland v Roper* [2004] IRLR 4.

8.13   Often the employer will provide that the employee has a contractual entitlement to a bonus subject to the attainment of given targets. Where such targets are not easily measurable, disputes may arise. In a case concerning the payment of an ill-health pension the Court of Appeal held that the pension scheme formed part of the employee's remuneration package under the employee's contract of employment and it was implicit in the contract of employment that the employer's functions should be discharged in good faith.[6]

Implied terms

8.14   Absolute discretion is where an employer has complete discretion as to whether to consider the eligibility of an employee for a bonus at all together with the amount of any bonus awarded.

8.15   In *Lavarack v Woods of Colchester Ltd*,[7] Mr Lavarack's service agreement provided that he was entitled to 'such bonus (if any) as the directors [...] shall from time to time determine'. His bonus formed a substantial part of his remuneration package. When the parties fell out he successfully claimed wrongful dismissal and argued that damages should include the loss of future bonuses. The Court of Appeal held by a majority that Mr Lavarack could not recover damages for loss of a chance.

8.16   Other cases have refined the position further. However, an express statement that any bonus is discretionary does not mean that the employee will have no contractual rights in relation to the manner in which the discretion is exercised.[8]

8.17   Simply using the word 'discretionary' may not suffice as all relevant circumstances will be taken into consideration in determining whether there are contractual elements.[9]

8.18   When exercising discretion an employer must take care to:

● reach a decision in good faith;

● not act capriciously, arbitrarily or irrationally (*Clark v Nomura*)[10];

● not breach the implied term of trust and confidence (*Attrill v Dresdner Kleinwort and Commerzbank*[11] and *Transco plc v O'Brien*[12] [2002] – see 8.23)

---

6   *Mihlenstedt v Barclays Bank International Ltd* [1989] IRLR 522.
7   [1967] 1 QB 278.
8   *Small v Boots Co plc* [2009] IRLR 328.
9   *Small v Boots Co plc* [2009] IRLR 328.
10 [2000] IRLR 766.
11 [2013] EWCA Civ 394.
12 [2002] EWCA Civ 379.

8.19   In *IBM v Dalgleish*[13] (concerning the duty of trust and confidence in the context of making changes to a pension scheme) the Court of Appeal held that the test for a breach of the duty of good faith applicable to those exercising non-fiduciary powers under pension schemes and the employer's duty of trust and confidence is a rationality test equivalent to that of the public law test in *Wednesbury* (see 8.45 ff). In order to decide whether an employer's decision in a given case satisfies the rationality test the court may need to know what the employer's reasons were and about the decision-making process.

8.20   The employer or the person exercising the power must take account of relevant matters (and no irrelevant matters) and the decision must not be arbitrary, perverse or capricious. If, however, the employees can show a prima facie case that the decision is at least questionable, the evidential burden may shift to the employer to show what its reasons were. If there is no such evidence, an inference may be drawn that the decision lacked rationality. The test is one of commercial rationality and logic and not of reasonableness. No higher duty arises from reasonable expectations engendered by previous actions and communications.

Decisions made capriciously and in bad faith

8.21   In *Clark v BET plc*[14] Mr Clark's employment contract contained an obligation that his salary 'shall be reviewed annually and be increased by such amount, if any, as the board shall in its absolute discretion decide'. The High Court held that there was an obligation on BET to review Mr Clark's salary and to review upwards. The High Court stated that 'if the board had capriciously or in bad faith exercised its discretion so as to determine the increase at nil and therefore to pay Mr Clark no increase at all, that would have been a breach of contract. This is a case where BET have repudiated their obligation altogether …'. The court rejected the argument that there was no contractual right to a pay increase and highlighted the language of entitlement.

8.22   With regard to bonus, Mr Clark's contract provided that 'the executive will participate in a bonus arrangement providing a maximum of 60% of salary in any year' and BET would notify the employee of the performance measures and terms for vesting of bonus awards at the beginning of each financial year. The High Court held that the contract 'confers a right on Mr Clark to participate in a bonus scheme, and a bonus scheme which provides within its terms for a maximum of 60% bonus of salary'. Merely stating the word 'discretionary' did not necessarily mean that the terms of a bonus scheme are discretionary.[15]

---

13   [2017] WLR(D) 545.
14   [1997] IRLR 348.
15   *Small v Boots Co plc* [2009] IRLR 328.

8.23   In *Transco plc v O'Brien*,[16] Mr O'Brien claimed that his former employers were in breach of his contract of employment by failing to consider him for and subsequently offer the enhanced contractual redundancy payment referred to in their document 'Financial Packages 1996–2002'. The Court of Appeal held that to single out, as Transco did, an employee on capricious grounds and refuse to offer him the same terms as are offered to the rest of the workforce was a breach of the implied term of trust and confidence.

Irrational and perverse

8.24   In *Clark v Nomura*,[17] Mr Clark succeeded in his claim for non-payment of a discretionary bonus which was stated to be 'not guaranteed in any way' and 'dependent upon individual performance'. To succeed, he had to show that no reasonable employer would have exercised the discretion in that way. In this case, Mr Clark had been awarded no bonus (following his raising various concerns with the regulator) in contrast to other employees who were awarded substantial bonuses.

8.25   Mr Clark had made substantial profits for Nomura during the relevant period. The High Court held that the correct test was 'one of irrationality or perversity ... i.e. that no reasonable employer would have exercised his discretion in this way'. On the facts, the decision not to award any bonus at all was plainly perverse and irrational. Burton J stated:

> 'the employer cannot rely upon the fact that the employee has been dismissed to avoid liability for a bonus otherwise payable – i.e. he cannot, if he dismisses at or after the payment date, simply say that there is no bonus because the employee has no longevity because he has been dismissed. To allow for longevity as a separate factor risks the outcome that the employer can create lack of longevity simply by dismissing'.

8.26   *Clark v Nomura* has been followed in numerous decisions.[18]

8.27   In *Horkulak v Cantor Fitzgerald International*,[19] Mr Horkulak was recruited on the basis of an initial guaranteed bonus and in addition a discretionary bonus on the following terms: 'the company may, in its absolute discretion, pay you an annual discretionary bonus which will be paid within 90 days of the financial year-end ... the amount of which shall be mutually agreed by yourself, the chief executive of the company and the president of Cantor Fitzgerald Ltd Partnership, however the final decision shall be in the sole discretion of the president of Cantor Fitzgerald LP ...'.

---

16 [2002] EWCA Civ 379.
17 [2000] IRLR 766.
18 *Mallone v BPB Industries Ltd* [2002] ICR 1045; *CommerzbankAg v Keen* [2006] EWCA Civ 1536; *Dresdner Kleinwort Ltd v Attrill* [2013] EWCA Civ 394.
19 [2005] ICR 402.

8.28   Mr Horkulak resigned following alleged bullying and claimed wrongful dismissal. The High Court held that Mr Horkulak was entitled to a 'fair and rational assessment of his entitlement'. The Court of Appeal followed *Clark v Nomura*. A discretion provided for in a contract which is prima facie of an unlimited nature will be regarded as subject to an implied term that it will be exercised genuinely and rationally.

8.29   The High Court had been right to hold that Mr Horkulak was entitled to a bona fide and rational exercise of the employer's discretion as to whether to award him a bonus and in what amount. On the facts the employer had acted irrationally and perversely and so in breach of contract when it did not award a bonus to Mr Horkulak.

8.30   In *Commerzbank v Keen*,[20] the Court of Appeal emphasised that the test of irrationality when deciding not to award a bonus is not easily met: 'it would require an overwhelming case to persuade the court to find that the level of a discretionary bonus was irrational or perverse in an area where so much must depend on the discretionary judgment of the bank in fluctuating market and labour conditions'.

8.31   In *Mallone v BPB Industries plc*,[21] the award of nil share options where scheme rules provided that BPB had 'absolute discretion' to decide the proportion of options exercisable after termination was held by the Court of Appeal to be an irrational exercise of discretion on the facts. However, this does not mean that an employer must exercise its discretion reasonably; rather, an employer must not do so in such a way as to destroy the implied term of trust and confidence.[22]

Discretion v construction of contract terms

8.32   The Court of Appeal in *Brogden v Investec plc*[23] (see 8.08) upheld a High Court decision that Investec was entitled to pay two equity derivatives traders a nil bonus when the profit and loss account of the Structured Equity Derivative desk for which they worked showed a loss.

8.33   However, the Court of Appeal took a different approach to the High Court when deciding on what basis the bank was entitled to pay a nil bonus. The High Court concluded that it was within the bank's discretion to determine what was meant by the term 'economic value added' (EVA) in the bonus scheme rules. It held that the bank's decision could only be challenged if it could be shown that it had acted irrationally or in bad faith.

---

20   [2007] ICR 632.
21   [2002] IRLR 452.
22   *Midland Bank plc v McCann* UKEAT/1041/97.
23   [2016] EWCA Civ 1031.

8.34   The Court of Appeal, however, concluded that this was not a case that turned on the application of the bank's discretion. Instead, this was a case that turned on construction of contractual terms, in what the bank must have meant by the term 'EVA' in the contracts with its employees.

8.35   Ultimately this case is fact-specific and is therefore of limited application. However, it highlights the difficulty faced by both employers and employees in understanding when an employer's decision can be challenged as the exercise of discretion (in which additional considerations come into play) and when the dispute is simply about what the express terms of the contract mean.

4   NOTICE PERIODS

8.36   It is common for a financial institution to seek to exclude from the bonus round any employee who has given or received notice at the time bonuses would usually be paid. In order to avoid paying a bonus to an employee who has left or is under notice, a clear provision must be stated in the employment contract or the bonus scheme terms.

8.37   In *Rutherford v Seymour Pierce Ltd*,[24] the High Court rejected an employer's argument that a term should be implied into a bonus scheme that in order to be considered for an award under the bonus scheme Mr Rutherford had to be employed and not under notice at the date of payment.

8.38   It may also be possible for an employee to argue that an implied term of his contract is that an employer cannot terminate the employee's employment in order to avoid paying a bonus (*Takacs v Barclays Services Jersey Ltd*)[25].

8.39   In *Takacs,* the High Court declined to grant the defendant employer summary judgment in respect of its argument that the express term of the claimant's employment entitling it to terminate his employment on notice overrode any implied term of cooperation regarding his bonus entitlement. The High Court found that the employee's claim in relation to an implied term of cooperation had a real prospect of success.

5   TERMINATION IN REPUDIATORY BREACH

8.40   Employers may also have difficulty in dismissing an employee to avoid paying a bonus where the dismissal is not effected properly in accordance with the contract terms.

---

24   [2010] IRLR 606.
25   [2006] IRLR 877.

8.41   In *Geys v Société Générale, London Branch*,[26] Société Générale attempted to dismiss Mr Geys by paying him in lieu of notice. Its aim was to ensure that the date on which his employment ended meant that it could avoid having to pay him a substantially higher termination payment provided for under his contract of employment than where his employment would end after a specified date.

8.42   After he was informed of his immediate termination and escorted from the building (without at that point being given any clear notification that the right to pay him in lieu of notice had been exercised), Mr Geys instructed solicitors to write to his employer affirming his contract of employment. A majority of the Supreme Court held that his employment did not end until he later received unequivocal communication of his employer's decision to properly exercise its contractual right to summarily dismiss him by making a payment in lieu of notice (PILON). His employment had not ended automatically when Société Générale wrongfully repudiated it on the earlier date.

8.43   PILON clauses should clearly state that an employee has no entitlement to any bonus on termination if that is the employer's intention. Care should also be taken when drafting a PILON clause to ensure the payment to be made is easily identifiable and not to use unspecific language such as 'benefits' which may be construed so as to include bonus within the PILON calculation.

8.44   In *Faieta v ICAP Management Services Ltd*,[27] the claimant argued that a provision in his contract of employment providing for 'benefits' to be continued during a period of garden leave extended to a guaranteed minimum bonus provided for in the contract. While accepting that a bonus is clearly a 'benefit', the High Court held that in the context of the claimant's service agreement there was a distinction between 'bonus arrangements' in one clause and 'benefits' in a separate clause referring to private medical insurance, group life assurance and group income protection. Accordingly, the claim for bonus during garden leave failed.

6   WEDNESBURY 'REASONABLENESS': BRAGANZA V BP SHIPPING

8.45   The scope for challenging the exercise of discretion was arguably widened as a result of the Supreme Court's decision in *Braganza v BP Shipping*.[28] In this case (unrelated to bonuses) the Supreme Court held that an employer's decision not to pay death in service benefit to a deceased employee's widow (because the employee had committed suicide) was 'unreasonable' in the *Wednesbury* sense (the public law concept of reasonableness which allows the court to consider the process by which a decision was reached, not simply the outcome).

---

26   [2013] IRLR 122.
27   [2017] EWHC 2995 (QB).
28   [2015] UKSC 17.

8.46   Mr Braganza's contract with BP stated that a death in service benefit would not be payable in the event of his suicide. Following an investigation, BP concluded that suicide was the most likely explanation for Mr Braganza's disappearance at sea. The court found that BP Shipping had failed to direct themselves that they needed to find evidence of sufficient cogency commensurate with the seriousness of the finding of suicide.

8.47   However, the ability to argue a *Braganza* case is not straightforward. The 'reasonableness' test in *Wednesbury* is a difficult test to meet. The Supreme Court reached its decision on the basis that the choice was binary – either a payment was made or it was not. Bonus claims are usually based on multiple outcomes where there is little scope for intensive scrutiny of the decision-making process.

8.48   The *Braganza* argument was tested in *Paturel v DB Services*,[29] although Mr Paturel failed to persuade the court on the facts in his case that an award of one per cent of profits was one that no reasonable employer would have reached.

8.49   In *Hills v Niksun Inc*,[30] the Court of Appeal held that once the employee had shown that the employer had acted irrationally it is for the employer to show that it acted reasonably.

8.50   The exercise of discretion to pay commission was not broad and untrammelled and in that case the commission plan in issue set out a detailed process for the award of commission, which Niksun was obliged to follow.

7   ISSUES FOR FINANCIAL SERVICES FIRMS

8.51   When considering the question of whether a decision is perverse or irrational can a financial institution justify a low or nil bonus in the light of regulatory expectations and common law? Ultimately, a firm will still need to consider the terms of its scheme and abide by the case law outlined in this chapter. Compliance with the remuneration codes in itself will not be a 'get out'. An employer will need to show that a decision to apply malus or clawback does not breach the duty of trust and confidence.

8.52   Regulated financial institutions must comply with the regulators' rules and expectations on variable remuneration (see Chapter 7). In addition to challenges to the exercise of discretion, firms also need to consider other statutory restrictions such as the need to avoid unlawful discrimination when awarding bonuses.

8.53   When claiming compensation for loss of employment in the context of a statutory claim such as unfair dismissal or discrimination an individual will

---

29   [2015] EWHC 3659.
30   [2016] EWCA Civ 115.

be able to claim for a lost bonus and for variable pay that has accrued but not yet vested.

Practical guidance

- Ensure the terms of any bonus scheme or contract provisions regarding bonus are clearly and unambiguously drafted and dovetail together.

- Where relevant, ensure that any deferral, malus and clawback provisions are expressly authorised by the employee. Ideally the ability to impose such terms should be authorised by the signed employment contract in addition to remuneration policies, scheme rules and any award documentation.

- Ensure that employment contracts, scheme documents and award documentation state that a bonus will only be paid while the employee is employed and not under notice and may be frozen while the employee is suspended or under investigation.

- Include express provisions that the contractual terms override any prior discussions, agreements or arrangements and that any oral representations are not binding.

- Avoid making statements that could create a contractual expectation to a certain level of bonus.

- Ensure that malus and clawback decisions are applied consistently, fairly and robustly and provide reasons for the decision. Where appropriate, allow for a review/appeal process.

- Remember that the application of malus or clawback should not be used as a deterrent nor have no link to the misconduct: in such a case it may be challenged as a penalty.

- Make sure that the employer's discretion is clear and, where appropriate, unfettered.

- Maintain clear records when exercising discretion explaining the reasons for a bonus award (particularly when the award is expected to be low).

- Consider all relevant matters and no irrelevant matters when exercising discretion.

- If varying contractual terms of a scheme or entitlement, if unilateral amendment is not clearly permitted ensure that the employee's express or implied consent is obtained.

- If it is intended that the employer will have the ability to unilaterally amend the terms of awards previously granted, ensure that there is an explicit provision in the scheme rules or the award documentation that makes clear that the employer can do this and how.

CHAPTER 9

Performance Management and Remuneration Incentives

Paul Fontes, Partner and Susan Mayne, Consultant

1	Introduction	9.01
2	Guidance on risks to customers from financial incentives	9.05
3	Risks to customers from performance management at firms	9.11
4	MiFID II remuneration incentives	9.17
5	Incentives, remuneration and performance management in consumer credit firms	9.21

I INTRODUCTION

9.01   The Remuneration Codes considered in Chapter 7 are primarily concerned with the remuneration of firms' senior staff (or MRTs). Their focus is on ensuring that firms adopt remuneration policies that promote sound and effective risk management. However, as a result of concerns about the mis-selling of various financial products to consumers (most notably payment protection insurance or 'PPI'), the FCA has also had concerns about the way in which firms incentivise and manage their sales staff and other staff whose behaviour can influence customer outcomes. The FCA has therefore issued guidance on these issues to all firms which deal directly with retail customers and some small and medium-sized enterprise customers.[1]

9.02   Furthermore, in order to implement the remuneration provisions contained in the Markets in Financial Instruments Directive (2004/39/EC) (MiFID) and the Markets in Financial Instruments Regulation, in 2018 the FCA introduced the MiFID Remuneration Incentives Code in SYSC 19F of the FCA Handbook. The aim of the MiFID Remuneration Incentives Code is to ensure that firms do not remunerate or assess the performance of staff in a way that conflicts with their duty to act in the best interests of their clients.

---

1   FCA FG13/01 and FCA FG15/01.

9.03   Separate rules and guidance have been issued by the FCA for firms that carry out consumer credit activity and have staff who deal directly with customers. These rules and guidance do not apply to firms that come under any of the FCA's Remuneration Codes.

9.04   The rules and guidance are considered in detail in this chapter. They should also be considered alongside the accountability regime. The focus on increased accountability means those working in financial services are expected to take more responsibility for their actions and the behaviours at their firms. The FCA sees the regime as an opportunity for employees to feel empowered to fulfil better their responsibilities to customers and challenge undue pressure that may be placed upon them.

2   GUIDANCE ON RISKS TO CUSTOMERS FROM FINANCIAL INCENTIVES[2]

9.05   In January 2013 the FSA (as it then was) published its final guidance on the risks to customers of financial incentives. This guidance remains in effect and applies to all firms in retail financial services with staff who are part of an incentive scheme and deal directly with retail customer transactions.[3] The guidance was issued following a review of firms' sales incentives in 2011 that had found that most incentive schemes were likely to encourage staff to mis-sell and that these risks were not being properly managed.

9.06   The guidance does not prescribe rules as to how firms should incentivise staff, but it does set out clear standards. Firms should apply Principle 3 of its Principles for Business[4] and SYSC of the FCA Handbook when developing incentive schemes and should have in place a strategy to manage the risk of any mis-selling to consumers that might occur.

9.07   It is noted that the likelihood of mis-selling increases when the value of incentives available to sales staff increases or when incentives make up a high proportion of a remuneration package for sales staff. In particular, customers are likely to suffer if:

- the incentive scheme is based on sales volumes, fee income or similar measures;

- the incentive scheme includes features that are harder to manage;

- management does not understand how the incentive scheme works; and

---

2   FCA FG13/01.
3   Where an appointed representative has their own sales staff or advisers, the principal firm is responsible for managing the risks from incentive arrangements. The principal will therefore need to understand the appointed representative's incentive arrangements.
4   Principle 3 states that: 'A firm must take reasonable care to organise and control its affairs responsibly and effectively, with adequate risk management systems'.

- poor quality sales or mis-selling are not adequately reflected in the eligibility for, or the level of, incentive payments.

9.08   The guidance identifies certain features of incentive schemes that significantly increase the risk of mis-selling. These include:

- where an employee receives a disproportionate reward for marginal sales. An example would be where achieving a target level of sales increases the incentive for all sales over a period, not just those above the target;

- where a higher rate of incentive is earned with a higher volume of sales;

- where there is an inappropriately larger incentive for selling one product over another or where there is an inappropriate level of incentive for selling additional products ('add-ons'); and

- where basic pay may be reduced if targets are not met or where remuneration is wholly based on commission.

9.09   The guidance also gives examples of incentive scheme features that might reduce the risk of mis-selling such as:

- rewarding good compliance and introducing quality measures that reflect the fair treatment of customers;

- reducing or withdrawing incentives where the quality of sales is poor;

- clawback where incentive payments already received have to be repaid or offset against future incentives if, for example, products are subsequently cancelled;

- deferral of part of the incentive so that payment can be linked to ongoing sales quality results or customer complaints records; and

- the use of balanced scorecards where the scheme is not just based on sales volumes but will include other measures such as the quality of sales and customer satisfaction.

9.10   To manage these risks, the FCA recommends effective governance arrangements and controls to identify the increased risk of mis-selling from incentive schemes. These include:

- robust monitoring and controls to mitigate the risk of inappropriate behaviour during sales conversations;

- management information to identify patterns in sales activity that could indicate an increased risk of mis-selling. This information may include which sales staff are achieving high sales volumes and what products they are selling;

- proper management of sales managers' conflicts of interest;

- effective oversight and approval of incentive schemes by senior management; and

- an effective risk identification and mitigation process.

3   RISKS TO CUSTOMERS FROM PERFORMANCE MANAGEMENT AT FIRMS

9.11   In FG13/01 it was recognised that the risks relating to incentive schemes for sales staff could also apply in a similar way to performance management and in July 2015 the FCA published its finalised guidance on risks to customers from performance management at firms.[5] This guidance is aimed at all firms in retail financial services and applies particularly to sales staff.[6]

9.12   The guidance notes that throughout 2014 the FCA saw an increase in whistleblowing reports regarding poor performance management practices, specifically in sales areas. This gave rise to significant concerns that poor performance management was creating a risk of mis-selling due to the pressure to meet targets. The FCA referred to this as 'undue pressure', recognising that some pressure and targets are to be expected in the course of business.

9.13   Furthermore, it was recognised that there was an inherent conflict in the role of middle management who manage the conflicting objectives of having to meet sales targets whilst at the same time being responsible for the manner in which a product is sold. Firms must ensure that these conflicts are managed in such a way that customers are not adversely affected.

9.14   Performance management is defined broadly in the guidance. The FCA describes it as 'the process through which organisations manage how individuals and teams behave to achieve organisational objectives'. This includes:

● formal processes such as appraisals and underperformance procedures;

● sales targets (or their equivalent); and

● other less formal day-to-day interactions and communications between sales staff and managers about sales results that influence behaviour (both written and verbal).

9.15   The guidance sets out the following key points which firms should consider:

● the type of pressure applied to staff and whether this is managed appropriately. In particular, the FCA highlights: intensive micro-management of sales results; pressure to share sales results with peers and possible face-to-face humiliation; and performance management practices not reflecting the firm's stated policy and aims;

● whether there is any hidden 'undue pressure'. Firms must ensure that the 'tone from the top' is reflected in the management of frontline staff. The FCA notes that the continuous interactions between different levels of management

---

5   FCA FG15/10.
6   Where an appointed representative has their own sales staff or advisers, the principal firm is responsible for managing the risks of mis-selling. The principal will therefore need to understand the appointed representative's approach to performance management.

and with frontline sales staff, which is often not documented, can present one of the greatest risks and is an area where poor practice could be hidden from direct view. Firms must ensure that sales results do not dominate any such interactions at the expense of the fair treatment of customers;

- the FCA recognises the commercial importance of sales targets. However, targets should reflect different aspects of the sales process including how individuals ensure customers receive the product(s) they need. There must be a balance between commercial targets and consumer benefits; and

- firms must ensure they do not 'over-incentivise' or apply unrealistic targets and must use performance management to root out poor performance.

9.16   To mitigate the risks of mis-selling, firms should:

- ensure they have effective performance management processes in place;

- put in place adequate systems and controls to identify any poor performance management practices and review any communications to staff which might lead to undue pressure. Firms should also engage with staff to understand where there is any undue pressure, for example using exit interviews to gauge levels of pressure;

- consider whether disciplinary procedures and other documents, such as standards of conduct, should be amended to reflect the expectations on managers. Examples of 'misconduct' should include mis-selling and applying undue pressure on staff to mis-sell. Firms should make clear what disciplinary sanctions may apply in the event of breach;

- ensure that whistleblowing policies make clear that staff can complain to the regulator about any undue pressure to mis-sell;

- coach and train line managers to manage appropriately and provide them with practical tools for assessment of performance;

- analyse customer complaints to measure whether overt pressure leads to mis-selling; and

- focus on ensuring that financial incentives are appropriate and are determined using a range of factors (not just sales targets). A balanced scorecard can help reduce risk.

4   MIFID II REMUNERATION INCENTIVES

9.17   As noted at 9.02, the MiFID Remuneration Incentives Code (SYSC 19F of the FCA Handbook) was introduced in 2018. It applies to the majority of firms regulated by the FCA capturing:

- banks, building societies, designated investment firms and IFPRU investment firms;

- firms subject to the optional exemption in Article 3 of MiFID (eg financial advisors, corporate finance firms and venture capitalist firms operating in the UK);

- third country firms (third country investment firms and UK branches of non-EEA banks) in relation to activities carried on from an establishment based in the UK; and

- UK branches of EEA MiFID investment firms (unless they are UCITS or AIFM investment firms).

9.18   SYSC 19F implements the MiFID requirements on remuneration incentives and focuses on the remuneration and performance management of sales staff. The types of roles affected include client-facing front-office staff, sales force staff (and their line managers) and financial analysts whose marketing material may be used by sales staff to induce clients to make investment decisions. It therefore largely affects staff who would not be classified as MRTs under the other Remuneration Codes.

9.19   SYSC 19F provides that a firm providing investment services to clients must ensure that staff are not remunerated or assessed in a way that conflicts with the firm's duties to act in the best interests of its clients. In particular, incentives or sales targets should not encourage staff to recommend a particular financial product to a retail client when another product would better meet the client's needs.[7] In particular, it provides that:

- remuneration and similar incentives must not be solely or predominantly based on quantitative commercial criteria, and must take fully into account appropriate qualitative criteria reflecting compliance with applicable regulations, the fair treatment of clients and the quality of services provided to clients; and

- there must at all times be a balance between fixed and variable components of remuneration so that the remuneration structure does not favour the interests of the firm or its staff against the interests of any client.[8]

9.20   It can therefore be seen that the MiFID Remuneration Incentives Code reflects many of the themes raised in the FCA's guidance in FG13/01 and FG15/10 referred to at 9.05 ff. Indeed, specific reference is made to this guidance in the Code.[9]

---

7   SYSC 19F.1.3R.
8   SYSC 19F.1.4R.
9   SYSC 19.1.5G.

5   INCENTIVES, REMUNERATION AND PERFORMANCE MANAGEMENT IN CONSUMER CREDIT FIRMS

9.21   In 2018 the FCA published final rules[10] on staff incentives, remuneration and performance management in consumer credit firms. The rules affect firms that carry out consumer credit activity and have staff that deal directly with customers. The rules do not apply to firms subject to any of the provisions in the IFPRU, BIPRU, AIFM, UCITS or Dual Regulated firms Remuneration Codes or those subject to the MiFID Remuneration Incentives Code.

9.22   The provisions are set out in section 2.11 of the consumer credit sourcebook (CONC) in the FCA Handbook and came into force on 1 October 2018.

9.23   The purpose of the rules is to ensure that firms identify and manage the risks to customers that may arise out of their policies, practices and procedures for the remuneration or performance management of staff who interact with customers. Such risks may arise, for example, where staff remuneration (eg bonus or commission) is determined in whole or part by the volume or value of credit provided or debt collected or when appraisals or performance management focuses on targets or measures of the volume or value of credit provided or debt collected.

9.24   The rules require firms to establish, implement and maintain adequate policies and procedures to detect the risk of any failure to comply with regulatory obligations. Such measures may include:

- monitoring the nature of sales activities and debt collecting;

- collecting management information to enable the firm to monitor trends;

- establishing procedures to ensure appropriate actions are taken if staff are found to have behaved inappropriately; and

- maintaining arrangements to ensure oversight of remuneration and performance management arrangements.

9.25   The rules are likely to be of most relevance to senior managers who design or approve incentive schemes and performance management processes, line managers who implement them, compliance and risk management staff and staff who participate in an incentive scheme.

9.26   The FCA has also published non-Handbook guidance to provide more detailed help to consumer credit firms when implementing the final rules.[11] This guidance is not intended to be prescriptive and the FCA's approach remains proportionate: there is no one-size-fits-all approach. The FCA expects firms to manage their affairs responsibly and effectively with adequate risk management systems (in accordance with Principle 3). It also expects them to have a mitigation

10   PS18/7.
11   FG18/2.

strategy in place to manage risks to customers. In essence, a firm should identify, manage, monitor and report risks, where appropriate.

9.27 Much of the guidance echoes the guidance given in FG13/01 and FG15/10 referred to at 9.01. The key points are set out in at 9.28–9.31.

9.28 Firms should have adequate governance procedures in place to assess and regularly review incentive schemes, their risks and the effectiveness of controls. If an issue comes to light that may have a significant impact on customers, these should be identified and flagged to senior management who should in turn notify the FCA if the issues are sufficiently serious.

9.29 The guidance provides some non-exhaustive examples of schemes that are likely to increase the risk of customer harm. These examples are broadly similar to the types of schemes referred to in FG13/01 (see 9.05 ff). The FCA also cites some examples of how firms have taken action to reduce the risk of harm. These include:

- incentive schemes based purely on quality or customer service measures;

- reductions in, or disqualification from, bonuses for failing to meet quality standards;

- deferral or clawback of incentive payments;

- incorporating quality measures into incentive schemes such as balanced scorecards;

- cumulative or rolling target thresholds, the idea being that volume-based incentives based on a rolling average can reduce the immediate impact on an individual if they perform poorly in one month, thereby reducing the pressure on them; and

- recognising actions that are in the interest of customers within incentive schemes.

9.30 In a similar way to the guidance in FG15/10, the guidance in FG18/2 recognises that performance management (both formal and informal) can have a significant impact on staff behaviour. Firms are advised to consider the risks arising both from the design of their formal performance management process and from the way in which both formal and informal processes are implemented. The guidance highlights the following issues in particular:

- *Focus of performance management discussions*: firms should encourage appropriate behaviour by focusing on quality and customer outcomes rather than volume or profitability-based performance measures;

- *Volume-based or monetary targets v quality-based targets*: targets should not be predominantly about the number of sales, value of sales, cash collected, etc. Performance management should focus on quality scores, customer outcomes and employee development;

- *Use of disciplinary action*: the threat of disciplinary action for failure to meet monetary targets may incentivise poor behaviours;

- *Results affecting other decisions*: only approving holiday or offering promotion or development opportunities for staff who have met their targets can place undue pressure on staff;

- *Multiple targets for different elements:* where staff are measured on a range of different measures this could drive an inappropriate focus on elements of the targets they have not met; and

- *Publicising 'good' or 'poor' performance*: peer pressure could lead to increased risk; conversely, emphasis on good performance on quality measures/good customer outcomes could encourage good behaviours.

9.31   The FCA advises firms to carry out their own assessments of the adequacy of governance arrangements and controls in relation to risks. The guidance sets out examples of aspects of governance and controls that could help firms manage risks. These include ensuring that:

- firms identify, understand and assess the risks in incentive schemes and incorporate steps to mitigate them;

- quality monitoring is carried out by competent staff. The guidance suggests some of the aspects that firms should consider when designing an effective quality monitoring approach;

- firms collect sufficient information to be able to properly manage the risks relating to their incentive schemes and performance management arrangements;

- line management conflicts of interests are appropriately managed; and

- controls to mitigate the risks arising from incentive schemes or performance management are sufficiently effective to manage the risks they pose to customers.

CHAPTER 10

Whistleblowing in Financial Institutions

Elizabeth Graves, Partner, Fiona McMutrie, Principal Associate and Jessica Wicker, Senior Associate

I THE PUBLIC INTEREST DISCLOSURE ACT

10.01   The Public Interest Disclosure Act 1998 (PIDA), which amended the Employment Rights Act 1996 (ERA),[1] introduced whistleblowing protection for workers[2] in all firms (including but not limited to financial institutions). PIDA implemented provisions to protect individuals from detrimental action and dismissal as a result of them making a 'protected disclosure'.

10.02   For these purposes, a protected disclosure is a disclosure of information which, in the reasonable opinion of the person making the disclosure, tends to show one or more of the following: that a criminal act has, or is likely to be, committed; legal obligations are not being complied with; a miscarriage of justice has or will occur; health and safety is being endangered; the environment is being damaged; or that information about any of these acts is being concealed.[3] The disclosure of the failure to comply with a legal obligation may often cover disclosures made about regulatory breaches in the financial services context.[4] If this is the case, such a disclosure made in the prescribed way will attract protection under the PIDA provisions in ERA. PIDA itself (but see 10.28 ff) does not, however, require an employer to set up a whistleblowing channel or other means of notifying concerns to the employer.

10.03   A disclosure of information must be more than merely making a statement or communication, and information must be more than simply an allegation (although the disclosure may contain allegations).[5] The Court of Appeal has offered clarification on how information should be defined.[6] There should not be a rigid dichotomy between information and allegations. On the other hand, although sometimes a statement which can be characterised as an allegation will also constitute 'information' and amount to a qualifying disclosure within ERA, s 43B(1), not every statement involving an allegation will do so. Whether a particular statement amounts to a qualifying disclosure under s 43B(1) will depend on whether it falls within the requirements set out in that provision.

10.04   In simple terms, the ordinary meaning of giving 'information' is conveying facts. Grammatically, the word 'information' has to be read with the qualifying phrase, 'which tends to show [etc]'. In order for a statement to be a

---

1   Whistleblowing provisions are set out in ERA, ss 43A–43L.
2   A worker for these purposes is defined in ERA, s 230(3) ERA and ERA, s 43K and includes employee shareholders, homeworkers, workers undergoing training or work experience as part of a training course, agency workers and limited liability partnership (LLP) members. It also covers former workers.
3   ERA, s 43B.
4   Breach of a legal obligation can include breach of the employee's own employment contract provided the public interest test is satisfied (*Parkins v Sodexho* [2002] IRLR 109 and *Chesterton Global Limited v Nurmohamed* [2017] EWCA Civ 979).
5   *Kilraine v London Borough of Wandsworth* UKEAT/0260/15; *Cavendish Munroe v Geduld* UKEAT/2009/0195.
6   *Kilraine v London Borough of Wandsworth* [2018] EWCA Civ 1436.

qualifying disclosure according to these requirements, it has to have a sufficient factual content and specificity such as is capable of tending to show one of the matters listed in the legislation. A statement such as 'you are not complying with regulatory requirements' would be an allegation but too general and not contain sufficient factual content to be information such as to satisfy s 43(B)(1).

10.05   A qualifying disclosure must be made in accordance with prescribed conditions and to one of the prescribed persons listed in ERA, s 43. There are six routes:

(1) to the employer directly;

(2) to a legal adviser if made in the course of obtaining legal advice;

(3) to a minister of the Crown where the worker is engaged in Crown or public employment;

(4) to a 'prescribed person'– the FCA and the PRA are prescribed persons;

(5) elsewhere (eg to the police or non-prescribed regulator) in defined circumstances;

(6) elsewhere in exceptionally serious cases.

A qualifying disclosure under PIDA to a prescribed person such as a regulator will only be protected if the worker reasonably believes that the default falls within the remit of the regulator; and the information disclosed and any allegation contained in it are substantially true. A disclosure must be in the public interest, which has proved to be a contentious issue.

10.06   The Court of Appeal has held that a disclosure about a manipulation of company accounts resulting in lower commission figures for around 100 sales staff was in the public interest due to the nature of the wrongdoing, the number of affected employees, the size of the amounts involved and the employer's standing as a substantial and prominent London business.[7]

10.07   A worker making such a protected disclosure is protected from suffering a detriment[8] for making such a disclosure and, if an employee, any dismissal for this reason will be automatically unfair (regardless of whether the employee has qualifying service to bring an unfair dismissal claim),[9] with no upper limit on compensation. When assessing compensation, the level of compensation is affected by whether or not the whistleblower acted in good faith. In the case of a detriment (but not dismissal) suffered by a worker, this is treated as being done by the employee imposing the detriment and also by the employer. This should serve as an alert to senior managers and certified staff who risk an adverse finding against them affecting their fit and proper status.

---

7   *Chesterton Global Ltd v Nurmohamed* [2017] EWCA Civ 979; see also *Underwood v Wincanton plc* UKEAT/0163/15.
8   ERA, s 47B(1).
9   ERA, s 103A.

10.08   The Court of Appeal held in a recent case[10] that the directors were jointly and severally liable together with the employer for losses suffered by a whistleblower in circumstances where one director instructed the other to dismiss the whistleblower and the second director complied with the instruction. The employment appeal tribunal judgment that despite a dismissal being excluded from the ambit of a detriment[11] the instruction to dismiss and implementation of that instruction constituted detriments for the purposes of the whistleblowing provisions was upheld. This means that it is possible that an employee dismissed for making a protected disclosure will bring an unfair dismissal claim against their employer and also a detriment claim against the manager making the decision to dismiss. The manager may be personally liable for the post-dismissal losses on a joint and several basis with the employer.

10.09   In determining the reason for dismissal a tribunal must only examine the mental processes of those authorised to take the decision to dismiss and for this mental process an employer may be vicariously liable.[12]

2   PROTECT

10.10   Protect (previously named Public Concern at Work) is a whistleblowing charity which advises and assists people wanting to raise whistleblowing concerns. It established the Whistleblowing Commission which published a whistleblowing code of practice which sets out best practice for employers and advice for employees. The Commission recommended that the code should be taken into account in court cases and by regulators. The Department for Business, Energy and Industrial Strategy has also published a code of practice and guidance for employers on whistleblowing (March 2015).

3   WHISTLEBLOWING AND FINANCIAL INSTITUTIONS

10.11   While the PIDA provisions have been in force for nearly 20 years, it became clear that a culture of fear pervaded financial institutions, which prevented people from speaking out when aware of misconduct or other wrongdoing.

10.12   In June 2013, the Parliamentary Commission on Banking Standards (PCBS) published a report 'Changing banking for good'[13] which set out proposals for reform of the banking sector. The report noted that fear of consequences, even if misplaced, deterred bank employees from raising concerns about wrongdoing with their manager or employer. At the time of the report, the number of successful whistleblowers in banks was understood to be very low. Despite the

---

10   *Timis v Osipov* [2018] EWCA Civ 2321.
11   ERA, s 47B(2).
12   *Royal Mail v Jhuti* [2017] EWCA Civ 1632.
13   http://www.parliament.uk/documents/banking-commission/Banking-final-report-vol-ii.pdf.

widespread knowledge of LIBOR-rigging no employee was confident enough to 'whistleblow' by escalating the issue internally or notifying the regulator. Had staff come forward earlier, much of the damage caused by the scandal might have been averted. As noted in the report, 'whistleblowing in the financial services sector needs to be treated by firms not as inconvenient and potentially damaging, but as a valuable source of information for senior management'.[14]

10.13 The report included recommendations that banks put in place mechanisms to allow their employees to raise concerns internally and that the FCA and the PRA ensure these mechanisms are effective. Staff should have a clear understanding of their duty to report an instance of wrongdoing within the firm. Employee contracts and codes of conduct should include clear references to the duty to whistleblow and the circumstances in which they would be expected to do so. Accountability for ensuring that such safeguards are in place should rest with the non-executive director responsible for whistleblowing. This person should be given specific responsibility for the effective operation of the firm's whistleblowing regime. The report also referred to 'reward' for whistleblowers. The regulators, while welcoming the report's recommendations, concluded that introducing financial incentives for whistleblowers would be unlikely to increase the number or quality of the disclosures received from them.[15]

10.14 In February 2015 the FCA and the PRA launched a joint consultation[16] on their proposed measures to implement the report's recommendations and to formalise firms' whistleblowing procedures to build on existing good practice and to encourage a more consistent approach in the banking and insurance sector. The regulators' aim was to encourage a 'speak up' culture within financial institutions which had before been slow to face up to internal deficiencies. The consultation proposed a set of rules to apply to UK banks, building societies, credit unions (with assets of more than £25m), PRA investment firms[17] and insurers. It was expected that the proposed new whistleblowing mechanism could be used by a range of people who are aware of conduct in a firm that concerned them. This includes:

- employees;
- non-executive directors (NEDs) (who may be self-employed);
- former employees;
- secondees, interns or people on work experience placements;
- volunteers;
- agency workers;
- contractors;

---

14 'Changing banking for good', p 369.
15 FCA/PRA 'Financial Incentives for Whistleblowers' July 2014.
16 FCA CP15/4; PRA CP6/15.
17 Collectively known as 'relevant authorised persons' – see FSMA, s 71A.

- agents;

- employees of subsidiary firms, competitor firms, appointed representatives, or suppliers.

10.15 Not all of the people listed at 10.14 would qualify for protection under PIDA but the regulators felt that all should be able to use a firm's whistleblowing arrangements to raise concerns.

10.16 The conclusions of this consultation were published in policy statements in October 2015[18] reporting broad support for the proposed measures (see 10.28 ff). Firms that do not properly implement the new rules may find themselves in breach of the Principles of Business.[19]

4 REPORTING TO THE REGULATOR

10.17 As a 'prescribed person', regulators must report annually on the number of whistleblowing concerns raised with them.[20] This duty requires the regulators to provide an annual report on the number of whistleblowers and how many of these reports led to the regulators taking action on the information received. Where action is taken, the regulators will then be expected to provide a summary of action taken by them as a result of receiving the concern and of how the concerns impacted on their functions and objectives as a regulatory body. The data should be anonymised to protect the whistleblower's identity.

10.18 Most whistleblowing allegations are raised directly with employers and the legal protection afforded to whistleblowers by PIDA is biased in favour of such an approach.

10.19 However, workers who are wary of raising potential employer wrongdoing with the employer may report their concerns externally in certain circumstances and still retain protection against retaliatory conduct. A claimant who lodges a whistleblowing claim with an employment tribunal may also tick a box on the ET1 claim form indicating that he/she wishes the employment tribunal to provide a copy of the claim to the FCA. In this way, the worker can make the regulator aware of whistleblowing allegations that have been raised directly with the employer or others. However, one approved person or senior manager taking this action would need to carefully consider whether they are subject to any duty to make any disclosure directly to the regulator and if the 'tick box' on the ET1 form is the most appropriate way to discharge such obligation.

---

18 FCA PS15/24; PRA PS24/15, Whistleblowing in deposit takers, PRA designated investment firms and insurers.

19 In particular Principle 2 (due skill, care and diligence) and Principle 3 (management and control).

20 Prescribed Persons (Reports on Disclosures of Information) Regulations 2017 (SI 2017/507) which came into force on 1 April 2017.

10.20 Within six months of the end of a reporting period (which falls between 1 April and 30 March) each relevant prescribed person must report qualifying disclosures it has received and which it reasonably believes fall within its remit – so an annual report falls due on or before 30 September each year.

10.21 Critical to the preparation of a report is the need for confidentiality. The reporting regulations expressly require that the report must not contain any information which might identify the whistleblower or any other person to whom the disclosure relates.

10.22 Subject to those limitations, the report must address:

● the number of disclosures received in the previous 12 months, reasonably believed to be qualifying disclosures;

● in how many cases further action was deemed appropriate;

● an explanation of the prescribed person's functions, objectives and any statutory powers;

● a summary of the type of action taken in response to qualified disclosures;

● a summary of how the disclosed information has impacted on the ability of the prescribed person to perform its functions and meet objectives.

10.23 The FCA provides the same level of confidentiality and anonymity to any person who makes a disclosure to it. It has reported that in 2017/18 it managed 1,106 cases from whistleblowers of which 649 were qualifying disclosures within its remit and 307 were not but 150 could not be determined.[21] In that period it took action on 121 disclosures and was continuing to assess 128 intelligence cases from whistleblowers to determine whether it should take action. The FCA claims that whistleblowers have helped it to initiate enforcement investigations, conduct visits to firms and carry out in-depth and thematic reviews with firms. It now offers a meeting to all whistleblowers to build their trust and reflect the value the FCA places on them and has rolled out training to help all FCA staff recognise whistleblowers and treat disclosures appropriately. The FCA associates these measures with an increase in the whistleblowing intelligence it has received.

10.24 The FCA states on its website that whistleblowing information has helped it to:

● issue fines and warning letters to firms and individuals;

● vary and withdraw permissions; and

● intervene with other kinds of early involvement such as asking firms to change their business activity.

10.25 It was revealed in a Freedom of Information request response that the FCA was referring whistleblower reports to enforcement and intervention in

---

21 FCA Annual Report and Accounts 2017/18, chapter 3.

double figures. It is predicted that senior manager accountability will continue to boost reports and enforcement. The FCA's records showed that fitness and propriety was the subject of consistently high complaint levels in a recently recorded six-month period suggesting that this is a particular area where employees choose to blow the whistle on their colleagues.

10.26   The Bank of England and the PRA reported having received a total of 141 disclosures in the period from 1 April 2017 to 31 March 2018 which were assessed against PIDA and discrete statutory requirements applicable to the Bank of England and the PRA.[22] Of these, 116 were considered to be PIDA disclosure and 25 were not. All 116 qualifying disclosures were the subject of supervisory consideration from which:

- 7 cases (including 3 cases considered by the PRA originating from the FCA) were referred to the Bank Enforcement Litigation Division;
- 28 cases were referred to the FCA; and
- 1 case was referred to the National Crime Agency.

10.27   While none of these cases directly contributed to Bank enforcement activity or other intervention, 15 disclosures were of significant value and contributed to the discharge of regulatory activity, 30 were or may be in the future of value but not immediately actionable and/or did not meet current regulatory risk thresholds and 71 disclosures were of little value and unlikely to assist in the discharge of regulatory or supervisory activity.

5   THE REGULATORY WHISTLEBLOWING REGIME: AN OVERVIEW

10.28   The whistleblowing rules came into force on 7 September 2016 (although the requirement to appoint a whistleblowing champion – see 10.38 ff – came into force on 7 March 2016).

The whistleblowing rules currently apply to:

- deposit takers with over £250m in assets;
- PRA designated investment firms;
- insurers and reinsurers subject to Solvency II (see 7.256) and to the Society of Lloyd's and managing agents,

collectively known as 'relevant firms'.

10.29   For all other FCA/PRA regulated firms, the whistleblowing rules currently have the status of non-binding guidance. It was anticipated that the whistleblowing rules would become mandatory for all FCA/PRA regulated firms as part of the extension of the Senior Managers and Certification Regime (SMCR) in 2018 although the consultation papers on extending the SMCR have

---

22 Bank of England and PRA 'Prescribed Persons (Reports on Disclosures of Information) Regulations 2017, Annual Report 1 April 2017 – 31 March 2018'.

been silent on whistleblowing. The FCA has stated that once the rules have been in place long enough to assess their effectiveness, it will consider whether to apply them more widely to other firms it regulates.[23]

10.30   The rules for whistleblowing are set out in the FCA Handbook and the PRA Rulebook[24] and further guidance is provided in the PRA's supervisory statement SS39/15 as well as the policy statements referred to at 10.16.

10.31   The whistleblowing rules only apply to UK entities and UK branches of overseas firms (as detailed at 10.81 ff). Firms with managers based overseas but with responsibility for UK staff will need to be provided with appropriate training (see 10.88).

10.32   In summary, the rules require a relevant firm to:

- put internal whistleblowing arrangements in place that are able to handle *all* types of disclosure from *all* types of person;

- tell UK-based employees about the FCA and PRA whistleblowing services;

- require its appointed representatives and tied agents to tell their UK-based employees about the FCA whistleblowing service;

- inform the FCA if it loses an employment tribunal case with a whistleblower;

- present a report on whistleblowing to its board at least annually;

- appoint a whistleblowing champion;

- not include wording in a settlement or other agreement that limits an employee's right to blow the whistle.

10.33   There is no regulatory duty on a firm's staff to blow the whistle.

10.34   The whistleblowing rules were intended to prompt a cultural change within financial institutions but since implementation of the new rules there have been concerns that some firms are finding it hard to change. Lord Cromwell, the chairman of the All-Party Parliamentary Group on Fair Business Banking, has stated that the UK should follow the US system of awarding to the whistleblower a share of the fine imposed upon an infringing institution. Lord Cromwell's comments are set against reports that whistleblowers in the banking sector have been subject to intimidation and persecution despite the reforms.

6   REQUIREMENT TO INFORM STAFF OF REGULATORS' WHISTLEBLOWING SERVICES

10.35   The FCA and the PRA each run dedicated whistleblowing services that any person can use to report any concern about a financial institution. The

---

23   FCA PS15/24.
24   FCA SYSC 18; PRA – CRR firms – General Organisational Requirements 2A.

regulators require UK-based employees of relevant firms to be informed about the regulators' whistleblowing services, including how to contact them, the protections they offer and the kind of disclosures that can be made. There is no requirement to promote the regulators' whistleblowing services to other parties although firms may choose to do so.

10.36   Reporting to a regulator is not conditional upon a report first being made using a firm's internal arrangements.[25] A person can also report using a firm's internal arrangements and also to a regulator simultaneously and consecutively. This should be made clear in the firm's employee handbook or equivalent document.

10.37   ERA provides for external disclosure of a protected disclosure (under PIDA) to certain prescribed persons such as a regulator provided particular conditions are met (the worker reasonably believes the default lies within the regulator's remit and the information and the allegation are substantially true). By providing express provision for disclosure to an external body, the regulatory whistleblowing rules ensure that employees retain the legal protection afforded by PIDA for a protected disclosure notwithstanding disclosure to a third party (which would ordinarily be subject to additional pre-conditions). As a result, in addition to protection from disadvantage or harassment contained in the new rules, employees will suffer no disadvantage in approaching the FCA or the PRA directly.

7   WHISTLEBLOWING CHAMPION

10.38   The whistleblowing rules require firms to allocate responsibility for compliance with the whistleblowing rules to a 'whistleblowers' champion'.[26] The whistleblowers' champion must be a NED who is subject to the SMCR or a director or senior manager under the Senior Insurance Managers Regime (SIMR).

10.39   As a NED, the whistleblowers' champion will be at one remove from the day-to-day running of the business so will need to rely on guidance and advice from others with more immediate understanding of the workings of the firm. A firm should therefore consider requiring an appropriate senior manager to advise and assist the whistleblowers' champion to carry out their duties.

10.40   A firm must allocate to the whistleblowers' champion the responsibility for ensuring and overseeing the integrity, independence and effectiveness of the firm's policies and procedures on whistleblowing, including those intended to protect whistleblowers from being victimised because they have disclosed reportable concerns. The whistleblowers' champion need not have a day-to-day operational role handling disclosures (and so can be based anywhere provided

---

25 SYSC 18.3.6R(1).
26 SYSC 18.4.

he or she can perform the functions effectively) but must oversee systems and processes and have responsibility for overseeing the effectiveness of internal policies and procedures.

10.41 The champion should have a level of authority and independence within the firm and access to resources and information (including recourse to independent legal advice and dedicated training)[27] to enable them to carry out their responsibilities.

10.42 Financial groups have flexibility about how to allocate the responsibility for the whistleblowing champion. A firm that is part of a group may use a group entity senior manager (SMF7 or SIMF7) as a means of appointing a person from elsewhere in the group to perform the role for multiple ring-fenced group entities. In most large organisations, the role is allocated to the Chair of the Audit Committee.

10.43 The whistleblowers' champion must oversee the preparation of an annual report to the board about how the whistleblowing policies and procedures are working. This report is available to the FCA or PRA on request but is not made public.

10.44 The whistleblowers' champion must also oversee notification of the relevant regulator when an employment tribunal finds that a whistleblower has successfully brought a whistleblowing complaint in respect of a detriment suffered or being unfairly dismissed as a result of making a protected disclosure (see 10.46 ff).

8 THE INDEPENDENT WHISTLEBLOWING CHANNEL

10.45 Based on the FCA existing guidance on whistleblowing, the regulators set out measures[28] that relevant firms should take:

- respect whistleblowers' confidentiality;

- deal with anonymous disclosures;

- assess and escalate whistleblowing concerns within the firm as appropriate, and where justified, to either regulator or an appropriate law enforcement agency;

- track the outcome of whistleblowing reports;

- track what happens to an internal whistleblower to determine whether they are subsequently disadvantaged as a consequence of speaking out;

- provide feedback to whistleblowers;

- prepare written procedures (for example, in a staff handbook);

---

27 PRA SS39/15.
28 FCA CP15/4; PRA CP6/15.

- take all reasonable steps to ensure that no-one under the firm's control engages in victimisation against a whistleblower and to take appropriate measures against any person who does so.

10.46 Firms must establish and maintain an 'appropriate and effective' independent whistleblowing channel through which individuals can make disclosures of 'reportable concerns'. A firm will need to ensure therefore that while there may be different channels through which a concern may be considered it is important that a whistleblowing concern is looked at by the appropriate person(s) with the firm.

10.47 Vitally, the concern must be investigated, appropriately dealt with and the outcome recorded. If the disclosure may be a protected disclosure, a clear record of the reasons why any decision was reached will be helpful to demonstrate to a regulator that the proper processes were observed should the firm lose an employment tribunal case.

10.48 The PRA suggests[29] that larger firms may create an internal specialist unit to handle disclosures. Other firms may use third parties to provide aspects of the service.

10.49 Firms may wish to clarify that there may be another more appropriate route for some issues to be reported (such as grievances or customer complaints) but the whistleblowing channel can be used after such routes have been exhausted.

10.50 As noted at 10.45, whistleblowing arrangements must ensure the 'effective assessment and escalation' of concerns. It is accepted that not all disclosures will result in investigative action although the regulators expect due consideration to be given to each case and for this to be recorded. If appropriate, firms can filter out genuine whistleblowing reports and redirect other reports (such as grievances or customer complaints) that would be better dealt with by other areas of the organisation.

10.51 A firm must observe data protection requirements when setting up whistleblowing arrangements. To this end any hotline should be not for general purposes but for raising concerns of a 'whistleblowing' nature and staff should be told about the scope of the hotline and how it should be used, including a reminder that there are other complaints mechanisms for other types of grievance or concern. Any employees who handle the data from a whistleblowing hotline must treat the information they receive with strict confidentiality.

9 REPORTABLE CONCERNS

10.52 *Any person* (not just the firm's employees and workers) may be able to make anonymous and confidential disclosures via the whistleblowing channel

---

29 SS39/15.

which should be able to deal with *all* types of disclosure, not just disclosures covered by PIDA. Such general disclosures are known as 'reportable concerns'.

10.53 The whistleblowing rules impose an obligation to enable the reporting of a 'reportable concern'.

10.54 A reportable concern is defined in SYSC 18 as:

'a concern held by any person in relation to the activities of a firm, including:

(a) anything that would be the subject-matter of a protected disclosure under PIDA, including breaches of rules;

(b) a breach of the firm's policies and procedures; and

(c) behaviour that harms or is likely to harm the reputation or financial well-being of the firm.'

10.55 This definition is far wider than a PIDA protected disclosure so when receiving a concern, a firm should first assess whether the disclosure falls within the ambit of PIDA or is a reportable concern under the regulatory regime. There is no requirement, as there is under PIDA, for a reportable concern to be in the public interest.

10 HANDLING DISCLOSURES

10.56 The regulators have noted[30] that larger firms usually have specialist units that handle whistleblowing disclosures (often known as 'integrity' or 'ethics' functions). A firm should consider where this unit might sit in its organisational structure and how various functions (HR, Compliance, internal audit etc) should work together to ensure that all angles of a regulatory whistleblowing disclosure are covered.

10.57 Given the regulatory scrutiny and the risk of reputational damage associated with a whistleblowing complaint, it is essential that disclosures of concerns are brought to the attention of functions other than just HR. This would enable concerns to be addressed internally rather than be escalated externally, whether to an employment tribunal (if the concern is a protected disclosure), the regulator or even the press. Some firms set up corporate compliance hotlines so that workers can anonymously raise concerns internally.

10.58 SYSC 18.3 in the FCA Handbook sets out the internal arrangements that must be put in place:

---

30 FCA CP15/4; PRA CP6/15.

- the arrangements must be able to handle reportable concerns including where the individual has requested confidentiality or has made the disclosure anonymously;

- the arrangements must allow for disclosures to be made through a range of communication methods;

- a firm must ensure the effective assessment and escalation of a reportable concern including, where appropriate, to a regulator;

- a firm must include reasonable measures to ensure that if a reportable concern is made no person under the control of the firm engages in victimisation of that whistleblower. Firms can help to prevent any improper treatment of whistleblowers by those outside of its control by honouring requests for confidentiality;

- a firm should provide feedback to a whistleblower about a reportable concern, where feasible and appropriate;

- a firm should prepare and maintain appropriate records of reportable concerns and the firm's treatment of these reports, including the outcome;

- a firm should prepare and maintain up-to-date written procedures that are readily available to the firm's UK-based employees;

- a firm must prepare (i) an annual report to the firm's governing body on the operation and effectiveness of its systems and controls in relation to whistleblowing; (ii) prompt reports to the FCA about each case the firm contested but lost before an employment tribunal where the claimant based all or part of their claim on either detriment caused or being unfairly dismissed as a result of making a protected disclosure under PIDA;

- a firm must include appropriate training for (i) its UK-based employees; (ii) managers of UK based employees wherever the manager is based; and (iii) employees responsible for operating the firm's internal arrangements.

Malicious disclosures

10.59 Nothing in the rules prevents a firm from taking action against a person who has knowingly made false and malicious disclosures.[31] Therefore policies may contain a warning that such disclosures may result in disciplinary action. However, a true but malicious disclosure – and even a malicious disclosure which the complainant reasonably believed tended to show the type of wrongdoing concerned, even if turns out to be false – remains capable of protection under PIDA. Whether a disclosure is made in good faith is an issue relevant only to the quantum of compensation for the purpose of PIDA.

---

31 SYSC 18.3.2G(3)(b).

11 CONFIDENTIALITY OF DISCLOSURES

10.60 Firms must protect the confidentiality of whistleblowers, if this is requested. Whilst firms may choose to discuss with the whistleblower the advantages of disclosing their identity, firms must ensure that they are able to handle anonymous disclosures.

10.61 It should be noted that both workers and any other persons (not just a firm's employees) must be able to make anonymous and confidential disclosures.

10.62 Barclays Group and its chief executive James Staley were fined by the FCA and the PRA a total of £642,430 for the chief executive's failure to act with due skill, care and diligence in the way he acted in response to an anonymous letter received by Barclays in June 2016. Mr Staley had attempted to identify the author of the letter claiming to be from a Barclays shareholder. The letter contained various allegations, some of which concerned Mr Staley. Given his conflict Mr Staley should have maintained an appropriate distance; he should not have taken steps to identify the author. Mr Staley should have explicitly consulted fully with those with expertise and responsibility for whistleblowing in Barclays.

10.63 The investigation found this to be a breach of the requirement to act with due skill, care and diligence (individual conduct rule 2) but not a breach of the requirement to act with integrity (individual conduct rule 1).

10.64 Barclays was also made subject to special requirements under which it must report annually to the regulators detailing how it handles whistleblowing, including personal attestations from those senior managers responsible for the relevant systems and controls. This is the first case brought under the SMCR. While Mr Staley made no personal gain, both regulators viewed his conduct as sufficiently serious for each to impose a penalty of 10% of Mr Staley's relevant annual income. Mr Staley was also censured by the publication of the regulators' Final Notices

10.65 In practice, it can be difficult to carry out as full an investigation as possible where a whistleblower is unwilling to disclose their identity. Investigators looking into concerns reported by a whistleblower may be impeded from sharing direct evidence with those under investigation if doing so would alert other witnesses to the whistleblower's identity.

12 INFORMING AND TRAINING STAFF

10.66 As noted at 10.45 ff, firms must establish and maintain an 'appropriate and effective' independent channel through which 'reportable concerns' can be disclosed directly to the firm and this must be communicated to all workers.

10.67   Firms must also ensure that staff have an appropriate level of training for all UK-based employees on how and when to report concerns and, for managers of those employees, how to recognise such a report and how to deal with it.

10.68   For all UK-based employees, training should include:[32]

- a statement that the firm takes reportable concerns seriously;

- making clear to staff that they can report reportable concerns to the firm and the methods for doing so (eg face to face, over the telephone, by email or by post);

- examples of events that might prompt the making of a reportable concern;

- examples of action that the firm might take (including maintaining confidentiality) once it has received a reportable concern;

- information about sources of external support such as whistleblowing charities;

- how to maintain a whistleblower's confidentiality (this applies wherever the employees are based);

- how to assess and grade the significance of information disclosed (this applies wherever the employees are based);

- how to assist the whistleblower's champion when asked to do so (this applies wherever the employees are based).

10.69   For managers of UK-based employees (wherever the manager is based), training should also include:

- how to recognise a disclosure of a reportable concern;

- how to protect whistleblowers and ensure their confidentiality is protected;

- how to provide feedback;

- steps to ensure fair treatment of any person accused of wrongdoing by a whistleblower;

- sources of internal and external advice.

10.70   For managers, training will necessarily involve issues such as how to deal with complaints and preserving confidentiality but also how to recognise a reportable concern.

10.71   See 10.81 ff for whistleblowing obligations of UK branches of overseas firms.

---

32   SYSC 18.3.4G.

10.72   In a recent survey carried out by Ernst & Young[33] only 1 in 3 financial services respondents indicated an awareness of whistleblowing hotlines. This concerning figure suggests that there is work to be done in raising awareness among staff. The survey also revealed that 73% of those responding to the survey would consider providing information about potential fraud, bribery and corruption in their business to an external third party. A significant majority of these would go directly to a law enforcement agency or regulator. Such a tendency to disclose concerns externally will make it harder for firms to manage matters internally. It is therefore in firms' interests to ensure that staff are fully aware of the whistleblowing services and channel available to them and that they have full confidence in the firm's processes.

13   DUTY TO BLOW THE WHISTLE

10.73   There is no general regulatory duty to blow the whistle. However, a duty to report concerns may arise from the general employment duty of fidelity, which is an implied duty arising in all employment contracts. By its very nature, this duty may also give rise to a duty for employees or workers (not just those in a supervisory or managerial capacity) to answer questions honestly or to report misconduct or suspected misconduct of others.[34] There are also specific statutory whistleblowing obligations in pensions and health and safety law.[35]

10.74   Further, directors and senior employees may owe fiduciary duties to their employers. In such a position, they can be expected to disclose instances of wrongdoing.

10.75   Firms should also consider other obligations to notify the regulator arising elsewhere in the regulators' rules.[36] In particular, senior manager conduct rule 4 requires senior managers to disclose appropriately any information of which the regulator would expect reasonable notice. Senior employees are likely to have greater access to information pertinent to the regulator and also a superior understanding of the importance and relevance of certain matters.

10.76   Individual conduct rule 3 which applies to all staff (except for ancillary staff) requires that an employee must be open and cooperative with the FCA, PRA and other regulators. In practice this means that the individual must answer the regulators' questions, attend interviews and supply the appropriate level of information and documentation required. The individual is not obliged to report misconduct directly to the regulator unless there is an absence of internal procedures or unless he is one of the approved persons responsible for reporting

---

33   Ernst & Young EMEIA Fraud Survey 2017, 'Human instinct or machine logic: which do you trust most in the fight against fraud and corruption?'
34   *RGB Resources PLC v Rastogi* [2002] EWHC 2785 (Ch).
35   Pensions Act 2004; Management of Health and Safety at Work Regulations 1999 (SI 1999/3242), reg 14.
36   See for example FCA Supervision manual (SUP) 15.3 and Principles of Business PRIN 11.

such matters to the regulator. The regulator is likely to treat someone as having the responsibility for reporting matters to the regulator if the individual obstructs reporting in any way.[37]

14   EMPLOYMENT CONTRACTS AND SETTLEMENT AGREEMENTS

10.77   Although there is no general duty on workers to blow the whistle, firms must take appropriate steps to ensure settlement agreements and employment contracts are worded in a way that does not deter staff from whistleblowing.[38]

10.78   Settlements agreements and employment agreements should include wording which specifies that nothing in the agreement prevents a worker from making a protected disclosure. Further, settlement agreements should not include a warranty asking a worker to confirm that they have not made a protected disclosure and that they know of no information that could lead to them making a protected disclosure. The FCA suggests the following wording for a settlement agreement, although this is not required language:

> 'For the avoidance of doubt, nothing precludes [name of worker] from making a "protected disclosure" within the meaning of Part 4A (Protected Disclosure) of the Employment Rights Act 1996. This includes protected disclosures made about matters previously disclosed to another recipient.'

10.79   Firms have a discretion about whether to include such text in employment contracts and whether to request that the employment agencies it uses include such text in settlement agreements entered into with workers.

15   DETRIMENT AND FITNESS AND PROPRIETY

10.80   The FCA has indicated[39] that it would consider any evidence that a firm has acted to the detriment of a whistleblower as a serious matter and one that could affect the ongoing determination as to the fitness and propriety both of the firm and of relevant members of its staff. This is reinforced by the fact that any adverse employment tribunal decision must be reported to the regulators immediately.

---

37   Further guidance is at COCON 4 of the FCA Conduct Rules and Rule 3.4 of the PRA Conduct Rules.
38   SYSC 18.5.1; PRA – CRR firms – general organisational requirements 2A.6; PS24/15.
39   SYSC 18.3.9G.

16 UK BRANCHES OF OVERSEAS FIRMS

10.81 The FCA and the PRA have separately published whistleblowing rules for UK branches which applied from September 2017. The whistleblowing rules require firms to provide an appropriate level of training for UK-based employees; managers of UK-based employees, irrespective of where they themselves are located; and employees with responsibility for operating the firm's internal arrangements.[40]

10.82 The PRA proposed in its consultation paper[41] that for UK branches of overseas firms:

(a) UK branches of non-EEA banks and of both EEA and non-EEA insurers must inform their workers about the FCA and PRA's whistleblowing services; and

(b) any non-EEA banking group with both a UK branch and UK subsidiary which is subject to the whistleblowing rules must *inform* the staff of the branch of the subsidiary's whistleblowing arrangements (although this proposal does not apply to insurers).

10.83 The FCA proposed in its consultation paper[42] that UK branches of overseas banks must tell their UK-based employees about the regulators' whistleblowing services. It also proposed that where a branch of an overseas bank sits alongside a UK-incorporated bank that is subject to the FCA's whistleblowing rules, the UK-based staff of that branch should be informed of the subsidiary's whistleblowing arrangements.

10.84 Final policy statements were published[43] in 2017 setting out final rules.[44]

10.85 The FCA's rules affect UK branches of overseas (EEA and third country) banks and came into effect on 7 September 2017. The PRA's rules affect UK branches of non-EEA banks and non-EEA insurers and reinsurers.

10.86 The FCA adopted the consultation's proposal that UK branches of overseas banks should tell their UK-based employees about the regulators' whistleblowing services. It also adopted the proposal in (b) at 10.82 that a UK branch of an overseas bank that has a sister or parent company that is subject to the whistleblowing rules should inform staff in that branch that they are able to use the sister or parent company's whistleblowing arrangements. The communication must be included in the branch's employee handbook or other equivalent document. Branches are also reminded that they may continue to have concurrent reporting obligations to their home state regulator.

---

40 SYSC 18.3G.
41 PRA CP35/16.
42 FCA CP 16/25.
43 FCA PS17/7; PRA PS8/17.
44 These are set out in SYSC 18.3.g, FCA – CRR firms – general organisational requirements, para 2A.7.

10.87   Although the PRA published a further policy statement in April 2017[45] which made no changes to the proposed rules, it decided not to apply its whistleblowing rules to UK branches of EEA insurers as proposed in the consultation paper.

10.88   The PRA makes clear that it requires relevant non-EEA branches to inform all workers of what would constitute a protected disclosure; branch workers should be made aware of the protections afforded by PIDA (as implemented in the ERA). The requirement to make branch workers aware of the subsidiary's whistleblowing channel is to ensure that branch staff may make a protected disclosure through that internal channel.

10.89   The other whistleblowing rules are not required for UK branches although they remain good practice guidance.

17   OTHER EU LEGISLATION

10.90   Various EU legislation such as the Markets in Financial Instruments Directive (MiFID II) (see Chapter 9) and the Market Abuse Regulation also contain whistleblowing mechanisms and obligations. These obligations include requirements for market participants to have appropriate internal procedures in place allowing their employees to whistleblow in respect of the firm's obligations under that piece of legislation. The Market Abuse Regulation requires appropriate internal procedures for whistleblowing purposes and has a broad application to all employers who carry out activities that are regulated by financial services regulation. The FCA notes that the whistleblowing obligation in MiFID refers to implementing 'appropriate' internal procedures. Firms can tailor their programmes and personnel resources in a proportionate manner to appropriately mitigate risk, dependent on their business.

10.91   The FCA felt that it could not create a 'common platform' of whistleblowing requirements across the various pieces of EU legislation since this would result in the gold-plating of some standards and under-delivery of others. The FCA therefore proposed a new chapter in SYSC 18 in its Handbook to bring together domestic and EU whistleblowing requirements. SYSC 18.6 transposes the whistleblowing requirements in Article 73(2) in MiFID II for investment firms. It also signposts whistleblowing requirements in other EU legislation.

18   CHALLENGES FOR EMPLOYERS

10.92   A challenge for employers implementing a whistleblowing policy compliant with the requirements of the regulatory rules is to ensure that it is

45   PS8/17.

framed in language that is accessible to all staff. Whistleblowing policies can sometimes be legalistic and corporate in style and will need to be user-friendly so that all staff can clearly understand how to raise a concern. Specifically, an employee will need to understand the distinction between a qualifying disclosure under PIDA and a 'reportable concern' under the regulatory rules.

10.93 Employers will need to tread carefully to balance the degree of reassurance they can offer a whistleblower that they are acting upon his concerns against duties of confidentiality, data protection obligations or even protection of potential criminal evidence. In the meantime the employer should consider whether a disclosure requires further notification either internally to its governance committee and/or externally to a regulator.

10.94 Firms should also note that where a whistleblower suffers a detriment, this can call the firm's and a staff member's fitness and propriety into question. It should consider how to manage this.

10.95 Employers will need to reassure senior managers about their potential exposure. Mark Steward, director of enforcement at the FCA, has said that because the senior managers regime has realigned focus on individual responsibility there could be less focus on large-scale fines against firms. There may be an increase in litigation in cases where senior managers receive fines since individuals are less likely to be ready to pay fines. There is also a risk of staff who are the subject of a whistleblowing complaint (or who have mismanaged the handling of a concern) being disciplined. Senior managers are likely to challenge any such action taken against them.

10.96 In November 2018 the FCA published the results of a review on the whistleblowing rules for the banking sector, giving examples of good practice and setting out areas for improvement.[46]

FCA Review: FCA expectations

These include:

- senior management should not only ensure that effective whistleblowing arrangements are in place but also continuously assess how these are working in practice;

- up to date written procedures should be maintained which clearly explain that a whistleblowing concern to the FCA or the PRA is not conditional on a report being made using the firm's internal arrangements;

- documentation is key. An investigation process should clearly set out a clear and consistent approach and include information on how to

---

46 The review's findings can be read at https://www.fca.org.uk/publications/multi-firm-reviews/retail-and-wholesale-banking-review-firms-whistleblowing-arrangements.

protect a whistleblower's confidentiality, how to assess and grade the significance of information being disclosed;

- firms should document and embed the approach to preventing victimisation across the whistleblowing arrangements;

- firms should ensure a whistleblowing report is made annually to the governing body;

- firms should provide appropriate tailored training to various levels of staff.

These expectations simply reflect the rules already in place.

FCA Review: FCA findings

The FCA has also given helpful feedback on the arrangements that are already in place in many firms, highlighting where this shows good practice and identifying where things could be improved. This feedback includes the following:

- all firms have implemented or updated policies; however, many had not fully implemented the SYSC18 requirements;

- some firms have implemented a detailed step-by-step investigation process; however most firms needed to document and enhance these processes to ensure a consistent approach to assessing and escalating concerns;

- most firms have a variety of reporting channels; however, some firms incorrectly stated that individuals must raise whistleblowing concerns internally first before contacting the regulator;

- most firms are producing annual reports; however, some of these did not contain a sufficient level of information and analysis;

- all firms reviewed provide whistleblowing training; however most firms needed to improve the detail and most firms did not distinguish between the training provided to all employees, training given to managers and training given to persons operating the firm's internal arrangements (including investigation teams).

CHAPTER 11

Women in Finance and Gender Pay

Dawn Dickson, Partner and David Williams, Senior Associate

I SCOPE OF THIS CHAPTER

11.01   Eight in ten companies and public sector bodies in the UK have a gender pay gap that favours men.[1]

11.02   The UK has the fourth widest gender pay gap in Europe behind Estonia, the Czech Republic and Germany.[2]

---

1   The Guardian, 4 April 2018, 'Gender Pay Gap figures reveal eight in 10 firms pay men more'.
2   Eurostat Press Office 38/2018, 8 March 2018.

11.03   Bridging the UK gender pay gap in work has the potential to create an extra £150bn on top of business-as-usual GDP forecasts in 2025.[3]

11.04   This section of this chapter focuses on the gender pay gap reporting obligations of larger private and voluntary sector employers. It will cover the background to the introduction of gender pay gap reporting and the detailed requirements set out in the Equality Act 2010 (Gender Pay Gap Information) Regulations 2017 ('the GPG Regulations'),[4] which came into force on 6 April 2017. This requires larger employers to publish an annual report containing data on their gender pay gap.

2   BACKGROUND TO THE GPG REGULATIONS AND THE GENDER PAY GAP

11.05   Mandatory gender pay gap reporting for larger private and voluntary sector employers came into force on 6 April 2017.[5]

11.06   Mandatory gender pay reporting for many large public sector employers was introduced on 31 March 2017 (with the deadline for the first reporting date being no later than 31 March 2018).[6] Although this chapter focuses on the regulations applicable to the private and voluntary sectors, much of the commentary in this chapter on the reporting requirements will be useful to both public and private sector employers.

11.07   The gender pay gap is a statistical representation of the fact that average pay for men is greater than for women. Since 1997, the gap between men and women's average pay has been monitored in the UK by the Office for National Statistics in its Annual Survey of Hours and Earnings.

11.08   Section 78 of the Equality Act 2010 (EqA 2010) gives the government power to make regulations requiring private and voluntary sector employers to publish information relating to their gender pay gap. Section 78 allows for regulations to be made which prescribe:

- definitions of employers and employees covered by gender pay gap reporting;

- how to calculate the number of employees an employer has;

- the information which must be reported;

- the timing and when this information must be published (which cannot be more than once a year); and

- the form and manner in which information is to be published.

---

3   McKinsey & Company, McKinsey Global Institute, 'The Power of Parity: Advancing Women's Equality in the United Kingdom'.
4   SI 2017/172.
5   Equality Act 2010 (Gender Pay Gap Information) Regulations 2017 (SI 2017/172).
6   Equality Act 2010 (Specific Duties and Public Authorities) Regulations 2017 (SI 2017/353).

11.09   In July 2015 the government announced that it would seek to 'end the gender pay gap in a generation'. The government published a consultation paper on proposals to introduce a mandatory gender pay gap reporting requirement for non-public sector employers with a least 250 employees.[7] The paper contained information about the gender pay gap, its causes and the ongoing work in this area to narrow the gap, including Lord Davies work (see 11.94 ff) on increasing gender diversity on company boards and the 'Think, Act, Report' initiative which encouraged employers to consider gender equality issues on a voluntary basis and to put in place reporting mechanisms on gender pay gaps.

11.10   However, by February 2016 (with the response to the first consultation complete and the launch of a second consultation with draft regulations being published) only seven signatories had voluntarily published their gender pay gap.

11.11   The Equality Act 2010 (Gender Pay Gap Information) Regulations 2017 ('the GPG Regulations') came into force on 6 April 2017.[8] The draft regulations were published on 6 December 2016 together with an explanatory memorandum.

11.12   On 28 January 2017 Acas and the Government Equalities Office (GEO) published draft non-statutory guidance to help organisations in their compliance with the GPG Regulations. The final version of this Guidance was broadened to cover gender pay reporting requirements for public and private sector employers (the 'Managing Gender Pay Reporting' guidance which was published on 3 April 2017).[9] The Guidance does not have binding legal effect but is likely to be taken into consideration by the Equalities and Human Rights Commission (EHRC).

11.13   More recently Eversheds Sutherland[10] in partnership with Winmark have published a report entitled 'Seeing the Bigger Picture – our gender pay gap research report 2018', measuring the impact the GPG Regulations have had thus far.

11.14   The Report seeks to capture the impact of the GPG Regulations as employers have started to publish their data. Much media attention has focused on the headline gender pay gap figures and in 2019 there will be an added dimension as comparisons are made between employers' pay data year on year. Where pay gaps appear to be static or increasing, employers might be asked difficult questions.

11.15   The Report surveyed 84 senior Human Resources and Chief People Officers across various industry sectors and focused on gender pay gap causes, challenges, executive commitment and steps being taken to close gender pay gaps.

---

7   Government Equalities Office, 'Closing the Gender Pay Gap', Consultation which ended on 14 July 2015.
8   Equality Act 2010 (Gender Pay Gap Information) Regulations 2017 (SI (2017/172).
9   Acas, 'Managing Gender Pay Reporting'.
10   Eversheds Sutherland (International) LLP.

11.16   The key findings were as follows:

- 76% thought that gender pay gap reporting is going to help address the UK's gender pay gap;

- 50% were concerned that a continuing gender pay gap will impact on staff recruitment, engagement and retention;

- 70% believed that the UK gender pay gap will be significantly reduced by 2018;

- 45% believed that their executive team consider gender pay disparity to be a high or very high priority;

- only 24% have or will set a gender pay gap target;

- 51% have conducted equal pay audits over the last five years or informal equal pay reviews.

11.17   The Report also asked respondents about the main reasons for their gender pay gap results. The most popular responses from respondent organisations were a lack of senior females, occupational segregation and the effect of child rearing.

11.18   Respondents were also asked about how they were addressing the gender pay disparity in their organisations. The most common responses were through female recruitment and progression, improving family friendly and flexible working practices and through education outreach programmes.

11.19   When asked about the societal changes which would help close the gender pay gap, respondents felt that breaking down gender stereotypes would have the biggest impact. Respondents identified two themes in relation to breaking down gender stereotypes. First, transforming the UK's parenting bias whereby women are the primary carers towards more shared parenting; and, second, more effective promotion in education of STEM (science, technology, engineering and mathematics) subjects and careers to girls.

3   TERRITORIAL SCOPE OF THE GPG REGULATIONS

11.20   The scope of the GPG Regulations is set out under EqA 2010, s 78, which is Great Britain. However, see 11.28, 11.36–11.38 and 11.80 with regard to the position of employees working overseas.

11.21   In Northern Ireland where employment law is a devolved matter, s 19 of the Employment Act (Northern Ireland) 2016 sets out a gender pay reporting requirement. However, this section has not yet been brought into force and no draft regulations under this section have been brought forward. It is of note that the reporting requirements under the Northern Irish legislation go further than the GPG Regulations in a number of key respects, but this is outside the scope of this chapter.

4   OUTLINE OF THE GPG REGULATIONS AND WHAT IS REQUIRED

11.22   Large private and voluntary sector employers are required to publicise their gender pay gap by April each year. The first reports were published by 4 April 2018. The published results showed a median gender pay gap of 9.7%, significantly lower than the national gender pay gap of 18.4% recorded by the Office of National Statistics. Notably the financial services sector had the largest reported gender pay gap at 35.6%.

11.23   Crucially, the gender pay gap is a measurement of the difference between men and women's average earnings: it is not about men and women being paid differently for the same job (this is covered by equal pay legislation). However, there is a concern among employers that large pay gaps may prompt equal pay claims and carry evidential weight. Interestingly, we are increasingly seeing a reference in equal pay grievances and pre-litigation requests for information to gender pay gap reports.

11.24   The GPG Regulations apply to 'relevant employers' in Great Britain with at least 250 employees on the 'snapshot date' which is 5 April in the relevant year.[11] 'Employer' is not defined in the GPG Regulations but reg 14 clearly suggests that it would include companies, limited liability partnerships (LLPs), partnerships, limited partnerships, unincorporated bodies or any other type of employing entity.

11.25   In response to the consultation on the GPG Regulations the Financial Reporting Council recommended that the government consider allowing gender pay gap reporting on a group-wide basis for group companies to reflect the approach taken in other areas of corporate reporting, where disclosures are required to be provided at a consolidated level for group companies.

11.26   However, the government response was clear that each company in a group is to be considered as a separate entity for reporting purposes. The rationale was that this is a more meaningful measure. This means that the obligation is to prepare a gender pay report where organisations have at least 250 employees working for an individual entity.

11.27   'Employee' is not defined in the GPG Regulations, but the explanatory memorandum[12] provides that the wider definition of employment under EqA 2010, s 83 applies. This definition includes employees, casual workers and some contractors. However, the gender pay gap reporting duties themselves only apply in respect of 'relevant employees'.

11.28   'Relevant employee' was defined in the 2016 draft regulations as an employee who ordinarily works in Great Britain and whose contract is governed by UK legislation. This wording was removed from the GPG Regulations leaving

---

11   GPG Regulations, reg 1(2).
12   Issued on 6 December 2016 at the same time as the publication of the GPG Regulations.

it uncertain whether an overseas employee of a UK employer may be covered. Under the GPG Regulations a 'relevant employee' is an employee employed on the relevant snapshot date (5 April) with the exception of partners (including LLP members).[13] This issue is considered in more detail at 11.34 ff.

5   TIMING AND OBLIGATION TO PUBLISH GENDER PAY GAP DATA

11.29   Employers must initially analyse their gender pay gap and then publish it each April on their website if they have one. Where the employer does not have its own website the consultation on the draft regulations states that an employer may want to create a separate webpage for their gender pay gap information or publish on a website hosted by its parent company. There is no requirement to publish the information on a UK website.

11.30   The GPG Regulations allow employers to analyse and publish the required information any time within 12 months of the snapshot date. Employers therefore have a high degree of flexibility over when to analyse and publish their information. Information published must remain online for at least three years. The publication of an employer's gender pay gap statement must be accompanied by a signed statement confirming the accuracy of the report and can (but does not have to) include an explanatory narrative to explain the reasons for the gap that exists. The information published must be provided in a manner that is easily accessible to all employees and the public. Employers must upload the information to a government website.[14] The uploaded information must include all gender pay gap and bonus pay gap information.[15]

6   WHAT INFORMATION MUST BE PUBLISHED?

11.31   The Guidance (see 11.12) states that only the results of an organisation's gender pay calculations must be published. As a result, this does not pose any employee data protection issues given that statistical information is being published. However, in preparing the reports in relation to gender pay reporting employers should bear the data protection principles in mind as the preparation may involve the processing of personal data.

11.32   Regulation 2 of the GPG Regulations requires the following information to be published:

● The difference between the mean pay of relevant full pay male employees and that of relevant full pay female employees.

---

13   GPG Regulations, reg 1(2), (4) and (5).
14   Gov.uk, 'Report your gender pay gap data'.
15   Required by reg 2 of the GPG Regulations.

- The difference between the median pay of relevant full pay male employees and that of relevant full pay female employees. The median, which is used by the Office of National Statistics is thought to be the most accurate representation of the typical difference between the genders as the median figure is not affected by the small number of very high earners.

- The difference between the mean bonus pay of relevant male and female employees.

- The difference between the median bonus pay of relevant male and female employees.

- The proportions of relevant male and female employees who were paid bonus pay in the relevant 12-month period.

- The proportions of full pay male and female employees in four quartile pay bands, based on the employer's overall pay range. This will show how the gender pay gap changes across the organisation, at different levels of seniority.

11.33 In addition, a written statement signed by an appropriate senior individual must also be published confirming that the published gender pay gap information is accurate. This must be signed by a senior individual as follows:

- for companies and other organisations (except LLPs), a director or equivalent officer;

- for LLPs, a designated member of a LLP;

- for partnerships, a partner;

- for other unincorporated associations, a senior officer or a member of the governance of the organisation; and finally

- for other types of organisation, the most senior employee of the employer.[16]

7 WHICH EMPLOYEES ARE COUNTED TOWARDS GENDER PAY GAP REPORTING?

11.34 The GPG Regulations do not define 'employee'; however, it is clear that all relevant employees employed by the organisation on the snapshot date are counted and must be reported upon. It is understood that the wider definition of employment under the EqA 2010 applies (see 11.27).[17]

---

16 GPG regulations, reg 14.
17 EqA 2010, s 83.

11.35 This is also confirmed by the Guidance.[18] The explanatory memorandum[19] confirms that the wider definition of employment under s 83 of the EqA 2010 applies. This is understood to mean:

• an individual who works under a contract of service;

• an individual who works under a contract of apprenticeship; or

• an individual who works under a contract to do work personally.

This will include some contractors and casual workers.

11.36 A relevant employee to whom a gender pay gap reporting duty will apply was defined in the 2016 draft regulations as an employee who ordinarily works in Great Britain and whose contract of employment was governed by the UK legislation. The GPG Regulations omitted this wording which leaves open the potential for overseas employees of the UK employer to be covered.

11.37 The Guidance states that where an employer based in Great Britain employs an individual who is based permanently overseas that individual may be included within the definition of a 'relevant employee' and may count towards the 250 employee threshold for applicability of the GPG Regulations. This depends on whether there can be said to be a close connection with Great Britain. To determine whether an employee based overseas should be included, an employer should consider the case law on jurisdiction, which is beyond the scope of this book.[20] It should be noted that the Government response to the consultation suggested that the regulations cover 'those who are not based in Great Britain but are still regarded as being employees of employers within scope ... because of a close connection with Great Britain'.

11.38 The government website on the GPG Regulations states: 'As a general rule, you must count an employee based overseas if they have an employment contract subject to English, Scottish or Welsh law'.[21] In reality, the test is more complex and involves an analysis of a number of different factors.

11.39 For the purposes of the GPG Regulations a 'relevant employee' is simply an employee employed on the relevant snapshot date (5 April), excluding partners and members of LLPs.[22] This makes clear that firms and LLPs do not have to include the earnings of their partners or members in their gender pay gap reporting calculations. This remains the case even where some partners or members are included within the 250-person head count threshold. This is because partners take a share of the organisation's profits, which is not directly comparable with employees' pay.

---

18 Acas, 'Managing Gender Pay Reporting'.
19 Issued on 6 December 2016 at the same time as the publication of the GPG Regulations.
20 See *Lawson v Serco* [2006] ICR 250; *Ravat v Halliburton* [2012] UKSC 1.
21 https://www.gov.uk/guidance/gender-pay-gap-reporting-overview.
22 GPG Regulations, reg 1(2), (4) and (5).

11.40   However, employers are excluded from the gender pay reporting obligations incumbent upon organisations if employees receive less than full pay as a result of being on leave. Less than full pay can mean a reduced rate of pay or a nil rate.[23] This exclusion has been achieved by the inclusion of a definition of 'full pay relevant employee' which is a 'relevant employee who has not, during the relevant pay period, been paid at a reduced rate or nil as a result of the employee being on leave'. Such employees are however included in the calculation of whether an organisation meets the threshold of having 250 'relevant employees'. Only full pay relevant employees are taken into account on the snapshot date for the calculations relating to mean and median hourly rates of pay, or the proportion of male and female employees in each quartile. However, all relevant employees are included in the calculation of the gender bonus gap. The introduction of the term 'full pay relevant employee' aims to address the concern that the gender pay gap could appear greater if the employer had a significant number of female employees on statutory maternity pay or unpaid maternity leave around the snapshot date.

11.41   So far as part-time workers and job-sharers are concerned, each part-time worker and job-sharer must be counted as one employee. So, for example, if two individuals share a job, that will count as two individuals for the GPG Regulations reporting obligations.

11.42   Only full pay relevant employees are taken into account on the snapshot date for the calculations relating to mean and medium hourly rates of pay or the proportion of male and female employees in each quartile. However, all relevant employees are included in the calculation of the gender bonus gap (see 11.66).

11.43   Where agency workers or service companies are used, such individuals count as part of the headcount of the agency or service company that provides them.

11.44   Whether a non-executive director (NED) will be an employee for the purposes of the GPG Regulations will depend on the terms of their engagement. Do the facts and terms suggest that the NED is in employment 'under a contract personally to do work'? It is likely that a NED will be an employee for GPG Regulations reporting obligations. However, if the NED's services are provided via the medium of a personal service company then it is unlikely that they will fall within scope of the GPG Regulations.

8   CALCULATING THE GENDER PAY GAP

11.45   The gender pay gap is always expressed as a percentage. This percentage is calculated by working out the difference between the average pay of all male

---

23   This has been achieved by the inclusion of a definition of 'full pay relevant employee' which is a 'relevant employee who has not, during the relevant pay period, been paid at a reduced rate or nil as a result of the employee being on leave' (Regulation 1(2), GPG Regulations).

employees and the average pay of all female employees, and dividing that number by the average pay of all male employees. This is expressed as a formula:

Where A is average male pay, and B is average female pay, it is expressed as:

$$\frac{A - B}{A} \times 100$$

11.46   This has the result that a negative gender pay gap figure would be indicative of the fact that average pay of men is more than the average pay of women in the reporting organisation.

9   WHAT IS 'PAY'?

11.47   The GPG Regulations define pay with reference to the terms 'ordinary pay', 'bonus pay' and 'hourly rate of pay'.

Mean and median

11.48   In looking at the difference between the mean pay of relevant full pay male employees and relevant full pay female employees it is important to note that the mean is to be expressed as a percentage of the mean hourly rate of pay for relevant male employees.

11.49   In looking at the median hourly rates of pay it is essential to:

• list all relevant employees in the group in order of their earnings;

• identify the hourly rate paid to the individual who appears in the middle of the list; and

• calculate the difference in median hourly rates of pay for the relevant male and female employees expressed as a percentage of the medium hourly rate of pay for relevant male employees.

What earnings are taken into account when calculating the mean and median hourly rates of pay?

11.50   For the purposes of reporting on an organisation's gender pay gap, pay is divided into two categories: ordinary pay and bonus pay.

11.51   **Ordinary pay** includes basic pay, allowances (excluding the reimbursement of expenses), shift premium pay, pay for piecework and pay in relation to leave. Ordinary pay does not include overtime pay, pay in lieu of leave, benefits in kind (for example benefits provided through salary sacrifice arrangements), redundancy pay and termination payments.[24]

11.52 With specific reference to salary sacrifice arrangements, the Guidance makes clear that the amount that should be reported on is the gross amount after salary sacrifice deduction. This is because the employee has no contractual entitlement to the additional sum 'sacrificed' through such an arrangement.

11.53 In looking at the allowances which would be included in basic pay these would include allowances for duties connected with one's main duties such as first aid officer, allowances for working in a certain geographical area, recruitment and retention allowances and allowances for being on call. Allowances would also include those which assist employees to provide items such as cars or clothing. Whilst pay for leave is included in the definition of basic pay this would in practice only include cases where employees receive full pay, otherwise they are excluded altogether from the gender pay gap calculations.

11.54 **Bonus pay** which is included in both the headline gender pay gap (on a pro rated basis if necessary) and the separate gender bonus gap figures is defined as:

● remuneration in the form of money, vouchers, securities, securities options, or interests in securities; and

● which relates to profit sharing, productivity performance, incentive or commission.[25]

11.55 The definitions of 'securities', 'securities options' and 'interests in securities' have the same meaning as in s 420 of the Income Tax (Earnings and Pensions) Act 2003. Bonus pay specifically does not include ordinary pay, overtime pay or remuneration referable to redundancy or termination payments.

11.56 The 2016 draft regulations made reference to bonus payments that were 'received and earned' in the relevant period. This definition does not appear in the GPG Regulations and instead non-cash bonus awards (ie remuneration in the form of shares, share options and interests in securities) are deemed paid at the time when, and in the amount in respect of which, they give rise to taxable earnings income.

11.57 Both ordinary pay and bonus pay (as defined at 11.51 and 11.54) paid in the pay period spanning the snapshot date (5 April) are taken into account when calculating the mean and median hourly rates of pay for gender pay gap reporting purposes.

---

24 GPG Regulations, reg 3(1).
25 GPG Regulations, reg 4(1).

How do you calculate the hourly rate of pay?

11.58   The basic unit of data for the calculation of an organisation's gender pay gap is the 'hourly rate of pay'.[26] The GPG Regulations set out a six-step process for working out the correct rate which is as follows:

- **Step 1**: an organisation must identify all amounts of ordinary pay and bonus pay paid to employees in the relevant pay period. The pay period is the period in respect of which the employer pays the employee basic pay.[27] So for example in relation to a weekly-paid employee, the relevant pay period will be one week. The relevant pay period is the one within which the snapshot date of 5 April falls.

- **Step 2**: an organisation is then required to exclude any amount of ordinary pay that would normally fall to be paid in a different pay period.

- **Step 3**: in the case of bonus pay which is paid for a period other than the pay period (for example an annual bonus paid in April) an organisation must divide the amount by the length of the bonus period and multiply it by the length of the relevant pay period. The bonus pay is therefore pro rated for the relevant pay period. A year is always treated as 365.25 days for these purposes and a month is always treated as 30.44 days.

- **Step 4**: this requires organisations to add together the amounts identified under Step 1 (adjusted where necessary as described under Steps 2 and 3).

- **Step 5**: an organisation is then required to multiply the amount under Step 4 by the appropriate multiplier (7 divided by the number of days in the relevant pay period, which for a month is always treated as 30.44 days).

- **Step 6**: an organisation is then required to divide the amount by the number of working days in the week for that employee.[28]

11.59   There are three options for calculating an employee's weekly working hours depending on whether they work normal working hours, have no normal working hours or work and are paid on a piecework basis.

11.60   For an employee who has normal working hours that do not differ from week to week or over a longer period, the weekly working hours are the contractual hours under the contract in force for that employee on the snapshot date (5 April). The calculation methods for calculating an employee's weekly working hours are similar to those under the Employment Rights Act 1996 for calculating a week's pay. The Guidance[29] indicates that where an employee has fixed contractual hours which are the same every week they should be treated as having normal working hours even if they often work additional unpaid hours.

---

26   GPG Regulations, reg 2.
27   GPG Regulations, reg 5.
28   GPG Regulations, reg 6.
29   Acas, 'Managing Gender Pay Reporting'.

The Guidance[30] also states that even if the employee's normal hours do vary from week to week, it would not usually be reasonable or necessary to carry out a weekly working hours calculation where they have a fixed hourly rate of pay, as employers would apply this in all circumstances.[31]

11.61   In addition there are detailed rules specified within reg 7 of the GPG Regulations for the calculation of an employee's weekly working hours where they have no normal working hours or are paid on the basis of piece work but these are outside the scope of this chapter.

10 BONUS PAY

11.62   **Bonus pay** which is included in both the headline gender pay gap (on a pro rated basis if necessary) and the separate gender bonus gap figures is defined as:

● remuneration in the form of money, vouchers, securities, securities options, or interests in securities; and

● which relates to profit sharing, productivity performance, incentive or commission.[32]

11.63   The definitions of 'securities', 'securities options' and 'interests in securities' have the same meaning as in s 420 of the Income Tax (Earnings and Pensions) Act 2003. Bonus pay specifically does not include ordinary pay, overtime pay or remuneration referable to redundancy or termination payments.

11.64   It should be noted that remuneration in the form of shares and share options counts as bonus pay when the shares/options give rise to a liability to income tax; so employers will need to include the value of bonuses paid as shares at the time when the employee incurs a liability to pay income tax. If an employee has decided to defer an entitlement to bonus pay, for example in the case of a long-term incentive plan (LTIP), then that amount would not be captured until a later time when the amount does give rise to an income tax liability.

11.65   The position with regard to deferred cash bonus is more complex as there is no specific provision in the GPG Regulations specifying when a deferred cash amount should be deemed to be paid. Amounts of bonus pay count for gender pay gap and gender bonus pay calculations if they are 'paid to the employee' during the relevant period.[33] Any amounts deferred could therefore be argued to be excluded from the calculations with them being included at the point they are actually paid to the employee during the relevant pay period.

---

30 Acas, 'Managing Gender Pay Reporting'.
31 Page 30 of the guidance.
32 GPG Regulations, reg 4(1).
33 Under GPG Regulations, regs 6 and 10.

11   CALCULATING THE GENDER BONUS GAP

11.66   Fulfilling an organisation's obligations in relation to gender bonus gap requires the following data to be published:

- The difference in mean bonus payments paid during the 12-month period preceding the snapshot date (5 April) to male and female employees given as a percentage of the mean bonus pay received by male employees.[34]

- The difference in median bonus payments paid during the 12-month period preceding the snapshot date to male and female employees given as a percentage of the median bonus pay received by male employees.[35]

- The proportion of male and female employees who received bonus payments during the same 12-month period.[36] Two separate percentage figures need to be published and should include all relevant employees whether they have been on leave in the period or not.

The gender bonus gap is calculated using A as the mean (or median) bonus pay of all relevant male employees and B as the mean (or median) bonus pay for all relevant female employees, with the following formula being applied:

$$\frac{A - B}{A} \times 100$$

11.67   Only employees who received bonus pay during the period of 12 months ending on the snapshot date and who are still employed on the snapshot date are included in this calculation.

12   SALARY QUARTILES

11.68   Employers are obliged to report on the proportion of men and women in each of four pay bands. Employers must generate their own pay quartiles each containing the same number of employees. The proportion of male and female employees in each quartile must then be reported in percentage terms. The GPG Regulations[37] set out the following method:

(1) Calculate the hourly rate of pay for each male and female full pay relevant employee and then run them from lowest paid to highest paid.

(2) Divide the employees into four sections each comprising an equal (or as near as possible to equal) number of employees to produce the lower, lower middle, upper middle and upper quartile pay bands.

---

34 GPG Regulations, reg 10.
35 GPG Regulations, reg 11.
36 GPG Regulations, reg 12.
37 GPG Regulations, reg 13.

(3) Express the proportion of full pay relevant male employees as a percentage of the total number of full pay relevant employees in that band.

(4) Express the proportion of full pay relevant female employees as a percentage of the total number of full pay relevant employees in that band.

11.69   The idea behind the quartile obligation within the GPG Regulations is to help employers identify where women are situated in terms of their remuneration and if there are any obstacles to their pay progression. It also puts the spotlight on the gender reaching the more senior roles within an organisation.

13   NON-COMPLIANCE

11.70   Where employers do not comply with their gender pay gap reporting obligations there is no system of enforcement in place under the GPG Regulations and no specific penalties for employers. Instead the government has committed to:

● regular checks to assess levels of non-compliance;

● the production of sector data of employers reported gender pay gaps;

● publicise examples of employers who publish full and explanatory information and who demonstrate what it sees as exemplary practice.

11.71   Further it should be noted that although the GPG Regulations themselves do not provide any sanctions against employers, the explanatory memorandum[38] provides that a failure to comply with the GPG Regulations will amount to an 'unlawful act' within the meaning of s 20 of the EqA 2006 (see 11.74).

11.72   Despite this uncertain position, prior to the deadline for the first reporting data, Maria Miller (chair of the House of Commons Women and Equalities Committee) stated that companies that failed to file their gender pay gap data before the deadline should face tough sanctions (around 1,500 companies failed to comply by the reporting date although all companies required to report gender pay gaps have now done so). Rebecca Hilsenrath, chief executive of the EHRC, also suggested that the EHRC would start enforcement against employers that had not complied (although it remains unclear whether the EHRC has legal authority to do this).

11.73   For most financial institutions, the focus will be less on enforcement and more on how to tackle the gender pay gaps within their organisations (the finance sector reported a gender pay gap of 35.6% in the first reporting data).

11.74   Under EqA 2010, s 20, the EHRC can carry out an investigation into unlawful acts[39] and can issue unlawful act notices. The Government also states

---

38   Issued on 6 December 2016 at the same time as the publication of the GPG Regulations.
39   Any act 'contrary to a provision of the Equality Act 2010'.

that it will monitor levels of non-compliance and may decide to introduce enforcement mechanisms in due course.

11.75   However, it is difficult to see how a compelling argument could be made to the effect that a breach of the GPG Regulations was an unlawful act as s 78 of the EqA 2010 merely gives the government a power to make regulations to require employers to publish gender pay gap information rather than pose any requirements on employers.

11.76   Perhaps one of the most acute risks of failure to comply with the GPG Regulations is that this may attract adverse publicity and reputational damage given the fact that such failures can easily be determined by anyone wishing to research an employer's organisation. Failure to comply may have an impact on an employer's ability to recruit and attract the best people.

11.77   It is important to note, however, that an organisation's gender pay gap figures will not in most cases assist individuals in establishing discrimination in relation to pay which is a different matter covered by the equal pay legislation.

14   PROBLEM AREAS

Atypical workers

11.78   Casual workers or bank staff who are engaged directly by a relevant employer will fall within the scope of the GPG Regulations. This includes workers engaged under an umbrella contract or a zero hours contract. Contractors may also come within the scope of the GPG Regulations where employed under a contract to do work personally and with a degree of control being exercised over them.

11.79   Agency workers will generally be regarded as employed by the business that supplies them rather than by the end user of their services (see 11.43).

International employees

11.80   The definition of 'relevant employee' under the GPG Regulations as published did not exclude those ordinarily working outside Great Britain. Employees who work abroad on a permanent basis could therefore potentially be included within the scope of the reporting requirements and may require to be counted towards the 250-employee threshold. However, this is unclear. The Government response to the consultation on the draft regulations suggested that the GPG Regulations would cover employees not based in Great Britain but still regarded as being employees, and so they should be counted in the 250-employee threshold as they had a close connection with Great Britain. The Guidance[40]

40   Acas, 'Managing Gender Pay Reporting'.

suggested that, as a general rule, an employee based overseas will be within the scope of the GPG Regulations if they can bring a claim to an employment tribunal under the EqA 2010. Matters such as an individual having a contract subject to Great British jurisdiction, maintaining a connection with Great Britain such as a home and having UK tax legislation apply to their employment will be significant in determining this. See also 11.37.

Salary sacrifice

11.81   The value of salary sacrifice schemes has been excluded from the definition of pay in the GPG Regulations. Whilst this may lead to greater simplicity as such benefits are simply disregarded it may lead to anomalies as women may be more likely to take up some benefits under salary sacrifice arrangements where for example they assist with the cost of providing childcare.

Sign on, buy out and retention bonuses

11.82   It was unclear from the GPG Regulations whether recruitment and retention payments should be counted as ordinary pay or bonus pay. This affected which pay gap statistics such payments should be included in.

11.83   The definition of 'ordinary pay' in the GPG Regulations includes any sum paid with respect to the recruitment and retention of an employee. However, the position may be less clear where there is a performance condition attached to the payment of the bonus, in which case it is less likely that the payment is for the primary purpose of recruitment or retention of an employee. In this case, such a payment runs the risk of being classified as a bonus payment.

11.84   If a recruitment or retention bonus is paid (whether in part or in full) as a non-cash payment, this non-cash part must be treated as bonus pay for the purpose of reporting under the GPG Regulations.

11.85   Are employer and employee pension contributions into occupational pension schemes included? Regulation 1(3) states that ordinary and bonus pay should be calculated 'before deductions made at source (for example deductions in relation to income tax'). Therefore pay should be calculated before any employee pension contributions are deducted. However, employer contributions should probably not be included since they are not 'paid' to the employee for the purposes of calculating the hourly rate of pay (see 11.34). The explanatory memorandum[41] clarifies this, noting that since employer pension contributions go directly to a pension fund these do not affect the GPG calculations.

---

41   Issued on 6 December 2016 at the same time as the publication of the GPG Regulations.

The bonus period for exercise of options

11.86 Bonus pay in the form of securities, securities options and interests in securities is treated as paid at the time when, and in the amounts in respect of which, it gives rise to taxable earnings. This means that the amounts relevant for gender pay gap reporting will depend on the type of security or interest in security. Tax-advantaged securities options will generally not give rise to a tax charge when the option is exercised. However, it is unclear whether the amount of the option gain is an amount which should be reported under the GPG Regulations.

11.87 When a non-tax advantaged option is exercised and gives rise to income tax as taxable earnings it is generally considered better practice to use the period from the date of grant to the date of vesting as the performance period. Firms may want to offer an explanation in the supporting statement.

11.88 Where a bonus is paid in respect of a period that does not match the relevant pay period (see 11.58) an employer should refer to reg 6 of the GPG Regulations which provides that the bonus should be divided by the length of the bonus period and multiplied by the pay period.

How does the application of malus and clawback affect reporting?

11.89 There is no specific reference to malus and/or clawback in the final GPG Regulations or Guidance. However, the definition of bonus pay (see 11.62) makes clear that remuneration in the form of securities, securities options and interests in securities are treated as paid to the employee at the time, and in the amount in respect of which, they give rise to a liability to income tax. Therefore any calculation of bonus pay in relation to such forms of remuneration would be adjusted to reflect a malus deduction since the liability to income tax would not have arisen when the deduction is made. The position is different in the case of clawback since the bonus payment will already have been made and a liability to income tax will have arisen when the deduction was made.

11.90 As the purpose of the GPG Regulations is to compare pay awarded, a bonus pay calculation that does not take into account malus and clawback deductions arguably will not accurately reflect the true picture. Where malus or clawback applies, further information may need to be included in the report to explain how these deductions have affected the calculations.

LTIPs in the form of conditional awards or nil cost options

11.91 Share awards made to employees under long-term incentive plans (LTIPs) are ordinarily made either in the form of conditional awards or nil cost options. A conditional award will ordinarily be taxed when the award vests whereas an option will ordinarily be taxed at the time the award is exercised.

11.92   This means that LTIP awards granted as nil cost options fall within the definition of bonus pay for the relevant year depending on when a participant exercises the option. It is therefore possible that different LTIP participants could exercise a nil cost option granted at the same time in different tax years so that one employee's award might count towards the gender pay gap in one reporting year but another employee's award may not count until a later reporting year.

Bonus buyouts

11.93   The GPG regulations do not make clear whether bonus buyouts will be included in the definition of bonus. It is assumed that bonus buyouts will be included and employers should work on that basis and include an explanation in the accompanying statement.

15   WOMEN IN FINANCE CHARTER

Background to the Charter

11.94   Women have historically been under-represented at boardroom level in the UK. In 2010, women made up only 12.5% of the boards of FTSE 100 companies and a report by the Equality and Human Rights Commission (EHRC) in 2008 suggested that it would take more than 70 years to achieve gender-balanced boardrooms in the UK's largest 100 companies.[42]

11.95   The government at that time was concerned about the significant gender disparity at senior management levels of UK companies and at the prospect of such a slow rate of progress. Lord Mervyn Davies of Abersoch was, therefore, asked to complete a review to identify the barriers that were preventing women reaching the boardroom and to make recommendations as to what the Government and business could do to improve gender diversity at boardroom level in the UK.

Davies Report – reasons for a diverse board

11.96   On 24 February 2011, following a period of consultation and an online call for evidence, Lord Davies published a report in which he set out a business strategy to increase the number of women on boards of listed companies in the UK.[43] As well as including a discussion as to the reasons for the historically low number of female board appointments, the report also identified four business reasons in favour of having a diverse board. The first of these was to improve corporate performance.

---

42 Lord Mervyn Davies, 'Women on Boards' (2011).
43 Lord Mervyn Davies, 'Women on Boards' (2011).

11.97   The report presented evidence that single sex senior management teams tended to think the same way. It also included evidence that companies with more female directors achieved a 42% higher return in sales, 66% higher return on invested capital and 53% better return on equity compared with rivals. There was also found to be a reduced risk of insolvency where at least one board member was a woman. The second reason was that gender-balanced boards were more likely to focus on good corporate governance and this included identifying criteria for measuring strategy, monitoring its implementation, following conflict of interest guidelines and adhering to a code of conduct. The third and fourth reasons were to ensure that the UK was better able to access a wider talent pool (the report provided evidence that the female talent pool was being under-utilised at board level in the UK) and to enable companies to better understand their customers and improve their market responsiveness.

Davies Report – reasons for low female numbers and recommendations

11.98   The Davies Report identified a number of reasons for the under-representation of women at board level and this included a drop-off in female representation at an earlier stage in the workforce structure, specifically at the middle to senior management level. The Davies Report explained how male and female entry into the UK workforce was relatively equal and that this equality was maintained through junior management positions.

11.99   However, the rates of female attrition increased significantly at senior management level. The reasons for this were acknowledged as being complex. The report relied on evidence collated by a separate 'Your Loss' study which referenced possible contributing factors such as a lack of access to flexible working arrangements, difficulties in achieving work-life balance or disillusionment at a lack of career progression.[44] The report also commented on other possible reasons, including a decline in the number of executive directorships; the influence of informal networks and lack of transparent criteria and the way that executive search firms were operating; differences in the way that men and women were being mentored and sponsored; and gender traits, such as a tendency for women to undervalue their skills.

11.100   The Davies Report also made recommendations as to how the UK could increase the number of women on boards. This included a proposal that all FTSE 100 companies should aim for a minimum of 25% of female board representation by 2015, with one-third of new appointments being women. Quoted companies should be required to disclose each year the proportion of women they have on their board, the number of women in senior executive positions in the company and the number of women employees in the whole organisation.

---

44   C Ioannidis and N Walther, 'Your Loss' (2010).

11.101 The report also recommended that the Financial Reporting Council (FRC) should amend the Corporate Governance Code to require listed companies to establish a policy on boardroom diversity, including measurable objectives for implementing the policy. The recommendations were all 'business-led' and the Davies Report deliberately avoided proposing the implementation of any mandatory quota due to concerns of tokenism.[45] From 2012 onwards the UK Corporate Governance Code for premium listed companies, in support of Lord Davies' recommendations, has asked companies to report on their board diversity policy. In 2013 the government legislated[46] to require quoted companies to disclose in their annual strategic report the numbers of male and female board directors, senior managers and total employees.

Corporate Governance Code 2018

11.102 Reflecting these recommendations, the Corporate Governance Code 2018 directly addresses issues of diversity. Appointments and succession plans should be based on merit and objective criteria and should promote diversity of gender, social and ethnic backgrounds, cognitive and personal strengths.

11.103 The 2018 Code provides that the annual report should include a report on the company's policy on diversity and inclusion; how it links to company strategy; how it has been implemented; and how it has or will influence board composition. It must also contain the gender balance of those in the senior management and their direct reports. This may lead to duplication in annual reports but the FRC considers that consistency in the way that this is reported will provide meaningful data which can be tracked over time to help companies assess whether attempts to improve gender equality are succeeding.

11.104 Separately, the 2018 Code's guidance encourages boards and their committees to think about how the company's gender pay gap is being addressed.

11.105 In September 2018 the FRC published a report[47] based on research by Exeter University Business School assessing the current extent and manner of reporting by FTSE 350 companies on diversity at board and senior management levels in their annual reports. The report also identifies examples of reporting that lead the way in terms of quality. Whilst overall the trend in quality of reporting is upwards, the FRC states that it would have expected to find even more of the largest companies providing meaningful information about their approach to boardroom diversity and offering real insights into the actions they are taking to increase diversity. Interestingly, being a signatory to the Women in Finance Charter (see 11.119 ff) appears to have a positive effect, resulting in a commitment to progress.

---

45 Lord Mervyn Davies, 'Women on Boards' (2011).
46 Companies Act 2006, s 414C.
47 https://www.frc.org.uk/getattachment/62202e7d-064c-4026-bd19-f9ac9591fe19/Board-Diversity-Reporting-September-2018.pdf

Davies Report – Five Year Summary, October 2015

11.106 On 29 October 2015 Lord Davies published a further report in which he assessed the impact of the Davies Report on boardroom diversity levels in the UK. The report found that significant progress had been made since the original publication in 2011.

11.107 As at 1 October 2015, there were no male-only boards in FTSE 100 companies and women held 26.1% of board positions in those companies. This compared favourably to the position in 2011 when 21 FTSE 100 companies had all-male boards and women held only 12.5% of board positions in those companies. However, the report also captured how further work needed to be done to increase the number of women holding executive positions which, as at October 2015, was at 9.6% within the FTSE 100.

11.108 The October 2015 report recommended that the voluntary, business-led approach (rather than the introduction of mandatory quotas) should be continued for another five years.

Gender diversity in financial services firms

Gadhia Review

11.109 The work completed by Lord Davies helped to drive a general improvement in gender diversity at UK Plc board level. However, the degree of impact varied from sector to sector and the financial services industry had the biggest shortage of women at senior levels in comparison to all other sectors.[48] It was also the case that whilst many financial services firms had more women than men at junior levels, the probability of female progression from middle to senior levels was worse than in any other sector.[49]

11.110 The pronounced nature of the gender disparity in financial services prompted the government, in July 2015, to announce that Jayne-Anne Gadhia, Chief Executive of Virgin Money Plc, would undertake a review into representation of women in senior managerial roles in the UK's financial services sector.

11.111 Following a period of consultation, the Gadhia Review was published in March 2016.[50] It was based on data that had been collected from 200 firms, across 12 different financial sub-sectors, including banking groups, asset managers,

48 'Focus on the pipeline: Engaging the full potential of female middle managers', Everywoman (2012).
49 Oliver Wyman, 'Women in Financial Services' (2014).
50 Jayne-Anne Gadhia, 'Empowering Productivity Harnessing the Talents of Women in Financial Services' (2016).

venture capitalists and insurers. The data was collected by New Financial.[51] The research confirmed that in 2015, women made up only 14% of Executive Committees in the sector. There was also found to be a large difference within the sector in the number of women at both board and executive committee level, where female representation ranged from 7 to 31% and 10 to 24% respectively.

11.112 This data appeared to support the evidence received throughout the consultation process that problems with female under-representation were more pronounced in particular aspects of financial services. The research also confirmed that 25% of companies in the sample had no women on their executive committee; more than 60% had between 0% and 15% female representation and nearly 17% had no women on their boards. The research helped to demonstrate that little or no progress had been made in some firms, particularly on the executive side and that there was a 'permafrost' in the mid-tier, where women did not progress or where they were leaving the sector.

11.113 In an effort to address the gender disparity that was more prevalent in financial institutions, the Gadhia Review included three overarching recommendations. It also suggested that these could best be captured in a voluntary Charter, owned by HM Treasury, to which firms would be able to sign up.

Reporting

11.114 The Gadhia Review recommended that firms should set their own internal gender diversity targets but that they should publicly report on them and the progress made against them. It was hoped that increased transparency in this area would act as a catalyst for individual firms to review policies and practices that may have been holding women back from progressing in their careers, and that requiring firms to publish figures on gender would act to ensure more firms put in place strategies to tackle problems where they existed.

11.115 It was also the case that during the consultation process many participants said that the commentary provided by the firm to accompany the targets and progress made would be of equal importance to the metrics. It was felt that for firms at an early stage in their plans to tackle gender diversity, narrative reporting that described the context of what was being done to improve female representation would be almost as important as publishing the statistics.

Executive accountability

11.116 The second recommendation was that there should be executive accountability for improving gender diversity at all levels of the organisation and in all business units. This built on the broader regulatory changes that were being

---

51 New Financial are a think tank and forum and they are the official data partner for the Women in Finance Charter.

introduced across the financial services sector, particularly the introduction of the Senior Managers and Certification Regime (SMCR), which assigns executive accountability for specific roles and responsibilities.

11.117 The Gadhia Review also acknowledged that too often collective responsibility meant that, in practice, no one takes responsibility or accountability. It was also felt that whilst firms should be given discretion as to who in their senior executive team should take on responsibility for gender diversity issues, there was a strong case for this responsibility sitting with someone in a profit and loss line. This would help to reduce the risk of diversity becoming a silo issue, but also help to ensure that female under-representation, which appeared to be greatest in such roles, may be better addressed. The Gadhia Review also commented as to how there was a case for this responsibility being given to a man rather than a woman, once again reducing the risk that it was viewed by senior executives as a silo issue.

Remuneration

11.118 The final recommendation was that executive bonuses should be explicitly tied to achieving the internal targets which firms set for themselves. It would be up to the institution to determine how they would do this. The Gadhia Review observed how remuneration structures and links with variable pay can be a powerful tool to change behaviours and act as an important signal to executives.

The Women in Finance Charter

11.119 The government supported the recommendations put forward in the Gadhia Review and in March 2016 it launched the HM Treasury Women in Finance Charter, which asks firms to commit to implement the review's recommendations. Under the Charter, which applies to all financial services firms as defined by the Financial Conduct Authority (FCA), firms are required to:

- appoint one member of the senior executive team as being responsible and accountable for gender diversity and inclusion. Firms must do this within three months of signing the Charter. To date, almost all firms have chosen their chief executive or another 'C-suite' member to take on this role;[52]

- set and publish internal targets for gender diversity in senior management. This must include at least one numerical target and it should ideally be part of a package of targets designed to include gender diversity at senior levels. The Treasury has produced Guidance for firms who sign up to the Charter and this invites them to set targets for a range of activities including flexible

---

52   HM Treasury, 'Women in Finance Charter – a pledge for gender balance across financial services'. Guidance on the Charter is available at https://www.gov.uk/government/uploads/system/uploads/attachment_data/file/596259/HMT_Women_in_Finance_Charter_guidance__Mar_2017_.pdf.

working, recruitment, promotion and retention. Firms have discretion over detail of these targets and the Treasury encourages them to develop a narrative which explains the rationale for their targets and the plans that they have in place to achieve them;

- publish progress annually against these targets in reports on their website. Once set, and by no later than three months after signing up to the Charter, firms should make the Treasury aware of their internal targets. The targets should also be published on a dedicated webpage on the firm's website, which should be easily navigable with targets clear and easy to find. There should also be some narrative text explaining why the firm has chosen those targets and how they can help improve gender diversity in senior management. Firms must then report on an annual basis to the Treasury upon the progress made towards achieving them; and

- demonstrate to the Treasury how they have linked executive variable pay to delivery against their gender diversity targets. Firms do not have to publish details of how their targets are linked to senior executive pay but they do need to provide details of this to the Treasury. It is for firms to determine which employees are in scope and the proportion of bonuses affected and many firms have chosen to link executive variable pay to delivery of gender diversity targets through performance review objectives.[53]

July 2017 Survey

11.120 By March 2017, 122 firms collectively employing more than 500,000 people in the UK and making up almost half of the financial services sector, had signed up to the Charter.

11.121 In May 2017 New Financial surveyed those Charter signatories in an attempt to get a better understanding as to what impact the Charter has had on signatory companies, what benefits they were realising and what challenges they were facing in meeting their Charter commitments. New Financial published the results of this survey in July 2017.

11.122 They found that two-thirds of signatories believed that signing up would lead to permanent and sustainable change within their companies and across the financial services industry. The most popular reasons that companies chose to sign up were to demonstrate leadership on gender diversity and to do the right thing. Nearly 70% of signatories were considering extending the Charter principles to other diversity characteristics and nearly half said the Charter had prompted them to take specific actions in their approach to non-gender diversity.

---

53 HM Treasury, 'Women in Finance Charter – a pledge for gender balance across financial services'. Guidance on the Charter is available at https://www.gov.uk/government/uploads/ system/uploads/attachment_data/file/596259/HMT_Women_in_Finance_Charter_guidance__ Mar_2017_.pdf.

11.123 Fine tuning the mechanism linking pay to gender diversity targets was said to be the most challenging of the Charter requirements and signatories were concerned about publishing poor numbers or missing targets. The biggest challenge that signatories faced was ensuring that gender diversity remained high on the business agenda despite all the other pressures on the Financial Services industry.[54]

Annual review – March 2018

11.124 As at March 2018, 205 financial services firms had signed the Charter. The first annual review of the Charter was also published in March 2018. This review found that 78% of the first group of signatories either increased or maintained the proportion of women in senior management in the reporting period.

11.125 Attached to the March 2018 publication of figures is analysis of signatory data by New Financial. This shows there is a big range in ambition among signatories and clear differences by sector. New Financial[55] disclosed the following:

- Incorporating gender diversity targets into bonus awards or as part of a balanced scorecard approach are the most common way of linking targets to managers' pay.

- A fifth of signatories have already met or exceeded their targets.

- Two-thirds of signatories name men as the accountable executive for diversity and inclusion, as suggested by the Gadhia Review (so that diversity is not seen as a 'women's problem').

11.126 The annual review also set out ten suggested actions to achieve targets, including female leadership training, examining hiring practices and improving flexible working. Since the Charter launched in March 2018, over 85% of the signatories that set their Charter targets committed to a 50/50 gender split in senior roles by 2021.

11.127 As of 11 July 2018 a further 67 companies had signed up to the Charter, taking the total number of signatories to 272. This means that the Charter now covers over 760,000 financial services employees in the UK.[56]

---

54 HM Treasury, 'Women in Finance Charter: Signatories Survey 2017 Assessing the impact of the Charter on signatories and the benefits and challenges they face', New Financial (July 2017).
55 New Financial, Annual Review March 2018.
56 https://www.gov.uk/government/news/more-financial-services-firms-commit-to-improve-gender-diversity-at-the-top?utm_source=8b930ef1-42e9-4ff7-9e00-909e4004023c&utm_medium=email&utm_campaign=govuk-notifications&utm_content=immediate.

Women in Finance Summit 2018

11.128 At the Women in Finance Summit 2018, Megan Butler, the FCA Director of Supervision emphasised[57] that diversity is a key supervisory issue for the FCA. She noted that over the past year the industry's approach to gender has changed. She attributed this to the continuing success of the Women in Finance Charter, publication of the gender pay gap data and the MeToo movement.

11.129 Separately, in 2018 the Investment Association and the Hampton-Alexander Review wrote[58] to 35 FTSE 350 companies with low female representation at leadership level, calling for change. They singled out 14 companies in the FTSE 100 who were asked to explain their poor gender balance and to explain what steps they are taking to move towards the targets set out in the Hampton-Alexander Review.

Insurers and board policy on diversity

11.130 In a policy statement[59] the Prudential Regulation Authority (PRA) set out its requirement that Solvency II insurers and large non-Solvency II Directive firms should have a policy to promote diversity among board members. These requirements are designed to promote a diverse board composition to improve the effectiveness of the board, enabling it to run the business more prudently and ensure the firm's safety and soundness. The proposals implement existing industry initiatives to improve diversity on boards; the Organisation for Economic Co-Operation and Development (OECD0) guidelines for insurers; and the Financial Reporting Council's Corporate Governance Code 2018 (see 11.102 ff). The rule requiring insurers to have a diversity policy became effective on 9 April 2018.

11.131 The rule reflects the regulators' increasing awareness that a diverse board minimises excessive risk taking. Its rules are not prescriptive as it recognises that insurers themselves are best placed to determine the details of their policy to promote diversity as the areas requiring greater representation would differ across firms and because the needs of firms will vary. The PRA states, 'although measurable factors such as gender, age, tenure and race are important, diversity of approach, skills and experience are just as important to combat groupthink'.

---

57 FCA Women in Finance Summit 2018.
58 https://www.theinvestmentassociation.org/media-centre/press-releases/2018/1-in-10-ftse-350-companies-fall-short-on-gender-diversity-targets.html.
59 PRA PS1/18.

Sexual harassment and the role of the regulators

11.132 The House of Commons Women's and Equalities committee has called on regulators to place incentives on employers to tackle workplace sexual harassment.[60]

11.133 Megan Butler of the FCA told the committee that regulatory attention was a 'key incentive' for focusing the financial services industry on the problem of sexual harassment. The SMCR presently being rolled out across the industry is intended to hold leaders responsible for the cultural values of their businesses, and for determining whether key staff are 'fit and proper' for their roles. The 'fit and proper' test does not explicitly require a history of sexual harassment issues to be considered but it considers aspects of the individual's behaviours which may impact on fitness and propriety.

11.134 Ms Butler stated that firms should take these aspects into account when they look at whether their key individuals are fit and proper to do their roles.

11.135 The committee concluded that regulators who fail to take steps to address sexual harassment in their sectors are failing in their public sector equality duty and called on the government to require regulators to put an action plan in place to ensure regulated employers take action to protect workers from sexual harassment.

11.136 Crucially, the committee urged regulators to make it clear that sexual harassment by regulated persons is a breach of regulatory requirements by the individual and their organisation; that such breaches must be reported to the appropriate regulator; and that such breaches must be taken into account when considering the fitness and propriety (or equivalent) of regulated individuals and their employers. Perpetration of or failure to address sexual harassment in the workplace must be recognised as grounds for failing a fit and proper person test or having professional credentials removed.

---

60 https://publications.parliament.uk/pa/cm201719/cmselect/cmwomeq/725/72506.htm#_idTextAnchor032.

CHAPTER 12

Senior Managers and Certification Regime for Insurers

Sophie White, Partner and Susan Mayne, Consultant

I BACKGROUND TO THE SENIOR INSURANCE MANAGERS REGIME

12.01 The legislation that originally introduced the Senior Managers and Certification Regime (SMCR) did not extend this regime to insurers. However, the regulators were cognisant of the risks that could be posed by these firms and of the guidance on systems of governance in the EU Solvency II Directive[1] (Solvency II). As a consequence, the Senior Insurance Managers Regime (SIMR) was implemented by the Prudential Regulation Authority (PRA) as the regulatory framework for insurers. Its stated aim was to ensure that all larger

---

1 Directive 2009/138/EC.

insurers subscribed to an effective governance system which provided a clear allocation of responsibilities within firms, as well as increasing the individual accountability of senior managers and directors.

12.02 Article 42 of Solvency II provides that individuals with key functions within insurers (key function holders (KFHs)) should meet certain standards such as possessing the right professional skills and being of high integrity. The regulators aimed to implement a regime that met and exceeded the requirements in Solvency II that would be aligned with the regime for the banking sector.

12.03 The SIMR came into force in full, alongside the SMCR for banks and larger financial services firms, on 7 March 2016. The full SIMR originally applied only to the following institutions:

- UK insurers and reinsurers that are within the scope of Solvency II (sometimes referred to as Directive firms);[2]

- third-country insurance branches within the scope of the PRA's rules transposing Solvency II;

- The Society of Lloyd's and managing agents; and

- insurance special purpose vehicles (ISPVs).

12.04 Most of the SIMR rules were found in the Solvency II part of the PRA Rulebook (however, see 12.07 ff following extension of the SMCR). Financial Conduct Authority (FCA) rules and guidance are in the following parts of the FCA Handbook: Chapter 10 of the Supervision Manual (SUP); Code of Conduct Sourcebook (COCON); and Fitness and Propriety Sourcebook (FIT). PRA Supervisory Statement SS 35/15 and policy statements set out the PRA's approach to strengthening individual accountability in insurance.[3]

12.05 The PRA and the FCA introduced a proportionate individual accountability framework for insurers that were not within the scope of Solvency II (these firms are sometimes referred to as non-directive firms (NDFs)). Larger NDFs[4] were required to comply with a similar regime to the SIMR and smaller NDFs[5] had to comply with a streamlined version of the regime.[6]

12.06 Whilst the SIMR appeared to mirror the SMCR in many ways, there were key differences (see 12.38 ff).

---

2   Conversely, firms that are not subject to Solvency II are sometimes referred to as 'non-Directive firms' or NDFs.
3   See PRA PS22/15; FCA PS16/22 (PRA PS5/16 and PS27/16 for regulatory references).
4   Defined as having assets in excess of £25m.
5   A small NDF is a firm where the value of its assets for all the regulated activities it carries out is £25,000,000 or less. The FCA estimates that there are around 75 UK insurance firms that classify as small NDFs.
6   PS21/15.

2 EXTENSION OF THE SMCR REGIME TO INSURERS: AN OVERVIEW

12.07 The Bank of England and Financial Services Act 2016 amended the Financial Services and Markets Act 2000 (FSMA) to facilitate the extension of the SMCR across all regulated firms, including insurers and reinsurers. All insurers and reinsurers regulated by the FCA and/or the PRA are affected by the extension of the regime which builds on the SIMR and APER. The Approved Persons Regime (APER) was replaced with the SMCR for these firms from the commencement date of 10 December 2018. (See Chapters 1 and 2 for more detail on the extension of the regime.)

12.08 As the SIMR put in place a streamlined version of the SMCR the intention was to amend that regime to incorporate the other aspects of the SMCR that had not previously been included. The intention is to have a single accountability regime, but there will be some divergence between insurers and banking firms which reflect the differences in the respective regulatory frameworks (eg between CRD IV and Solvency II (see Chapter 7)) and the different business models.

12.09 In July 2017 both regulators published consultation papers on their proposals to align more closely the SMCR individual accountability regimes for the banking and insurance sectors whilst respecting the different business models as well as relevant EU legislation.[7] Policy statements were published in July 2018[8] extending the regime to insurers with effect from 10 December 2018. The FCA and PRA rules should be read together as applicable to insurers. PRA final rules were published in November 2018.[9] The FCA's final rules for insurers can be found in FCA Handbook Notice 58.

12.10 The PRA proposed a proportionate extension of the SMCR to insurers. Accordingly, from 10 December 2018 the *full* SMCR regime applied to those firms that were previously subject to the SIMR and large NDFs, namely:

- UK Solvency II firms;

- The Society of Lloyd's and Lloyd's managing agents;

- third country (re)insurance branches;

- insurance special purpose vehicles (ISPVs);

- large NDFs.[10]

12.11 Given the difference in size and nature of the different types of insurer that are now subject to the SMCR, a streamlined application of the regime applies

---

7   FCA CP17/26; PRA CP14/17.
8   FCA PS18/15; PRA PS15/18.
9   PRA PS27/18.
10   A firm where the value of its assets for all the regulated activities it carries out exceeds £25,000,000.

to small NDFs,[11] small run-off firms[12] and ISPVs. Details of this proportionate application are set out below. This proportionate approach is also adopted with regard to remuneration (see Chapter 8).

12.12   The PRA's key supervisory statement SS35/15 has been amended to reflect the detail of the extended regime (the July 2018 version of SS35/15 applies from 10 December 2018). This update also widens the application of the supervisory statement to include large NDFs. The amendments include setting out the PRA's expectations of how the statutory duty of responsibility[13] should be observed by senior managers (SMs) and directors at insurers as well as expectations on the content of statements of responsibility (SoRs) (see 12.60 ff) and management responsibilities maps (see 12.89 ff). The FCA has also published a policy statement setting out its expectations on how the Duty of Responsibility will apply to insurers and solo regulated firms.[14]

12.13   The SMCR has been extended to insurers by way of amendments to the SIMR that was previously implemented for larger insurers and there is a new Insurance – Certification Part to the Solvency II section of the PRA Rulebook, along with corresponding new parts for large NDFs and small NDFs, as well as amendments to existing sections of the PRA Rulebook relating to the SIMR.

12.14   Despite the streamlined approach mentioned at 12.11, *all insurers* are subject to the following:

- The certification regime[15] (see Chapter 3).

- Fit and proper tests (see Chapter 3).

- Conduct rules (currently called conduct standards under the SIMR) (see Chapter 6).

- Senior managers regime. Some features of the SMR do not apply to small NDFs and ISPVs. For these firms, the existing higher level governance requirements continue to apply (see Chapter 2).

- Senior management functions (SMFs). Not all insurers are subject to the same list of SMFs.

- Prescribed responsibilities. The full list of prescribed responsibilities will apply to Solvency II firms and large NDFs. There are fewer prescribed responsibilities for small NDFs, third-country branches and ISPVs. Prescribed responsibilities will not apply to EEA branches.

---

11 A small NDF is a firm where the value of its assets for all the regulated activities it carries out is £25,000,000 or less.
12 Defined as a firm with less than £25,000,000 technical provisions that no longer have permission to write or acquire new business.
13 FSMA, s 66B(5) (Condition C).
14 FCA PS18/16.
15 This will implement the provisions in FSMA, ss 63E and 63F that will apply to these firms by virtue of the Bank of England and Financial Services Act 2016.

12.15 The regulators have also made rules for the notification to them of conduct rule breaches by holders of a SMF or by employees to whom the conduct rules apply.

12.16 There is also a new rule relating to the provision of handover information and materials in relation to the performance of a new SMF or new responsibility. This rule applies to Solvency II firms and large NDFs. Further information on handovers can be found at 2.61 ff.

12.17 The PRA will also facilitate the approval process for transfers of individuals between banking and insurance firms.

FCA Summary of extended application of SMCR to insurers and reinsurers

Tools	Solvency II & large NDFs	Small NDFs and small run-off firms	EEA branches	Non-EEA branches	ISPVs
Senior Management Functions (FCA only)	● Executive director ● Partner ● Other overall responsibility ● Compliance oversight ● Money laundering reporting officer ● Chair of nominations committee ● Chair of the with-profits committee ● Conduct risk oversight officer (Lloyd's)	● Executive director ● Partner ● Compliance oversight ● Money laundering reporting officer	● EEA branch senior manager ● Money laundering reporting officer	● Executive director ● Partner ● Compliance oversight ● Money laundering reporting officer ● Other local responsi-bility	● Executive director ● Partner ● Compliance oversight
Duty of responsibility	All firms	All firms	All firms	All firms	All firms
Prescribed responsibility	19 in total, 3 FCA only	9 in total, 3 FCA only	N/A	14 in total, 3 FCA only	4 in total, 2 FCA only
Statements of responsibility	All firms	All firms	All firms	All firms	All firms
Responsibilities maps	Yes	No	Yes	Yes	No
Handover procedures	Yes	No	No	No	No

Tools	Solvency II & large NDFs	Small NDFs and small run-off firms	EEA branches	Non-EEA branches	ISPVs
Overall responsibility	Yes	No	No	Yes	No
Certification regime	All firms	All firms	All firms	All firms	All firms
Fit and proper	All firms	All firms	All firms	All firms	All firms
Conduct rules	All firms	All firms	All firms	All firms	All firms
Criminal records checks for senior managers and NEDs	All firms	All firms	All firms	All firms	All firms
Regulatory references	All firms	All firms	All firms	All firms	All firms

12.18   Details of the extended regime are set out at 12.47 ff. For more detail on the specific elements of the SMCR, reference should be made to the relevant chapters in this book.

Extended regime: transitional arrangements[16]

12.19   The regulators consulted[17] over transitional arrangements for firms and staff transferring from the SIMR and APER to the SMCR and set out their proposals in PS15/18 and PS18/15. The regulators recognised that, given the differences in scale, it was appropriate to approach conversion to the SMCR in a proportionate and flexible way. APER remained in place until the start of the new regime on 10 December 2018 ('Commencement').

Transitional provisions

Firms must have identified certification staff before Commencement but have 12 months from Commencement to complete the initial certification process. Senior managers and certification staff must have been identified and trained on the conduct rules by Commencement. Firms have 12 months to train other staff on the conduct rules.

Conversion

12.20   If an individual was approved for their role under the old regime and the equivalent role existed in the senior managers regime the firm did not need to apply

---

16 FCA CP17/41; PRA CP28/17.
17 FCA CP17/41, PRA CP28/17

for re-approval. Any application for approval of a role that did not require pre-approval under the SMCR which had not been approved prior to Commencement automatically lapsed on Commencement. Small NDFs and small run-off firms did not have to apply for re-approval for their approved individuals. No extra checks were required.

Checking for approvals

12.21   Firms were required to check the updated Financial Services Register after Commencement to ensure they held the correct approvals after automatic conversion had taken place.

Statements of responsibility

12.22   All senior managers at Solvency II firms and large NDFs were required to have a statement of responsibilities in place at Commencement. The PRA proposed that these statements did not have to be submitted automatically to the PRA by insurers on Commencement, but they could be requested from firms as part of the PRA's ongoing supervision.

Prescribed responsibilities

12.23   The PRA proposals are aimed at integrating the prescribed responsibilities of the existing banking SMCR and the SIMR while respecting the differences between banking firms and insurers.

Certification and conduct rules

12.24   Certification as fit and proper will take place 12 months after Commencement. This means that insurers will not have to issue a certificate to any employee until this later date. Firms do not need to obtain regulatory references for certification employees until the time they decide to issue a certificate. However, individual conduct rules will apply to certification staff from Commencement.

12.25   Firms must therefore know who their certification staff are from Commencement and ensure they meet the conduct rules from this date.

12.26   Firms will not be required to obtain regulatory references for existing employees who will be performing the same role after Commencement.

Practical guidance: regulatory references

- Ensure that processes are in place to provide and request regulatory references and that record retention systems are appropriate to safely store required information about ex-employees in compliance with the regulatory rules and data protection legislation.

- Ensure that you fully understand the requirements of the regulatory references regime and that those staff who may be asked to provide references understand the rules.

- Ensure that senior managers understand their own responsibilities to ensure that adequate records are kept and systems and controls maintained.

Other conduct rules staff

12.27 Firms are given 12 months from Commencement to prepare to apply the conduct rules to other conduct rules staff (ie those staff to whom the conduct rules apply who are not senior manager or certification staff).

Practical tip: training

- For the purposes of providing training on the conduct rules, ancillary staff should be identified and appropriate training on the conduct rules should be put in place for *all other staff*. Senior managers and certified staff should understand the conduct rules and how they apply to them by Commencement.

- Arrange training for staff on:
    - the statutory duty of responsibility (senior managers only);
    - fitness and propriety assessments (senior managers and HR) (F&P assessments and certification will come into force 12 months after Commencement, or sooner if a firm so chooses);
    - conduct rules and performance management (all staff other than ancillary staff);
    - regulatory references (all staff other than ancillary staff; those who will provide regulatory references should be given detailed training).

Overlap rule

12.28 There may be cases when an individual is applying to perform a PRA senior insurance management function (SIMF) and a FCA controlled function at the same time. In this case an 'overlap rule' will be applied. In such a case, a firm does not need to seek separate approval from the FCA and the PRA. Instead an individual will apply just once to a regulator and the overlap rule ensures the approval covers both roles.

Failure to submit a conversion notification

12.29 If a Solvency II firm or large NDF did not submit a conversion notification it will be in breach of regulatory requirements. Approvals under APER will lapse and the individual will not have senior management regime approval, which leaves the individual carrying out their role without approval to do so and the firm will be in breach. If a firm is in this situation it must re-apply for approval of individuals through the full SMCR application process, including mandatory criminal records checks and regulatory references.

Applications for approval to take effect on or after Commencement

12.30 Firms should note that applications submitted to take effect on or after Commencement (using the SMCR forms) must meet the majority of the SMCR application requirements, even if submitted before the start of the new regime. This includes criminal records checks, but will not include regulatory references as the rules requiring firms to provide these will only come into force at Commencement.

New forms

12.31 There are new versions of forms for dual regulated firms reflecting the statutory and regulatory requirements of the SMCR.

Appointed representatives

12.32 The Bank of England and Financial Services Act 2016 did not give the regulators the power to extend the SMCR to appointed representatives (ARs). Elements of APER are therefore retained for ARs.

Transfer of SMFs from insurance firms to banking firms

12.33 The PRA proposes to enable an individual who has been approved for a SMF in an insurance firm to be treated equivalently to an individual who has been approved for a SMF in a banking firm. The process will be streamlined so that an individual can move from a SMF at a banking firm to a SMF at an insurance firm and vice versa by submitting Short Form A or Form E.

12.34 The PRA published a consultation paper[18] which set out proposed rules for certain consequential technical changes in relation to the extension of the regime to larger insurers already covered by the SIMR. The PRA has also published a note clarifying that SIMFs are automatically redesignated as SMFs. Insurers must, however, update their scope of responsibilities to reflect the change to statements of responsibility. There were no changes to the matters consulted on in the PRA's policy statement PS27/18.

Transition to the SMCR

The employment implications for both larger and smaller authorised firms are significant. All regulated firms have to identify their certified populations and put in place procedures for assessing the fitness and propriety of senior manager and certification staff (the first certification should take place 12 months after commencement of the regime). Annual assessments are normally carried out at the same time as annual appraisals and the two processes are intricately connected.

Separately, communication strategies should be implemented to ensure staff understand what is happening and what this means for them.

The most senior approved persons carrying out controlled functions under APER will likely convert to SMFs; other approved persons will become certification staff and their existing approvals will lapse when the new regime begins. Up until 10 December 2018, APER remained in force. Employment documentation from recruitment to departure should be reviewed and revised to reflect the requirements of the new regime.

---

3   SIMR – THE OLD REGIME IN OUTLINE

12.35 The SIMR in many ways mirrored the SMCR but had certain key differences and sometimes used different terminology for certain details (for example 'conduct rules' under the SMCR were called conduct standards under the SIMR). Terminology has been standardised under the extended SMCR regime. The SIMR replaced APER for those firms to which it applied (see 12.07). Under the extended regime, APER no longer applies to insurers and reinsurers.

12.36 Under the SIMR, senior insurance managers (SIMs) were, like senior managers, individuals who carried out key functions known as senior insurance management functions (SIMFs).[19] Such individuals had to comply with conduct standards (broadly the same as conduct rules for senior managers under the SMCR). These standards were extended to non-executive directors (NEDs) in 2017. The rules on SIMs included sharing a PRA SIMF and the allocation of

---

18   CP20/18.
19   PRA Rulebook – Insurance – Senior Insurance Management Functions.

responsibilities. Insurers covered by the regime had to prepare governance maps (similar to management responsibilities maps).

12.37 Conduct standards applied directly to individuals performing a SIMF but not to any other staff. As the SIMR did not have a certification regime, there were no certified staff who needed to comply with the standards.

4 DIFFERENCES BETWEEN THE SMCR AND THE SIMR

12.38 Apart from differences in terminology, the key difference between the SIMR and the SMCR is that the SIMR did not include a certification regime. This meant that below SIMs there were no staff who needed to be approved as fit and proper and certified as such.

12.39 Conduct standards applied to SIMs but not to other staff, in contrast to the SMCR where conduct rules apply to nearly all staff other than specified categories of ancillary staff (under FCA rules) and to senior manager and certified staff (under PRA rules). In practice, many firms apply the individual conduct rules to all staff working for them to ensure consistency of high standards.

12.40 The statutory duty of responsibility under the SMCR which applies to senior managers did not apply to SIMs. This now applies to all senior managers and guidance is provided on this duty by both the FCA and the PRA.

12.41 The criminal offence of reckless misconduct also did not apply to SIMs under the SIMR. This is now extended to all senior managers.

Practical guidance: implementation of the SMCR regime

- Amend employment documentation. For example, employment contracts for certified staff after Commencement should include a condition that the offer is made subject to continued certification as fit and proper (although certification as fit and proper will not be required until 12 months after Commencement) and a warranty that the candidate has disclosed all information that may be relevant to their fitness and propriety and receipt of a satisfactory regulatory reference (including an updated regulatory reference which discloses misconduct that impacts on fitness and propriety).

- Implement processes to annually assess senior managers and certified persons as fit and proper to perform their jobs. Decide who will undertake the appraisal.

- Amend employment documentation for approved persons that will become senior managers to include, for example, an agreement to comply with the conduct rules, an obligation to assist with handovers (and, if required, upkeep an ongoing record compliant with regulatory handover obligations) and a provision making continued employment subject to continued regulatory approval.

- Ensure that senior managers' contracts include provision that their duties may be reallocated during any period of absence without this constituting a breach of contract.

- Ensure that individuals who will be senior managers understand the statutory duty of responsibility and are provided with training on their obligations and responsibilities. Ensure that senior managers are provided with appropriate guidance and assistance.

- Decide the policy on handovers. Will the firm require a living handover document to be maintained? (This requirement for handovers applies only to firms currently covered by the SIMR.)

Table 1: Summary of the SM&CR tools

Tools	Solvency II & Large NDFs	Small NDFs & Small Run – off firms	EEA Branches	Non-EEA Branches	ISPVs
Senior Management Functions[1] (FCA only)	SMF 3 - Executive Director Function SMF 13 - Chair of the Nomination Committee Function SMF 15 - Chair of the With-Profits Committee Function SMF 16 - Compliance Oversight Function SMF 17 - Money Laundering Reporting Function SMF 18 - Other Overall Responsibility Function SMF 23b - Conduct Risk Oversight (Lloyd's) Function SMF 27 - Partner Function	SMF3 - Executive Director Function SMF16 - Compliance Oversight Function SMF17 - Money Laundering Reporting Function SMF 27 - Partner Function	SMF21 - EEA Branch Senior Manager SMF17 - Money Laundering Reporting Function	SMF3 - Executive Director Function SMF 15 - Chair of the With-Profits Committee Function SMF16 - Compliance Oversight Function SMF17 - Money Laundering Reporting Function SMF22 - Other Local Responsibility Function	SMF3 - Executive Director Function SMF16 - Compliance Oversight Function
Duty of Responsibility	Applies to all firms				
Prescribed Responsibilities	19 in total, 3 FCA only	9 in total, 3 FCA only	N/A	16 in total, 3 FCA only	5 in total, 2 FCA only
Statements of Responsibilities	Applies to all firms				
Responsibilities Maps	✓	✗	✓	✓	✗
Handover Procedures	✓	✗	✗	✗	✗
Overall Responsibility	✓	✗	✗	✓	✗
Certification Regime	Applies to all firms				
Fit and Proper	Applies to all firms				
Conduct Rules	Relevant to all firms				

1   Note that these functions only apply where the firm already has someone fulfilling the role or if it is a required function for the firm type

2   Note this includes the person(s) responsible for the with-profits advisory arrangement where relevant

5   SENIOR MANAGERS

Senior insurance managers – the old regime

12.42   Under the SIMR, SIMs had to be pre-approved by the PRA before they could undertake their role. In this respect, the SIMR mirrored the SMCR for senior managers. SIMs performed SIMFs prescribed by the PRA.

12.43   The PRA published supervisory statement SS35/15 (updated in July 2018 to reflect the requirements of the extended SMCR) to provide guidance to insurers on implementing aspects of the regime, including assessing the fitness and propriety of SIMs to undertake SIMFs. Reference should be made to Chapter 2 for further detail.

12.44   The statutory framework of the SIMR contained fewer obligations than under the SMR.

12.45   The scope of the SIMFs under the SIMR only applied in relation to a firm's UK-regulated activities – however the fact that an individual was located outside the UK did not mean that they could not perform a SIMF on behalf of a firm.

12.46   The PRA did not require pre-approval of senior individuals located overseas whose responsibilities in relation to the UK are limited to developing the group's overall strategy.[20] The PRA's focus is on those individuals who, irrespective of their location, are directly responsible for implementing the group's strategy at UK firms.

6   EXTENDED REGIME: SENIOR (INSURANCE) MANAGERS, SENIOR MANAGER FUNCTIONS AND PRESCRIBED RESPONSIBILITIES

Senior management functions

12.47   Rules on the SMR can be found in the relevant parts of the PRA Rulebook,[21] the FCA's rules and guidance on its corresponding SMCR and the PRA's supervisory statement SS35/15. SIMs became senior managers (SMs) under the new regime. SMs perform SMFs which are a type of controlled function under FSMA, s 59AZ. The PRA did not propose any further change to the set of PRA SIMFs that was already in place under the SIMR and each was included in the new SMCR. In the PRA consultation paper these were referred to as S(I)MFs in recognition that they were senior *insurance* management functions as referred to in the PRA Rulebook *and* SMFs under FSMA although these are now renamed as SMFs. Which SMFs apply to a particular firm depends on what

---

20   SS35/15, para 2.11.

21   Insurance – Senior Management Functions, Insurance – Allocation of Responsibilities, Conditions Governing Business, and Insurance – Fitness & Propriety for large NDFs; also SS5/16 'Corporate governance: Board responsibilities'.

type of SMCR firm it is. The PRA supervisory statement SS35/15 sets out more detail about PRA SMFs.

12.48 The regulators also amended terminology and acronyms to be aligned more closely with that for the banking regime.

12.49 The PRA executive functions are:

- SMF1 – chief executive;
- SMF2 – chief finance function;
- SMF4 – chief risk function;
- SMF5 – head of internal audit;
- SMF6 – head of key business area;
- SMF7 – group entity senior manager;
- SMF20 – chief actuarial function;
- SMF20a – with-profits actuary;
- SMF23 – chief underwriting function;
- SMF23a – underwriting risk oversight function (Lloyds only);
- SMF24 – chief operations.

12.50 In addition to the PRA senior management roles the FCA proposed five executive functions as FCA SMFs in Solvency II firms and large NDFs. These are:

- SMF3 – executive director;
- SMF23b – conduct risk oversight officer (Lloyd's only);
- SMF18 – other overall responsibility;
- SMF16 – compliance oversight;
- SMF17 – money laundering reporting officer.

12.51 There are also oversight SMF for Solvency II firms and large NDFs:

- SMF13 – chair of nominations committee (FCA);
- SMF15 – chair of the with-profits committee (FCA);
- SMF9 – chair of the governing body (PRA);
- SMF10 – chair of the risk committee (PRA);
- SMF11 – chair of the audit committee (PRA);
- SMF12 – chair of the remuneration committee (PRA);
- SMF14 – senior independent director.

See 12.67 for the SMFs that apply to small NDFs, small run-off firms and ISPVs.

12.52 Under the SMCR, only NEDs that perform specific roles will be SMs. However, even if they are not SMs, conduct rules, fit and proper requirements and regulatory references apply to all NEDs.

12.53 The FCA introduced 'overall responsibility' and 'other overall responsibility' requirements (SMF18 and SMF22 functions) to all Solvency II firms and large NDFs. This means that such firms will need to make sure that every activity, business area and management function of the firm has a SM with overall responsibility for it.

12.54 Overall responsibility means that a SM has ultimate responsibility for managing or supervising a function; briefs and reports to the governing body about their area of responsibility; and puts matters for decision about their area of responsibility to the governing body. Where a senior executive is the most senior person responsible for an area of the firm's business but they do not perform any other SMF they may be allocated the 'other overall responsibility' function, SMF18.

12.55 It is not possible to divide or share an overall responsibility but it is possible to allocate overall responsibility for the same area or activity to two or more SMs where that is appropriate.

12.56 The SMCR allows someone to cover for a SM without that person needing to be approved where the absence is temporary or reasonably unforeseen and the appointment is for less than 12 consecutive weeks.

Territorial limitation

12.57 There is no territorial limitation on the SMR so the regime will apply to anyone performing a SM role whether they are based in the UK or overseas. There is also no territorial limitation for SMs in EEA branches so that the SMR will apply to anyone performing a SM role whether they are based in the UK or overseas.

Sharing a management function

12.58 The amended SS35/15 includes the expectation that PRA SMFs and prescribed responsibilities can be shared but not split between two or more SMFs. This means that where two or more individuals share a SMF or prescribed responsibility each will be deemed fully accountable for all the responsibilities inherent in or allocated to that SMF. The PRA expects to see a clear explanation and justification of how the relevant responsibilities are allocated or shared between the individuals responsible for the SIMF, along with reporting lines and lines of responsibility for each individual.

12.59   The FCA clarifies that it is not possible to divide an overall responsibility but two or more SMs can share overall responsibility for the same area or activity.

Statement of responsibilities

12.60   The record of the scope of responsibilities[22] that was required to be maintained and kept-up-to-date under the SIMR will be re-named a statement of responsibilities (SoR) but is identical in substance. SoRs are a FSMA requirement and will also apply to small NDFs and ISPVs. Small NDFs already produced scope of responsibilities documents under the SIMR so the key change was that these documents must be submitted with an approval application.

12.61   Every SM must have a SoR which sets out their role and what they are responsible for. SoRs should be updated and re-submitted whenever there is a significant change in responsibilities.

12.62   SoRs must:

- include the full set of responsibilities for each individual;

- reflect how the business model, complexity, risk profile and size of firm affect each SM's responsibilities.

12.63   The FCA provides that Solvency II firms must keep records of their SoR documents for ten years. Large and small NDFs are required to keep records for six years. The FCA sets out guidance in its Handbook.[23]

Holding more than one SMF

12.64   The FCA clarifies that where someone intends to hold more than one SMF that person will need to apply for approval for each function. Only one SoR is needed but it must describe all of their responsibilities.

12.65   Where a SM applies to perform a PRA and a FCA SMF at the same time the 'overlap rule' may be applied, which means that a firm does not need to seek separate approval from both regulators.

Sharing a SMF

12.66   SS25/15 sets out the PRA's guidance on sharing a SMF. In certain circumstances and only where appropriate and justified, including but not limited to job-sharing arrangements, a firm may allow more than one person to be

---

22   See PRA Rulebook – Allocation rules which apply to all KFHs, including holders of a S(I)MF at Solvency II insurers and large NDFs.
23   SUP10C.11.

responsible for a single SMF. There must be a clear explanation and justification of how the relevant responsibilities are allocated or shared along with reporting lines and lines of responsibility for each individual. Where two individuals share a SMF, both are fully accountable for all the responsibilities allocated to that SMF.

Small NDFs and ISPVs

12.67   As indicated above, small NDFs were subject to fewer requirements than larger insurers under the SIMR; this approach is maintained under the extended SMCR regime. For small NDFs the FCA introduces three SMFs (and the PRA designates three functions).[24] For ISPVs, FCA SMF3 and SMF16 and PRA SMF1, SMF2 and SMF9 apply.

12.68   SoRs apply to small NDFs which must submit this alongside an approval application.

12.69   There are fewer prescribed responsibilities for small NDFs in line with the regulators' proportionality approach.

Prescribed responsibilities

12.70   Prescribed responsibilities (PRs) are intended to ensure that a SM is accountable for key conduct risks. PRs are specific responsibilities must be given to a SM and are set out in SYSC24 of the FCA Handbook and in the PRA Rulebook. They are additional to the responsibilities that are part of a SM's role.

12.71   EEA branches do not need to apply the PRs because they remain subject to Home State supervision. They apply to all other firms within the regime.

12.72   The SM who is allocated a PR should be the most senior person responsible for that area. The PR must be clearly allocated and should normally be held by a single person, except where a firm can show that dividing or sharing a responsibility is appropriate and justifiable.

12.73   The FCA and the PRA proposed 19 PRs in total. Of these 19 PRs, eight are shared between the PRA and the FCA; eight have been allocated by the PRA only; and three are FCA only. All these PRs apply to Solvency II firms and large NDFs. A reduced number of PRs apply to small NDFs, small run-off firms and ISPVs. The three FCA-only PRs are:

---

24   FCA – SMF3 – executive director, SMF16 – compliance oversight, SMF17 – money laundering reporting officer; PRA – SMF25 – small insurer senior management function, SMF20 – small insurer chief actuary function, SMF20a – small insurer with-profits actuary function.

- A PR for meeting firms' obligations under the FCA's Code of Conduct (COCON) to ensure that the firm trains its staff in the conduct rules and complies with the FCA notification requirements.

- A Client Asset Sourcebook (CASS) compliance PR.

- A PR for overseeing the firm's policies and procedures for countering the risk that the firm might be used to further financial crime.

12.74   Each PR should normally be held by only one person. Firms will only be able to divide or share a PR in limited circumstances and where they can show that this is appropriate and justifiable.[25] If a firm divides or shares a PR they will need to show why this is justified and confirm that this does not leave a gap. For example, it would be justifiable to share a function or responsibility as part of a job share, where departing and incoming SMs work together temporarily as part of a handover, or where a particular area of a firm is run by two SMs. Where responsibilities are shared or divided, this will need to be clearly explained in the SoR. Each SM will be jointly accountable for the responsibilities.

Overall responsibility requirement

12.75   The FCA has applied an overall responsibility requirement to all Solvency II firms and large NDFs (see 12.62, 12.63 and Chapter 2). This means that these firms will need to ensure that every activity, business area and management function has a senior manager with overall responsibility for it. The SMF18 only applies when an individual with overall responsibility as described does not hold any other FCA or PRA SMF.

12.76   The FCA noted that many banking firms experienced difficulty understanding this requirement so it has set out the following steps that insurance firms might wish to consider:

- Firms should consider what activities, business areas and management functions they have.[26]

- Once a firm has set these out the next step is to think about who has overall responsibility at the most senior level for each of these.

- The most senior person with overall responsibility might be an existing SM, such as the chief executive, an executive director or the senior manager responsible for compliance oversight.

- Where a senior manager has overall responsibility[27] for an activity, business area or management function this will need to be clearly set out in their SoR and reflected in the responsibilities map.

---

25   FCA PS18/15.
26   Firms may find it useful to refer to the general concepts in Annex 1 of SYSC 4.
27   The scope of the overall responsibility rule is the same as the scope of the conduct rules: this means it applies to a firm's regulated and unregulated financial services activities.

12.77   The FCA has extended[28] to responsibilities under the overall responsibility requirement the 12-week rule whereby a person can cover for an approved person or a senior manager without being approved where the absence is temporary or reasonably unforeseen and the appointment is for less than 12 consecutive weeks. The rule applies whatever the reason for the SM's absence.

Statutory Duty of Responsibility

12.78   Every senior manager also has a Duty of Responsibility (see Chapter 2) under the extended regime. This means that if a firm breaches a regulatory requirement the SM responsible for that area could be held accountable if they did not take reasonable steps to prevent the breach occurring. The burden of proof lies with the regulator to show that the SM did not take reasonable steps to avoid the breach occurring. Criteria to be taken into account when deciding whether to take action against a SM for breach are set out in the FCA's Decision Procedure and Penalties Manual. The FCA has published a policy statement[29] which sets out how it will apply the duty of responsibility to insurers and FCA solo regulated firms. Guidance is provided on the duty of responsibility by the PRA in its supervisory statement SS35/15.

12.79   Under the extended regime the PRA and the FCA applied the statutory duty of responsibility to all SMs and NEDs at insurers (see 2.173 ff). This new duty of responsibility has been established by adding a fourth element to FSMA, s 66B(5). This means that the regulators are able to take action against a SM for misconduct if:

- the firm contravenes, or has contravened, a regulatory requirement;

- at the relevant time, the SM was responsible for the management of any of the firm's activities in relation to which the contravention occurred; and

- the SM did not take such steps as a person in the senior manager's position could reasonably be expected to take to avoid the contravention occurring or continuing.

12.80   If the regulator wishes to take action for misconduct, it will be for the regulator to set out why it appears that the SM did not take reasonable steps. The PRA includes wording on its expectations on the new duty of responsibility in SS35/15.[30] The FCA sets out its expectations on the duty for insurers and solo regulated firms in its policy statement PS18/16 and in DEPP 6.2.9.

12.81   The FCA states that when deciding to take action, it will look at all the circumstances of the case including the seriousness of the breach, the person's position, responsibilities and seniority and the need to use enforcement powers

---

28   FCA PS18/15.
29   FCA PS18/16.
30   Paras 2.94-2.13. The wording is expected to be suitable for both insurance and banking firms.

effectively and proportionately.[31] Sometimes the regulator will take action against a SM, sometimes against a firm and sometimes against both.

12.82 The FCA emphasises that the duty of responsibility merely requires that SMs take reasonable steps. Even if they do not, no liability arises under the duty without associated firm misconduct. The FCA will consider the following when deciding whether a SM's actions were reasonable: delegation; the establishment of reporting lines; staff appraisal processes; role transition handovers; risk identification; expansion and restructurings; external professional advice, transaction monitoring; and collective decision-making. The PRA gives as examples of the considerations it will have: the size, scale and complexity of the firm; what expertise and competence the SM had; what steps or alternative actions the SM could have taken; the SM's actual responsibilities and the relation between those responsibilities and the responsibilities of other SMs in the firm; whether the SM delegated any functions and the overall circumstances and environment at the firm.

12.83 When determining the extent of a SM's responsibilities the FCA or PRA will consider an individual's SoR although the regulator may look beyond this where appropriate. Individuals should keep records of the steps that they take in case questions are raised. Individuals should note that any relevant FCA investigation is likely to take into account that each SM is also under a Code of Conduct (COCON) obligation to take reasonable steps to make sure that the business of the firm for which they are responsible complies with the firm's record keeping obligations. A SM's failure to take reasonable steps in relation to record keeping may, apart from the duty of responsibility, amount to misconduct.

Handover of responsibilities

12.84 The regulators have added a new rule requiring Solvency II insurers and large NDFs to take all reasonable steps to ensure a SM is provided with all the information and materials they would reasonably expect in order to perform a new SMF or new responsibilities. This mirrors the FCA equivalent requirement for the banking sector. The FCA suggests that one way of handing over responsibilities could be for the predecessor to prepare a suitable handover note. This could be a document that is regularly maintained and kept up to date by a senior manager (see Chapter 2). The PRA has endorsed the FCA approach on handovers[32] which it believes codifies best practice. The PRA is maintaining its policy which it believes reinforces a culture of accountability.

12.85 What is 'reasonable steps' will vary from case to case, depending on the circumstances.

---

31 The criteria for using enforcement powers are set out in the Decision and Procedure and Penalties Manual.
32 PRA PS15/18.

12.86 The FCA has clarified[33] that it is not mandatory to prepare a handover certificate. Whilst this is one way that firms can meet the handover requirements, there may be cases where this is impractical.[34]

12.87 Firms should also have arrangements for an orderly transition between SMs. It is for firms to decide how to ensure this happens. The FCA notes that a handover policy and ensuring SMs are aware and trained could help firms show the reasonable steps that they have taken to give a new SM the information and materials they need to do their job effectively, even if the previous SM leaves suddenly.

12.88 Firms should also have in place a policy explaining how they comply with this requirement and maintain adequate records of the steps they have taken.

Practical guidance

The regulators propose to apply the handover of responsibilities rule to departing senior managers in Solvency II insurers and large NDFs, mirroring the FCA equivalent requirement for the banking sector. This rule has thrown up practical issues of how to ensure compliance when, say, a senior manager leaves on bad terms. There are a variety of approaches to managing this issue, including requiring a 'living handover document' to be prepared and updated regularly and ensuring compliance with handover obligations is contained in employment documentation.

Governance maps/management responsibilities maps

12.89 Insurers were required under the SIMR[35] to maintain a governance map which was the insurers' equivalent of a management responsibilities map. This showed the key functions in the firm and the relevant individuals responsible for those functions along with their lines of accountability and responsibility.

12.90 Governance maps for Solvency II insurers (other than ISPVs and small run-off firms) and large NDFs are renamed 'management responsibilities maps' (MRMs) under the extended regime. The PRA's expectations on SoRs and MRMs are set out in the updated SS35/15. MRMs must be drafted in a clear and complete way with a consistent structure and appropriate and proportionate level of detail. There is no requirement for a MRM for small NDFs and small run-off firms.[36]

12.91 MRMs will not present a major change to insurers as they are identical in substance to governance maps. The FCA rules on MRMs are set out in

---

33 FCA PS18/15.
34 See SYSC 25.9.8.
35 PRA Rulebook – Insurance – Allocation of Responsibilities 5; SS35/15, para 2.29.
36 FCA PS18/15, para 2.61.

SYSC 25.2.3. There is no obligation to create two separate MRMs for the FCA and the PRA.

12.92   These maps must be kept up to date and submitted alongside any application for approval to either the FCA or the PRA, as appropriate. The requirements do not apply to small NDFs, small run-off firms and ISPVs. These firms will still need to keep up-to-date records of apportionment of responsibilities in line with SYSC 2.

12.93   Firms which operate within a group should note that the SMCR applies to legal entities individually, rather than to a group as a whole. It is not, therefore, appropriate for firms to submit one MRM for the entire group.[37]

Overlap rule

12.94   There may be cases where a SM applies to perform both a FCA and PRA SMF at the same time. In such a case the FCA applies an 'overlap rule'.[38] For example, if a firm is seeking approval for an SMF2 – chief finance officer who will also be appointed to the board (SMF3 – executive director) at the same time, then they only need to make one application to the PRA. The overlap rule ensures the approval covers both roles. The overlap rule only applies if the firm's application for PRA approval states that the person will also be performing an FCA designated SMF. Where the overlap rule does not apply, firms should apply to the FCA for approval of the FCA SMF. The regulators will still hold the individual to account for both halves of their role.

12.95   The overlap rule applies to FCA governing functions only. For example, if an individual is put forward for an SMF2 (a PRA function) and an SMF16 compliance oversight function, which is a FCA 'required function' the firm must apply to both the PRA and the FCA separately.

7   CERTIFICATION REGIME

12.96   Under the old SIMR there was no certification regime. The introduction of a certification regime is the biggest single change under the extended regime for insurers. Insurers are now responsible for assessing their certified staff as fit and proper to carry out their certification functions. This means that insurers will need to identify employees who perform certification functions; assess whether such staff are fit and proper at the point of recruitment and annually thereafter; and issue a certificate to the employee if satisfied the employee is fit and proper. The rules on certification are set out in the PRA Rulebook[39] and FCA rules.

---

37   FCA PS18/15, para 2.53.
38   SUP10C.9.8; see also guidance in SUP10C.9.9G.
39   Insurance – Certification and Insurance – Fitness & Propriety; see Chapter 3 for FCA rules.

12.97   If a firm decides that an employee is not fit and proper after an assessment then it must notify the person in writing, setting out what steps (if any) it proposes to take in relation to that individual and the reasons for proposing this.

Certification

There is a significant variation between firms about how to treat a certified employee that 'fails' a fitness and propriety (F&P) assessment. Some firms have proceeded straight to termination without 'passing GO'. It now seems clear that such an approach is likely to result in an unfair dismissal finding if no consideration is given as to how that employee might be retained, whether in an alternative role or subject, say, to remediation or supervision for a period of time. Termination should not be a kneejerk reaction. Awards of compensation in tribunal are likely to be high given that a regulatory reference must record the reason for dismissal and thereby render it unlikely that the individual will work in the sector again.

Territorial application

12.98   The FCA states that the certification regime is limited to people performing a certification function who are either based in the UK or, if based outside the UK, have contact with UK clients. The exception to this is where a person is a material risk taker (MRT) (see Chapter 7) under Solvency II regulations on remuneration for whom there is no territorial limitation.

12.99   In an EEA branch, the certification regime will only apply to individuals based in the UK and will not extend to people based outside the UK even if they deal with a UK client.

Who is in the regime?

12.100   The extended regime introduced a certification regime which is aligned as closely as possible with the population that is identified for the purpose of applying the firm's remuneration policy.[40] This includes members of the governing body, persons who effectively run the firm or have other key functions and other categories of staff whose professional activities have a material impact on the firm's risk profile.[41]

12.101   For small NDFs the PRA certification regime encompasses only members of the governing body (other than PRA/FCA approved persons or NEDs) rather

---

40 EU Solvency II Delegated Regulation, Article 275.
41 'Significant harm function' in FSMA, s 63E(5) 'requires the person performing it to be involved in one or more aspects of the firm's affairs, so far as relating to a regulated activity and ... those aspects involve, or might involve, a risk of significant harm to the firm or any of its customers'.

than including all members of the governing body and all employees who report directly to the governing body.[42]

12.102 The PRA provides that all key function holders (KFHs) at Solvency II insurers, large NDFs and ISPVs should be designated as being in a certification function unless that function is a SMF or a FCA controlled function or they are a NED.

12.103 Additionally, certification functions include MRTs[43] for Solvency II insurers and large NDFs that are 'large firms'.[44] Large firms are required to maintain records showing the identity of these MRTs. The following functions as a minimum should be considered to be certification functions:

- investment management;
- claims management;
- underwriting and pricing of products;
- reinsurance;
- capital management;
- liquidity management;
- operational systems and controls;
- information technology;
- managing material risk takers (for large firms).

12.104 The FCA sets out the roles that it considers to be certification functions as follows:

- significant management function;
- proprietary traders;
- CASS oversight function;
- functions subject to qualification requirements;
- client dealing function;
- algorithmic traders;
- material risk takers;

---

42 PRA PS15/18, para 1.5.
43 Employees whose professional activities have a material impact on the firm's risk profile. The PRA proposes to define these MRTs in line with the Solvency II remuneration requirements and so can be identified in accordance with SS10/16.
44 A firm with annual premium income (gross of reinsurance) of more than £1bn in each of the previous three financial years, or with assets (including any reinsurance) related to regulatory activities of more than £10bn at the end of each of the last three financial years.

- Anyone who supervises or manages a person performing a certification function.

12.105 The PRA thus have a slightly different set of certification functions. The FCA's wider set of certification functions reflects the different statutory objectives of the regulators.

12.106 Small run-off firms are deemed not to have any certification functions although they will still need to assess the fitness and propriety of persons performing a key function.[45]

FCA Table of Certification Functions

Certification function	Overview
Significant management function (based on current CF29)	These individuals perform functions that would have been Significant Influence Functions under the FCA's Approved Persons Regime.
	These important roles can seriously affect the way the firm conducts its business.
Functions subject to qualification requirements	These are set out in the FCA's Training and Competence Sourcebook.
	For example, life insurers should identify individuals:
	• advising on long-term care insurance contracts
	• overseeing administrative functions for insurance contracts that are life policies and for pension schemes
	• giving advice or performing activities related to pension transfers (current CF30s)
Anyone who supervises or manages a Certified Function (directly or indirectly), but is not a Senior Manager	This will ensure that people who supervise certified employees are held to the same standard of accountability. It also ensures a clear chain of accountability between junior certified employees and the Senior Manager ultimately responsible for that area.
	For example, if a firm employs a customer-facing financial adviser, every manager above them in the same chain of responsibility will have to be certified (until the Senior Manager approved under the SMR is reached).
Material risk takers	For dual-regulated insurers, these individuals are those that Solvency II firms already need to identify under Solvency II regulations on remuneration.
	Solvency II firms need to identify those individuals whose professional activities have a material impact on the firm's risk profile. This function does not apply to firms which are not subject to the Solvency II requirements on remuneration.

---

45 PRA Rulebook – Insurance – Fitness and Propriety 2.

Certification function	Overview
The client dealing function	This function has been expanded from the current CF30 function to apply to any person dealing with clients, including retail and professional clients and eligible counterparties. This will cover people who: ● advise on investments (other than a non-investment insurance contract) and perform other related functions, such as dealing and arranging ● deal, as principal or agent, and arrange (bring about) deals in investments ● act in the capacity of an investment manager and all functions connected with this ● act as a bidder's representative
Proprietary traders (covered by current CF29) CASS oversight function (current CF10a)	These individuals perform functions that would have been Significant Influence Functions under the FCA's Approved Persons Regime. These important roles can seriously affect the way the firm conducts its business. These roles are unlikely to apply to most insurance firms.
Algorithmic trading	This function includes people with responsibility for: ● approving the use of a trading algorithm or a material part of one ● approving the use of a material amendment to a trading algorithm or a material part of one, or the combination of trading algorithms ● monitoring or deciding whether or not the use or deployment of a trading algorithm is or remains compliant with the firm's obligations This role is unlikely to apply to most insurance firms.

More than one certification function

12.107 The FCA states that if a person performs more than one certification function, a firm must certify that the individual is fit and proper to carry out each function although this can be done as part of the same assessment process. If a SM also performs a certification function that is closely linked to their role as a SM the FCA states that they will not need to be certified under the certification regime. However, if the certification function is very different to the activity they are performing as a SM they will also need to be certified.

Temporary appointment

12.108 Any individual whose appointment is solely to cover the absence of an employee in a 'certification function' whose absence is reasonably unforeseen and is for less than four weeks is deemed to be excluded.

Assessment of fitness and propriety

12.109 Firms are required to ensure that anyone carrying out a certification role is fit and proper to carry out that role and to issue certificates *annually* for employees in certification functions. Certified staff will not appear on the FCA public register, unlike SMs, although the FCA is consulting over a separate public register which will include details of certified staff.

FCA flowchart on who is defined as certified staff

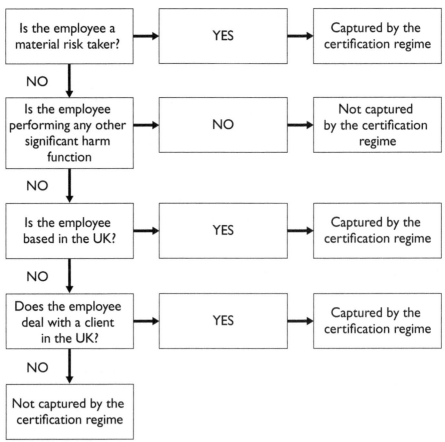

8 TRANSFERS OF INDIVIDUALS BETWEEN INSURANCE AND BANKING FIRMS

12.110 After the extension of SMCR to all insurers the PRA proposes to enable S(I)Ms within insurers to be treated equivalently to SMFs within banking firms. This would enable applications for approval to be made of an individual moving from a SMF at a banking firm to a S(I)MF at an insurance firm.

9 NON-EXECUTIVE DIRECTORS

12.111 The PRA recognises that NEDs who are in scope of the SMR do not manage a firm's business in the same way as executive directors. It therefore provides that the potential accountability of NEDs is restricted to those activities for which they are responsible.[46] The PRA expects the SoRs of NEDs in scope of the SMR to be less extensive than those of executive SMs but they must provide some detail.

12.112 Firms must assess the fitness and propriety of notified NEDs who are not within the scope of the SMR periodically and comply with certain notification requirements. NEDs within scope of the SMR must be assessed as fit and proper in the same way as other SMs.

12.113 NEDs who are subject to pre-approval by the PRA or FCA were previously directly subject to the conduct standards under the SIMR, including those applicable only to SIMs. Breaches of conduct standards by NEDs are directly enforceable by the PRA using its powers under FSMA.[47] Firms are also required[48] to require all members of the management body including notified NEDs to observe conduct standards 3.1–3.3 and 3.7–3.8.

12.114 Under the extended regime, the FCA conduct rules apply to all directors, whether or not they are also senior managers.[49] The FCA rules apply to a firm's regulated and unregulated financial services activities.

12.115 NEDs who are subject to pre-approval by the PRA or the FCA are directly subject to all the conduct rules, including those only applicable to SMs. Conduct rules NEDs are directly subject to PRA individual conduct rules 1–3 and PRA senior manager conduct rules 7–8 (see 12.118 ff).

12.116 The PRA conduct rules apply to those employees holding a senior manager or certification function, including employees holding a SMF on a temporary basis.[50] The PRA rules also apply in relation to a firm's regulated

---

46 SS35/15.
47 SS35/15, paras 3.29–3.33.
48 PRA Rulebook – Insurance – Conduct Standards 2.2.
49 FCA PS18/15.
50 PRA PS15/18.

and unregulated business activities. See also 12.122 for application of the PRA conduct rules to notified NEDs under the extended regime.

12.117 The requirements to be 'open and co-operative with the FCA, the PRA and other regulators' (conduct standard 3.3 – see 12.120) and to 'disclose appropriately any information of which the FCA or PRA would reasonably expect notice' (conduct standard 3.7 – see 12.121) are particularly important for NEDs. If any director has concerns about the firm or its management and governance the PRA expects them to press for remedial action and if the concerns are not addressed to alert the PRA.[51]

10   CONDUCT STANDARDS/CONDUCT RULES

12.118 Under the old SIMR regime PRA conduct standards applied to individuals performing a SIMF specified by the PRA or a controlled function specified by the FCA.

12.119 The Insurance-Conduct Standards and Large Non-Solvency Firms – Conduct Standards parts of the PRA Rulebook applied directly to a person who performed a SMF or who was responsible for a 'key function'. Additionally, certified staff and 'Conduct Rules NEDs' were also required to comply with the PRA conduct standards.[52] The PRA also refers to its conduct standards as conduct rules under the extended regime. The FCA conduct rules which apply to insurers have a wider application than the PRA's rules (see 12.120–12.121). More information about conduct rules is set out in Chapter 6. The conduct rules apply directly to the staff covered by them under the extended regime.

PRA individual conduct rules

12.120

- Individual conduct rule 1: *You must act with integrity*

- Individual conduct rule 3.2: *You must act with due skill, care and diligence*

  The PRA expects all SIMs or relevant NEDs to exercise their business skills with appropriate levels of attention and care and to provide adequate explanations of their activities.[53]

- Individual conduct rule 3.3: *You must be open and co-operative with the FCA, the PRA and other regulators*

---

51   PRA's approach to banking supervision, June 2014, para 88.
52   SS35/15.
53   SS35/15, para 3.10.

The PRA expects individuals to use their firm's mechanisms for reporting information to the regulators. Relevant factors in assessing compliance include:

– whether a person has provided information into the firm's mechanisms appropriately;

– whether the person has taken steps to influence a decision so as not to report to the regulator;

– whether the person has acted in a way intended to obstruct the reporting of information to the regulator;

– the way in which the person has operated, managed or overseen the mechanisms;

– the way in which a person has responded to a regulator's requests.[54]

PRA SM conduct rules

12.121

● Conduct rule 3.4: *You must take reasonable steps to ensure that the business of the firm for which you are responsible is controlled effectively*

If the firm's strategy is to enter higher-risk areas then the degree of control and strength of monitoring will be higher.[55]

● Conduct rule 3.5: *You must take reasonable steps to ensure that the business of the firm for which you are responsible complies with the relevant requirements and standards of the regulatory system*

A firm's KFH must take reasonable steps both to ensure the firm's compliance with regulatory requirements and standards and to ensure all staff are aware of the need for compliance. The KFH must take reasonable steps to ensure the business has operating procedures and systems which include well-defined steps for compliance.[56]

● Conduct rule 3.6: *You must take reasonable steps to ensure that any delegation of your responsibilities is to an appropriate person and that you oversee the discharge of the delegated responsibility effectively*

The PRA does not expect a KFH to personally manage the business on a day-to-day basis and the extent to which this is done will depend on a number of factors including the nature, scale and complexity of the business. The PRA states that authority for dealing with part of the business should only be delegated when a KFH has reasonable grounds for believing that the delegate has the necessary capacity, competence, knowledge, seniority or skill to deal with the issue.[57]

---

54   SS35/15, para 3.14.
55   SS35/15, paras 3.17–3.18.
56   SS35/15, paras 3.19–3.20.
57   SS35/15, paras 3.21–3.23.

- Conduct rule 3.7: *You must disclose appropriately any information of which the FCA or PRA would reasonably expect notice*

  This conduct standard goes beyond conduct standard 3.3 which primarily applies to responses from individuals to requests from a regulator. Conduct standard 3.7 imposes a greater duty on KFHs to disclose any information the relevant regulator would reasonably expect. This includes making a disclosure in the absence of any request or enquiry from the relevant regulator.[58]

- Conduct rule 3.8: *When exercising your responsibilities, you must pay due regard to the interests of current and potential future policyholders in ensuring the provision by the firm of an appropriate degree of protection for their insured benefits*

  The PRA expects KFHs to exercise sound and prudent management over the business areas for which they are responsible. Suitable due diligence should be applied to major transactions and KFHs should also apply due care and attention in the appropriate management of any conflicts of interest.[59]

12.122 Under the extended regime, the PRA requires certified employees (other than a KFH) and SMs to comply with conduct rules 3.1–3.3. Any KFH other than a notified NED must comply with conduct rules 3.4–3.8 and notified NEDs must comply with conduct rules 3.1–3.3 and 3.7–3.8.

12.123 When assessing compliance with conduct rules 3.4–3.8 the PRA expects a firm to take the following into account:

- whether the person exercised reasonable care when considering the information available;

- whether the person reached a reasonable conclusion upon which to act;

- the nature, scale and complexity of the firm's business;

- the person's role and responsibility; and

- the knowledge the person had, or should have had, of any regulatory concerns.[60]

Assessing compliance with a conduct rule

12.124 When assessing whether an individual's conduct was either consistent with or complied with a conduct rule, the PRA expects the context in which a course of conduct was undertaken to be taken into account, including the:

- precise circumstances of each individual case;

---

58 SS35/15, paras 3.24–3.26.
59 SS35/15, paras 3.27–3.28.
60 SS35/15, para 3.16.

- characteristics of the particular function performed by the individual in question; and

- behaviour to be expected in that function.[61]

Examples of matters that will be taken into account when assessing compliance with a conduct rule are set out in the PRA's supervisory statement SS35/15.

12.125 An individual will only be in breach of the conduct standards where they are *personally culpable*. This may arise where:

- an individual's conduct was deliberate; or

- the individual's standard of conduct was below that which would be reasonable in all the circumstances.[62]

12.126 Firms and groups must have suitable procedures in place to monitor the conduct of individuals who are performing a key function.[63]

12.127 Importantly, the conduct standards only apply to an individual's conduct in relation to the firm's (or group's) activities in which they work. This means that actions in the individual's private life are not relevant *unless* this behaviour could or did affect the individual's ability to follow the standards more generally.[64] The way in which a person behaves in their private life may then be relevant to any assessment by the PRA or by the firm itself of the individual's fitness and propriety.

12.128 The PRA suggests that the conduct rules may be required through a staff handbook and then through subsequent staff contract updates. A firm should ensure that relevant staff are aware of their obligation to observe these rules.

Breaches of conduct rules

12.129 The Bank of England and Financial Services Act 2016 introduces provisions in FSMA that requires notification by firms to the PRA and FCA where: (a) a firm takes disciplinary action against either a person in a controlled function, a director, or an employee, for a reason specified in the rules made by the regulator (FSMA, s 64C); or (b) the firm is of the opinion that there are grounds on which the approval of an individual could be withdrawn (FSMA, s 63(2A)).

12.130 A breach of a conduct rule by an individual, including details of any related disciplinary action taken by a firm against that individual is generally expected to be material to the assessment of their fitness and propriety. The PRA therefore expects insurance firms and groups to notify it if they know that

---

61 SS35/15.
62 SS35/15, para 3.5.
63 PRA Rulebook – Insurance – Fitness and Propriety 2.3.
64 SS35/15, para 3.8.

an individual covered by the conduct standards has not complied with any of the conduct rules.[65] Where a firm has reported a breach of a conduct rule and subsequently takes disciplinary action against the person for matters relating to the breach, the firm should make a separate notification to the PRA of the disciplinary action.[66] Rules are set out in the Notifications part of the PRA Rulebook.

FCA conduct rules

12.131 Under the extended regime, the FCA conduct rules apply to a senior manager, certified employee, all NEDs who are not SMs (known as 'notified NEDs') *and* all other employees other than ancillary staff.[67] The Financial Services (Banking Reform) Act 2013 empowered the regulators to write rules of conduct that could apply to all employees. Firms can apply the conduct rules to all their employees if they choose, but the regulatory obligations to train staff in the conduct rules and to notify breaches do not apply to staff outside those to whom the rules must apply.

12.132 The FCA conduct rules apply to a firm's regulated and unregulated financial services activities.[68] This is narrower than for the banking regime where the conduct rules apply to everything an employee does on behalf of a bank.

12.133 The FCA applies its conduct rules to EEA branches but only to staff in such branches in relation to matters that are within the UK's scope of responsibilities as the host state regulator. As with the certification regime, the conduct rules do not apply to employees based outside the UK.

12.134 The FCA's conduct rules are the same as the PRA's except that it has two additional individual conduct rules:

- *You must pay due regard to the interests of customers and treat them fairly.*

- *You must observe proper standards of market conduct.*

12.135 The three generic conduct standards will apply directly to certified employees as conduct rules.

Training

12.136 Firms must take all reasonable steps to ensure certified staff and others to whom the conduct rules apply understand how those conduct rules apply, including providing training.

---

65 PRA Rulebook – Insurance – Fitness and Propriety 4.3; PRA Rulebook Fundamental Rules 7, SS35/15, para 3.34.
66 SS35/15, paras 3.35–3.36.
67 The FCA sets out an exhaustive list of roles it considers to be ancillary.
68 The FCA clarifies that conduct issues that have an impact on its objectives will not be limited to the regulated areas of a firm's business.

Notifications of breach of conduct rule

12.137 The regulators also require notifications about disciplinary action that mirror those for other regulated firms. For employees to whom the conduct rules apply a firm must notify the PRA or FCA as appropriate within seven days where the disciplinary action relates to any action, failure to act, or circumstance that amounts to a breach of any conduct rule.

12.138 The PRA has made rules[69] to require firms to notify the regulators:

- where a firm takes disciplinary action against either a person in a controlled function, a director or an employee for a reason specified in the rules; or

- where the firm is of the opinion that there are grounds on which the approval of an individual could be withdrawn.

The FCA rules on notification apply as for other financial services firms (see Chapter 6).

12.139 These rules mirror those for other financial services firms. In particular, notification is required within seven business days where the disciplinary action relates to any action, failure to act, or circumstance that amounts to a breach of any conduct rule.[70]

12.140 Where a firm has reported a breach of a conduct standard and subsequently takes disciplinary action against that person for matters relating to the breach, the firm should make a separate notification to the PRA of the disciplinary action.[71]

12.141 Further, the PRA expects that firms will report to the PRA and the FCA details of known breaches, including those that do not come to the firm's attention until after the person concerned has left the firm. Firms should consider whether the person was a KFH for the firm at the time the breach is thought to have occurred.[72]

12.142 The new notification requirements do not affect firms' obligations to report concerns about an individual's conduct under existing rules and principles such as SUP 15 and FCA Principle 11. Firms should also note that for all FCA conduct rules staff other than SMs, firms must notify the FCA annually of any breaches; if there have been no breaches, a nil return must be made. For senior managers, conduct rule breaches should be notified within seven business days using Form C on the FCA's Connect system.

---

69 In the PRA Rulebook – Notifications Part.
70 This will therefore apply to all SMFs and conduct rules NEDs, certified staff and other staff to whom the conduct rules apply.
71 SS35/15, para 3.35.
72 SS35/15, para. 3.36.

12.143 The PRA's approach is different since it requires notification within seven business days in relation to all PRA SMs, notified NEDs and other employees (including certified staff) subject to the conduct rules.

12.144 If a firm takes disciplinary action in relation to a conduct rule breach but the employee appeals or plans to appeal, this should still be reported to the regulator.

11 ASSESSING FITNESS AND PROPRIETY

12.145 When assessing whether an individual is fit and proper to perform a key function, firms and groups should apply the rules in Insurance – Fitness and Propriety in the PRA Rulebook along with the EU Solvency II Delegated Regulation and also have regard to the EIOPA guidelines on systems of governance. For more detail on assessing fitness and propriety see Chapter 4.

12.146 Regard must be had to an individual's:

● honesty, integrity and reputation;

● competence and capability; and

● financial soundness.

The PRA will also consider these factors when deciding fitness and propriety and when considering honesty, integrity and reputation it will have regard to all relevant matters which may have arisen in the UK or elsewhere.[73] The PRA expects firms who identify any matter which might be relevant to an assessment of fitness and propriety to promptly and fully investigate and to take appropriate action.[74] More detail on fitness and propriety assessments are set out in Chapters 3 and 4.

12.147 The FCA has set out the fit and proper test and the evidence it expects firms to gather when making their fit and proper assessments of senior managers, NEDs and certified staff. See Chapter 3.

12.148 The FCA is applying the fit and proper assessment to NEDs who are not SMs.

12.149 The FCA specifies that the fit and proper assessment should take into account relevant FCA rules around the qualifications, training, competence and personal characteristics required for that role.

---

73 SS35/15, paras 4.2–4.11.
74 SS35/15, para 3.7.

12.150 For new appointees to SMFs and for the appointment of other new KFHs, certified staff and NEDs the PRA expects regulatory references and the Financial Services Register to be an important independent source of information.[75]

12.151 The PRA suggests that firms may wish to consider whether internal procedures such as pre-employment questionnaires for candidates might be relevant to elicit information on past business conduct.[76] If a firm becomes aware of information that may be relevant to an assessment of fitness and propriety it should make reasonable enquiries to establish the circumstances of the conduct and its relevance to an assessment of fitness and propriety.

12.152 For an ongoing assessment the PRA believes that most firms will have a regular cycle of appraisals and performance reviews that can form a baseline requirement for this assessment. Additional checks can be carried out taking into account the nature and level of an individual's responsibilities.[77]

Criminal background checks and criminal offences

12.153 Under the APER application processes firms and candidates had to declare if a candidate had a criminal record, including any spent convictions that the employer had a legal right to know. This will continue for SM applications. The FCA requires firms to undertake a criminal records check as part of each SM approval application. This will ensure that the information that the candidate has provided is accurate and complete. The requirement will also apply to NEDs who are not SMs where a fitness requirement already applies to them. There are no criminal records checks required for certified staff.

12.154 The PRA also requires criminal background checks for SMs or other KFHs.[78]

12.155 In order to satisfy this requirement a firm should get an application form from the Disclosure and Barring Service (DBS) or umbrella body in England and Wales. In Scotland the equivalent procedure involves Disclosure Scotland and in Northern Ireland, AccessNI.

12.156 If the candidate is employed by a contractor the firm should ask the contractor to obtain the certificate.[79]

12.157 Conviction for a criminal offence will not automatically mean an application will be rejected.[80] The regulators state that they will consider each

---

75 PRA Rulebook – Insurance – Fitness and Propriety 3.1; SS35/15, para 4.9.
76 SS35/15, para 4.10.
77 SS35/15, para 4.11.
78 PRA Rulebook – Insurance – Fitness and Propriety 2.4.
79 SS35/15, para 4.12.
80 SS35/15, para 4.6.

application on a case-by-case basis, having regard to a range of factors which may include the:

- seriousness of, and circumstances surrounding, the offence;

- explanation offered by the convicted person;

- relevance of the offence to the proposed role;

- passage of time since the offence was committed; and

- evidence of the individual's rehabilitation.[81]

12.158 The FCA clarifies that it will require a criminal records check for every application for a SMF even if that person already performs a role in the firm or group (this is not required by the PRA). However, it does not require annual criminal records checks (although firms may choose to do this as part of their ongoing fit and proper assessments).[82] The FCA also suggests that if a candidate for a SMF has spent considerable time overseas in the last six years, firms should consider carrying out a criminal records check in those jurisdictions.[83]

12.159 See also Chapters 3 and 4.

12 REGULATORY REFERENCES

12.160 The regulatory references regime for insurers[84] originally extended to:

- Solvency II insurance firms;

- The Society of Lloyd's;

- Lloyd's managing agents;

- third-country branch undertakings (other than Swiss general insurers) in relation to the activities of their establishment in the UK ('third-country branch undertakings');

- UK Insurance Special Purpose Vehicles;

- large non-Solvency II Directive firms (NDFs).

12.161 Under the extended regime from 10 December 2018 *all* insurers seeking to appoint someone to a SM or certified role must request a regulatory reference from the candidate's past employer mirroring the regime for the banking sector.[85] The rules on regulatory references are set out in more detail in Chapter 5. The requirement also applies to all NEDs who are not SMs. The FCA rules on regulatory references are set out in SYSC 22.

---

81 SS35/15, para 4.6; see also FCA FIT.
82 FCA SUP 10C.10.23A.
83 FCA PS18/15, para 4.12.
84 PRA Rulebook – Insurance – Fitness and Propriety; SS35/15, para 5.
85 FCA PS18/15; PRA SS35/15.

12.162 A regulatory reference must cover the previous six years of employment. A firm requesting a reference must make such a request of all relevant former employers or organisations at which the individual is or was a NED and any firms at which the candidate performed:

- a SIMF;

- a SMF;

- another controlled function;

- a certification function;

- a notified NED function or credit union NED function; and/or

- any other KFH.[86]

12.163 Other references should be requested from any other employers other than firms for which the candidate has performed a role.

12.164 Where a firm (A) requests a reference from another full scope regulatory reference firm (B) firm B should make it clear that the request is subject to the requirements in Insurance – Fitness and Propriety by referring to the regulatory reference template.

12.165 If firm A requests a reference from a firm that is not a full scope regulatory reference firm it should specify the information that should be included.

Recruiting from overseas: regulatory references

12.166 Where there are jurisdictional legal restrictions on obtaining information the regulators expect firms to take reasonable steps to obtain references from all current and former employers. Such steps may include:

- approaching all current and former overseas employers;

- explaining that UK regulation requires them to request certain information on candidates for certain functions and to specify the information they require; and

- collecting as much of this information as the overseas employers are legally able and willing to provide.[87]

12.167 The PRA states that while regulatory reference firms must take reasonable steps to obtain information from overseas firms the PRA will take into account any demonstrable legal impediments. Evidence of legal constraints may include relevant correspondence with the overseas employer or a legal opinion.[88]

---

86 SS35/15, para 5.5.
87 SS35/15, para 5.11; SYSC 22.
88 SS35/15, para 5.12.

Recruiting internally – regulatory references

12.168 A firm need not obtain a regulatory reference from another firm which is within the same group provided internal policies and procedures enable the requesting firm to access all the relevant information.[89]

Timing of request for a reference

12.169 In some cases it may not be possible to obtain a reference before applying to a regulator for approval on behalf of a SIMF.

12.170 If the current employer is a UK listed company, the individual's resignation may trigger an obligation to issue a regulatory notification under Listing Rule 9. A request for a reference would put the employer on notice of the employee's impending resignation.

12.171 The PRA states that the requirement for firms to satisfy themselves that candidates for a SMF are fit and proper before applying for approval still applies. In such a case, where it is not possible to obtain the references before applying for approval, a firm must:

- explain in the application for approval why it was not possible to obtain all prior regulatory references;

- confirm that the candidate is nonetheless fit and proper and list the evidence relied on;

- commit to obtaining all necessary regulatory references as soon as reasonably practicable subject to legal restrictions and to take appropriate action if a reference discloses adverse information, including, if appropriate, revoking an offer of employment or terminating employment.[90]

12.172 If a firm cannot obtain a reference because doing so would trigger a market-sensitive notification it must do so before the PRA can approve the candidate. If the firm cannot obtain a reference for another reason it must obtain and consider all references necessary to confirm its conclusions as to the candidate's fitness and propriety no later than one month before the application is due to be determined.[91] Similar FCA rules apply in SYSC 22.

---

89 PRA Rulebook – Insurance – Fitness and Propriety 2.5(2).
90 SS35/15, para 5.18.
91 SS35/15, para 5.20.

Providing regulatory references

12.173 A firm that receives a request for a regulatory reference must include all information which it reasonably considers to be relevant to the hiring firm's assessment of that individual's fitness and propriety.[92]

Agreements and settlements

12.174 The obligation to provide a regulatory reference applies to every firm notwithstanding any agreement or arrangement it may have entered into with an individual prior to or on termination of their employment. This includes a COT3 agreement reached with the services of Acas.

Regulatory reference template

12.175 Regulatory reference firms must supply information about the candidate using the mandatory regulatory reference template (see Appendix 1). In response to questions E and F and covering the period beginning six years before the reference request date and ending on the date of the reference the following information must be provided:

- a description of any conduct breaches if they culminated in disciplinary action[93] and the outcome of such disciplinary action;

- whether the firm concluded that the candidate was not fit and proper.[94]

12.176 Suspensions imposed pending an internal investigation do not need to be notified to the regulators nor included in a regulatory reference. A suspension imposed as a disciplinary sanction must be disclosed in a regulatory reference and may need to be reported.

12.177 Reduction/recovery of remuneration need only be included if it is imposed as a disciplinary action due to a conduct breach.

12.178 In addition to this mandatory information a firm must also provide all information of which it is aware that it reasonably considers to be relevant to the requesting firm's assessment of the candidate's fitness and propriety. This information is requested in section G as 'all relevant information'. This section should not duplicate information given elsewhere as it is intended to capture other information which may be relevant to an assessment of fitness and propriety. This section can also be used to give further information on a breach including mitigating circumstances.[95]

---

92 PRA Rulebook – Insurance – Fitness and Propriety 3; SS35/15, para 5.22.
93 See FSMA, s 64C.
94 SS35/15, para 5.31.
95 SS35/15, paras 5.35–5.41.

12.179 Disclosures in section G (all other relevant information) are subject to the same six-year time limit except for serious matters. Firms are expected to make their own assessment of what misconduct may be serious to warrant inclusion but this may include misconduct involving serious dishonesty or conduct that would have caused the firm to dismiss the individual in accordance with its internal code of conduct if it had been discovered while the individual was still working there.

Right of reply

12.180 There is no statutory or regulatory right to reply to a reference but an individual may be given a right to comment in the interests of fairness. If a firm decides to allow this, it has no obligation to revise a reference.

Updating a reference

12.181 From 7 March 2017 firms have been required to revise a regulatory reference where they later become aware of matters that would cause them to draft the reference differently if the reference were being given now. This updating obligation applies for a period of six years, starting on the date when the individual's employment terminated.[96]

12.182 A disclosure in a regulatory reference may also refer to misconduct that occurred more than six years earlier but which subsequently comes to light, if the misconduct is sufficiently serious.

12.183 A firm that provides an updated reference must only provide it to the employee's current employer.[97]

12.184 The PRA draws attention[98] to additional requirements on firms to disclose misconduct to either the regulators or other firms. Where a firm discovers misconduct a number of existing rules require firms and individuals to disclose this to the PRA.[99]

Legal obligations

12.185 As detailed in Chapter 5, firms also have statutory and common law obligations both to an ex-employee and future employer when providing a reference and these should always be complied with.

---

96   SS35/15, para 5.51.
97   PRA Rulebook – Insurance – Fitness and Propriety 3.
98   SS35/15, para 5.55.
99   Fundamental Rule 7, individual conduct standard 3 and senior insurance manager conduct standard 4, Insurance – Fitness and Propriety 4.3.

13 WHISTLEBLOWING

12.186 The whistleblowing regime (see Chapter 10) has applied to Solvency II insurers and reinsurers, the Society of Lloyd's and managing agents since its inception.

CHAPTER 13

FCA Enforcement and the SMCR

Jake McQuitty, Partner

I INVESTIGATIONS INTO SENIOR MANAGEMENT – THE FCA'S ENFORCEMENT POWERS

13.01 The Financial Conduct Authority (FCA)[1] is responsible for regulating the conduct of firms and individuals in the UK's financial services sector. It is the FCA's stated belief that 'misconduct, if undetected or unaddressed causes a loss of confidence and trust in the operation of our markets, as well as financial loss to consumers and firms'. The FCA can investigate and sanction both firms and individuals for breaches of its rules, with the aim of ensuring 'that the sanction is sufficient to deter the firm or individual from re-offending, and deter others from offending'.

---

1 Prior to 1 April 2013, the FCA was named the Financial Services Authority (FSA). For ease of understanding, we have referred to the FCA throughout.

13.02 With the introduction of the Senior Managers and Certification Regime (SMCR) in March 2016, accountability for institutional and individual misconduct is under increased scrutiny. In analysing the statistics for the FCA's enforcement activity against individuals between the 2008 economic crisis and today it is hoped to provide some insight into the FCA's decision-making, and the lessons that can be learnt.

2   GENERAL STATISTICAL ANALYSIS OF 2008–2018 ENFORCEMENT DECISIONS

13.03 The table at Appendix 1 summarises some useful statistics on the FCA's successful enforcement decisions against individuals, where fines were imposed, across a ten-year period.

13.04 It is clear from this data that both the number of individuals subject to final notices from enforcement decisions and the quantum of the average fine levied peaked in 2012. Since this peak, on average, the FCA has made fewer enforcement decisions, and proportionately less of the FCA's fines have been directed at individuals, when considered as a percentage against the total fines levied in any given year. Recently, however, the quantum of the fines has begun to increase, despite fewer cases being brought. Whether or not this trend is set to continue and/or is related to the introduction of the SMCR remains to be seen.

13.05 Across the ten-year period analysed the largest fines have been levied against individuals who:

- engaged in market abuse;

- traded on insider information; or

- deliberately misled customers via provision of unsuitable advice or deceptive promotional materials.

13.06 Since 2014, the FCA has included, in its short description of reasons for issuing a fine (published on the FCA website) details of which rules for regulated persons and/or other guidance have been breached. In this way, the FCA has started to ascribe a clearer connection between the misconduct and the FCA's rules and guidance.

13.07 It is also important to note that, in addition to the FCA's ability to levy fines against individuals, its enforcement powers also include the power to make prohibition orders. Such orders prohibit individuals from working in regulated financial services on the basis they are no longer deemed to be 'fit and proper'. Prohibition orders are part of the FCA's regulatory toolkit aimed at ensuring and maintaining high standards of conduct in the industry.

13.08 In contrast to fines, which are punitive sanctions for past conduct, prohibition orders regulate (mis)conduct into the future. Prohibition orders are imposed where the regulator considers the individual presents an ongoing risk to consumers and/or markets. The FCA can prevent individuals from performing any function in relation to regulated activities (see the case of Paul Flowers at 13.26 ff), or can reduce the scope of regulated activities, prohibiting individuals from working in any positions with significant influence.

13.09   The number of open FCA investigations, into both individuals and firms, continues to increase, having risen 113% in two years, from 247 investigations in March 2016 to 527 investigations at 11 June 2018. Of those investigations, 306 (58%) are into individuals, five of which are senior managers, and 221 (42%) are into firms. Some of this increase is attributable to the fact the FCA will now, as a matter of routine, consider opening investigations into accountable and responsible individuals at the same time as it commences an investigation into the firm (normally, the individual's employer).

13.10   However, while the number of investigations continues to rise, the FCA has said that firms and individuals should expect that many of these will be closed with no action taken. This is because the FCA increasingly treats an investigation as a precursor to reaching a decision on whether regulatory action is necessary. In effect, the FCA says the purpose of the investigation is to gather the evidence and ascertain what happened. The FCA also says that in most cases it has no preconceived notion of whether there has been a breach. Whilst this may be reassuring, the increase in volume of investigations into individuals where the FCA may not yet have formed a view as to whether there is potential wrongdoing means more individuals will find themselves in the regulatory spotlight, with all the potential stigma attached to being under investigation, waiting to find out if the FCA intends to take any action.

13.11   Such situations also cause considerable difficulty for individuals seeking employment into a regulated role in financial services. This is because, under the FCA's rules, they are obliged to inform prospective employers that they are the subject of investigation when the outcome is far from certain and, on the FCA's own account, there is a real possibility the investigation will be closed with no further action.

13.12   Although there appears to be a potentially high number of conduct investigations in the pipeline, there are relatively few which involve or are likely to involve breaches of the SMCR rules – and only one published decision so far, concerning the CEO of Barclays Bank. In order therefore to understand how the FCA is likely to interpret and apply the SMCR, where there has been a breach, it is useful first to consider some of the key enforcement decisions involving senior individuals which pre-dated the introduction of the SMCR.

3 FCA ENFORCEMENT DECISIONS PRIOR TO THE INTRODUCTION OF THE SMCR

Anthony Claire, Nicolas Bower and Peter Halpin – prohibition orders and a cumulative fine of £928,000

13.13   In November 2014 the FCA imposed a cumulative fine of £928,000 on the CEO, finance director and marketing director of the Swinton Group. The Swinton Group was also fined £7.38M for product mis-selling. Finally, the FCA also issued prohibition orders, which, for the first time, banned senior executives for cultural failings.

13.14   The FCA felt that the culture at the Swinton Group was one where high-pressure sales tactics, from which the directors stood to benefit, were allowed to pervade the organisation. Anthony Clare, the former finance director, was criticised for missing indications that a sales-focused culture was developing within the firm that could lead to the unfair treatment of customers. Similarly, Nicolas Bower failed to ensure that the design, development and marketing of monthly 'add on' insurance products was achieved in a way that treated customers fairly. The FCA felt that the directors had not properly considered the requirement to treat customers fairly 'beyond offering a competitive customer proposition', and that fair treatment was being put at risk by the drive for profits.

13.15   The former CEO, Peter Halpin, received similar criticism regarding the fair treatment of customers, but also, according to the FCA, failed to ensure that management information provided to the board was sufficiently accurate, reliable and fit for purpose. As a result, the board placed undue weight on erroneous management information that was 'inadequate to obtain proper assurance that the risk of mis-selling the monthly add-on products had been adequately mitigated'.

13.16   The FCA commented that 'these three directors should have recognised the risk to customers and redressed the balance so that the drive to maximise profits did not jeopardise the fair treatment of customers'. This case was an early indicator of the weight the FCA continues to place on 'tone from the top' and the impact the culture of an organisation has on ensuring that customers are not exposed to undue risk.

Peter Cummings – fine of £500,000

13.17   Contributing £11,277,283 to the subtotal of fines levied against individuals in 2012 was Peter Cummings, who, according to the FCA, was knowingly concerned in a contravention by the Bank of Scotland of Principle 3 of the FCA's Principles for Business (the requirement to have adequate risk controls), and also individually failed to comply with Principle 6 of the FCA's Principles for Approved Persons (the requirement to act with due skill, care and diligence when performing a regulated function). The FCA fined him £500,000 on 12 September 2012.

13.18   Mr Cummings was appointed as chief executive of the corporate division of the Bank of Scotland. This division's portfolio was high risk, with a specific focus on sub-investment grade lending, and therefore particularly vulnerable to a downturn in the economic cycle. Mr Cummings pursued an aggressive growth strategy, without – in the view of the FCA – appreciating that any high-risk business and lending strategy required a proportionately robust level of control and oversight. Mr Cummings therefore 'failed to take reasonable steps to assess, manage or mitigate the risks involved' in the division. This growth strategy also contrasted with statements in the firm's internal business plan.

13.19   In addition to failing to focus on the inherent riskiness of the business, Mr Cummings failed 'to take reasonable care to ensure that the corporate division adequately and prudently managed a significant number of high value transactions which showed signs of stress' upon the start of the financial crisis and impending economic downturn. Instead he 'continued to direct the corporate division to lend in a way that increased credit and concentration risk, increasing the vulnerability of the portfolio'.

13.20   Mr Cummings was personally involved in the oversight of stressed transactions, and in the sanctioning of high-value/high-risk transactions throughout the period. In conjunction with a pervasive culture of optimism in the business, the FCA found Peter Cummings had failed to act prudently in (i) setting targets and (ii) responding to the changing economic environment, despite weaknesses in the control framework being highlighted to him.

13.21   In the decision notice, the FCA was also critical of the incentive structure for staff, with its focus on revenue rather than risk, and the FCA expressed concerns on the quality, reliability and utility of management information being relayed to senior management.

13.22   The Peter Cummings decision is inextricably linked to the case against the Bank of Scotland, due to his involvement in the breach of regulatory requirements by the firm. However, the overarching conclusion of the FCA has important repercussions for individual accountability under the SMCR. The FCA stated that 'senior managers holding significant influence functions must take responsibility for ensuring that appropriate regard is paid to the risks of the business, recognising that a higher risk business strategy will require a commensurately higher and more robust control framework'.

13.23   Despite this statement, other senior managers at the Bank of Scotland were not subject to enforcement investigations at the time. The FCA's approach in this regard was criticised in Andrew Green QC's 'Report into the FSA's enforcement actions following the failure of HBOS' (for further details see Chapter 1). Whilst the report concluded that the investigation into Mr Cummings was reasonable, Andrew Green QC concluded that 'the FCA gave no proper consideration to the investigation of any other individuals including former members of the Board (such as the former Group Chief Executive Officer, Andy Hornby, and the former Chairman, Lord Stevenson)'.

4   OTHER CASES OF NOTE

13.24   The data in Appendix 1 to this chapter is compiled from cases where the FCA:

(1) was successful in its enforcement endeavours; and

(2) decided to levy a fine against the individuals involved.

13.25   However, in addition to the data and individual cases discussed at 13.13 ff, other cases exist outside of these strict parameters, which provide useful insight into the FCA's approach.

Paul Flowers – prohibition order

13.26   The FCA's decision to impose a prohibition order on Paul Flowers[2] serves as a useful reminder of the wide-ranging sanctions available to the FCA, over and above the imposition of fines, and its ability to impose these sanctions for a variety of reasons. Whilst not guilty of market abuse, insider trading or misleading financial promotions, Mr Flowers was deemed 'not a fit and proper person' for a position in any regulated activity, due to his 'disregard for the standards and requirements he was expected to meet, in particular during the period he held a position of trust and influence' as chairman of the Co-op Bank.

13.27   Whilst in this role, between 22 May 2011 and 7 May 2014, the FCA said Paul Flowers:

● used his work mobile telephone for personal use to call a premium rate chat line on at least nine occasions, in breach of the company's expense policy;

● used his work email account to send and receive sexually explicit messages, and discuss purchasing, taking and offering to provide illegal drugs, in breach of the company's Code of Conduct for Directors, and the computer use policy.

13.28   After stepping down from his role as Chairman, Mr Flowers was subsequently convicted for possession of illegal drugs, including cocaine and ketamine. The FCA found these circumstances particularly egregious as the behavioural standards expected were well known to him, his failings spanned a significant period of time, and his misconduct occurred notwithstanding the fact that he had agreed to uphold high standards both as an approved person, and as a Methodist minister.

13.29   The decision to impose a prohibition order was taken to support the FCA's 'operational objective of promoting and enhancing the integrity of the UK financial system'. The Executive Director of Enforcement and Market Oversight at the time said that 'the role of Chair occupies a unique place of

2   See https://www.fca.org.uk/publication/final-notices/paul-john-flowers-2018.pdf.

trust and influence. The Chair is pivotal in setting expectations of a company's culture, values and behaviour. Mr Flowers failed in his duty to lead by example and to meet the high standards of integrity and probity demanded by the role'. It is noteworthy that the FCA took this decision despite the fact that Mr Flowers was not found deficient against his regulatory operational responsibilities, or guilty of misconduct in the performance of his work duties. Instead, the decision to impose a prohibition order relied on character-based concerns regarding his private life. The FCA's decision highlighted that a directors' private life *can* extend into professional concerns, and regulatory sanctions.

13.30   Based on the parameters of the Fit and Proper Test for Approved Persons (FIT) in the FCA Handbook, the FCA can assess fitness and propriety against a person's honesty, integrity, reputation, competence and capability, and financial soundness (FIT 1.3.1BG) (see Chapter 4). According to the FCA, a failure to meet these grounds, and the 'attendant negative publicity' risked 'undermining consumer and market confidence'. The Paul Flowers decision is a reminder to directors of regulated firms that the FCA's FIT test and its resulting enforcement powers extend beyond strict regulatory concerns.

John Pottage – reversal of FCA fine by the Upper Tribunal

13.31   The decision of the Upper Tribunal (Tax and Chancery Chambers) in *John Pottage and the Financial Services Authority*[3] is also particularly noteworthy, as it was the first time the FCA had tried to penalise a senior manager for inadequate supervision, rather than actual personal wrongdoing.

13.32   This case related to Mr Pottage's conduct between 4 September 2006 and 31 July 2007, where, as CEO with responsibility for wealth management businesses of corporate entities, through which UBS AG and UBS Wealth management (UK) Ltd operated, he was – according to the FCA – 'the only individual with full regulatory responsibility for all aspects of compliance with the regulatory regime'.

13.33   In this role, the FCA believed that Mr Pottage had failed to take reasonable steps to ensure that the business of the firm complied with the requirements and standards of the regulatory system. In its view, Mr Pottage ought to have spent 'substantial and significant time' ensuring that the governance and risk management frameworks operated effectively. It was argued by the FCA that Mr Pottage failed to:

- conduct adequate initial assessments of the business upon his appointment;

- complete continuous monitoring; and

- question assurances that there were no fundamental deficiencies in the design and operational effectiveness of governance and risk management systems.

---

3   FS/2010/33; see https://assets.publishing.service.gov.uk/media/5752b95640f0b64328000020/ John_Pottage.pdf.

13.34   According to the FCA, these failures led to 'serious and widespread flaws in the business' which went undetected.

13.35   Whilst the FCA's decision to fine Mr Pottage £100,000 was overturned by the Upper Tribunal, the case provided useful insight into what the Tribunal, as an independent judicial body and having heard the evidence in full, considered to be the key criteria for determining whether a senior individual was personally accountable for regulatory failings within a firm. The Tribunal articulated these criteria as follows:

(1)   where a control failure in a business becomes apparent, whether the CEO – from his unique position of oversight – assessed the wider implications of that failure to the business as a whole and took reasonable steps to address the failure;

(2)   whether the senior individual was personally culpable for the failings identified;

(3)   a CEO is not required to design, create or implement controls personally – his is a role of oversight;

(4)   where the senior individual has delegated a task or role, whether this was appropriate and if so whether it was delegated to an appropriately qualified individual;

(v)   whether the senior individual took reasonable steps to ensure that the business has compliant systems and controls. What is required to be done by way of 'reasonable steps' depends on all the circumstances.

13.36   Although it pre-dates the introduction of the SMCR, this case remains a useful precedent and an early insight into what would ultimately feature in the SMCR. For instance, some of the criteria outlined by the Tribunal are now mirrored in the SMCR, such as the requirement that senior managers take 'reasonable steps' to prevent or minimise a breach of regulatory requirements.

Barry Tootell and Keith Alderson

13.37   Although the FCA failed to get its man in the *Pottage* case, subsequently the PRA were considerably more successful in the case of two senior executives from the Co-operative Bank Plc ('Co-op Bank').

13.38   In August 2015, the Prudential Regulation Authority (PRA) publicly censured the Co-op Bank for, among other things, failing to have in place adequate risk management systems. The PRA found that the Co-op Bank's failings had the potential to weaken the firm and reduce its resilience.

13.39   The PRA also investigated the involvement of senior management in these failings and subsequently, on 15 January 2016, it prohibited Barry Tootell, the former CEO of the Co-op Bank and Keith Alderson, the former managing director of the Co-op Bank's Corporate and Business Banking Division, from holding a significant influence function in a PRA authorised firm for breaches related to the running of the Co-op Bank. The PRA also fined Mr Tootell £173,802 and Mr Alderson £88,890. These fines represented a 30% early settlement discount on the original fines proposed.

13.40 In its published decisions, the PRA explained that it had found Mr Tootell and Mr Alderson failed to exercise due skill, care and diligence in carrying out their roles at the Co-op Bank during two periods of time: for Mr Tootell, the period between 1 January 2009 and 10 May 2013; and for Mr Alderson, the period between 1 August 2009 and January 2011. This failure constituted a breach of Statement of Principle 6 of the Statements of Principle and Code of Practice for Approved Persons.[4]

13.41 The PRA also found that both men were knowingly concerned in the contravention by the Co-op Bank of Principle 3 of the Principles for Businesses (the requirement to have in place adequate risk management systems) during the relevant period.[5] Under the Financial Services and Markets Act 2000 (FSMA), s 66, the regulator has the power take enforcement action against an approved person if they are found to have been knowingly concerned in a breach of a regulatory requirement by their firm.

13.42 The FCA has said that in order to establish that an approved person was 'knowingly concerned' in a breach of a regulatory requirement by their firm, the regulator must establish that the individual in question had knowledge of the facts that caused the breach, but it is not necessary to show that he or she had knowledge that a breach had actually occurred. Nor is it necessary for the regulator to prove that the approved person had acted dishonestly to find that they had been knowingly concerned in a breach of regulatory requirements.

13.43 In relation to the conduct of each individual, the PRA found that:

(1) Mr Tootell was centrally involved in a culture within the Co-op Bank which encouraged prioritising the short-term financial position of the firm at the cost of taking prudent and sustainable actions to secure the firm's longer-term capital position;

(2) Mr Tootell did not take adequate steps to ensure that the Co-op Banking Risk team, for which he was ultimately responsible, was properly structured and organised to enable it to provide proper independent challenge and guidance to the first line business of the Co-op Bank. As CEO, Mr Tootell played a significant role in the Co-op Bank managing its finances and capital position

---

4   The FSA Statements of Principle and Code of Practice for Approved Persons applied to Mr Tootell from 1 January 2009 to 31 March 2013 and the PRA's Statements of Principle and Code of Practice for Approved Persons applied from 1 April 2013 to 10 May 2013.

5   Although the Principles for Businesses were replaced with effect from June 2014 by the PRA Fundamental Rules, the FSA Principles for Businesses applied to Co-op Bank in the Relevant Period up to 31 March 2013 and the PRA's Principles for Businesses in the Relevant Period from 1 April 2013 to 13 May 2013.

in a manner that was not in line with the firm's own stated cautious risk appetite;

(3) Mr Alderson did not take reasonable steps to ensure that Co-op Bank adequately assessed risk arising across the Britannia Corporate Loan Book; and

(4) Mr Alderson did not escalate specific risks inherent in the Britannia Corporate Loan Book sufficiently clearly to Co-op Bank's formal risk management processes. As a result, the risks could not properly be considered, and nor could the appropriate actions be taken to mitigate them.

13.44 As a consequence of these failings, the PRA said the Co-op Bank's culture was materially adversely affected – resulting in an environment in which some staff felt inappropriately pressured to meet targets. Whilst the PRA accepted that there was no improper intent on the part of Mr Alderson and Mr Tootell to influence culture or behaviours, the consequence of the environment created by their failings meant that a more optimistic view on the bank's impairment position was ultimately taken than would otherwise have been the case. In turn, this undermined the bank's safety and soundness. The PRA therefore found that Mr Tootell's and Mr Alderson's breaches had the clear potential to affect the safety and soundness of the Co-op Bank and the PRA concluded that they were not fit and proper persons to carry out a significant influence function at a PRA authorised firm on the grounds of a lack of competence and capability.

13.45 The PRA recognised that Mr Tootell and Mr Alderson did not deliberately or recklessly breach regulatory provisions and no findings of dishonesty or lack of integrity were made in relation to them. The PRA also acknowledged that, by settling the cases against them, Mr Tootell and Mr Alderson had accepted responsibility for the fact they fell short of the PRA's expected standards.

13.46 In the press statement accompanying the published findings, Andrew Bailey, the then Deputy Governor, Prudential Regulation, Bank of England and CEO of the PRA said:

> 'Banks that are not well governed have the potential to pose a threat to UK financial stability. The actions of Mr Tootell and Mr Alderson posed an unacceptable threat to the safety and soundness of the Co-op Bank which is why we have decided a prohibition is appropriate in these cases. This action makes clear that there are serious consequences for senior individuals who fall short of the PRA's expectations. The new Senior Managers Regime, which will be introduced in March, will further ensure that senior managers are held duly responsible for their actions.'

13.47 Mr Bailey's comments clearly demonstrate how this case was perceived as a precursor to the SMCR. Nevertheless, as the rest of this chapter explains, the regulators have so far struggled to find a case which can meaningfully back up the intent of the new regime, reinforcing the messages of the cases outlined involving Messrs Claire, Bowyer, Halpin, Cummings, Flowers, Tootell and Alderson.

5   FCA/PRA ENFORCEMENT DECISIONS AGAINST SENIOR INDIVIDUALS SINCE THE SMCR

The introduction of the SMCR – a brief recap

13.48   The introduction of the SMCR was the result of recommendations put forward by the UK Parliamentary Commission on Banking Standards (see Chapter 1).

13.49   The stated aim of the SMCR is to remove ambiguous and bureaucratic structures that have blurred the lines of responsibility and put in place a regime which will strengthen market integrity and prevent consumer harm by focusing on robust governance, increasing senior manager accountability and setting better conduct standards for staff at all levels.

13.50   The SMCR requires individuals who hold key roles and responsibilities, such as those carrying out senior management functions, to be approved by the FCA. Thereafter firms are legally required to ensure that they have procedures in place to assess individuals' fitness and propriety at least annually (see Chapter 4).

13.51   Should a firm fail to meet any of the FCA's requirements, the senior manager responsible could be held to account if they fail to take reasonable steps to prevent or stop the breach (see Chapter 2).

13.52   At present, the SMCR applies to banks, insurers and some other large firms. The FCA is, however, extending the SMCR to all regulated firms with effect from 9 December 2019.

6   FCA/PRA ENFORCEMENT POWERS SINCE THE SMCR

13.53   Since the introduction of the SMCR, neither the FCA nor the PRA have taken on any new enforcement powers. This means that the same investigation and enforcement challenges that existed prior to the SMCR remain, particularly the challenge of proving a senior manager failed to take reasonable steps – where the burden of proof is on the FCA to show this was not the case.

13.54   However, the SMCR does create greater clarity in determining responsibility for various functions, especially among senior managers. Statements of responsibilities and management responsibilities maps now pinpoint who is responsible for what within a financial institution. This transparency means that the FCA is now more likely to consider and treat enforcement against individuals as a priority from the outset of an investigation, rather than as something to consider once it has completed its investigation into the firm.

13.55   The FCA is able to enforce both fines and prohibition orders against individuals. In order to determine the appropriate level of financial penalty, the FCA applies the following five-step framework which involves:

(1) depriving an individual of the financial benefit derived from the breach;

(2) assessing the seriousness of the breach;

(3) assessing mitigating and aggravating factors;

(4) adjusting the fine for deterrence; and

(5) applying settlement discount.

13.56 Interestingly, there appears to be no correlation between the level of fine and whether or not a prohibition is ordered. For example, the lowest fine since the introduction of the SMCR was made in May 2016 for £10,000 against Mr Joint for his failure to exercise due skill, care and diligence in managing the business of Joint Aviation. Mr Joint was a director (with approval to perform the CF1 controlled function), responsible for the misapplication of client insurance premiums of around £150,000 which, instead of being paid to the insurer(s), had been used to pay Joint Aviation's business expenses. As well as being fined, Mr Joint was prohibited from performing any significant influence functions in relation to any regulated activity carried on by any authorised person, exempt person or exempt professional firm.

7   ENFORCEMENT DECISIONS – MARCH 2016 TO PRESENT

13.57 Since March 2016, the FCA/PRA has fined 22 individuals (as at time of writing), with total fines in aggregate of £2,611,125. It should, however, be noted that not all of these 22 individuals occupy senior management roles and only one of these fines concerns a breach of the SMCR (see 13.70).

13.58 Over the period analysed, the most common reasons for fines on senior management individuals are market abuse and a lack of fitness/propriety in the relevant financial area, in particular, the failure to manage conflicts of interest and the mishandling of client money.

13.59 Interestingly, despite the introduction of the SMCR, there has been a decrease in fines against senior managers. Notably, in the two months preceding the introduction of the SMCR in March 2016, fines on individuals came to a total of £15,118,500; however, following the introduction of the SMCR, fines against individuals to the end of the year equalled just £832,146. This fall in fines has been widely noted and the FCA has been quick to assert that it has not 'gone soft'.

13.60 In 2017, the total fines on individuals was even lower than in 2016, at just £435,879, with fines ranging from £10,000 to £105,000. Of all FCA fines, fines against individuals made up just 0.19%.

13.61 In 2018 FCA fines for individuals have been much greater; by November these were already at £1,343,100, making up 6.01% of the total FCA fines for the year. This is presumably in an effort to deflect concerns about the enforcement of the SMCR.

8 EXAMPLES OF ENFORCEMENT DECISIONS

13.62 Of the 22 fines against individuals, two of these are noteworthy because they relate to senior individuals and they therefore provide some insight into where regulatory expectations are set and are likely to be set in relation to the SMCR. The first case concerns John Radford, which was a finding on the basis of breaches pre-dating the introduction of the SMCR; and the second concerns Jes Staley, the only fine so far for breach of the SMCR.

John Radford

13.63 The case concerning John Radford is notable because it touches on the reasonable steps test outlined in the decision concerning John Pottage.

13.64 On 30 August 2018, the FCA published its final decision notice in respect of John Radford. In that notice, the FCA found Mr Radford had breached Statements of Principle 6 (due skill, care and diligence) and 7 (the requirement to ensure a firm complies with the relevant requirements and standards of the regulatory system) in his capacity as a CF1 director at One Call Insurance Services Limited ('One Call'). The FCA also found Mr Radford lacked an adequate understanding of the FCA's Client Money Rules and consequently failed to ensure that One Call protected its client's money in accordance with those rules and Principle 10 of the FCA's Principles for Businesses (the requirement to arrange adequate protection for clients' assets). The breaches were said to have occurred between 14 January 2005 to 12 August 2013.

13.65 As a consequence of these breaches, Mr Radford was fined £468,600 and prohibited from having any responsibility for client money and/or insurer money in relation to any regulated activity carried on by any authorised person, exempt person or exempt professional firm.

13.66 During the majority of the relevant period, until September 2011, Mr Radford was responsible for client money at One Call. He was required to ensure that One Call protected client money by complying with Principle 10 and the Client Money Rules. However, the FCA found that Mr Radford lacked adequate understanding of the Authority's requirements in relation to client money. In summary, this meant Mr Radford:

(1) failed to take reasonable steps to inform himself of the relevant regulatory requirements;

(2) failed, in his role as CF1 and CEO of One Call, to respond adequately to warnings from One Call's external auditor that it may be in breach of the Client Money Rules;

(3) failed to take reasonable steps to ensure that One Call properly assessed the basis on which it held client money, and then failed to establish the necessary systems and controls to handle that client money in accordance with the Client Money Rules; and

(4) as a result of (1) to (3), he failed to ensure that One Call complied with the rules and requirements of the Client Money Rules. The result was that from December 2009 One Call inadvertently then spent for its own benefit monies over and above those due to it in commission, fees and charges earned, resulting in a substantial client money deficit of approximately £17.3m.

13.67 The FCA found that this may have led to a significant competitive advantage for One Call – because it could offer insurance products at lower prices – and it exposed customers to significant risk of loss.

13.68 The FCA said that Mr Radford's failings were particularly serious because he was oblivious to certain key risks and he failed to take reasonable steps to manage those risks. The FCA went on to say it would expect those reasonable steps to have included comprehensive and regular reviews of One Call's terms of business to confirm that the risk transfer provisions were effective. The FCA also criticised Mr Radford for making a series of assumptions concerning risk, relying on statements made by third parties, without taking independent steps to satisfy himself as to the robustness and reliability of those statements, such as by seeking expert advice.

13.69 Mr Radford's failure to seek advice or conduct regular reviews was further aggravated by his failure to reconsider his views following queries raised by One Call's external auditor. On the basis of those queries, the FCA said Mr Radford should have taken steps to reconsider his views and check the correct position. Most likely this would have meant issues could have been discovered and the size of the deficit, and therefore the risk to the customer, would have been remedied sooner.

Jes Staley

13.70 As at the date of writing, the only FCA/PRA financial penalty for breach of the SMCR was against the CEO of Barclays Group, Jes Staley. Were it not for the 30% early settlement discount, the FCA would have imposed a financial penalty of £458,900 on Mr Staley, with a PRA fine against him for the same amount. Mr Staley was fined for breaches of Individual Conduct Rule 2 – the requirement to act with due skill, care and diligence.

13.71 Mr Staley was approved by the FCA to carry out the SMF1 (chief executive) function at Barclays under the SMCR.

13.72 Investigations surrounding Mr Staley followed two letters which were sent to the Group Board. The first was authored by an individual claiming to be a long-term institutional shareholder of the Barclays Group. It raised concerns over the appointment of an employee who Mr Staley had known at a previous employer, questioning Mr Staley's dealings with the employee including his recruitment in which Mr Staley had been involved. Unknown at the time to Mr Staley, Barclay's Group Compliance considered the first letter to be a whistleblow and a whistleblowing case was opened. Mr Staley did not consider it to be a whistleblow and considered that the accusations were false and malicious.

13.73 Mr Staley emailed a copy of the letter to a friend and former colleague and, separately, discussed the letter with another friend.

13.74 A second letter was received in June 2016. It was anonymous and expressed similar concerns to those in the first letter. Mr Staley considered this second letter could fall within the scope of Barclays' whistleblowing policy and believed the two letters were part of a campaign to attack said employee and Barclays. Unknown to Mr Staley at the time, the second letter was logged as a whistleblowing case.

13.75 Mr Staley asked Barclay's Group Security to identify the author of the first letter. However, shortly after this request was made, Mr Staley was advised that he should not try to identify the author. Mr Staley was also informed that the letter was being treated as a whistleblow and would be dealt with in accordance with Barclays' whistleblowing policy.

13.76 Mr Staley later understood that, as the allegations were unsubstantiated, the first letter was no longer being treated as a whistleblow and so concluded that he could decide how to proceed in relation to it. He again tried (and went to great lengths) to discover the identity of the author of the first letter.

13.77 In early 2017, Barclays Board became aware of Mr Staley's attempt to identify the author of the first letter. Barclays undertook its own investigation and reported it to the FCA and PRA.

13.78 Following the FCA's investigation, it was found that Mr Staley had failed to:

(1) identify that he had a conflict of interest in relation to the first letter and failed to take appropriate steps to mitigate this conflict;

(2) be objective by distancing himself from the investigation;

(3) maintain the independence of the Group Compliance's investigation by trying to identify the author;

(4) exercise impartial judgment by discussing the first letter with two individuals outside of Barclays Group; and

(5) maintain confidence in Barclays' whistleblowing policy and the protection it affords to whistleblowers.

13.79 Although in this case there was no financial loss, Mr Staley had compromised the value of the important resource of whistleblowing by which the financial services industry and regulators can identify poor behaviours. The risk (and no doubt the fine) was exacerbated given the high profile of Mr Staley and Barclays within the financial services industry and Barclays' revenue, rather than this being indicative of a wider issue in the industry.

9 WHAT IS IN THE PIPELINE, BASED ON FCA'S PUBLIC STATEMENTS IN ITS ANNUAL BUSINESS PLAN AND RECENT SPEECHES IN 2017/18?

Extending the SMCR

13.80   The SMCR has been live for banks and deposit takers since March 2016. In July 2017, the FCA and PRA consulted on extending the SMCR to all FSMA regulated firms. This will come into effect on 9 December 2019 and will affect around 47,000 firms in total.

13.81   The roll-out of the SMCR to all FCA authorised firms next year will no doubt lead to yet more investigations into individuals and potentially more FCA decisions being contested and referred to the FCA's Regulatory Decisions Committee and the Upper Tribunal.

10   FCA/PRA ENFORCEMENT TRENDS

13.82   Mark Steward (FCA Director of Enforcement and Market Oversight) has defended the assertion that the rise in investigations opened represents a return to the 'shoot first and ask questions later' policy announced by Martin Wheatley (the FCA's former Chief Executive) in 2012. However, with the introduction of the SMCR, there is undoubted pressure on the regulators to show that the new accountability and conduct rules deliver results.

13.83   As described earlier in this chapter, the increase in new investigations being opened (and at an early stage) is bad news for individuals who will potentially find themselves facing less well-formulated cases, with the FCA starting investigations before it has gathered all the evidence, established what happened and reached preliminary views on whether there was a rule breach. Even if an investigation is subsequently dropped that will not spare the senior manager from the loss of time taken up defending the case, the potential stigma resulting from being under investigation and the associated stress and anxiety.

Harder to resolve by agreement

13.84   Enforcement investigations involving individuals tend to be hard-fought and therefore time-consuming and costly for the FCA to pursue. In a talk given in January 2017, the Head of the FCA Enforcement division, Mark Steward, spoke about how the FCA expected actions against senior managers to be harder to resolve by agreement. Mr Steward said that the FCA does not expect 'senior managers to agree so readily to pay high fines to resolve cases. We expect there will be more contest and more litigation.' This view is consistent with the difficulties encountered previously by the FCA in successfully proving its case against senior individuals, such as Mr Pottage, as described at 13.31 ff. Nevertheless, it has been suggested that the SMCR's rules concerning identification of accountable individuals, along with more explicitly documented governance and management information, such as detailed management responsibility maps, will make it easier for the FCA to identify who was responsible and whether they reasonably discharged that responsibility.

13.85   Although a senior manager under investigation is more likely to take his or her case to the Upper Tribunal for a decision, it is not yet certain there will be any meaningful increase in the number of those cases – when compared to the period prior to SMCR – particularly given the FCA's comments concerning the volumes of cases it expects will be discontinued with no public outcome. The FCA has said it will use enforcement investigations as a diagnostic tool – to establish what happened – and that this is likely to result in the FCA discontinuing a higher proportion of enforcement investigations than has been the case in prior years.

II   INDIVIDUAL RESPONSIBILITY

13.86   There has been concern about the pressures of the SMCR on individuals in senior positions, indeed that the SMCR may dissuade individuals from taking on such responsibilities. To this, the FCA has said that the SMCR is not a means of shifting corporate liability onto individuals because the firm's liability is a jurisdictional fact in any action against an individual.

13.87   At the New York University Program on Corporate Compliance and Enforcement on 31 March 2017, Mark Steward maintained that action against firms, including heavy financial penalties, will not soften as a result of the SMCR. That said, the concern surrounding the pressures on individuals continues and the SMCR is often cited by individuals as a reason for leaving a senior manager role or rejecting the offer of a role. Ultimately, if this were to become a common trend it would be directly at odds with the purposes of the SMCR – because it would result in a loss of talent in the form of experienced senior managers, thereby increasing the risk of poor management decisions and of badly managed firms.

APPENDIX

2008	
No. of individual enforcement fines	19
Subtotal of FCA fines for individuals	£899,826.11
Total fines in 2008	£22,706,526.00
Percentage of FCA fines attributed to individuals	3.96%
Average fine for individuals in 2008	£47,359.27
2009	
No. of individual enforcement fines	21
Subtotal of FCA fines for individuals	£1,820,567.00
Total fines in 2009	£35,005,522.00
Percentage of FCA fines attributed to individuals	5.20%
Average fine for individuals in 2009	£86,693.67
2010	
No. of individual enforcement fines	52
Subtotal of FCA fines for individuals	£9,555,681.50
Total fines in 2010	£89,121,281.50
Percentage of FCA fines attributed to individuals	10.72%
Average fine for individuals in 2010	£183,763.11
2011	
No. of individual enforcement fines	34
Subtotal of FCA fines for individuals	£9,888,811.00
Total fines in 2011	£66,144,839.00
Percentage of FCA fines attributed to individuals	14.95%
Average fine for individuals in 2011	£290,847.38
2012	
No. of individual enforcement fines	27
Subtotal of FCA fines for individuals	£11,277,283.00
Total fines in 2012	£311,569,256.00
Percentage of FCA fines attributed to individuals	3.62%
Average fine for individuals in 2012	£417,677.15
2013	
No. of individual enforcement fines	20
Subtotal of FCA fines for individuals	£4,988,738.00
Total fines in 2013	£474,263,738.00

Percentage of FCA fines attributed to individuals	1.05%
Average fine for individuals in 2013	£249,436.90
2014	
No. of individual enforcement fines	13
Subtotal of FCA fines for individuals	£2,907,900.00
Total fines in 2014	£147,431,800.00
Percentage of FCA fines attributed to individuals	1.97%
Average fine for individuals in 2014	£223,684.62
2015	
No. of individual enforcement fines	22
Subtotal of FCA fines for individuals	£6,689,474.00
Total fines in 2015	£905,219,078.00
Percentage of FCA fines attributed to individuals	0.74%
Average fine for individuals in 2015	£304,067.00
2016	
No. of individual enforcement fines	15
Subtotal of FCA fines for individuals	£2,820,646.00
Total fines in 2016	£22,216,446.00
Percentage of FCA fines attributed to individuals	12.70%
Average fine for individuals in 2016	£201,474.71
2017	
No. of individual enforcement fines	8
Subtotal of FCA fines for individuals	£435,879.00
Total fines in 2017	£229,515,303.00
Percentage of FCA fines attributed to individuals	0.19%
Average fine for individuals in 2017	£54,484.88
2018 (to November)	
No. of individual enforcement fines	7
Subtotal of FCA fines for individuals (to date)	£1,343,100.00
Total fines in 2018 (to date)	£22,348,612.00
Percentage of FCA fines attributed to individuals	6.01%
Average fine for individuals in 2018 (to date)	£191,871.43

Average Fine

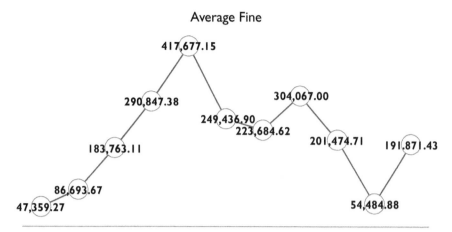

2008 2009 2010 2011 2012 2013 2014 2015 2016 2017 2018

Number of Individual Enforcement Cases Resulting in a Final Notice and a Fine

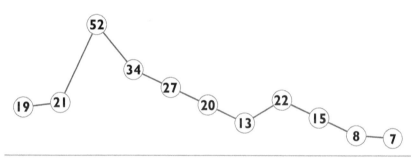

2008 2009 2010 2011 2012 2013 2014 2015 2016 2017 2018

SYSC 22 Regulatory references

Note: Italic text denotes defined terms. The definitions can be found in the Glossary to the FCA Handbook at https://www.handbook.fca.org.uk/handbook/glossary/.

Chapter 22

Regulatory references

22

22.1 Application

General application

22.1.1 **R** This chapter applies to all *firms* (subject to ■ SYSC 22.1.5R).

Activities covered

22.1.2 **G** This chapter is not limited to *regulated activities* or other specific types of activities.

Territorial scope and overseas firms

22.1.3 **R** There is no territorial limitation on the application of this chapter, subject to ■ SYSC 22.1.5R and ■ SYSC 22.1.6R.

22.1.4 **G** One effect of ■ SYSC 22.1.3R is that the obligation to provide a reference can apply even if the *employee* worked in an overseas office of the *employer*.

22.1.5 **R** This chapter does not apply to:

    (1) an *overseas firm* that does not have an establishment in the *United Kingdom*;

    (2) a *UCITS qualifier* (see section 266 of the *Act* (Disapplication of rules));

    (3) an *AIFM qualifier*; or

    (4) an *incoming EEA firm* that is an *EEA pure reinsurer*.

22.1.6 **R** For an *incoming firm* or any other *overseas firm*, ■ SYSC 22.2.2R (Obligation to give references) only applies if the current or former *employee* in question (defined as "P" in ■ SYSC 22.2.2R) is or was an *employee* of its *branch* in the *United Kingdom* and only relates to their activities as such.

22.1.7 **R** (1) In order to decide whether someone is an *employee* of a *branch*, the *Glossary* definition of *employee* is applied to the *branch* as if the *branch* and the *firm* of which it forms part were separate *firms*.

    (2) For the purpose of (1), paragraph (4A)(c) of the definition of *employee* (someone employed elsewhere in the *group*) does not apply.

411

22.2 Getting, giving and updating references: the main rules

Obligation to obtain references (applicable to SMCR firms)

22.2.1   **R**   (1) If an *SMCR firm* (A) is considering:

    (a) permitting or appointing someone (P) to perform a *controlled function*; or

    (b) issuing a certificate under the certification regime for P;

    (as explained in more detail in rows (A) and (B) of the table in ■ SYSC 22.2.3R), A must take reasonable steps to obtain appropriate references from:

    (c) P's current *employer*; and

    (d) anyone who has been P's *employer* in the past six years.

  (2) A must take reasonable steps to obtain the reference before the time in column two of the applicable row in the table in ▨ SYSC 22.2.3R. If A does not obtain it within that time it must take reasonable steps to obtain it as soon as possible thereafter.

  (3) A must in particular request:

    (a) the information in ■ SYSC 22.2.2R(1) to (3); and

    (b) (if P's current or previous *employer* is also an *SMCR firm*) the information in ■ SYSC 22.2.2R(4) (questions (A) to (F) of Part One of ■ SYSC 22 Annex 1R).

  (4) When deciding what information to request under (1), A must have regard to the factors in ■ SYSC 22.2.2R(5) (Factors set out in ■ SYSC 22 Annex 2R).

Obligation to give references

22.2.2   **R**   (1) A *firm* (B) must provide a reference to another *firm* (A) as soon as reasonably practicable if:

    (a) A is considering:

      (i) permitting or appointing someone (P) to perform a *controlled function*; or

      (ii) issuing a certificate under the certification regime for P; or

      (iii) appointing P to another position in the table in ■ SYSC 22.2.3R;

      (as explained in more detail in the table in ■ SYSC 22.2.3R);

22

(b) A makes a request, for a reference or other information in
respect of P from B, in B's capacity as P's current or former
employer;

(c) B:

(i) is P's current *employer*; or

(ii) has been P's *employer* at any time in the six year period
preceding the request in (1)(b); and

(d) A indicates to B the purpose of the request.

(2) B must disclose to A in the reference all information of which B is
aware that B reasonably considers to be relevant to A's assessment of
whether P is fit and proper.

(3) B is only required to disclose under (1) and (2) something that
occurred or existed:

(a) in the six years before the request for a reference; or

(b) between the date of the request for the reference and the date B
gives the reference; or

(c) (in the case of serious misconduct) at any time.

[**Note:** See ■SYSC 22.5.10G and ■SYSC 22.5.11G for *guidance* on the
meaning of serious misconduct]

(4) Where B is an *SMCR firm*:

(a) B must in addition disclose the information in questions (A) to (F)
of Part One of ■SYSC 22 Annex 1R (Template for regulatory
references given by SMCR firms and disclosure requirements); and

(b) B must disclose the information in (a) whether or not A is an
SMCR firm.

(5) When deciding what information to give to A under (1) to (3), B must
have regard to the factors in ■SYSC 22 Annex 2R (Factors to take into
account when asking for and giving regulatory references).

22.2.3 R Table: What positions need a reference

Position	When to obtain reference	Comments
(A) Permitting or appointing someone to perform an *FCA controlled function* or a *PRA controlled function*.	One *month* before the end of the application period	Where a request for a reference would require: (a) the *firm* requesting the reference; (b) the *employer* giving the reference; or (c) any other *person*;

Position	When to obtain reference	Comments
	to make a mandatory disclosure prior to P disclosing to its current *employer* that such application has been made, the date is the end of the application period.	
(B) Issuing a certificate under section 63F of the *Act* (Certification of employees by authorised persons).	Before the certificate is issued	This includes renewing an existing certificate.
(C) Appointing someone to any of the following positions (as defined in the *PRA Rulebook*): (a) a notified non-executive director; (b) a credit union non-executive director; or (c) a key function holder.	Not applicable	SYSC 22.2.1R (obligation to obtain a reference) does not apply to a *firm* appointing someone to the position in column (1). However SYSC 22.2.2R does apply to a *firm* asked to give a reference to a *firm* appointing someone to the position in column (1).

Note 1: Mandatory disclosure means an obligation in any applicable laws, regulations or rules to declare or disclose information to the public.

Note 2: P refers to the *employee* or ex-*employee* about whom the reference is given as defined in more detail in SYSC 22.2.1R and SYSC 22.2.2R.

Note 3: The application period means the period for consideration referred to in section 61 of the *Act* (Determination of application).

Obligation to revise references: The main rule (applicable to SMCR firms)

22.2.4　**R**　If at any time:

(1) an *SMCR firm* (B) has given a reference under ▨ SYSC 22.2.2R to another *firm* (A) about an *employee* or ex-*employee* of B (P);

(2) B was also an *SMCR firm* when it gave the reference in (1);

(3) either of the following applies:

(a) B is aware of matters or circumstances that mean that if B had been aware of them when giving that reference, this chapter would have required B to draft the reference differently; or

(b) the following applies:

(i) B has since giving the reference reached conclusions of the type described in question (E) of Part One of ■SYSC 22 Annex 1R or taken disciplinary action of the type described in question (F) of Part One of ■SYSC 22 Annex 1R; and

22

      (ii) if B had taken or reached those conclusions or actions within
the six year period referred to in Part One of
■ SYSC 22 Annex 1R, this chapter would have required B to
draft the reference differently; and

  (4) it would be reasonable to consider the differences in (3) to be
significant for an assessment by A of the fitness and propriety of P for
the role at A for which the reference was given;

B must:

  (5) make reasonable inquiries as to the identity of P's current *employer*;
and

  (6) give A details of those differences in writing as soon as reasonably
practicable, unless ■ SYSC 22.2.5R says that B does not have to do so.

22.2.5   **R**   B does not need to update A if:

  (1) A is no longer a *firm*;

  (2) P has not yet been *employed* by A (because, for example, P is still
working their notice period with B) and it is no longer intended for A
to *employ* P;

  (3) A is no longer P's *employer*; or

  (4) despite making reasonable enquiries under ■ SYSC 22.2.4R, B does not
know whether P is still *employed* by A.

22.2.6   **R**   This *rule* sets out time limits about the obligation to update a reference in
■ SYSC 22.2.4R.

  (1) If B still *employs* P, ■ SYSC 22.2.4R applies throughout the period B
remains *employed*.

  (2) If B no longer *employs* P, the obligation to update ends six years after
P ceased to be *employed* by B.

  (3) If B no longer *employs* P and the matters or circumstances are not
serious misconduct by P, B does not have to disclose something if it
did not occur or exist in the six year period ending on the date B
gave the original reference. This limitation applies in addition to the
one in (2).

[**Note:** See ■ SYSC 22.5.10G and ■ SYSC 22.5.11G for *guidance* on the meaning
of serious misconduct]

415

Obligation to revise references: Finding out who the current employer is (all firms)

22.2.7   **R**   If at any time:

(1) an *SMCR firm* (B) has given a reference under ■SYSC 22.2.2R to another *firm* (A) about an *employee* or ex-*employee* of B (P);

(2) B asks A whether P is still an *employee* of A; and

(3) B gave A the reference no more than six years ago;

A must answer that question as soon as reasonably practicable, even if B does not tell A why it wants to know that information.

22

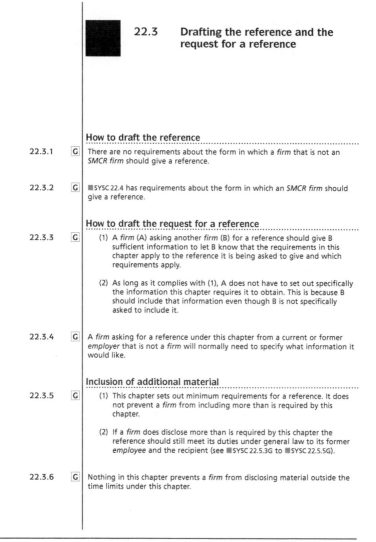

22

22.3 Drafting the reference and the request for a reference

How to draft the reference

22.3.1 G There are no requirements about the form in which a *firm* that is not an *SMCR firm* should give a reference.

22.3.2 G ■SYSC 22.4 has requirements about the form in which an *SMCR firm* should give a reference.

How to draft the request for a reference

22.3.3 G (1) A *firm* (A) asking another *firm* (B) for a reference should give B sufficient information to let B know that the requirements in this chapter apply to the reference it is being asked to give and which requirements apply.

(2) As long as it complies with (1), A does not have to set out specifically the information this chapter requires it to obtain. This is because B should include that information even though B is not specifically asked to include it.

22.3.4 G A *firm* asking for a reference under this chapter from a current or former *employer* that is not a *firm* will normally need to specify what information it would like.

Inclusion of additional material

22.3.5 G (1) This chapter sets out minimum requirements for a reference. It does not prevent a *firm* from including more than is required by this chapter.

(2) If a *firm* does disclose more than is required by this chapter the reference should still meet its duties under general law to its former *employee* and the recipient (see ■SYSC 22.5.3G to ■SYSC 22.5.5G).

22.3.6 G Nothing in this chapter prevents a *firm* from disclosing material outside the time limits under this chapter.

Appendix 1

SYSC 22 : Regulatory references

Section 22.4 : Drafting the reference:
detailed requirements for full scope
regulatory reference firms

22.4 Drafting the reference: detailed requirements for full scope regulatory reference firms

Drafting the reference: detailed requirements for SMCR firms

22.4.1 |G| ■ SYSC 22 Annex 1R (Template for regulatory references given by SMCR firms and disclosure requirements) has two purposes:

    (1) to set out what information an *SMCR firm* should disclose under ■ SYSC 22.2.2R(4); and

    (2) to provide a template that an *SMCR firm* should use when giving a reference under this chapter.

How to draft the reference

22.4.2 |R| (1) An *SMCR firm* must use the template in Part One of ■ SYSC 22 Annex 1R (Template for regulatory references given by SMCR firms and disclosure requirements) when giving a reference under this chapter to another *firm* (A).

    (2) A *firm* may make minor changes to the format of the template in Part One of ■ SYSC 22 Annex 1R when giving a reference under this chapter, provided that the reference includes all the information required by ■ SYSC 22 Annex 1R.

    (3) This *rule* applies even if A is not an *SMCR firm*.

22.4.3 |G| (1) ■ SYSC 22.4.2R does not stop an *SMCR firm* including matters in the reference not required by the template in ■ SYSC 22 Annex 1R.

    (2) An *SMCR firm* may include the material required by the template and additional material in the same document.

    (3) Any additional material should not alter the scope of any of the questions in the templates.

22.4.4 |G| An *SMCR firm* should use the template in ■ SYSC 22 Annex 1R (Template for regulatory references given by SMCR firms and disclosure requirements) even if the *firm* asking for the reference does not specifically ask it to.

SYSC 22 : Regulatory references

22

PRA requirements

22.4.5   **R**   *B* may combine in a single reference what the *PRA's rules* require and what this chapter requires.

419

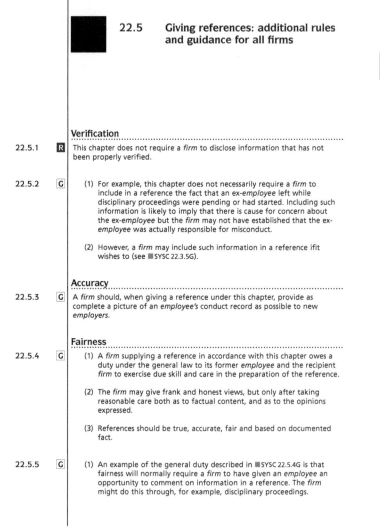

**22.5   Giving references: additional rules
            and guidance for all firms**

Verification

22.5.1   **R**   This chapter does not require a *firm* to disclose information that has not
                   been properly verified.

22.5.2   **G**   (1) For example, this chapter does not necessarily require a *firm* to
                       include in a reference the fact that an ex-*employee* left while
                       disciplinary proceedings were pending or had started. Including such
                       information is likely to imply that there is cause for concern about
                       the ex-*employee* but the *firm* may not have established that the ex-
                       employee was actually responsible for misconduct.

                   (2) However, a *firm* may include such information in a reference if it
                       wishes to (see ▪SYSC 22.3.5G).

Accuracy

22.5.3   **G**   A *firm* should, when giving a reference under this chapter, provide as
                   complete a picture of an *employee's* conduct record as possible to new
                   employers.

Fairness

22.5.4   **G**   (1) A *firm* supplying a reference in accordance with this chapter owes a
                       duty under the general law to its former *employee* and the recipient
                       firm to exercise due skill and care in the preparation of the reference.

                   (2) The *firm* may give frank and honest views, but only after taking
                       reasonable care both as to factual content, and as to the opinions
                       expressed.

                   (3) References should be true, accurate, fair and based on documented
                       fact.

22.5.5   **G**   (1) An example of the general duty described in ▪SYSC 22.5.4G is that
                       fairness will normally require a *firm* to have given an *employee* an
                       opportunity to comment on information in a reference. The *firm*
                       might do this through, for example, disciplinary proceedings.

22

(2) Paragraph (1) does not mean that the *firm* should provide an opportunity to comment on the reference itself, as opposed to the allegations on which it is based.

(3) A *firm* may have given the *employee* an opportunity to comment on allegations that are later included in a reference even though, at the time that the *firm* is giving that opportunity, no reference is being contemplated. That may mean that the *firm* gives the *employee* their opportunity to comment on the allegations some time before the reference is prepared.

(4) Paragraph (1) does not mean that a *firm* will be unable to include an allegation in a reference if it has offered the *employee* an opportunity to comment on the allegation but the *employee* has unreasonably refused to do so.

(5) Where a *firm* should have given an *employee* an opportunity to comment on an allegation if the allegation is to be included in a reference, this chapter requires the *firm* to give the *employee* that opportunity rather than merely to leave the allegation out of the reference.

(6) Paragraph (5) may mean that where the *firm* has not given its *employee* an opportunity to comment on a matter at the time it first arose, it will have to give the *employee* the opportunity around the time that the *firm* is preparing the reference.

(7) The obligation to give an *employee* an opportunity to comment does not mean that there is a wider duty to investigate whether there are facts that show that there has been a conduct breach (see ■SYSC 22.5.18G).

(8) This chapter does not require the *employee's* views to be included in the reference. Instead the *firm* should take those views into account so far as appropriate when deciding whether something should be disclosed and how the disclosure is drafted.

Outsourcing

22.5.6 |G| The requirements in this chapter for a *firm* (B) to give a *firm* (A) a reference also apply where A has outsourced the collection of that information to another (unregulated) third party, where B has been made aware that the unregulated third party is acting on behalf of A.

Circumstances in which the ex-employee left

22.5.7 |G| The obligation to give a reference for an *employee* or ex-*employee* applies however the *employment* ended or is going to end. For example, it applies whether it ended through resignation, redundancy, dismissal or fixed term work, a secondment or temporary work coming to an end.

Missing or incomplete information

22.5.8 |G| (1) If a *firm's* records do not cover the maximum periods contemplated by ■SYSC 22.2.2R or ■SYSC 22 Annex 1R (Template for regulatory references given by SMCR firms and disclosure requirements), the *firm* should note that in the reference.

(2) A *firm* should not include a warning of the type described in (1) as a matter of routine. It should only be included if there is a genuine need to include it.

All relevant information: Calculation of six year period for disclosure

22.5.9 |G| (1) In general there is a six year limit on what should be disclosed under ■ SYSC 22.2.2R(1) to (3).

(2) Where the matter to be disclosed consists of a single course of conduct (such as market manipulation) the six year period does not begin until that course of conduct has come to an end. This means that individual events that occurred more than six years ago may still be within the six year limit.

(3) This *guidance* is also relevant to the six year time limits for updating references in ■ SYSC 22.2.6R.

All relevant information: Removal of six year period

22.5.10 |G| (1) ■ SYSC 22.2.2R(1) to (3) normally has a six year time limit. ■ SYSC 22.2.2R(3)(c) removes that time limit for serious matters. This paragraph (■ SYSC 22.5.10G) and ■ SYSC 22.5.11G have *guidance* about this. This *guidance* is also relevant to the time limits for updating references in ■ SYSC 22.2.6R.

(2) The removal of the time limit does not mean that the time that has elapsed since the matter occurred is irrelevant. The length of time that has elapsed is relevant to deciding whether the matter is serious. In general, the longer ago the matter occurred, the less likely it is still to be serious for these purposes.

(3) In determining whether something is serious for these purposes, the key question is how important the information still is for the requesting *firm's* assessment of the *employee's* fitness for the function that they are going to perform.

(4) In considering what is relevant, a *firm* should, in particular, have regard to ■ SYSC 22.5.4G (Fairness).

(5) The table in ■ SYSC 22.5.11G provides *guidance* on some of the factors which a *firm* should take into account when determining whether a matter is serious.

(6) The *guidance* in this paragraph and in the table in ■ SYSC 22.5.11G is only designed for the purposes of this chapter. It does not, for example, apply for the purposes of ■ SUP 15 (Notifications to the FCA), *DEPP* or *EG*.

22.5.11 |G| Table: Examples of factors to take into account when deciding whether old misconduct is sufficiently serious to disclose

22

Factors to take into account	Comments
(A) Whether P has committed a serious breach of individual conduct requirements.	Individual conduct requirements has the same meaning as in Part Two of SYSC 22 Annex 1R (Template for regulatory references given by SMCR firms and disclosure requirements).
	Factors to take into account in deciding whether the breach is serious include the following.
	(1) The extent to which the conduct was deliberate or reckless.
	(2) The extent to which the conduct was dishonest.
	(3) Whether the breaches are frequent or whether they have continued over a long period of time. The fact that breaches were frequent or repeated may increase the likelihood that they should be disclosed since the breaches may show a pattern of non-compliance.
	(4) The extent of loss, or risk of loss, caused to existing, past or potential investors, depositors, policyholders or other counterparties or customers.
	(5) The reasons for the breach. For example, where the breach was caused by lack of experience which has been remedied by training or further experience, it is less likely that the breach will still be relevant.
(B) Whether the conduct caused B to breach requirements of the *regulatory system* or P was concerned in a contravention of such a requirement by B and, in each case, whether P's conduct was itself serious.	(1) The factors in (A) are relevant to whether P's conduct was serious.
	(2) The seriousness of the breach by B is relevant. The factors in (A) are also relevant to this.
	(3) A breach by B of certain requirements is always likely to be serious under (2). Breach of the *threshold conditions* is an example. However that does not mean that P's involvement will automatically be serious.
(C) Whether P's conduct involved dishonesty (whether or not also involving a criminal act).	Dishonesty is an important factor but it is not automatically decisive in every case. For instance, a small one-off case of dishonesty many years ago may not be sufficiently serious to require disclosure.
(D) Whether the conduct would have resulted in B's dismissing P, had P still been working for B, based on B's disciplinary policies and the requirements of the law about unfair dismissal.	

423

Factors to take into account	Comments
(E) Whether the conduct was such that, if B was considering P for a role today and became aware of the historical conduct, B would not employ P today notwithstanding the time that has passed.	

Note 1: P refers to the *employee* about whom the reference is being written.

Note 2: B refers to the *firm* giving the reference.

Breach of APER

22.5.12 [G]

(1) An example ofinformation that may be relevant under
    ■ SYSC 22.2.2R(1) to (3) is the fact that the *employee* has breached a
    requirement in *APER*.

(2) This means that any *firm* (not just one that is an *SMCR firm*) should
    consider whether it needs to disclose a breach ofindividual conduct
    requirements (as defined in Part Two of ■ SYSC 22 Annex 1R (Template
    for regulatory references given by SMCR firms and disclosure
    requirements)) when giving a reference under this chapter.

Agreements not to disclose information

22.5.13 [R]

A *firm* must not enter into any arrangements or agreements with any *person*
that limit its ability to disclose information under this chapter.

22.5.14 [G]

■ SYSC 22.5.13R covers all types of agreements and arrangements. For
example:

(1) it is not limited to an agreement or arrangement entered into when
    the *employee* leaves;

(2) it applies however the *employment* ends (see ■ SYSC 22.5.7G); and

(3) it covers a "COT 3" Agreement settled by the Advisory, Conciliation
    and Arbitration Service (ACAS).

22.5.15 [G]

A *firm* should not give any undertakings to supress or omit relevant
information in order to secure a negotiated release.

22.5.16 [G]

The obligation to supply information to another *firm* under this chapter will
apply notwithstanding any agreement prohibited by ■ SYSC 22.5.13R.

Time in which to respond to reference requests

22.5.17 [G]

The *FCA* expects that normally a *firm* should issue a reference under this
chapter within six weeks of being asked to.

SYSC 22 : Regulatory references   Section 22.5 : Giving references: additional
rules and guidance for all firms

22

Duty to investigate allegations

22.5.18   G   (1) A *firm* should, wherever feasible, conclude investigative procedures
before the *employee* departs.

(2) However, this chapter does not create a duty to investigate alleged
misconduct by an *employee* or former *employee*.

(3) There are several reasons why a *firm* may find it appropriate to
investigate potential misconduct by an *employee* or former *employee*,
including:

(a) assessing the actual and potential damage resulting from
misconduct;

(b) identifying other individuals potentially culpable or accountable
for the breach;

(c) satisfying itself that the *SMF manager* responsible for the areas
where the misconduct occurred took reasonable steps to prevent
or stop it; and

(d) (where the *employee* has *remuneration* susceptible to malus or
clawback) enabling it to consider whether any adjustments are
justified.

Criminal record checks

22.5.19   G   A *firm* giving a reference need not include information from a criminal
records check it has carried out under Part V of the Police Act 1997
(Certificates of Criminal Records, &). The recruiting *firm* should carry out a
criminal records check itselfif necessary. ■ SUP 10C.10.16R requires an *SMCR
firm* to carry out such a check when appointing an *SMF manager*.

Appendix I

SYSC 22 : Regulatory references

Section 22.6 : Giving and updating
references: additional rules and guidance for
SMCR firms

22.6 Giving and updating references: additional rules and guidance for SMCR firms

Omitting or supplementing mandatory disclosures

22.6.1 | G | (1) A *firm* may have concluded that an *employee* is unfit or has breached *COCON* or *APER* (as described in questions (E) to (F) of Part One of ◼ SYSC 22 Annex 1R (Template for regulatory references given by SMCR firms and disclosure requirements)). The *firm* may later become aware of facts or matters causing it to revise its original conclusions.

(2) If so, the *firm* may decide not to disclose in a reference its conclusion or may qualify its conclusion with supplementary information.

22.6.2 | G | (1) A *firm* may have concluded that an *employee* is unfit or has breached *COCON* or *APER* (as described in questions (E) to (F) of Part One of ◼ SYSC 22 Annex 1R (Template for regulatory references given by SMCR firms and disclosure requirements)). However the *firm* may consider that the disclosure is incomplete without including mitigating circumstances.

(2) For example, if the *firm* is reporting a breach of *COCON* it may consider that the breach is very uncharacteristic of the *employee* and that they have had an exemplary record since then. In that case, the *firm* should include those views.

Requirement to consider whether there has been a conduct breach

22.6.3 | G | (1) If a *firm* has taken disciplinary action of the type referred to in question (F) in Part One of ◼ SYSC 22 Annex 1R (Template for regulatory references given by SMCR firms and disclosure requirements) against an *employee* and is asked to give a reference about that *employee*, the *firm* should (if it has not already done so) consider whether the basis on which it took that action amounts to a breach of any individual conduct requirements covered by question (F).

(2) If the *firm* decides that the basis on which it took that action does amount to a breach of those requirements, it should include that disciplinary action in the reference under question (F).

(3) Paragraph (2) applies even if the grounds of the disciplinary action did not include such a breach of individual conduct requirements.

SYSC 22 : Regulatory references

Section 22.6 : Giving and updating
references: additional rules and guidance for
SMCR firms

22

(4) The requirement in (1) is disapplied for disciplinary action taken before certain specified dates, where a *firm's* records do not record whether previous conduct subject to disciplinary action amounted to a breach. The date differs between different types of *SMCR firms*. ■SYSC TP 5 and ■SYSC TP 7 set out those specified dates and other details.

(5) The obligation to consider whether there was a conduct breach does not mean that there is a wider duty to investigate whether there are facts that show that there has been a conduct breach (see ■SYSC 22.5.18G).

All relevant information: Interaction with mandatory disclosures

22.6.4 | G | (1) ■SYSC 22.2.2R(1) to (3) may require an *SMCR firm* to disclose information that goes beyond the mandatory minimum information in Part One of ■SYSC 22 Annex 1R (Template for regulatory references given by SMCR firms and disclosure requirements).

(2) This may mean, for instance, that a *firm* should in some cases disclose a conclusion that an *employee* or former *employee* has breached *COCON* or *APER* where that conclusion was reached outside the time limits in Part One of ■SYSC 22 Annex 1R.

Updating references fairly

22.6.5 | G | (1) ■SYSC 22.5.1R to ■SYSC 22.5.5G (Verification, accuracy and fairness) also apply to updating a reference under ■SYSC 22.2.4R.

(2) Therefore fairness may require a *firm* to have given an *employee* an opportunity to comment on an allegation if it is included in an update to a reference.

22.7   **Getting references: additional
rules and guidance for SMCR firms**

22

Intra-group transfers

22.7.1   **R**   (1) This *rule* applies when:

(a) an *SMCR firm* (A) would otherwise have to ask another *person* (B)
for a reference under ■SYSC 22.2.1R; and

(b) A and B are in the same *group*.

(2) A need not ask for a reference from B if there are adequate
arrangements in place under which A has access to the same
information sources as B to the extent that they are relevant to
things A has to ask B under ■SYSC 22.2.1R (Obligation to obtain
references).

(3) If A only has access to some of the information sources in (2), A may
ask for a reference that only covers the sources to which A does not
have such access.

(4) If A, in accordance with this rule, does not ask for a reference or a
full reference it must access the information resources referred to in
this *rule* and get the relevant information within the time specified
by ■SYSC 22.2.3R.

22.7.2   **G**   (1) ■SYSC 22.7.1R means that a *firm* recruiting someone from another
member of its *group* is not required to request a reference from the
other where the *group* has centralised records or alternative measures
in place to ensure sharing of relevant information between its
members.

(2) The recruiting *firm* should be satisfied that the centralised or
alternative measures ensure relevant information is made available as
part of the fit and proper assessment of the recruit.

Who should be asked to give a reference

22.7.3   **G**   The *Glossary* definition of *employer* covers more than just a conventional
employer and so it may not always be obvious who a *person's employer* is.
Therefore an *SMCR firm* appointing someone to a position that requires a
reference may have to get the *employee's* help in identifying their previous
employers.

SYSC 22 : Regulatory references

22

22.7.4	G	(1) ■ SYSC 22.2.1R (Obligation of an *SMCR firm* to try to obtain a reference) applies even if the ex-*employer* is not a *firm*.
		(2) An *SMCR firm* should take all reasonable steps to try to obtain the reference in these circumstances. However, the *FCA* accepts that the previous *employer* may not be willing to give sufficient information.

Asking for a reference to be updated

22.7.5	G	(1) ■ SYSC 22.2.1R (Obligation of an *SMCR firm* to try to obtain a reference) applies even if the *employer* has already got a reference for the *employee*. For example:
		(a) an *SMCR firm* should have a reference whenever it renews the certificate of a *certification employee*; and
		(b) changing jobs within the same *SMCR firm* may require a reference.
		(2) However, the *SMCR firm* does not necessarily need to obtain a new reference each time (a) or (b) above occurs. That is because an existing reference will very often still be appropriate for the purpose (see ■ SYSC 22.7.6G to ■ SYSC 22.7.8G).

22.7.6	G	If an *SMCR firm* (A):
		(1) appoints someone (P) to a *certification function* position;
		(2) obtains a reference from an ex-*employer*; and
		(3) later wishes to renew P's certificate under the certification regime;
		it is unlikely that A will need to ask for another reference from that ex-*employer* or ask for it to be reissued unless there is a change in P's role of the type described in ■ SYSC 5.2.17G (major changes in role).

22.7.7	G	(1) If an *SMCR firm* (A):
		(a) appoints someone (P) to a *certification function* or an *approved person* position;
		(b) obtains a reference from an ex-*employer* (B); and
		(c) later wishes to:
		(i) appoint P to another *certification function* or *approved person* position; or
		(ii) keep P in the same *certification function* but make a change in P's role of the type described in ■ SYSC 5.2.17G (major changes in role), whether that change is made at a time when the certificate has not yet come up for renewal or at the time it is being reissued; or
		(iii) move P from a *certification function* to an *approved person* position or vice versa;

A should consider whether to ask B to reissue or amend its reference.

(2) A may decide that it is not necessary to ask B to reissue or amend its reference. For example, A may decide that:

(a) the existing reference already covers everything necessary; or

(b) (where B is not a *firm*) B will not give any further information.

22

22.7.8   [G]   If:

(1) a *firm* (A) appoints someone (P) to a *certification function* or *approved person* position;

(2) A obtains a reference from an ex-*employer* (B);

(3) later P transfers to a *certification function* or an *approved person* position withan *SMCR firm* in A's *group* (C);

(4) B's reference is:

(a) addressed to all *firms* in A's *group*; or

(b) otherwise drafted so that it is clear that C may rely on it; and

(5) C does not need to ask for the reference to be reissued or amended, taking account of ■SYSC 22.7.6G and ■SYSC 22.7.7G;

C may be able to rely on that reference without asking B to give another one.

When references are to be obtained

22.7.9   [G]   If an *SMCR firm* is unable to obtain a reference by the time in column two of the table in ■SYSC 22.2.3R, it should still try to obtain the reference as soon as possible afterwards.

22.7.10   [G]   (1) Where an *SMCR firm* needs to fill a vacancy for a *certification function* which could not have reasonably been foreseen, the *FCA* recognises that it may not be reasonable to expect the *SMCR firm* to obtain references prior to issuing a certificate.

(2) In such cases, the *SMCR firm* should take up the reference as soon as reasonably possible.

(3) If a reference obtained later raises concerns about the person's fitness and propriety, the *SMCR firm* should revisit its decision to issue the person with a certificate.

22.7.11   [G]   (1) Although this chapter (see ■SYSC 22.2.3R) only requires an *SMCR firm* to try to get a reference for a *person* it is recruiting to perform an *FCA controlled function* or a *PRA controlled function* towards the end of the application process, the *FCA* would normally expect a *firm* to have obtained the reference before the application for approval is made.

22

(2) The main examples of circumstances in which it would be reasonable
for a *firm* to delay getting a reference are where asking for a
reference earlier will create a serious risk of:

   (a) breaching the confidentiality of a wider commercial or corporate
transaction;

   (b) prematurely triggering the need for a public announcement; or

   (c) the *candidate* not applying for the position in the first place
because it would reveal to the *candidate's* current *employer* the
proposed move too soon.

(3) The *FCA* may consider that it needs to see the information in a
reference before it reaches a decision. If so, it may formally ask for
that information and extend the time period in which it has to make
its decision until it gets the reference. ■ SUP 10C.10.28G gives
additional details about requests for further information and the
effect they have on the period of time the *FCA* has to make a
decision about an application.

(4) *SMCR firm* are reminded that the *Act* itself requires a *firm* to be
satisfied that a *candidate* is fit and proper before it makes an
application for approval (see ■ SUP 10C.10.14G for more detail).
■ SYSC 22.7.11G(2) does not affect that obligation.

22.8   Additional rules and guidance for all firms

Policies and procedures

22.8.1   **R**   A *firm* must establish, implement and maintain policies and procedures that are adequate for the purpose of complying with the obligations in this chapter.

22.8.2   **G**   ■ SYSC 22.8.1R does not require a *firm* to create or keep records that are not required under ■ SYSC 22.9.1R (General record keeping rules) or another *rule*.

Appointed representatives

22.8.3   **R**   This chapter applies to a *firm's appointed representatives* as well as to the *firm*.

22.8.4   **R**   When ■ SYSC 22.8.3R applies to an *SMCR firm*, the requirements of this chapter for firms that are not *SMCR firms* apply in place of the requirements that only apply to *SMCR firms*.

22.8.4A   **R**   (1) The *approved person's authorised approved person employer* is responsible for compliance with ■ SYSC 22.8.3R in the case of a requirement:

   (a) to give a reference about an *approved person* whose approval is under ■ SUP 10A.1.15R to ■ SUP 10A.1.16BR (Appointed representatives);

   (b) to update any such reference; and

   (c) under ■ SYSC 22.2.7R in relation to any such *person*.

   (2) In any other case, each *principal* of the *appointed representative* in question is responsible for compliance with ■ SYSC 22.8.3R.

   (3) If another *principal* of the *appointed representative* has accepted responsibility for the obligation in ■ SYSC 22.8.3R, that *principal* is responsible in place of the other *firms* in (1) or (2).

22.8.5   **G**   One effect of ■ SYSC 22.8.4R is that when an *appointed representative* appoints an *approved person* under ■ SUP 10A.1.16BR (appointed representatives of an *SMCR firm*) there is no requirement for the *appointed representative* or its *principal* to request a reference.

22

22.8.6	G	(1) A *firm* should ensure that its *appointed representative* gives a reference when another *firm* (or its *appointed representative*) asks that *appointed representative* to give a reference in accordance with this chapter.

(2) A *firm* is not responsible for its *appointed representative's* giving references if another *principal* has accepted responsibility for this.

Getting and giving a reference where the employee has worked in a group or on secondment

22.8.7	G	If:

(1) a *firm* (A) is thinking of employing someone (P);

(2) P is *employed* by a group services company (D) that is not a *firm*;

(3) P (in their capacity as an *employee* of D) performs a function or service for a *firm* (B) in the same *group* as D such that P is also an *employee* of B; and

(4) A intends to appoint (P) to a position that entitles A to obtain a reference from B;

then:

(5) (if A is an *SMCR firm*) A should ask both B and D for a reference;

(6) B is obliged to give the reference if A asks it to (whether or not A is an *SMCR firm*);

(7) B should ask D to provide it with the information needed to provide a reference in accordance with this chapter;

(8) D may give a reference but (as it is not a *firm*) it is not obliged to; and

(9) D and B may give a single joint reference.

22.8.8	G	■SYSC 22.8.7G also applies where:

(1) D is not in the same *group* but has seconded P to B; and

(2) P (in their capacity as an *employee* of D) performed any function or services for B such that P was also an *employee* of B.

22.8.9	G	If:

(1) a *firm* (A) is thinking of appointing someone (P) to a position that entitles A to obtain a reference from another *firm* (B); and

(2) P was an *employee* of other members of B's *group* as well as of B;

then:

(3) (if A is an *SMCR firm*) A should ask all the group members that *employed* P for a reference;

(4) B should give a reference if A asks it to (whether or not A is an *SMCR firm*);

(5) P's *employers* in that group (including any that are not *firms*) may give a single joint reference; and

(6) if the reference is being provided on a consolidated group basis, it should be clear what information is relevant to which *employer* within the *group*.

22

22

22.9 Records

General record keeping rules (applicable to SMCR firms)

22.9.1 **R**

(1) An *SMCR firm* must arrange for orderly records to be created and kept that are sufficient to enable it to comply with the requirements of this chapter.

(2) This *rule* only applies to records in relation to the following questions in Part One of ■ SYSC 22 Annex 1R (Template for regulatory references given by SMCR firms and disclosure requirements):

(a) question (E) (fit and proper); and

(b) question (F) (disciplinary action).

Time limit for records to be kept (applicable to SMCR firms)

22.9.2 **G**

■ SYSC 22.9.1R does not have an express time limit for which a *firm* should retain the records as its effect is that those time limits are the same as the time limits in ■ SYSC 22 Annex 1R (Template for regulatory references given by SMCR firms and disclosure requirements).

Reduction in disclosure obligations where there are limited record keeping requirements (all firms)

22.9.3 **R**

A *firm* does not breach the requirements of this chapter by failing to include information in a reference that it would otherwise have to include if:

(1) the reason for the omission is that the *firm* does not have the necessary records; and

(2) neither ■ SYSC 22.9.1R nor any other requirement of or under the *regulatory system* requires the *firm* to have those records.

22.9.4 **G**

If a *firm* is asked to give a reference in circumstances where the record keeping requirements in ■ SYSC 22.9.1R do not apply:

(1) it is still required to give the reference;

(2) it should give the reference based on the records it does have; and

(3) it will not breach the requirements of this chapter by failing to include information in a reference if the reason for this is that it does

not have the necessary records, as long as it is not required to have those records by some other requirement in the *Handbook* outside this chapter or some other requirement of or under the *regulatory system*.

Effect of previous record keeping requirements (applicable to SMCR firms)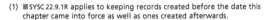

22.9.5   G   (1) ■ SYSC 22.9.1R applies to keeping records created before the date this chapter came into force as well as ones created afterwards.

(2) An *SMCR firm* does not breach the requirements of this chapter by failing to include something in a reference or by failing to have records because it destroyed the relevant records before the date this chapter came into force in accordance with the record keeping requirements applicable to it at the time of destruction.

(3) (1) also applies to records created before this chapter (or the relevant provision of this chapter) first applied to the *firm*.

(4) (2) also applies if the *firm* destroyed the records before this chapter (or the relevant provision of this chapter) first applied to it.

436

SYSC 22 : Regulatory references

22

437

Template for regulatory references given by SMCR firms and disclosure requirements

22

Part One: Form of Template

Guide to using this template:

Each question must be answered. Where there is nothing to disclose, this should be confirmed by ticking the "No" box for the relevant question.

In this template:

•"we" / "our firm" refers to the firm or firms giving the reference (as set out in either 1A or 1B below) ;

•"individual" refers to the subject of the reference (as set out in 2 below); and

•"your" refers to the firm requesting the reference (as set out in 3 below).

	Information requested	Response
1A	Name, contact details and firm reference number of firm providing reference; or	
1B	Names, contact details and firm reference numbers (where applicable) of group firms providing a joint reference	
2	Individual's name (i.e. the subject of the reference)	
3	Name, contact details and firm reference number of firm requesting the reference	
4	Date of request for reference	
5	Date of reference	

The answers to Questions A to F cover the period beginning six years before the date of your request for a reference and ending on the date of this reference

Question A

Has the individual:

(1) performed a certification function for our firm; or

(2) been an approved person for our firm.

Answer:

Yes

No

Question B:

Has the individual performed one or more of the following roles in relation to our firm:

(1) notified non-executive director;

(2) credit union non-executive director; or

SYSC 22 : Regulatory references

The answers to Questions A to F cover the period beginning six years before the date of your request for a reference and ending on the date of this reference

(3) key function holder (other than a controlled function).

Answer:

Yes

No

Question C:

If we have answered 'yes' to either Question A or B above, we set out the details of each position held below, including:

(1) what the controlled function, certification function or key function holder role is or was;

(2) (in the case of a controlled function) whether the approval is or was subject to a condition, suspension, limitation, restriction or time limit;

(3) whether any potential FCA governing function is or was included in a PRA controlled function; and

(4) the dates during which the individual held the position.

Answer:

Question D:

Has the individual performed a role for our firm other than the roles referred to in Questions A and B above:

Answer:

Yes

No

If 'yes', we have provided summary details of the other role(s), e.g. job title, department and business unit, below.

Question E:

Have we concluded that the individual was not fit and proper to perform a function:

Answer:

Yes

No

If 'yes' and associated disciplinary action was taken as a result, please refer to Question F below.

If 'yes', and no associated disciplinary action was taken as a result, we have set out below the facts which led to our conclusion.

Question F:

We have taken disciplinary action against the individual that:

(1) relates to an action, failure to act, or circumstances, that amounts to a breach of any individual conduct requirements that:

(a) apply or applied to the individual; or

(b) (if the individual is or was a key function holder, a notified non-executive director or a credit union non-executive director for your firm) the individual is or was required to observe under *PRA* rules (including if applicable, *PRA* rules in force before 7 March 2016); or

(2) relates to the individual not being fit and proper to perform a function.

Answer:

Yes

SYSC 22 : Regulatory references

The answers to Questions A to F cover the period beginning six years before the date of your request for a reference and ending on the date of this reference
No
If 'yes', we have provided below a description of the breaches (including dates of when they occurred) and the basis for, and outcome of, the subsequent disciplinary action.
Question G:
Are we aware of any other information that we reasonably consider to be relevant to your assessment of whether the individual is fit and proper? This disclosure is made on the basis that we shall only disclose something that:
(1) occurred or existed:
(a) in the six years before your request for a reference; or
(b) between the date of your request for the reference and the date of this reference; or
(2) is serious misconduct.
Answer:
Yes
No
If 'yes', we have provided the relevant information below.

Part Two: Definitions used in Part One

Section One of Part Two of this annex defines terms used in this annex.

Section Two of Part Two of this annex modifies the meaning of certain requirements in Part One and has material about completing the template.

Section One: Meaning of certain terms and phrases	
Defined term or phrase	**Meaning**
B	B refers to the *employer* or ex-*employer* giving the reference as defined in more detail in SYSC 22.2.1R and SYSC 22.2.2R.
P	P refers to the *employee* or ex-*employee* about whom the reference is given as defined in more detail in SYSC 22.2.1R and SYSC 22.2.2R.
A finding or conclusion by B that P was not fit and proper to perform a function (see questions (E) to (F) of the template)	This means a finding or conclusion by B where:
	(a)B assesses the continuing fitness and propriety of P as an *approved person* in accordance with the requirements of the *regulatory system*, including when carrying out this assessment under section 63(2A) of the *Act* (annual assessment of *approved persons* by an *SMCR firm*); or
	(b)B assesses the fitness and propriety of P when B is proposing to issue a certificate under section 63F of the *Act* (Certification of employees by *SMCR firms*) for P.
	Paragraph (b) applies whether the certificate is being issued for the first time or is being renewed.
Individual conduct requirements	Individual conduct requirements mean any of the following:
	(a)*COCON*;
	(b)*APER*;

22

Section One: Meaning of certain terms and phrases	
Defined term or phrase	Meaning
	(c)the *PRA's* Individual Conduct Standards or Senior Manager Conduct Standards in:
	(i) Chapter 3 of the Part of the *PRA Rulebook* called Insurance – Conduct Standards;
	(ii) Chapter 3 of the Part of the *PRA Rulebook* called Large Non-Solvency II Firms – Conduct Standards; and
	(iii) Chapter 2 of the Part of the *PRA Rulebook* called Non-Solvency II firms - Conduct Standards; or
	(d)the *PRA's* Individual Conduct Rules or Senior Manager Conduct Rules in:
	(i) Chapters 2 and 3 of the Part of the *PRA Rulebook* called CRR Firms: Conduct Rules; and
	(ii) Chapters 2 and 3 of the Part of the PRA Rulebook called Non-CRR Firms: Conduct Rules.
Function (as referred to in questions (E) to (F))	A function means a function as an *approved person* or *certification employee*.
Disciplinary action	Disciplinary action has the same meaning as in section 64C(2) of the *Act* (Requirement for authorised persons to notify regulatory of disciplinary action), which is:
	(a)the issue of a formal written warning; or
	(b)the suspension or dismissal of P; or
	(c)the reduction or recovery of any of P's remuneration.
	This definition applies even if B is not an *SMCR firm*.
Notified non-executive director, credit union non-executive director and key function holder	These terms have the same meaning as they do in the *PRA Rulebook*.
Certification function, approved person, controlled function and PRA controlled function	These terms have the same meaning as they do in the *Glossary*.
Potential FCA governing function	Potential FCA governing function means a function:
	(a)that would have been an *FCA controlled function* but for:
	(i)SUP 10A.11 (Minimising overlap with the PRA approved persons regime) (when that section was in force); or
	(ii)SUP 10C.9 (Minimising overlap with the PRA approved persons regime);
	(b)but instead is included in a *PRA controlled function* under the parts of the *PRA Rulebook* listed in SUP 10C.9.6G.
Section Two: Supplementary requirements	
Item of template for which supplemental requirements apply	Supplemental requirements

| Section One: Meaning of certain terms and phrases | |
Defined term or phrase	Meaning
Questions (E) and (F)	If:
	(a)the finding or disciplinary action was reached or taken by another member of B's *group* with the authority to do so; and
	(b)the finding or disciplinary action relates to conduct by P relating to the carrying on of activities (whether or not *regulated activities*) by B;
	this question applies to such finding or disciplinary action in the same way as it does to findings or disciplinary action made or taken by the *firm* itself.
Question (F)	This question is subject to SYSC TP 5.4.5R and SYSC TP 7.4.4R (where there is no need to disclose disciplinary action that took place before certain dates if the *firm's* records do not show whether there was a breach ofindividual conduct requirements).
The whole of Part One of this annex	The template to be used by a *firm* in giving a reference consists of everything in Part One of this annex except for the "Guide to using this template" paragraph.

22

SYSC 22 : Regulatory references

22

Factors to take into account when asking for and giving regulatory references

22

Matters to take into account	Comments
(A)Any outstanding liabilities of that person from commission payments	
(B)Any relevant outstanding or upheld complaint from an *eligible complainant* against P	
(C)Section 5 of the relevant Form A in SUP 10A Annex 4 (Application to perform controlled functions under approved persons regime) or SUP 10C Annex 3 (Application to perform senior management functions)	
(D)FIT 2 (Main assessment criteria)	
(E)The persistency of any life policies sold by P	This only applies if SUP 16.8.1G(1) (Persistency reports from insurers) applies to B

Note: P refers to the *employee* or ex-*employee* about whom the reference is given as defined in more detail in SYSC 22.2.1R and SYSC 22.2.2R.

SYSC 22 : Regulatory references

SYSC 18 Whistleblowing

Note: Italic text denotes defined terms. The definitions can be found in the Glossary to the FCA Handbook at https://www.handbook.fca.org.uk/handbook/glossary/.

Chapter 18

Whistleblowing

18.1   Application and purpose

Application
....

18.1.1   G   [deleted]

18.1.1A   R   This chapter applies to:

(1) a *firm*;

(2) in relation to the *guidance* in ■SYSC 18.3.9G, every *firm*;

(3) in relation to ■SYSC 18.3.6R and ■SYSC 18.3.10R, *EEA SMCR banking firms* and *third-country SMCR banking firms* only in relation to a *branch* maintained by them in the *United Kingdom*; and

(4) in relation to ■SYSC 18.6.1R to ■SYSC 18.6.3G (Whistleblowing obligations under MiFID):

(a) a *UK MiFID investment firm*, except a *collective portfolio management firm*; and

(b) a *third country investment firm*; and

(5) in relation to ■SYSC 18.6.4G to ■SYSC 18.6.5G (Whistleblowing obligations under other EU legislation), a *person* within the scope of the identified *EU* sectoral and cross-sectoral legislation.

18.1.1AA   G   *Firms* are reminded that for the purpose of ■SYSC 18 (except for ■SYSC 18.3.9G) "*firm*" has the specific meaning set out in paragraph (8) of that definition in the *Glossary*, namely:

(a) "(8) (in ■SYSC 18, with the exception of the *guidance* in ■SYSC 18.3.9G):

(a) a *UK SMCR banking firm* except a *small deposit taker*; and

(b) a firm as referred to in Chapter 1.1 of the PRA Rulebook: Solvency II Firms: Whistleblowing Instrument 2015."

18

18.1.1B   R   In this chapter, a reference to a provision of the Employment Rights Act 1996 includes a reference to the corresponding provision of the Employment Rights (Northern Ireland) Order 1996.

448

SYSC 18 : Whistleblowing

18.1.1C   [G]   A *firm* not referred to in ■SYSC 18.1.1AR may adopt the *rules* and *guidance* in this chapter as best practice. If so, it may tailor its approach in a manner that reflects its size, structure and headcount.

Purpose

18.1.2   [G]   (1) The purposes of this chapter are to:

    (a) set out the requirements on *firms* in relation to the adoption, and communication to *UK*-based *employees*, of appropriate internal procedures for handling *reportable concerns* made by *whistleblowers* as part of an effective risk management system (■SYSC 18.3);

    (b) set out the role of the *whistleblowers' champion* (■SYSC 18.4);

    (c) require *firms* to ensure that *settlement agreements* expressly state that *workers* may make *protected disclosures* (■SYSC 18.5) and do not include warranties related to *protected disclosures*;

    (ca) implement the whistleblowing obligation under article 73(2) of *MiFID*, which requires *MiFID investment firms* (except *collective portfolio management firms*) to have in place appropriate procedures for their employees to report potential or actual infringements of *MiFID* and *MiFIR* (■SYSC 18.6);

    (cb) outline other *EU*-derived whistleblowing obligations similar to those in article 73(2) of *MiFID*, some of which may also be applicable to *MiFID investment firms* (■SYSC 18.6);

    (d) outline best practice for *firms* which are not required to apply the measures set out in this chapter but which wish to do so; and

    (e) outline the link between effective whistleblowing measures and fitness and propriety.

(2) [deleted]

18.1.3   [G]   [deleted]

18

449

18.3   Internal arrangements

Arrangements to be appropriate and effective

18.3.1   **R**   (1) A *firm* must establish, implement and maintain appropriate and effective arrangements for the disclosure of *reportable concerns* by *whistleblowers*.

(2) The arrangements in (1) must at least:

    (a) be able effectively to handle disclosures of *reportable concerns* including:

        (i) where the *whistleblower* has requested confidentiality or has chosen not to reveal their identity; and

        (ii) allowing for disclosures to be made through a range of communication methods;

    (b) ensure the effective assessment and escalation of *reportable concerns* by *whistleblowers* where appropriate, including to the *FCA* or *PRA*;

    (c) include reasonable measures to ensure that if a *reportable concern* is made by a *whistleblower* no *person* under the control of the *firm* engages in victimisation of that *whistleblower*;

    (d) provide feedback to a *whistleblower* about a *reportable concern* made to the *firm* by that *whistleblower*, where this is feasible and appropriate;

    (e) include the preparation and maintenance of:

        (i) appropriate records of *reportable concerns* made by *whistleblowers* and the *firm's* treatment of these reports including the outcome; and

        (ii) up-to-date written procedures that are readily available to the *firm's UK*-based *employees* outlining the *firm's* processes for complying with this chapter;

    (f) include the preparation of the following reports:

        (i) a report made at least annually to the *firm's governing body* on the operation and effectiveness of its systems and controls in relation to whistleblowing (see ■ SYSC 18.3.1R); this report must maintain the confidentiality of individual *whistleblowers*; and

        (ii) prompt reports to the *FCA* about each case the *firm* contested but lost before an employment tribunal where the claimant successfully based all or part of their claim on either detriment suffered as a result of making a protected

18

disclosure in breach of section 47B of the Employment Rights Act 1996 or being unfairly dismissed under section 103A of the Employment Rights Act 1996;

(g) include appropriate training for:

   (i) *UK*-based *employees*;

   (ii) *managers* of *UK*-based *employees* wherever the *manager* is based; and

   (iii) *employees* responsible for operating the *firms'* internal arrangements.

18.3.2 G (1) When establishing internal arrangements in line with ■SYSC 18.3.1R a *firm* may:

   (a) draw upon relevant resources prepared by whistleblowing charities or other recognised standards setting organisations; and

   (b) consult with its *UK*-based *employees* or those representing these *employees*.

(2) In considering if a *firm* has complied with ■SYSC 18.3.1R the *FCA* will take into account whether the *firm* has applied the measures in (1).

(3) A *firm* may wish to clarify in its written procedures for the purposes of ■SYSC 18.3.1R(2)(e)(ii), that:

   (a) there may be other appropriate routes for some issues, such as employee grievances or consumer complaints, but internal arrangements as set out in ■SYSC 18.3.1R(2) can be used to blow the whistle after alternative routes have been exhausted, in relation to the effectiveness or efficiency of the routes; and

   (b) nothing prevents *firms* taking action against those who have made false and malicious disclosures.

18.3.3 G (1) A *firm* may wish to operate its arrangements under ■SYSC 18.3.1R internally, within its *group* or through a third party.

(2) *Firms* will have to consider how to manage any conflicts of interest.

(3) If the *firm* uses another member of its group or a third party to operate its arrangements under ■SYSC 18.3.1R it will continue to be responsible for complying with that *rule*.

Training and development

18.3.4 G A *firm's* training and development in line with ■SYSC 18.3.1R(2)(g) should include:

(1) for all *UK*-based *employees*:

   (a) a statement that the *firm* takes the making of *reportable concerns* seriously;

   (b) a reference to the ability to report *reportable concerns* to the *firm* and the methods for doing so;

18

  (c) examples of events that might prompt the making of a *reportable concern;*

  (d) examples of action that might be taken by the *firm* after receiving a *reportable concern* by a *whistleblower,* including measures to protect the *whistleblower's* confidentiality; and

   information about sources of external support such as whistleblowing charities;

 (2) for all managers of *UK*-based *employees* wherever the *manager* is based:

  (a) how to recognise when there has been a disclosure of a *reportable concern* by a *whistleblower;*

  (b) how to protect *whistleblowers* and ensure their confidentiality is preserved;

  (c) how to provide feedback to a *whistleblower,* where appropriate;

  (d) steps to ensure fair treatment of any *person* accused of wrongdoing by a *whistleblower;* and

  (e) sources of internal and external advice and support on the matters referred to in (a) to (d);

 (3) all *employees* of the *firm,* wherever they are based, responsible for operating the *firm's* arrangements under ■ SYSC 18.3.1R, how to:

  (a) protect a *whistleblower's* confidentiality;

  (b) assess and grade the significance of information provided by *whistleblowers;* and

  (c) assist the *whistleblowers' champion* (see ■ SYSC 18.4) when asked to do so.

18.3.5 |G| Where a *firm* operates its arrangements under ■ SYSC 18.3.1R through another member of its *group* or a third party it should consider providing the training referred to in ■ SYSC 18.3.4G(3) to the *persons* operating the arrangements by the *group* member or third party.

Reporting of concerns by employees to regulators

18.3.6 **R** This *rule* applies to an *EEA SMCR banking firm* and a *third-country SMCR banking firm.*

 (1) A *person* subject to this *rule* ('P') must, in the manner described in (2), communicate to its *UK*-based *employees* that they may disclose *reportable concerns* to the *PRA* or the *FCA* and the methods for doing so. P must make clear that:

  (a) reporting to the *PRA* or to the *FCA* is not conditional on a report first being made using P's internal arrangements;

  (b) it is possible to report using P's internal arrangements and also to the *PRA* or *FCA;* these routes may be used simultaneously or consecutively; and

  (c) it is not necessary for a disclosure to be made to P in the first instance.

 (2) The communication in (1) must be included in the *firm's* employee handbook or other equivalent *document.*

18.3.6A	G	For the purposes of ■SYSC 18.3.6R(1) the possibility for P's *employees* to disclose *reportable concerns* to the *PRA* or to the *FCA* does not override any obligation of P or its *employees* to report breaches to P's *Home State regulator* of matters reserved by an *EU* instrument to that regulator.
18.3.7	R	*Firms* must ensure that their *appointed representatives* or, where applicable, their *tied agents*, inform any of their *UK*-based *employees* who are *workers* that, as *workers*, they may make *protected disclosures* to the *FCA*.

Appointed representatives and tied agents

18.3.8	G	*Firms* are encouraged to invite their *appointed representatives* or, where applicable, their *tied agents* to consider adopting appropriate internal procedures which will encourage *workers* with concerns to blow the whistle internally about matters which are relevant to the functions of the *FCA* or *PRA*.

Link to fitness and propriety

18.3.9	G	The *FCA* would regard as a serious matter any evidence that a *firm* had acted to the detriment of a *whistleblower*. Such evidence could call into question the fitness and propriety of the *firm* or relevant members ofits staff, and could therefore, if relevant, affect the *firm's* continuing satisfaction of *threshold condition* 5 (Suitability) or, for an *approved person* or a *certification employee*, their status as such.

Additional rules for UK branches

18.3.10	R	(1) This *rule* applies where an *EEA SMCR banking firm* or a *third-country SMCR banking firm* has:

    (a) a *branch* in the *United Kingdom*; and

    (b) a *group* entity which is a *UK SMCR banking firm*.

(2) An *EEA SMCR banking firm* and a *third-country SMCR banking firm* must, in the manner described in (3), communicate to the *UK*-based *employees* ofits *UK branch*:

    (a) the whistleblowing arrangements of the *group* entity that is a *UK SMCR banking firm*; and

    (b) indicate that these arrangements may be used by *employees* of its *UK branch*.

(3) The communication in (2) must be included in the *branch's* employee handbook or other equivalent *document*.

18

453

18.4   The whistleblowers' champion

18.4.1   G   (1) A *UK SMCR banking firm* is required under ■SYSC 24.2.1R to allocate the *FCA*-prescribed senior management responsibility for acting as the *firm's whistleblowers' champion*.

(2) ■SYSC 18.4.2R requires the appointment by an insurer of a *director* or *senior manager* as its *whistleblowers' champion*.

(3) This section sets out the role of the *whistleblowers' champion*.

(4) The *FCA* expects that a *firm* will appoint a *non-executive director* as its *whistleblowers' champion*. A *firm* that does not have a *non-executive director* would not be expected to appoint one just for this purpose.

18.4.2   R   An *insurer* must appoint a *director* or *senior manager* as its *whistleblowers' champion*.

18.4.3   R   A *firm* must assign the responsibilities set out in ■SYSC 18.4.4R to its *whistleblowers' champion*.

18.4.4   R   A *firm* must allocate to the *whistleblowers' champion* the responsibility for ensuring and overseeing the integrity, independence and effectiveness of the *firm's* policies and procedures on whistleblowing (see ■SYSC 18.3 (Internal Arrangements)) including those policies and procedures intended to protect *whistleblowers* from being victimised because they have disclosed *reportable concerns*.

18.4.5   G   The whistleblowers' champion:

(1) should have a level of authority and independence within the *firm* and access to resources (including access to independent legal advice and training) and information sufficient to enable him to carry out that responsibility;

(2) need not have a day-to-day operational role handling disclosures from *whistleblowers*; and

(3) may be based anywhere provided he can perform his function effectively.

18

18.4.6 G   The role of a *whistleblowers' champion*, before the introduction of his or her responsibilities under those provisions of ■SYSC 18 which are to come into force on 7 September 2016, includes oversight of the *firm's* transition to its new arrangements for whistleblowing.

18

18.5   Settlement agreements with workers

18.5.1   **R**   A *firm* must include a term in any *settlement agreement* with a *worker* that makes clear that nothing in such an agreement prevents a *worker* from making a *protected disclosure*.

18.5.2   **E**   (1) *Firms* may use the following wording, or alternative wording which has substantively the same meaning, in any *settlement agreement*:

"For the avoidance of doubt, nothing precludes [name of worker] from making a "protected disclosure" within the meaning of Part 4A (Protected Disclosures) of the Employment Rights Act 1996. This includes protected disclosures made about matters previously disclosed to another recipient."

(2) Compliance with (1) may be relied on as tending to establish compliance with ■SYSC 18.5.1R.

18.5.3   **R**   (1) *Firms* must not request that *workers* enter into warranties which require them to disclose to the *firm* that:

(a) they have made a *protected disclosure*; or

(b) they know of no information which could form the basis of a *protected disclosure*.

(2) *Firms* must not use measures intended to prevent *workers* from making *protected disclosures*.

18

18.6 Whistleblowing obligations under MiFID and other EU legislation

Whistleblowing obligations under MiFID

18.6.1 **R** (1) A *UK MiFID investment firm* (except a *collective portfolio management investment firm*) must have appropriate procedures in place for its employees to report a potential or actual breach of:

(a) any *rule* implementing *MiFID*; or

(b) a requirement imposed by *MiFIR* or any *EU regulation* adopted under *MiFID* or *MiFIR*.

(2) The procedures in (1) must enable employees to report internally through a specific, independent and autonomous channel.

(3) The channel referred to in (2) may be provided through arrangements made by social partners, subject to the Public Interest Disclosure Act 1998 and the Employment Rights Act 1996 to the extent that they apply.

[**Note:** article 73(2) of *MiFID*]

18.6.2 **R** ■SYSC 18.6.1R applies to a *third country investment firm* as if it were a *UK MiFID investment firm* (unless it is a *collective portfolio management investment firm*) when the following conditions are met:

(1) it carries on *MiFID or equivalent third country business*; and

(2) it carries on the business in (1) from an establishment in the *United Kingdom*.

18.6.3 **G** When considering what procedures may be appropriate for the purposes of ■SYSC 18.6.1R(1), a *UK MIFID investment firm* or a *third country investment firm* may wish to consider the arrangements in ■SYSC 18.3.1R(2).

Whistleblowing obligations under other EU legislation

18.6.4 **G** In addition to obligations under *MiFID*, similar whistleblowing obligations apply to miscellaneous *persons* subject to regulation by the *FCA* under the following non-exhaustive list of *EU* legislation:

(1) article 32(3) of the *Market Abuse Regulation*, as implemented in section 131AA of the *Act*;

18

(2) article 71(3) of the *CRD* (see ■ IFPRU 2.4.1R in respect of *IFPRU investment firms*);

(3) article 99d(5) of the *UCITS Directive* (see ■ SYSC 4.1.1ER in respect of *UK UCITS management companies*, and ■ COLL 6.6B.30R in respect of *depositaries*); and

(4) article 24(3) of the *securities financing transactions regulation*.

18.6.5   ☐G   Depending on the nature of its business, in addition to ■ SYSC 18.6.1R, a *MiFID investment firm* may, for example, be subject to one or more of the requirements in ■ SYSC 18.6.4G.

SUP 10C7.3 G Guidance on how the other overall responsibility function applies

TABLE: EXAMPLES OF HOW THE OTHER OVERALL RESPONSIBILITY FUNCTION APPLIES

Example	Comments
(1) 'A' is appointed to perform the executive *director function* and to perform a potential *other overall responsibility function* for the same *firm*.	A only needs approval to perform the executive *director function*.
(2) 'A' is approved to perform the *other overall responsibility function*. Later, A is appointed to perform the executive *director function* for the same *firm*.	A requires approval for the *other overall responsibility function* when A is first appointed. When A is later approved to perform the executive *director function*, A stops performing the *other overall responsibility function*. The *firm* should use Form E to apply for approval for A to perform the executive *director function*.
(3) 'A' is appointed to perform the *PRA's* Head of Key Business Area *designated senior management function* and to perform a potential *other overall responsibility function* for the same *firm*.	A only needs approval to perform the *PRA's* Head of Key Business Area *designated senior management function*. It does not make any difference whether the potential *other overall responsibility function* that A performs is connected to the *PRA's* Head of Key Business Area *designated senior management function*.
(4) 'A' is approved to perform the *other overall responsibility function*. Later, A is appointed to perform the *PRA's* Head of Key Business Area *designated senior management function* for the same *firm*.	A requires approval for the *other overall responsibility function* when A is first appointed. When A is later approved to perform the *PRA's* Head of Key Business Area *designated senior management function*, A stops performing the *other overall responsibility function*.

Example	Comments
(5) 'A' is appointed to perform: (a) the *compliance oversight function* for one *firm* (Firm X) in a group (which may or may not be a *relevant authorised person*); and (b) a function coming within the scope of the *other overall responsibility function* for another *firm* (which is a *relevant authorised person*) in the same group (Firm Y).	A needs approval to perform the *compliance oversight function* for Firm X and the *other overall responsibility function* for Firm Y.
(6) 'A' is appointed to be head of sales and to report directly to the *firm's governing body* about this. This function also comes within the *PRA's* Head of Key Business Area *designated senior management function*.	A only needs approval to perform the *PRA's* Head of Key Business Area *designated senior management function*.
(7) 'A' is appointed to take on some functions that come within the *other overall responsibility function*. Later, A is appointed as chief risk officer.	On A's first appointment, A will need to be approved to perform the *other overall responsibility function*. On being appointed as chief risk officer, the answer for example (4) applies because being chief risk officer is a *PRA-designated senior management function*. A will stop performing the *other overall responsibility function*.
(8) 'A' is appointed to a role that comes within the *other overall responsibility function*. Later, the firm reorganises and A's role comes within the *PRA's* Head of Key Business Area *designated senior management function*. A's role does not otherwise change.	The answer for example (7) applies.
(9) 'A' is appointed to a role that comes within the *PRA's* Head of Key Business Area *designated senior management function*. It is also a potential *other overall responsibility function*. Later, the *firm* reorganises—A's role stays the same but now it falls outside the *PRA's* Head of Key Business Area *designated senior management function*.	On A's first appointment, A only needs approval to perform the *PRA's* Head of Key Business Area *designated senior management function*. Following the reorganisation, the *firm* has three months to get approval for A to perform the *other overall responsibility function*. This three-month period applies because the relevant *PRA* rules keep the *PRA's* Head of Key Business Area *designated senior management function* in place, which means that the *other overall responsibility function* does not apply during that period. The relevant *PRA* rules can be found in Chapter 2 of the part of the *PRA* rulebook titled 'Senior Management Functions'.

Example	Comments
(10) 'A' is appointed to a role that comes within the *PRA's* Head of Key Business Area *designated senior management function*. A also performs a potential *other overall responsibility function*. A gives up the *PRA* role but carries on with the potential *other overall responsibility function*.	The answer to example (9) applies.
(11) 'A' is appointed as an executive director. A then resigns and takes up a job with the same *firm* coming within the *other overall responsibility function*.	On A's first appointment, A will need to be approved to perform the executive *director function*. A will need to get approval to perform the *other overall responsibility function* before A gives up being a director.

Note (1): A potential *other overall responsibility function* means a function that would have come within the *other overall responsibility function* but is excluded by *SUP 10C.7.1R(2)*.

Note (2): A potential *other overall responsibility function* should be recorded in A's *statement of responsibilities* and in the *firm's management responsibilities map*.

Submitting statements of responsibilities: examples of how the requirements work

SUP 10C.11.18 G 07/03/2016

The table in *SUP 10C.11.19G* gives examples of how the requirements in this section for submitting *statements of responsibilities* work in different cases.

SUP 10C.11.19 G 07/03/2016 RP

Table: examples of how the requirements for submitting statements of responsibilities work

Example	Comments
(1) A *firm* applies for approval for A to perform the executive *director function* and the *money laundering function*.	There should be a single *statement of responsibilities* document that covers the two functions. The combined document should be included with the application for approval.
(2) Firm X applies for approval for A to perform the executive *director function*. Firm Y applies for approval for A to perform the *money laundering function*. Both *firms* are *relevant authorised persons*.	There should be separate *statements of responsibilities* for each *firm*. This is the case even if Firm X and Firm Y are in the same group.
(3) A *firm* applies for approval for A to perform an *FCA-designated senior management function* and a *PRA-designated senior management function*. The arrangements in *SUP 10C.9* for *FCA* functions to be absorbed into *PRA* ones do not apply and so there are separate applications to the *FCA* and *PRA*.	The single *statement of responsibilities* document should cover both the *FCA* and the PRA functions.

Example	Comments
(4) A has approval to perform the executive *director function*. Later, A is to be appointed to perform the *money laundering function* for the same *firm*. This will also result in substantial changes to A's duties as an executive director.	The *firm* should not use Form J to notify the changes to A's duties as an executive director. The *firm* should submit a revised single *statement of responsibilities* document along with the application to perform the *money laundering function*. The single *statement of responsibilities* document should cover both functions. The part relating to A's duties as an executive director should be updated.
(5) A has approval to perform the executive *director function*. Later, A is to be appointed to perform the *PRA's* chief risk officer *designated senior management function* for the same *firm*. This will also result in substantial changes to A's duties as an executive director.	The *firm* should not use Form J to notify the changes to A's duties as an executive director. The *firm* should submit a revised single *statement of responsibilities* document along with the application to perform the *PRA* function. The *firm* should not submit the revised single *statement of responsibilities* document separately to the *FCA*. Instead, it should include it as part of the application to the *PRA*. The single *statement of responsibilities* document should cover both the *FCA* and the *PRA* functions. The part relating to A's duties as an executive director should be updated.
(6) A has approval to perform the *money laundering function*. The approval to perform the *money laundering function* is subject to a condition. The *firm* is applying to vary that condition.	The *firm* should include a revised *statement of responsibilities* with the application. The *firm* should not use Form J. It should submit a revised *statement of responsibilities* along with the application to vary the approval.
(7) A has approval to perform the executive *director function* and the *money laundering function* for the same *firm*. The approval to perform the *money laundering function* is subject to a condition. The *firm* is applying to vary that condition. As part of the same arrangements, there are to be substantial changes to A's job as an executive director.	The *firm* should not use Form J to notify the changes to A's duties as an executive director. The *firm* should submit a revised single *statement of responsibilities* document along with the application to vary the approval for the *money laundering function*. The single *statement of responsibilities* document should be updated and should cover both functions.

Example	Comments
(8) A has approval to perform the executive *director function* and the *PRA's* chief risk officer *designated senior management function* for the same *firm*. The arrangements in *SUP 10C.9* for *FCA* functions to be absorbed into *PRA* ones do not apply and so there are separate *FCA* and *PRA* approvals. The approval to perform the *PRA's* chief risk officer *designated senior management function* is subject to a condition. The *firm* is applying to vary that condition. As part of the same arrangements, there are to be substantial changes to A's job as an executive director.	The *firm* should not use Form J to notify the changes to A's duties as an executive director. The *firm* should submit a revised single *statement of responsibilities* document along with the application to vary the *PRA* function. The *firm* should not submit the revised document separately to the *FCA*. Instead it should include it as part of the application to the *PRA*. The single *statement of responsibilities* document should cover both the *FCA* and the *PRA* functions and should be updated.
(9) A has approval to perform the executive *director function* and the *money laundering function* for the same *firm*. Sometime later, A is to give up the *money laundering function* and take up the *PRA's* chief risk officer *designated senior management function*. This will involve major changes to A's role as executive director.	The answer to example (5) applies. The application to the *PRA* to perform the *PRA* function should be accompanied by a single document that: (1) contains the *statement of responsibilities* for the new function; (2) contains the revised *statement of responsibilities* for the executive *director function*; and (3) reflects the fact that A is no longer performing the *money laundering function*.
(10) A *firm* has approval for A to perform the executive *director function* and the *money laundering function*. A then ceases to perform the *money laundering function* but continues to perform the executive *director function*.	The *firm* must submit: (a) Form C for the *money laundering function*; (b) Form J; and (c) a single updated *statement of responsibilities* document that covers the executive *director function*.
(11) A has approval to perform the executive *director function* and the *PRA's* chief risk officer *designated senior management function* for the same *firm*. Later, A gives up his role as chief risk officer.	The *firm* must submit: (a) Form C for the *PRA* function; (b) Form J; and (c) a single updated *statement of responsibilities* document that covers the executive *director function*. The *firm* should not submit the revised single *statement of responsibilities* document separately to the *FCA*. Instead, it should include it as part of the notification to the *PRA*.

Example	Comments
(12) A has approval to perform the executive *director function*. Later, A is to be appointed to perform the *money laundering function* for the same *firm*. The application is rejected.	The single *statement of responsibilities* document submitted as part of the application will no longer be correct as it reflects the proposed new approval. If the only changes to the single document in the version sent with the application are ones, clearly and exclusively tied to the new function, the *firm* will not need to amend the document as the changes will automatically fall away. In any other case (for instance if the application is approved conditionally), it is likely that the *firm* will need to update it using Form J. In any case, the *FCA* may contact the *firm* to agree a revised single *statement of responsibilities* document.
(13) A has approval to perform the executive *director function*. Later, A is to be appointed to perform the *money laundering function* for the same *firm*. This will not result in any changes to A's duties as an executive director. However, there have been some insignificant changes to A's role as an executive director since the *firm* submitted the most recent single *statement of responsibilities* document. The changes are not connected to A's appointment to perform the *money laundering function*.	The answer for example (4) applies. The single *statement of responsibilities* document should be updated to cover the changes to A's duties as executive director, as well as covering A's new money laundering role. It does not matter that the changes to A's role as an executive director are not significant.
(14) A has approval to perform the executive *director function*. Later, A's business unit grows in size and so the *firm* needs to apply for A to be approved to perform the *PRA's* Head of Key Business Area *designated senior management function*. However, A's responsibilities do not change.	The *firm* should submit a revised single *statement of responsibilities* document along with the application to perform the *PRA* function. The *firm* should submit a single *statement of responsibilities* document that covers both the *FCA* and the *PRA* functions. It should not submit the revised single *statement of responsibilities* document separately to the *FCA*. Instead, it should include it as part of the application to the *PRA*.

Example	Comments
2(15) Firm X has a *branch* in the *United Kingdom*. Firm Y is a *UK* authorised *subsidiary*3 of firm X. Firm X is a *third-country relevant authorised person* and firm3 Y is a *UK relevant authorised person*. Both *firms* apply for approval for the same individual (P) to perform the executive3*director function*.	There should be separate *statement of responsibilities* for P for each *firm*.
The single *statement of responsibilities* document means the single document described in *SUP 10C.11.13D*	

APPENDIX 5

FCA Policy statement PS18/4: Credit card market study

Figure 1: Firm Checker Tool

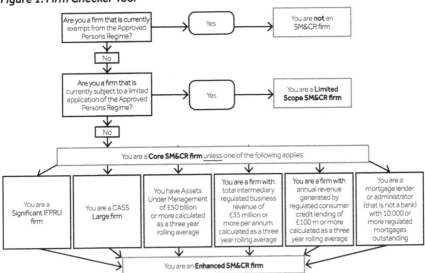

Table 1: Table of Firm Types

Firm type	Description
Limited Scope Firm	Firms that have fewer requirements than Core firms. This covers all firms that currently have a limited application of the Approved Persons Regime, including: • limited permission consumer credit firms • all sole traders • authorised professional firms whose only regulated activities are non-mainstream regulated activities • oil market participants • service companies • energy market participants • subsidiaries of local authorities or registered social landlords • insurance intermediaries whose principal business is not insurance intermediation and who only have permission to carry on insurance mediation activity in relation to non-investment insurance contracts • authorised internally managed Alternative Investment Funds (AIFs)
Core Firm	Firms that will have a baseline of SM&CR requirements applied.
Enhanced Firm	A small proportion of solo-regulated firms that will have to apply extra rules.

Table 2: Prescribed Responsibilities

Handbook PR Ref.	Description
All Core and Enhanced Firms	
(a)	Performance by the firm of its obligations under the SMR, including implementation and oversight
(b)	Performance by the firm of its obligations under the Certification Regime
(b-1)	Performance by the firm of its obligations in respect of notifications and training of the Conduct Rules
(d)	Responsibility for the firm's policies and procedures for countering the risk that the firm might be used to further financial crime
(z)	Responsibility for the firm's compliance with CASS (if applicable)
Authorised Fund Managers	
(za)	Responsibility for an AFM's value for money assessments, independent director representation and acting in investors' best interests. This PR only applies to AFMs. For more details, see CP17/18, MS15/2.3 – Asset Management Market Study: Final Report and PS18/8.
Enhanced Firms	
(c)	Compliance with the rules relating to the firm's Responsibilities Map
(j)	Safeguarding and overseeing the independence and performance of the internal audit function (in accordance with SYSC 6.2)
(k)	Safeguarding and overseeing the independence and performance of the compliance function (in accordance with SYSC 6.1)
(l)	Safeguarding and overseeing the independence and performance of the risk function (in accordance with SYSC 7.1.21R and SYSC 7.1.22R)
(j-3)	If the firm outsources its internal audit function, taking reasonable steps to make sure that every person involved in the performance of the service is independent from the persons who perform external audit, including: • supervision and management of the work of outsourced internal auditors • management of potential conflicts of interest between the provision of external audit and internal audit services
(t)	Developing and maintaining the firm's business model
(s)	Managing the firm's internal stress-tests and ensuring the accuracy and timeliness of information provided to the FCA for stress-testing

Table 6: Application of the SM&CR to branches

Element	EEA Branches	Non-EEA Branches
SMFs	SMF21 – EEA Branch Senior Manager	SMF19 – Head of Third Country Branch
	SMF17 – Money Laundering Reporting Officer (MLRO)	SMF3 – Executive Director
		SMF16 – Compliance Oversight
		SMF17 – Money Laundering Reporting Officer (MLRO)
Prescribed Responsibilities	N/A	a) Performance by the firm of its obligations under the Senior Managers Regime, including implementation and oversight
		b) Performance by the firm of its obligations under the Certification Regime
		b-1) Performance by the firm of its obligations in respect of notifications and training of the Conduct Rules
		d) Responsibility for the firm's policies and procedures for countering the risk that the firm might be used to further financial crime
		z) Responsibility for the firm's compliance with CASS
		aa) Responsibility for management of the firm's risk management processes in the UK
		ff) Responsibility for the firm's compliance with the UK regulatory system applicable to the firm
		ee) Responsibility for the escalation of correspondence from the PRA, FCA and other regulators in respect of the firm to the governing body and/or the management body of the firm or, where appropriate, of the parent undertaking or holding company of the firm's group
		(za) Responsibility for an AFM's value for money assessments, independent director representation and acting in investors' best interests
Certification Regime	Yes	
Conduct Rules	Yes	

GC18/4: Senior Managers and Certification Regime – Proposed guidance on statements of responsibilities for FCA firms

Example 9: SMF18 - Other Overall Responsibility Function in an Enhanced firm

Senior management function	Description of senior management function	Tick SMF applied for or held					Effective Date
		Core firms				Enhanced SMCR firms	
		Limited scope SMCR firms	UK core SMCR firms	EEA core SMCR firms	Third country branches		
SMF 18	Other Overall responsibility					☑	09/12/2019

Please provide a title for this overall responsibility	Please provide further details of this overall responsibility	Is this overall responsibility shared? If 'Yes' please provide, the name(s), IRN(s) and/or job title(s) of the individual(s) you are sharing this responsibility with (where known)
Human Resources	I am responsible overall for the Human Resources (HR) Function of XXX Group ltd, which focuses on implementing the Group HR's Policy, oversight and management of staffing and organisational approach to HR with regard to employees and management within XXX Ltd and YYY Ltd, including but not limited to internal appointments, hiring new employees, graduate scheme, compensation policy and employees' benefits, organisational development programme, performance management, employee relationship management, learning and development, employee engagement and training.	No
	For this purpose, my role involves supervising and monitoring the activities of the HR function in relation to: Professional development of employees; Talent management and acquisition; Creating and delivering policy in relation to bonuses and other performance-based compensation; The management of the risks held within the HR function including updating the Risk Log; Please review the HR function contained in the responsibilities map of XXX ltd for full details.	

Example 10: SMF24 – Chief Operations Function in an Enhanced firm

Senior management function	Description of senior management function	Tick SMF applied for or held					Effective Date
		Core firms				Enhanced SMCR firms	
		Limited scope SMCR firms	UK core SMCR firms	EEA core SMCR firms	Third country branches		
SMF 24	Chief Operations					☑	09/12/2019

Please provide a title for this overall responsibility	Please provide further details of this overall responsibility	Is this overall responsibility shared? If 'Yes' please provide, the name(s), IRN(s) and/or job title(s) of the individual(s) you are sharing this responsibility with (where known)
Customer service	I am accountable for all related issues to the Board.	No

Guide for FCA solo regulated firms

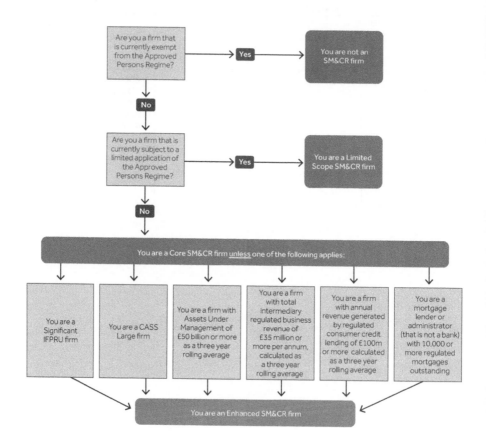

Territoriality and the Certification Regime for UK firms

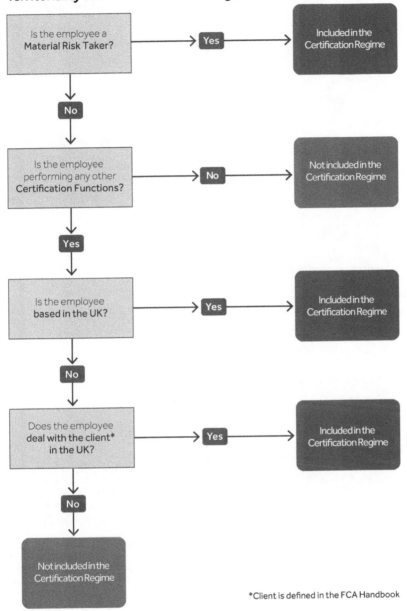

*Client is defined in the FCA Handbook

Territoriality and the Certification Regime for branches

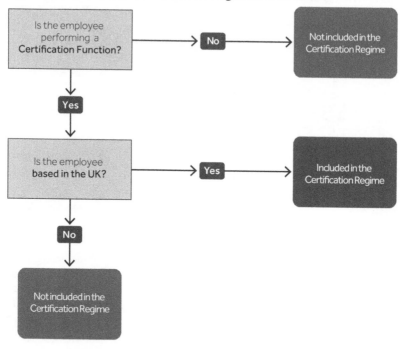

Example firms

Throughout this guide, our 3 example firms show how each of the elements might apply to different types of firm. These examples are non-exhaustive and purely illustrative - you will need to consider how the rules apply to your circumstances.

A

Firm A

Firm A is an Enhanced firm within a global banking group. It employs 3000 staff, performing a variety of roles for the UK entity, some of whom hold roles in scope of the Certification Regime. Two of the firm's 5 Non-Executive Directors are Senior Managers of other group entities.

B

Firm B

Firm B is a medium-sized IFA and mortgage broking firm incorporated as a limited company. The firm falls within the Core tier and has 40 staff. This includes 2 Executive Directors and 30 advisers, all of whom give investment or mortgage advice. Six of the remaining staff do not advise but perform various functions connected to financial services. Two of the remaining staff are not involved in financial services activities at all. The firm has a governing body with three Non-Executive Directors, one of whom acts as the firm's Chair.

C

Firm C

Firm C is a dental practice incorporated as a limited company. It is a Limited Permission Consumer Credit firm and is therefore a Limited Scope firm.

Index